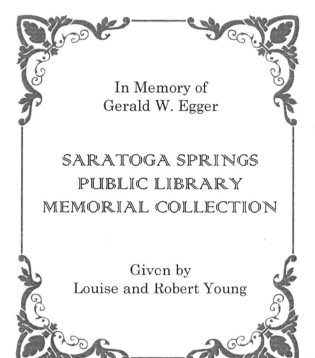

CIVIL WAR DYNASTY

Civil War Dynasty

The Ewing Family of Ohio

Kenneth J. Heineman

NEW YORK UNIVERSITY PRESS
New York and London

NEW YORK UNIVERSITY PRESS
New York and London
www.nyupress.org

References to Internet websites (URLs) were accurate at the time of writing.
Neither the author nor New York University Press is responsible for URLs that
may have expired or changed since the manuscript was prepared.

LIBRARY OF CONGRESS CATALOGING-IN-PUBLICATION DATA
Heineman, Kenneth J., 1962–
Civil War dynasty : the Ewing family of Ohio / Kenneth J. Heineman.
p. cm.
Includes bibliographical references and index.
ISBN 978-0-8147-7301-7 (cl : alk. paper)
ISBN 978-0-8147-7302-4 (e-book)
ISBN 978-0-8147-9070-0 (e-book)
1. Ohio—History—Civil War, 1861-1865. 2. United States—History—Civil War,
1861–1865—Campaigns. 3. Ewing family. 4. Ewing, Thomas,—1829-1896.
5. Sherman, William T. (William Tecumseh), 1820-1891—Family. I. Title.
E525.H45   2012
973.7'471—dc23   2012027274

New York University Press books are printed on acid-free paper,
and their binding materials are chosen for strength and durability.
We strive to use environmentally responsible suppliers and materials
to the greatest extent possible in publishing our books.

Manufactured in the United States of America
10 9 8 7 6 5 4 3 2 1

Arms and the man I sing, who first made way,
Predestined exile, from the Trojan shore
To Italy, the blest Lavinian strand.
Smitten of storms he was on land and sea
By violence of Heaven, to satisfy
Stern Juno's sleepless wrath; and much in war
He suffered, seeking at the last to found
The city, and bring o'er his fathers' gods
To safe abode in Latium; whence arose
The Latin race, old Alba's reverend lords,
And from her hills wide-walled, imperial Rome.

The *Aeneid*

GILBERT D. HEINEMAN (1919–2002)
Guadalcanal, Bougainville, New Georgia

TERRY G. HEINEMAN (1947–2008)
South Vietnam

CONTENTS

ACKNOWLEDGMENTS

Every student of history owes a great debt to the organizations and archivists who make reconstruction of the past possible. The Kansas State Historical Society, the Ohio Historical Society, the University of Notre Dame Archives, the Library of Congress, and the National Archives are treasures—as are their respective staffs.

I must express great appreciation to Nicole McDaniel at Angelo State University, as well as to her industrious students in English 4360, Professional Editing—including Amanda Cooper, Cate Cuba, Mindy Armitage, Tyler Carson, Christine Stone, John Phair, and Patricia Larson. I also greatly appreciate the encouragement given to me by my senior scholars, notably Arnoldo DeLeon and Joe Zheng. Their professional engagement, as well as their friendship, has meant much to me since my arrival in 2009.

Before I came to Texas, I had spent eighteen years in Lancaster, Ohio, home of the Ewing dynasty. It is entirely due to the efforts of the fine folks at the Fairfield Heritage Association (FHA) and the Sherman House Museum that I developed an interest in the Ewing family. To Diane Eversole, Joyce Harvey, and Frank and Laura Bullock: thank you for persuading me in 2005 that it would be a good idea for me to grow a beard, wear a heavy woolen outfit, and play General Hugh Ewing on a hot fall evening at the former Ohio fairgrounds. Subsequently, I had the pleasure of joining Andy McGreevy, an Ohio University–Lancaster history colleague, on FHA-sponsored tours of Gettysburg and Springfield.

I must also thank one Ohioan and three Pennsylvania friends for their insights on Civil War–era politics: Chris Phillips, Randall Miller, Michael Birkner, and Van Beck Hall. As a graduate student at Pitt, I always knew Van Beck Hall was well read. After one conversation with him at a meeting of the Pennsylvania Historical Association at which he rattled off numerous works related to the economic history of the Kanawha Valley saltworks, however, I realized something else: he is always the smartest man in any room.

Debbie Gershenowitz at NYU Press believed in this project and worked tirelessly to see it come to fruition. She is, without a doubt, the best book editor I have ever had.

Finally, I thank Theresa Heineman and our two wonderful children, Natalie and Grace, for their encouragement. Working on this book has been a lot like going back to graduate school, but so much better than the first time around because of their presence in my life.

Introduction

Ellen Ewing Sherman had seen her share of death. At William Tecumseh Sherman's encampment near Vicksburg, Mississippi, she had toured abandoned entrenchments laden with blood. It was during Ellen's visit with her husband in the summer of 1863 that their son Willie had fallen sick. He died before Ellen could reach her parents in Lancaster, Ohio. That same fall, Ellen's mother, Maria Boyle Ewing, entered the final stages of a terminal illness. Her father, Thomas Ewing, had already suffered a series of heart attacks since the beginning of the war.[1]

If the deaths of Maria and Willie had shaken Ellen to her core—followed by the loss of another child while Sherman was marching through Georgia— her father's decline was devastating. He had always been a source of calm in Ellen's turbulent life. By sheer willpower Ewing had rallied so he could continue his law practice in Washington. He collapsed while presenting a case before the U.S. Supreme Court in 1869. Remarkably, Ewing was not yet counted out. Now, two years later, Ellen sat by her father's bedside in Lancaster on a deathwatch. Her husband kept his distance, harboring mixed feelings of gratitude and resentment toward the man who had taken him in when his own father died and to whom he owed so much.[2]

As Ewing's life slipped away on October 26, 1871, his reputation had already assumed legendary proportions. He was the impoverished "Salt Boiler" of Virginia's Kanawha Valley who had gone on to become a U.S. senator and serve in the administrations of Presidents William Henry Harrison and Zachary Taylor. Although Ewing had not known Taylor before his 1848 campaign, he found him to be a lively storyteller and keen observer of human foibles. Taylor had an honored place at Ellen's wedding in 1850—a fact Sherman underscored when trying to impress military superiors and prospective business associates.[3]

In his first Senate term (1831–37), Ewing sat next to the prickly Henry Clay of Kentucky and behind the eloquent Daniel Webster of Massachusetts. Ewing often mediated disputes between these rival leaders of the Whig Party, and he became especially close to Webster. Indeed, Webster and Ewing were like impish schoolboys, whispering wry observations about their colleagues in Latin lest anyone might be listening. Whether in committee meetings or in debates on the Senate floor, Ewing gained equal measures of respect and bile as "the Logician of the West." Webster believed he had never met a more intelligent man, while Treasury Secretary William Meredith, who also served in Taylor's cabinet, said of Ewing: "His reasoning was like a sledgehammer, and woe betide the antagonist who mistook its weight." Even a few of his critics acknowledged him as a "statesman" who was "inclined to be what some would term 'jovial.'"[4]

His Scots-Irish forebears had bequeathed to him a commanding physique. He stood six feet tall, and though he weighed 260 pounds, it was mostly muscle, not fat, that tipped the scales. Old-timers in Lancaster recalled that when Ewing had simultaneously served as prosecuting attorney for Athens and Fairfield Counties, he had led a posse in pursuit of outlaws. Locating the fugitives in a farmhouse, Ewing charged up a flight of stairs and then launched his fists into the largest member of the gang. Amid breaking furniture and bones, he hogtied his quarry. His companions had a rougher time, so Ewing turned his attention to the rest of the gang. Seeing an opportunity, Ewing's prisoner loosened his binding enough so he could get to his feet, jump out the second-story window, and escape on a horse provided by a relative.[5]

Ewing's private legal practice proved to be both consequential and, on occasion, peculiar. In 1828, Ewing represented a Lancaster man accused of having had sexual relations with a horse. Ewing won the defamation suit and collected the princely sum of $500. That same year, Ewing received admittance to practice law before the U.S. Supreme Court. He made quite an impression, and in later years when he entered the Supreme Court the justices interrupted their deliberations to shake his hand. American jurists, when recommending case law to their younger cohorts, urged them to read less Blackstone and more Ewing.[6]

He tendered his most important—and unsolicited—legal advice to President Abraham Lincoln. In November 1861, the *U.S.S. San Jacinto* intercepted the British ship *Trent*, which was conveying two agents of the Confederate States of America—James Mason and John Slidell—to Europe. The British government viewed the Union Navy's action as tantamount to an act of war. Secretary of State Henry Seward, and public opinion in the North generally, favored keeping Mason and Slidell prisoners even if it meant war with Britain. Alarmed, Ewing lectured Lincoln in international law and argued that the United States could not defeat the Confederacy while fighting Britain. (Among friends, Ewing characterized Seward as "a low, vulgar, vain demagogue.") In need of a legal framework to justify the release of the Confederates, Lincoln accepted Ewing's rationale but gave him little credit.[7]

At home in Lancaster, Ewing solicited clients by engaging in athletic competitions. In one such exhibition, Ewing demonstrated his physical prowess by hurling an ax over the Fairfield County Courthouse. This same attorney that played roughneck for the locals took a complex case involving land claims in St. Louis. Ewing realized that understanding Spanish might prove useful in interpreting earlier land titles, so he locked himself in his study for six weeks and became fluent. For his fee, Ewing obtained a large portion of downtown St. Louis.[8]

When Ewing set a goal for himself he became an unstoppable force of nature. If he became interested in real estate speculation, then his objective was to be among those who developed St. Louis and Leavenworth, Kansas. If in need of a better burning fuel for boiling brine at his salt wells, then Ewing would become the father of coal mining in southeastern Ohio. If Ewing required more efficient transportation networks for his salt and coal, then he would construct canals and railroads to link Lancaster to New York City, Pittsburgh, Wheeling, and the Kanawha Valley.[9]

Most importantly, if in need of political protection, then Ewing would cultivate friends and family. He formed law partnerships with such men as Illinois senator Orville Hickman Browning, a confidant of Lincoln, and Henry Stanbery, a Lancaster relative who later served as attorney general for President Andrew Johnson. These political and familial alliances were no small matter. Daniel Webster introduced Ewing to the Boston businessmen who provided a good portion of the capital to build his canals and railroads.

Cousin James Gillespie Blaine, the Republican Speaker of the U.S. House of Representatives and the party's 1884 presidential candidate, joined the Ewing family in the mining of Ohio coal.[10]

Ewing kept the wine cellar and humidor well stocked when travelers from the Upper South came through Lancaster on Zane's Trace—which linked to the National Road all the way to Washington. Henry Clay and Andrew Johnson knew they could always find good cheer at the Ewing mansion on Main Hill. When he served as secretary of the Interior, Ewing rented the Blair House, which had space enough for entertaining. With his legal practice in the 1840s having netted nearly $1,000 a month, Ewing was well able to spend money to make more money.[11]

As with business, law, and politics, so it was with love: nothing could deter Ewing. In this case, the prize was Maria Boyle, the attractive and bright niece of Philemon Beecher, a prominent Lancaster attorney and member of Congress. Although Maria was Irish Catholic and Thomas of Irish Presbyterian descent, the sentiment among the Blaines, Boyles, Ewings, and Gillespies could be summarized thus: they were the exiles of Donegal and Londonderry seeking religious and economic freedom. For Thomas Ewing this meant his religion was the U.S. Constitution. For Maria Boyle, while the path to God went through Rome one still had to coexist peacefully in Protestant Ohio. Consequently, they reared their six children in the Catholic faith, with frequent visits to their Blaine kin so that they would be socially at ease with the Protestant majority.[12]

Thomas and Maria Ewing raised their two daughters and four sons in the contrasting worlds of Lancaster and Washington. The eldest child, Philemon (b. 1820), was likely the only thirteen-year-old in America who could say he had dined in the White House and camped in the foothills of Appalachia. Although Phil Ewing spent his legal career in Ohio and acquired no national reputation, he knew his way around the corridors of power in Washington. He was also a rare confidant of his mercurial brother-in-law, William Sherman. Phil's intimate knowledge of Washington politics helped save Sherman's military career more than once during the Civil War.[13]

The Ewings' daughters, Ellen (b. 1824) and Maria Theresa (b. 1837), received the most intensive religious instruction of the children. Maria went to the Sisters of Visitation in Washington, while Ellen attended Catholic boarding schools in Somerset, Ohio, and Georgetown. It was at the Georgetown (Washington) convent of the Sisters of Visitation that Ellen became friends with several members of the Mudd family—one of Maryland's prominent Catholic families. (The Mudd and Ewing families had a connection that preceded Ellen's enrollment at the Georgetown convent. Sister Catherine

Mudd of Maryland was among the founding faculty affiliated with St. Mary's Academy in Somerset.)[14]

From her mother, Ellen developed a religious devotion that might have led her to take vows but for her love of the red-headed Sherman boy. From her father, Ellen inherited keen skills of observation. It was doubtful that any adulterer or drunkard in Lancaster, St. Louis, or Washington escaped Ellen's notice. Like her father, Ellen kept track of enemies and allies. To her husband's dismay, Ellen envied Maria Theresa, who had been able to remain physically close to their parents.[15]

As the second eldest son, Hugh Ewing (b. 1826) had his father's girth, as well as his love of literature and thirst for adventure. What he lacked, especially in his younger years, was focus. Hugh was also more of an idealist than his father. Of the boys, Hugh appeared most comfortable hunting and playing war in the dense woods of southeastern Ohio. He certainly knew his way around taverns and billiards tables but remained a stranger to advanced mathematics. For those reasons, Hugh proved to be one of the most popular cadets to ever flunk out of the U.S. Military Academy at West Point. He was also a welcome companion to have in the goldfields of California. Few would have predicted that Hugh was destined to become a fine general in the Union Army, serving honorably at South Mountain, Antietam, Vicksburg, and Missionary Ridge.

Tom Ewing (b. 1829) looked like a leaner version of his father. He possessed a first-rate intellect and made the most of his education at Brown. In contrast to Hugh, Tom had ambitions to be just as prominent as his father in business, law, and politics. Having served as his father's personal secretary when he led the Interior Department, Tom knew all of Washington's back channels of influence. Like his father, Tom was politically pragmatic and thoroughly logical. Unlike either Thomas or Hugh, Tom was reserved, as if always on guard against potential threats. He was the only Ewing son who rejected his mother's Catholicism and became Presbyterian—much to his sister Ellen's sorrow.

Tom moved to Kansas in the 1850s, hoping to achieve fame and fortune. While he did not acquire fortune, Tom became chief justice of the Kansas Supreme Court and won fame of a kind during the Civil War. General Thomas Ewing Jr. fought William Quantrill's Confederate guerrillas and, after the 1863 Lawrence Massacre, issued General Order Number 11, which, at bayonet point, removed from their homes ten thousand Missouri residents suspected of aiding the insurgency. In 1864, Tom Ewing saved St. Louis from capture, decisively defeating a Confederate force several times larger than his own at Pilot Knob, Missouri.

When Dr. Samuel Mudd of Maryland stood accused of aiding John Wilkes Booth in his flight from Washington after the assassination of Lincoln, Tom Ewing served as his aggressive legal counsel. He also assisted Henry Stanbery in the defense of President Johnson at his Senate impeachment trial. Of the brothers, Tom Ewing had the dirtiest war and the most controversial legal and political career. Though Sherman's relations with Hugh and Charles Ewing during and after the war were sometimes tense, he always showed Tom the greatest deference.

Charles Ewing (b. 1835) was the youngest, shortest, and only golden-haired son of Thomas and Maria. As a teenager, Ellen practiced her mothering skills on Charley in an effort to make him an obedient child. She failed. Charley was a scamp with quick mental and physical reflexes—useful attributes to have, since he had a talent for finding trouble. His studies at the University of Virginia immersed him in Greek philosophy and the pastimes of the southern gentry. Fifteen years junior to Sherman, he idolized his brother-in-law. As a captain in the Thirteenth U.S. Infantry, Charley was wounded at Vicksburg while leading a desperate charge against Confederate positions. He fought at Missionary Ridge and marched through Georgia and the Carolinas, ending the Civil War with the rank of general and the distinction of being the most sought-after bachelor in Washington.

Thanks to Hugh, Tom, and Charley, as well as to the great renown achieved by his son-in-law Sherman, Thomas Ewing became known at the end of war as "the Father of Generals." It was rare for one family to produce so many capable military commanders, placing the Ewings in the exceptional company of Ohio's "Fighting McCooks" and the Virginian Jacksons. What made the Ewing brothers particularly remarkable was the size and pro-southern culture of the community from which they sprang, as well as their privileged background.

Lancaster at the outbreak of the Civil War was a county seat of 4,303, as well as a transportation hub that encompassed a winding route between Virginia's Kanawha Valley and Columbus, the capital of Ohio. From this small community sprang five Union generals and two of the first soldiers to receive the Medal of Honor. Lancaster and Fairfield County men filled the ranks of the Sixty-First Ohio Volunteer Infantry and served in at least eleven other Ohio regiments. They fought in nearly every major battle in the eastern and western theaters, including Antietam, Atlanta, Chancellorsville, Gettysburg, and Vicksburg.[16]

Despite impressive service to the Union, much of Lancaster, Fairfield County, southern Ohio, and, indeed, its western neighbors preferred either neutrality in the war or an outright Confederate victory. Ulysses Grant recalled that in his southern Ohio hometown most residents despised Lincoln. Moreover, Grant continued, "There were churches in that part of Ohio where treason was preached regularly, and where, to secure membership, hostility to the government, to the war, and to the liberation of the slaves, was far more essential than a belief in the authenticity or credibility of the Bible."[17]

Grant's characterization of southern Ohio rang true. On the eve of the Civil War, roughly a quarter of the residents of the Old Northwest were either southern born or the children of southerners. The founders of Ohio— notably, Thomas Worthington, Nathaniel Massie, and Simon Kenton—were Virginians. This was not surprising, since there was a fifteen-county area in southern Ohio known as the Virginia Military District—land set aside for Revolutionary War veterans from the Old Dominion. Indeed, Ohio's original capital, Chillicothe, was in the Virginia Military District. Ohio's first settlers tended to be ardent states' rights Democrats, as was true of their southern kin. Populist on economic matters, such people often assumed that businessmen were dishonest as a matter of course. Tellingly, when they felt cheated in a commercial transaction, they claimed they had been "Yankeed."[18]

Although many southern transplants had migrated to the Old Northwest because of their inability to compete economically against slave labor, they harbored more hatred for African Americans than for white planters. To them, blacks were the carriers of crime, disease, and moral debasement. In 1802, when Thomas Worthington helped draft the Ohio Constitution, he opposed granting citizenship to blacks. Ohio's Virginian-bred leaders prohibited blacks from testifying in court, barred their children from public schools, denied them the vote, and required African Americans to post a $500 bond that had to be signed by two white men if they wished to remain in the Buckeye State. After Lincoln called for volunteers to put down the southern rebellion in April 1861, Ohio Democrats in the legislature sponsored a bill to ban interracial marriage. Their intention was to place Republicans on the record as supporting interracial sex and to divert attention from South Carolina's attack on Fort Sumter.[19]

Ohio, Indiana, and Illinois were hotbeds of antiwar and antiblack sentiment, leading Republicans and some prowar Democrats to refer to their foes as "Copperheads"—after the poisonous snakes that were abundant in the Ohio River Valley. Ohio produced a number of important opponents of the war and the emancipation of the slaves. Columbus was home to Samuel Medary, who had been the editor of the state's Democratic newspaper, the *Ohio Statesman*, and a proslavery territorial governor of Kansas. Medary was not one to mince words. When Whigs in 1845 tried to repeal Ohio's antiblack

laws, Medary's *Statesman* asked: "Are you ready to be on a level with the niggers in the political rights for which your fathers contended? Are you ready
to share with them your hearths and your homes?"[20]

Medary's racial attitudes did not soften with the passage of time. During the Civil War, Medary, who by then was editing the *Columbus Crisis*,
castigated "the half-witted usurper" Lincoln and his emancipation policy.
Medary approvingly quoted a Chillicothe antiwar activist who argued that
"every white man in the North, who does not want to be swapped off for a
free nigger, should vote the Democratic ticket."[21]

In the congressional district adjacent to and north of Fairfield County,
Samuel "Sunset" Cox mocked Unionists and rallied House Democrats
against Lincoln. Meanwhile, U.S. representative George Pendleton of Cincinnati joined George McClellan on the Democrats' presidential peace ticket in
1864. Pendleton charged Republicans with having gone to war under false
pretenses. While deceitfully claiming that the North was fighting to preserve
the Union, Lincoln, so Pendleton alleged, was leading "an armed crusade for
the abolition of slavery." Both Pendleton and Cox warned that freed slaves
would invade Ohio—which already had the largest black population in the
Old Northwest—if the South lost the war.[22]

Most notorious among all the Copperheads was Congressman Clement Vallandigham of Dayton. Vallandigham opposed emancipation and pay
raises for Union troops. He expressed his criticism of military recruiting so
intemperately that he had the singular distinction of being deported from
Union territory. From exile in Canada, Vallandigham ran for governor of
Ohio in 1863. His campaign song, which mocked the abolitionists' "Battle
Cry of Freedom," spoke volumes:

> We will hurry to the polls boys
> From the East and from the West,
> Shouting Vallandigham and Freedom,
> And we'll teach the oppression's crew,
> With the niggers and the rest,
> To shout Vallandigham and Freedom!

Vallandigham racked up impressive tallies in Fairfield County and the neighboring Virginia Military District but decisively lost the Connecticut Yankee–
dominated Western Reserve near Lake Erie.[23]

In Lancaster, antiwar Democrat Edson Olds ended up jailed in 1862 for
his efforts to disrupt military conscription. From a prison cell in New York
City, Olds won a special election as Lancaster's representative to the Ohio

House of Representatives. Lancaster's antiwar Democratic newspaper, the *Eagle*, praised Olds and luridly editorialized against emancipation and the enlistment of blacks into the Union Army: "The Negro is a barbarian. His method of making war is by the destruction and massacre of women and children, as well as men, by the perpetuation of atrocities that makes humanity shudder."[24]

Well acquainted with the state's noxious political divisions, Thomas Ewing positioned himself on the slavery issue between the extremes of the abolitionist Western Reserve and the stridently antiblack Virginia Military District. The senior Ewing and son Tom desired to preserve the Union without abolishing slavery, hoping it could be contained in the South. This made them wary supporters of Lincoln and enthusiastic backers of Andrew Johnson. Hugh, on the other hand, became an abolitionist. Even Ellen, who had never previously had a political disagreement with her father, embraced abolition as both a military necessity and an act of vengeance against the South—the latter sentiment being one that Sherman did not share.

In addition to the racial antagonisms that poisoned attitudes toward emancipation and preservation of the Union, there were angry Democratic charges that the struggle against the South was a rich man's war and a poor man's fight. Antiwar Democrats in the North contended that conscription fell heavily upon working-class men. Few poor males, especially Irish Catholic immigrants, could afford to hire a substitute for $300 to serve in their place. Rising businessmen such as John D. Rockefeller of Cleveland and Andrew Carnegie of Pittsburgh avoided military service. Financier Thomas Mellon of Pittsburgh urged his sons to stay out of the war. In New York, attorney Grover Cleveland and businessman Theodore Roosevelt Sr. hired substitutes.[25]

Overall, only 2 percent of Union soldiers came from the ranks of professionals and businessmen. Factory workers and craftsmen accounted for 40 percent of the Union's 2.1 million troops, a proportion that was several times larger than their share of the North's population. When working-class males in the North went off to war, whether as volunteers or as conscripts, they often left behind wives, mothers, sisters, and children with little means of financial support. Consequently, class tensions on the northern home front were never far beneath the surface during the Civil War.[26]

Paradoxically, even as Lincoln dispatched Union troops to New York City in 1863 to put down an anticonscription riot that took at least 105 lives, his son Robert was sitting out the war at Harvard. Robert Lincoln claimed that he wanted to serve but that his frantic mother objected. After his graduation near the end of the war, Robert Lincoln went into the military. Lincoln, however, received an assignment to Washington, away from combat. Given how many prominent young men were able to evade military service, the Ewing brothers proved exceptional, leading by example and acting from a strong sense of civic obligation—even at the risk of their lives.[27]

Then again, given that the Ewing brothers had spent part of their formative years at the doorstop of Appalachia and were of Scots-Irish descent, they may have been close in culture and heritage to the southern warriors against whom they fought. The bulk of the troops who marched through Georgia and the Carolinas with Charley Ewing, after all, were not gentlemen Yankee clerks from the East. They were often enough uncouth western farm boys, with the highest proportion of Sherman's command coming from Ohio.

During the war Thomas Ewing had a strained relationship with Radical Republicans and the Lincoln administration, viewing the president as the best of a sorry lot of politicians. Senator John Sherman of Ohio, who kept politically, but not emotionally, close to his brother's relations, was harsher, regarding Lincoln as a disaster. Senator Sherman even tried to persuade the Republican Party not to renominate Lincoln. Thomas Ewing and John Sherman, as well as Phil, Hugh, and Tom, battled Secretary of War Edwin Stanton when he seemingly (and repeatedly) questioned General Sherman's sanity and loyalty to the Union. They also tried to temper the Radical Republican senator Benjamin Wade of Ohio and his Committee on the Conduct of the War. With Tennessee senator and committee member Andrew Johnson on board, the Ewings fought Wade, who, as Ulysses Grant complained, appeared interested in promoting Union officers more for their abolitionist beliefs than for their competency.[28]

With the end of the Civil War, the divisions that had beset the nation, Ohio, and Lancaster did not quickly recede. Thomas Ewing, Tom Ewing, and Henry Stanbery were vocal critics of the Radical Reconstruction of the South that Senator Wade proposed. They also continued their feud with Stanton, whose dismissal by Johnson triggered the president's impeachment. It was with this history in mind that the *New York Times*, in publishing its obituary of Thomas Ewing, took a position close to his Radical Republican enemies. "Mr. Ewing," the *New York Times* concluded, "was a man of the old generation in politics, a stately figure, honorable, high-toned, without fear and above reproach, but unfitted for these times of change and progress by a conservatism which clings to the past, and refuses to see any good in the future."[29]

Just before the end of his life Thomas Ewing received communion in the Catholic Church. There was no little irony to his gesture. Ewing had paid a political price for being married to a Catholic and for raising his children in the church. Angry nativists had prevented him from securing the vice presidential slot on the Whig ticket in 1848. In his stead, the Whigs' anti-Catholic faction chose Millard Fillmore, who ascended to the presidency following Taylor's death. (Fillmore later ran for president as the candidate of the nativist American Republican Party.) Even though Ewing had not converted until on his deathbed, his family had become revered and reviled as one of the most prominent Catholic families in the Old Northwest.[30]

Much of the state government of Ohio closed for business on the day of Ewing's funeral. In Washington, most federal offices were shuttered, with the Department of Interior draped in black. His pallbearers included Senator Sherman and Henry Stanbery, as well as Ohio governor Rutherford B. Hayes. Before the Civil War Ewing had praised Hayes's legal mind and predicted that he would make his mark on national politics. During the war, Hayes had commanded the Twenty-Third Ohio while Hugh Ewing led the Thirtieth Ohio—both part of the Kanawha Division, which saw action in western Virginia, South Mountain, and Antietam. Hayes felt a debt of honor to both father and son.[31]

Ewing's funeral Mass was said at St. Mary's in Lancaster, an imposing structure at the top of Main Hill that he had helped construct in 1864 as a monument to his wife. Cincinnati archbishop John Baptist Purcell delivered the eulogy, after which the funeral procession went to St. Mary's Cemetery at the city's outskirts.[32]

As the years passed, Thomas Ewing and his brood of generals faded from local and national memory. If recalled at all, Thomas Ewing received a passing mention as the father-in-law of General Sherman, although a few biographers noted that he had been politically powerful and protective of his daughter Ellen. For their part in history, Hugh, Tom, and Charley Ewing became nearly invisible, obscured by the shadow of their famous brother-in-law. Given this state of affairs, it is time to tell a tale of westward expansion, disunion, war, and high-stakes politics as seen by a close-knit family that shaped an era as much as the era shaped them.

On the central political issue of the Civil War and Reconstruction, the status of blacks in America, the Ewings charted a moderate course. They were repelled, in varying degrees, by the virulent racism of many northern Democrats and the black and white poverty they saw firsthand in the South. At the same time, the Ewings' extended family had little patience with Radical Republicans. In both the political and military arenas, the Ewings grappled with slavery and emancipation. Whether liberating slaves in the March through Georgia or advancing the political career of Andrew Johnson, the Ewings were at the center of the national debate on race relations.

The Ewings' skepticism of equal rights for blacks, and their limited goal of fighting a war to preserve the Union, embodied the views of the majority of Border State prowar Democrats and Republicans in 1861. Mounting casualties and escalating war, however, polarized the northern electorate and changed the political objective from fighting to preserve the Union with slavery to fighting for abolition. Thomas Ewing, Tom Ewing, and William Sherman reluctantly came to accept the abolition of slavery but did not believe that blacks merited political and social equality on a par with whites. Tom Ewing had commanded black volunteers and treated them more decently than was the case with many other Union officers. His African American troops in turn gave him good marks. But in the end, Tom Ewing and his family did not change their stance on civil rights and were consequently placed, along with Sherman and Johnson, on a collision course with the Radical Republican Congress.

Once passions over the war subsided in the North, the Radical Republicans lost ground and the court of public opinion swung sharply against them. In place of a spirit of vengeance there arose sympathy and admiration for the Confederate soldiers. The narrative of the Civil War that came into prominence twenty years after Sherman's March hailed the brave Yankees and the gallant southerners of "The Lost Cause" who had fought nobly at Gettysburg. In this emerging narrative, the Ewing family fell into disrepute or disappeared outright.[33]

Contrary to the romanticized view of the Civil War that many white northerners and southerners embraced after Robert E. Lee's surrender to Grant, the conflict had its share of ignoble events. Indeed, it can be fairly argued that the North won precisely because certain commanders were willing to fight more viciously than their southern foes—whose own hands bore the blood of massacred black Union troops and unarmed civilians.

Sherman became a reviled figure in Dixie because his troops did something far worse than kill their foes in battle—they destroyed southern property and psychologically emasculated Confederate soldiers who were unable to return home from Virginia to defend their families. Neither Sherman nor Charley Ewing ever regretted these tactics. They believed that South Carolina had started the war and Ohio was going to finish it—no matter the economic cost and mental anguish inflicted on the South.

Tom Ewing felt no differently. The anti-insurgency tactics he used in Missouri, and his battle of annihilation with Confederate forces, had, like Sherman's March, contributed to Union victory. If crushing the Missouri insurgency in the aftermath of the 1863 Lawrence Massacre required the removal of ten thousand civilians who had provided aid to the guerrillas, then Tom Ewing would remove them. Faced with a Confederate force several times larger than his own at Pilot Knob, Missouri, in 1864, a foe that tortured and executed Union prisoners, Ewing gave no quarter.

Unfortunately for the reputations of the Ewings and Sherman, after the Union armies disbanded and the martial ardor of the Yankees cooled, the North seemed to become ashamed of its win-at-any-cost warriors. While southerners deified Lee and erased Confederate president Jefferson Davis from their "Lost Cause" narrative, northerners placed Lincoln, rather than Sherman, or even Grant, at the heart of the Union narrative. Significantly, the North's idealized Lincoln would not be the president who approved Sherman's March and Tom Ewing's General Order Number 11; he would be the gentle Lincoln who desired reconciliation with the South.

As the battlefield experiences of Hugh, Charley, Sherman, and especially Tom Ewing illustrated, three Civil Wars were being fought. The first and most familiar war was the one of Union and Confederate armies clashing in conventional combat at Antietam and Gettysburg. The desperate battles became the spine of "The Lost Cause," glorious contests fought between two equally admirable forces.

The second and less familiar war—a war largely unknown to Americans today—was the struggle against guerrilla insurgents and the targeting of civilians. This war took the lives of fifty thousand civilians. Tom Ewing's Civil War, in terms of the brutality directed against combatant and noncombatant, equaled what Sherman inflicted on the South in 1864 and 1865. To understand the Civil War in all its dimensions requires studying the Ewing brothers' response to guerrillas and the insurgents' civilian support network in Missouri, western Virginia, Georgia, and the Carolinas.[34]

Finally, the third Civil War was one that the Ewings and Lincoln appreciated all too well. This front was the political contest fought by antiwar northern Democrats against the Unionists. There was a direct relationship between the electoral prospects of Republicans and prowar Democrats in the North and the military progress of Union forces. Repulsing Lee at Antietam in 1862 made the issuance of the Emancipation Proclamation possible, even though, as Thomas Ewing warned Lincoln, it gave ammunition to racist Copperhead Democrats in the Old Northwest. Sherman's capture of Atlanta and Tom Ewing's defense of St. Louis in 1864 secured Lincoln's reelection. There could never be a separation of military policy and electoral politics—a fact of life well understood by the Ewings.

Rediscovering the Ewings provides a window on the importance of family networks in nineteenth-century American politics. This family helped advance Andrew Johnson to the White House (and saved him from impeachment), paved the way for Sherman to become one of America's greatest soldiers, and kept the Union out of war with Britain. Thomas Ewing combined his business and political interests and practiced constitutional law at the highest level. The power he wielded, while laying the foundation for his sons' military careers during the Civil War, also served the larger purpose of preserving the Union and economically developing the West.

Finally, the Ewings represented one of the most socially and politically prominent "blended" families in Civil War–era America. Although the ancestors of the Ewing, Boyle, Blaine, and Gillespie families had fought each other in Ireland's sectarian wars, they became Americans at ease in Catholic and Presbyterian pews. While Scots-Irish and Irish Catholics conducted bloody feuds in Belfast, Boston, New York, and Philadelphia, the Ewings' relations came to each other's aid. If there had been any doubt as to whether an American could be loyal to the Roman Church and the Constitution— and this was the doubt nineteenth-century nativists raised—the military and political records of the Ewings gave proof of their patriotism. In the religious culture wars of the nineteenth century, there were important figures such as the Ewings who reserved their ammunition for real battlefields.

* * *

Chapter 1 will chart Thomas Ewing's path from impoverished Appalachian salt boiler to formidable Washington political player. The political context of Ewing's battles with Presidents Andrew Jackson and John Tyler, as well as his business ventures prior to 1850, receive particular attention. Further, the cultural context of Ohio and western politics and society in the early nineteenth century will be analyzed.

Chapter 2 focuses on Thomas Ewing's marriage, children, kinship ties, and Catholic religious practice. The introduction of William Sherman into the Ewing household, failed efforts to bring the belligerent John Sherman under control, and John Sherman's later redemption are part of this story. We will discuss the adventures of three of the Ewing brothers: Hugh, Tom, and Charley. While Hugh Ewing flunked out of West Point and headed to the California goldfields, Tom Ewing served as his father's assistant in the Interior Department and witnessed his father's (losing) opposition to the Compromise of 1850. Thomas Ewing opposed the 1854 Kansas-Nebraska Act and watched with disgust when armed Missourians crossed into territorial Kansas to vote for its admission to the Union as a slave state. Tom and Hugh Ewing went to Kansas to practice law, speculate in real estate, and politically battle the proslavery forces.

In chapter 3, we will survey Thomas Ewing's role in the 1860 presidential election and his subsequent participation, along with Tom, in the 1861 Washington Peace Convention. By a quirk of fate, Hugh, Charley, and William Sherman, along with U. S. Grant, found themselves in the middle of what was then the bloodiest moment of the Civil War as fighting broke out in St. Louis between secessionists and Unionists. Hugh Ewing returned to Ohio to join the invasion of western Virginia in the summer of 1861. The Ewing family intervened with President Lincoln to protect Sherman from charges that he was insane, while Thomas Ewing and John Sherman presided over the establishment of the Union Party in Ohio, bringing together moderate Republicans and prowar Democrats. The senior Ewing also took it upon himself to save Lincoln from war with Great Britain.

As the events of 1862 unfold in chapter 4, we will explore Hugh Ewing's embrace of abolition even as his father warned Lincoln that a policy of emancipation would play into the hands of the Copperheads and throw the Old Northwest to the antiwar Democrats. In the aftermath of the bloody battle of Shiloh, the Ewings once again fought to save Sherman's reputation. While Charley Ewing languished as a prison guard at Alton, Illinois, Hugh Ewing and the Kanawha Division played critical roles in the Union Army's victories against Lee at South Mountain and Antietam. Meanwhile, Tom Ewing resigned as chief justice of the Kansas Supreme Court to assume command of a Kansas regiment. He distinguished himself in Missouri and Arkansas. Subsequently promoted to brigadier general, Tom Ewing battled a vicious guerrilla insurgency along the Kansas-Missouri border.

In chapter 5, Hugh Ewing, Charley Ewing, and William Sherman held a family reunion in Mississippi. General Grant's Vicksburg campaign of 1862–63—followed by the desperate battle of Missionary Ridge in Tennessee—brought notoriety and pain to the Ewing brothers. Both were in the thick of combat, with Charley Ewing wounded and Hugh Ewing all too accurately calling his troops "the Forlorn Hope."

Shortly after the guns at Vicksburg fell silent, Confederate guerrilla William Quantrill's troops executed 175 men and boys in Lawrence, Kansas. General Tom Ewing issued General Order Number 11. Ewing's military response to the guerrilla insurgency would not be matched in scale until the federal government relocated tens of thousands of Japanese immigrants and their children during World War II.

In Ohio, the Copperheads nominated the exiled Clement Vallandigham for governor as pro- and antiwar partisans escalated their feud. Losing Ohio to the Copperheads in 1863 would have made Lincoln's reelection in 1864 all the harder and would have hampered war mobilization given that the Buckeye State provided the third-largest number of troops to the Union cause.

Chapter 6 emphasizes the interplay between presidential politics and the brutal military clashes of 1864. Sherman, Charley Ewing, and an army of one hundred thousand advanced toward Atlanta while Grant racked up enormous casualties in the eastern theater against Lee. After antiwar Democrats in the North captured control of their party and nominated former Union general George McClellan and Ohio congressman George Pendleton for president and vice president, respectively, Lincoln's sense of desperation grew. Moderate Republicans chose Tennessee Democrat Andrew Johnson, a Unionist and ally of the Ewing family, as Lincoln's running mate to appeal to prowar voters outside the Republican Party.

Sherman's capture of Atlanta in September 1864 improved Lincoln's political position. Aware of that fact, Confederate general Sterling Price launched an invasion of Missouri with the intention of capturing St. Louis and shifting northern political momentum away from Lincoln. Only Tom Ewing's troops stood in the way of a much greater Confederate force.

After the battle of Pilot Knob, Charley Ewing and sixty thousand Union troops launched what was then the most audacious campaign in American military history. As a member of Sherman's staff responsible for overseeing the behavior of troops, providing supplies, and acting as troubleshooter at large, Charley Ewing took a crucial backstage role in the march through Georgia in 1864. Hugh Ewing, exhausted from three years of close combat, remained behind in Kentucky to deal with a guerrilla insurgency. Tom Ewing, promoted to the rank of major general for his decisive victory at Pilot Knob, Missouri, turned down Sherman's invitation to join him in Georgia, choosing to resign his commission and take up a law practice in Washington. Only Charley Ewing would be present at the creation of the legend of General William T. Sherman.

In chapter 7, Sherman's troops marched through the Carolinas and greatly contributed to the ending of the military conflict. While the shooting stopped in April 1865, a political war between Radical Republicans and moderate Republicans and War Democrats commenced. Sherman found himself in trouble with War Secretary Edwin Stanton and Senator Ben Wade, thanks in part to the generous surrender terms he had given Confederate general Joe Johnston in North Carolina. The Ewing family once again rallied to Sherman's side.

Meanwhile, Tom Ewing became one of the most despised men in the North by defending Dr. Samuel Mudd and a few others prosecuted for complicity in the assassination of Lincoln. With Ewing family member and law partner Henry Stanbery serving as President Johnson's attorney general, Tom Ewing and his father crossed swords with the Republican radicals. Paradoxically, the post–Civil War era opened with a military trial—that of Dr. Mudd—and closed with the Senate impeachment trial of Johnson—defended by Stanbery and the Ewings.

1

"The Devoted Band of Leonidas"

Thomas Ewing's Ascent

Turn but your eyes on modern Greece and remember how short the time since she was sunk to the lowest stage of political and moral degeneration—her degeneracy, her abject slavery, a by-word, a reproach among the nations. She sued for foreign aid, but no Christian arm was raised to free her from her infidel oppressors. She at length aroused herself from her lethargy—her chains burst asunder, and the deeds of her modern sons have eclipsed even the glory of her ancient heroes. Year after year, with a comparatively feeble force she has swept the seas of the fleets, and the land of the armies of her invaders. But her foes multiply by defeat, and fleets and armies thicken on her coast. Though like the devoted band of Leonidas, she may be wasted in conquest and fall in the arms of victory. Though like Spain, she may be sold by treachery or crushed by overwhelming power: yet she will never sink again to slavery.
—Thomas Ewing Sr., 1825

Near an Irish river called the Boyne in 1690 the fate of English parliamentary rule, as well as the future of Ireland's Protestant colony, hung in the balance as two armies closed for battle. On one side stood the Dutchman William of Orange, representing England's parliament and the Scottish Presbyterians who had settled in Ulster province. Against William III loomed the ousted English King James II, backed by French troops and Irish Catholics—the latter determined to punish the Protestants who had "stolen" their lands. At battle's end James II fled the field, pursued by troops whose ranks included Captain Charles Ewing.[1]

The Scots-Irish Presbyterians who served under Charles Ewing at the Boyne were products of generations of strife. An Irish uprising in 1641 resulted in the destruction of one-seventh of the Protestant population of Ulster. In the 1650s, Puritan general Oliver Cromwell had tried to pacify Ireland, setting into motion a cycle of war and famine that led to the deaths of five hundred thousand Catholics and one hundred thousand Protestants. Unfortunately for Ireland, William III's victory failed to secure the peace for either Protestant or Catholic. Desperate poverty stalked Irish and Scots-Irish alike, while the English Anglicans regarded the latter as an expendable military buffer against the former.[2]

Unwilling to endure any longer the miserable economic and political conditions of Ireland, the Ewings joined tens of thousands of their Presbyterian brethren in the trek to the American colonies. Charles Ewing's heirs settled in New Jersey. Other Scots-Irish headed to Lancaster, Pennsylvania, and frontier Virginia. In the mountains of western Virginia, they named a county "Orange" to honor William III and established a government that viewed individual liberty as a first principle. Looking at the rough-hewn Ulster clans, who bore such names as MacCracken and MacIntyre, Charles Lee, a Virginian of Anglican pedigree, derided the "Mac-ocracy" of the frontier.[3]

The Scots-Irish called their new homes "the Best Poor Man's Country in the World." But while they acquired land, peace eluded the Scots-Irish. In the course of the eighteenth century they took up the musket and tomahawk time and again to fight the native tribes, acquiring in the process reputations as restless adventurers and accomplished warriors. Moravian missionaries, sharing Anglican disdain for Ulster's refugees, claimed they felt safer among Cherokee tribesmen than in "the Irish settlements."[4]

Eight months after American revolutionaries clashed with British troops at Concord, Massachusetts, George Ewing, the great-grandson of Charles Ewing, enlisted as a private in the Second New Jersey, a regiment in the Continental Army. For most of 1776, Ewing and the Second New Jersey skirmished with British forces in the Lake Champlain region of New York. Much of the ground over which the Second New Jersey fought had been contested in the French and Indian War twenty years earlier. George Ewing observed in his journal that he encamped at a base built atop the remains of Fort William Henry—the scene of a major British defeat in 1757.[5]

Although Ewing had a reputation as a soft-spoken, scholarly man, fellow soldiers noted his leadership qualities. Just shy of his twenty-third birthday, he transferred from the Second New Jersey to become a subaltern (lieutenant) in the Third New Jersey. Outside Philadelphia in 1777, Ewing participated in his first large-scale engagements, standing among twelve thousand citizen soldiers arrayed against fifteen thousand well-trained British troops.[6]

Sir William Howe's forces delivered hammer blows to the Third New Jersey at Brandywine (September 1777) and Germantown (October 1777). Defeated, the Continental Army abandoned Philadelphia and settled in for winter quarters at Valley Forge, Pennsylvania. Recognized for his steadfastness in battle, superior officers chose Ewing to be among the one hundred men to receive formal instruction in the manual of arms. Baron Friedrich

Thomas Ewing Sr. (1789–1871). The "Father of Generals," Thomas Ewing was a U.S. senator, a U.S. secretary of the Treasury, a U.S. secretary of the Home Department (Interior), an attorney, a real estate developer, and a confidant to Whig presidents William Henry Harrison and Zachary Taylor. (Courtesy of the University of Notre Dame Archives.)

von Steuben taught the Americans how to drill like soldiers and curse like Prussians.[7]

The suffering of the Continental soldiers at Valley Forge was as at least as bad as what they had experienced at Brandywine. Nearly two thousand Americans perished at Valley Forge, the majority from dysentery, influenza, and pneumonia. By May 1778, George Ewing's health was precarious. He received an honorable discharge and a pocketful of worthless Continental currency. Ewing never regretted his military service, but neither did he draw attention to it until near the end of his life, when he sought a government pension to help him pay his debts.[8]

After his discharge, George Ewing married Rachel Harris, a Scots-Irish farmer's daughter whose dowry consisted of little more than a love for classical Greek literature in English translation. They migrated to western Pennsylvania, where Ewing attempted to support his growing family as a schoolteacher and farmer. Making little progress in Pennsylvania, the Ewings relocated to West Liberty, Virginia, near the Ohio River settlement of Wheeling. It was in the frontier community of West Liberty, on December 28, 1789, that Rachel gave birth to Thomas Ewing, the sixth of their seven children.[9]

At the age of three Thomas Ewing took a flatboat down the Ohio River to Marietta in the Northwest Territory. Aside from the loss of a teenaged member of their party to quicksand near the Muskingum River, the journey westward had been uneventful. The Ewing family settled into a fortified blockhouse at a place aptly named Waterford, and then traveled to another garrison called Olive Green.[10]

Prior to the Ewings' arrival, the Congress of the Confederation, a precursor of the U.S. Congress, had adopted the Northwest Ordinance, which organized the frontier territory that became the states of Ohio, Indiana, Illinois, Michigan, and Wisconsin. The Northwest Ordinance of 1787, which Thomas Jefferson helped draft, prohibited slavery in America's "First West." Eastern politicians, however, were slower in providing security for settlers. Thomas Ewing sensed the uneasiness of the adults around him at Olive Green, an uneasiness that turned to grim resolve when tribesmen ambushed, killed, and scalped Abel Sherman. Abel had been among the first members of the large Sherman family to depart Fairfield County, Connecticut, for the Northwest Territory.[11]

Olive Green's residents might have rested easier had they known that 260 miles to the north, three thousand American soldiers were poised to destroy the military power of the Shawnee and Miami tribes. Under the leadership of Revolutionary War veteran Anthony Wayne and a hard-charging junior officer named William Henry Harrison, American forces won a decisive victory at Fallen Timbers in August 1794. Minor skirmishes continued for the next several months until the warring tribes signed the Treaty of Greenville in 1795. White settlers subsequently felt safer in venturing further from their garrisons.

Leaving Olive Green, the Ewings ended up in Athens County, Ohio, where they built a home and cleared land for farming. The family supplemented their larder with fishing expeditions on the Ohio River. During one fishing trip in 1796, George Ewing received an invitation to dine with a group of Shawnee who were hunting deer. Admitting to being simultaneously intrigued and terrified of the Indians, Thomas Ewing listened intently to their version of Fallen Timbers. They appeared good-natured enough despite their defeat and generously offered the seven-year-old a fine treat of cooked puppies and venison. Although he lost his appetite, young Ewing appreciated the tribesmen's instruction in fishing, as well as their vivid storytelling.[12]

Thomas Ewing's eldest sister, Abigail, taught him how to read prose, while an alcoholic neighbor introduced him to English poetry. He soon devoured the King James Bible, one of the few books in the house other than *Aesop's Fables* and Oliver Goldsmith's 1766 novel *The Vicar of Wakefield*. Ewing found Chronicles to be incomprehensible, while the Gospels of Matthew, Mark, Luke, and John riveted, perplexed, and, finally, let him down: "The four Gospels puzzled me. I took them to be narratives of four different advents, lives, and crucifixions of our Savior in which he had passed through the same scenes; and I was greatly disappointed when my father explained away that crowning miracle."[13]

The Ewings and their neighbors were determined to advance education in the Appalachian wilderness. In 1803, they donated raccoon pelts that one community member took to Boston and sold to purchase fifty-one books. It was thus that the first free, or "circulating," library in the Old Northwest came into existence. (Two other libraries in the Old Northwest were by subscription only, which meant that few could afford to check out their books.) The Ewings' friends colorfully called their new institution "the Coonskin Library." Thomas Ewing, who had chipped in ten raccoon pelts—"all my hoarded wealth"—dove into the books.[14]

Neighboring farmers and fieldhands so enjoyed young Ewing's voice that they entreated him to read to them as they worked. Since several of the books Ewing borrowed from the Coonskin Library lacked covers, he had no idea that on one occasion he was reciting from Virgil's *Aeneid*. Ewing's audience, after a heated discussion, concluded that "the ungrateful Latins" needed to behave more respectfully toward their womenfolk. Less judgmental of Virgil's characters than the farmworkers had been, Ewing decided that he should learn to read the *Aeneid* in its original language. Through repeated copying and recitation, Latin eventually became Ewing's second tongue. He enjoyed its structure and logic, finding it occupied his mind while he performed dull chores. His subsequent discovery of mathematics and Greek philosophy further delighted him.[15]

George Ewing spared no effort in providing for his family, attempting to make a go of farming as well as starting a salt-boiling business venture. Prosperity, however, eluded the Ewing household. Having grown into a physically imposing young man, Thomas Ewing set off in 1809 for the Kanawha Valley in Virginia, determined to earn enough money to help support his family and to pay for a college education. He promised to return home to assist with planting and harvesting.[16]

Covering the two-hundred-mile distance on foot and keelboat, Ewing arrived in Charleston, Virginia, to engage in the hardest labor of his life. Near the Great Kanawha and Elk Rivers, Charleston had become the nation's most important producer of salt. Extraction was a labor-intensive process. Sinking wells fifty feet deep with pick and shovel in search of salt brine was just the beginning. Hundreds of huge kettles boiled the brine and required a host of workers to tend fires and stir water. Two dozen kettles typically burned three to five cords of wood for each batch. Salt workers harvested the forests for fuel until the exploitation of coal created a new mining industry. It took two hundred gallons of brine to make a single bushel of salt, which, in the early 1800s, sold for $2. By 1814, the Kanawha Valley produced 640,000 bushels of salt annually.[17]

Thomas Ewing chopped wood and filled, fired, and stirred kettles. The work left him coated with soot and salt—both of which remained welded to his skin in spite of regular baths. Most of Ewing's fellow salt boilers were males between the ages of fifteen and thirty-nine. The Kanawha salt wells were not for the very young or the aged. Women, especially refined women, were scarce in the Charleston area. Ewing admitted that on the rare occasions when he encountered a well-attired woman he became tongue-tied, not feeling worthy of such company. There were also slaves working among the salt boilers. A thousand slaves resided among five thousand whites in Kanawha County—the largest concentration of African Americans Ewing had encountered up to that time. The salt operators valued their slaves, reserving dangerous jobs for the white, mostly Scots-Irish, workers. This was a recipe for racial animosity.[18]

For six years Thomas Ewing divided his time among the Kanawha saltworks, the family farm, and an academic academy in Athens, Ohio, that had been founded in 1804 by a few of the area's leading citizens. With the $400 he earned annually in Charleston, he kept debt collectors from his father's door and paid for his college tuition. When he ran out of funds in Athens, he returned to the Kanawha Valley, taking his texts with him so he could study during rest breaks. It was a tribute to his self-discipline that, although caked in salt and exhausted, he taught himself French. His teachers, and members of the academy's trustees, were so impressed with Ewing that they waived the Greek language requirement. In 1815, Ewing became the first graduate of Ohio University—itself the first public college in the Old Northwest. Trustee Charles Sherman, a relative of the ill-fated Abel Sherman, urged him to move to Lancaster, Ohio, and read law. Ewing agreed.[19]

The town that became Thomas Ewing's home had only just been carved from the wilderness. Located in the foothills of Appalachia, Lancaster had red and white oak trees six feet in diameter. Sugar maples and black walnuts were abundant, as were magnolias and dogwoods, whose springtime blossoms lit the landscape. The indigenous buckeye trees with their peculiar green leaves and inedible brown nuts gave Ohio its state nickname and a quip: "What is a Buckeye? Why it's a worthless nut." Turkeys, white-tailed deer, squirrels, panthers, and wolves roamed Lancaster's forests. The streams were filled with perch and bass.[20]

Twenty-five thousand years earlier, the Wisconsin Glacier had flattened northern Ohio, Indiana, and Illinois, while in southern Ohio it had pushed up mountains and left behind narrow river valleys—among them the Muskingum, Hocking, and Scioto. All three waterways flowed into the Ohio River, though the Hocking, where Lancaster was sited, lacked the depth to support year-round commercial navigation.[21]

As had been true with the Ewings, penetration into the Northwest Territory had been along the Ohio River. It took an ambitious land speculator in Wheeling named Ebenezer Zane to grasp the money-making potential in building an overland road. Having persuaded Congress in 1796 to give him land grants in exchange for his efforts, Zane built a 230-mile westward "trace" or pathway between Wheeling and Limestone (later Maysville), Kentucky. Zane sited settlements on the Muskingum River (Zanesville) and the Hocking (Lancaster). The trace also linked to the preexisting settlement of Chillicothe on the Scioto before it once again touched the Ohio River.[22]

Established in 1800, "New Lancaster" had a strong Pennsylvania Scots-Irish and German presence. Pennsylvania settlers imposed the Philadelphia grid on their new town, creating perfectly square blocks and streets named Broad, Chestnut, Locust, and Walnut. At their places of business, Pennsylvanians posted signs in English and German. The founders of Lancaster's first

newspaper, which evolved into a Democratic Party organ, named their publication *Der Adler (The Eagle)*. They eventually published it in English.[23]

The next largest collection of settlers hailed from Virginia and Kentucky,
followed by natives of New England. Connecticut people like the Shermans
lived in wood-framed homes that often had low ceilings and small porches.
The Virginians built homes of brick. Prosperous Scots-Irish Virginians had
houses with high ceilings, Palladian windows, and expansive verandas. Lancaster's southern migrants built homes that were designed to vent heat in the
summer, while New England settlers sought to retain warmth in the winter.
Their respective architectural strategies made sense in regions with consistently cool or warm temperatures. Unfortunately for both groups, Lancaster
had "southern" summers and "northern" winters.[24]

By the time Ewing came to Lancaster in 1815, the settlement of eight hundred was prospering as a trading center and county seat. Zane's Trace was
now a true road, twenty feet wide and with the marshy sections backfilled.
Pennsylvania, Virginia, and Kentucky settlers who traveled Zane's Trace
helped swell Ohio's population from 230,000 in 1810 to 400,000 five years
later. Farmers herded up to two hundred head of cattle or hogs at a time
along the road between Lancaster and Zanesville. Fifty-four taverns lined the
route from Wheeling to Limestone, including Chillicothe's notorious Red
Lion. Families went to Lancaster for the services of a blacksmith or a lawyer.
Men went to Chillicothe looking for locally distilled corn liquor and whores.
Chillicothe, in the words of one critic, fully deserved its reputation as "a town
of drunkards and a sink of corruption."[25]

Since Charles Sherman was a respected young attorney and graduate
of Dartmouth, his recommendation carried weight. Philemon Beecher, an
attorney from a prominent Connecticut family and the former speaker of the
Ohio House of Representatives, had assented to Sherman's request that he
meet Ewing. Beecher was not prepared for the strapping rustic who entered
his law office. Ewing looked as if he could thrash every man at Chillicothe's
Red Lion tavern. Ewing's erudite and deliberate manner further took Beecher
aback. And then there was Ewing's simple earnestness. Beecher told Ewing
that if he wanted to read law with him then he would be required to study
Blackstone's *Commentaries*. He asked if Ewing had heard of this legal classic.
Ewing replied that he had memorized the four volumes since his graduation.
Beecher realized Ewing was not joking.[26]

Ewing read law with Beecher and boarded with his family, helping with
the household chores. Among the members of the Beecher household were
Philemon's nieces, Maria and Susan Boyle, who had moved in following their
mother's death. Their father, Hugh Boyle, had served as clerk of the common

Maria Boyle Ewing (1801–64), mother of generals, enforcer of discipline, and defender of the Catholic faith. (Courtesy of the University of Notre Dame Archives.)

pleas court since 1803—and continued in that position for several decades. His history was sketchy.

Boyle had the ability—some would have called it the Irish gift—to talk a lot without providing any incriminating specifics. He told friends that his parents had sufficient means to send him to schools in France. Exactly what a Catholic youth from Donegal would have learned in revolutionary France beyond anticlericalism and military drill, Boyle did not elaborate. After his return, Boyle, for reasons never fully explained, attracted the notice of the English authorities. His parents felt it prudent for him to leave Ireland in 1791 at the age of eighteen. Apparently, it had not been sufficient for his kin that Boyle just cross the Atlantic—he headed deep into the Virginia frontier and went to work for an uncle.[27]

While on a business trip to Brownsville, Pennsylvania, outside Pittsburgh, Boyle met a fellow Donegal man named Neal Gillespie. The Gillespies were a growing family of Catholics who felt no need to fight the religious wars of their forebears. Neal Gillespie's granddaughter, Maria, for instance, married a Scots-Irish Presbyterian named Ephraim Blaine, whose own ancestors had defended Londonderry against a Catholic siege. When Blaine ran for a local office and nativists accused him of being a secret Catholic, he asked the parish priest to write a public letter for his campaign. The priest, an old friend of the Gillespies, readily complied: "This is to certify that Ephraim L. Blaine is not now and never was a member of the Catholic Church; and furthermore, in my opinion, he is not fit to be a member of any church."[28]

Boyle fell in love with Gillespie's daughter, Eleanor. They married and departed for Chillicothe in 1798—the destination of many native and adopted Virginians like Boyle. Hugh and Eleanor Gillespie Boyle, however, found raucous Chillicothe to be a less than ideal place in which to raise a family, so they relocated to Lancaster in 1801. Graced with a gregarious personality, Boyle was a get-along, go-along kind of fellow. Ignoring the strictures of the Catholic Church against joining secret societies, Boyle helped establish the local Masonic Lodge. His social position became firmly solidified when his wife's sister, Susan Gillespie, met and married Philemon Beecher, who was twenty years her senior. Beecher, like Ephraim Blaine, was Presbyterian.[29]

Maria Boyle was four years old when her mother died in 1805 from complications related to the birth of a second daughter. Hugh Boyle was overwhelmed: he did not know how to raise an infant and a four-year-old by himself. His Beecher in-laws came to the rescue. Susan Gillespie Beecher made sure that her late sister's girls were instructed in the Catholic faith—no easy feat, since Lancaster did not have an assigned priest or church. For that matter, the first Catholic parish in Ohio would not be founded until 1818 in Somerset—an eighteen-mile trip from Lancaster on Zane's Trace.[30]

From the moment Thomas Ewing moved in with the Beechers, Maria Boyle had felt drawn to him. He was generous with his time to the children of the household, entertaining them with tales of valor he had heard from Shawnee braves and Revolutionary War veterans. There was no doubting Ewing's strong work ethic. After a year of study with Beecher, Ewing received admittance to the Ohio Bar. Beecher made him a partner in his legal practice and placed him in charge of the office when he left for Congress in 1817. Charles Sherman sought out Ewing to join him in court, where they enjoyed a string of victories as defense attorneys.[31]

In 1818, having been appointed prosecuting attorney for Athens and Fairfield counties, Ewing became a local legend. Tasked with prosecuting a band of thieves, he first had to have them arrested. This proved difficult, since, as Ewing recounted, "The Sheriff was absent—the Deputy Sheriff drunk, so that I [had to] take charge of the enterprise or let the rascals escape." Ewing deputized a posse and led the assault on the criminals' lair. He was likely the only prosecutor in Ohio who could quote lengthy passages of *Don Quixote* from memory and land a takedown punch. Maria Boyle fell in love.[32]

Ewing had been entranced with Maria since he first laid eyes on her. As he confessed, she gave him a feeling of being "reborn." Given her age, Ewing was discreet but still let Maria know that she was special to him. By 1819, when he proposed marriage, Maria accepted—with conditions. First, they would be married by a priest. Second, they would raise their children Catholic. Ewing, who was not religiously sectarian, agreed to Maria's terms. He also stood aside as Maria became the religious enforcer in their household. In truth, Ewing's reading tastes did not trend toward theology, so for him choosing a faith was a matter best left to those who were better informed.[33]

As the 1820s commenced, Ewing's circle of friends grew and prospered—with a notable exception. Charles Sherman suffered a major setback as a consequence of having agreed in 1813 to serve as the U.S. collector of internal revenue for the Third Ohio District. Lacking Ewing's business acumen, Sherman had accepted payment in notes drawn from local banks. (Sherman's practice ran toward criminal law rather than commercial—unlike Ewing's, which worked in both areas.) In 1817, the federal government insisted that collectors remit payment in either gold or U.S. Bank notes. Caught off guard, Sherman found himself saddled with an enormous debt. Although his appointment to the Ohio Supreme Court in 1823 was a great honor and kept his household afloat financially, the Shermans had no margin for error.[34]

Always on the hunt for legal talent, Ewing brought Zanesville attorney Henry Stanbery into the Beecher practice in 1824. A native of New York, Stanbery's physician father had moved his family to Zanesville in 1814. He attended Washington College in western Pennsylvania and then read law in Zanesville. The twenty-one-year-old Stanbery impressed contemporaries. As friends recounted, Stanbery loved "Latin maxims, which he regarded as the very embodiment of terse wisdom." He was a detail-oriented attorney, careful in both his writing and speaking to rely upon evidence, not emotion, to arrive at conclusions.[35]

It was no mystery as to why Ewing had recruited Stanbery; he was, temperamentally, a younger version of himself. Friendship aside, however, Ewing gave Stanbery the least desirable cases, including the settlement of a festering dispute over the ownership of a cow. Stanbery wryly observed afterwards that he had never again worked so long on a case for so little money—and at that, the parties in the dispute had stiffed him and paid only half of his $5 fee. (Ewing reserved for himself the more interesting and lucrative case of the Lancaster politician who stood accused of having sexual relations with a horse.) Like Ewing, Philemon Beecher appreciated Stanbery's character and intellect. In 1829, Beecher's daughter Frances married Stanbery. This marriage forged a familial and political link with the Ewings and Gillespies that continued after Philemon Beecher's death in 1839 and spanned two generations.[36]

The firm of Beecher, Ewing, and Stanbery kept busy. All three served as defense counsel in 1824 for an extremely difficult case. Jacob Shafer, a man of considerable financial means, had shot and killed a Licking County neighbor in a dispute over a fence. A grand jury indicted Shafer for premeditated murder, since he had armed himself before confronting the victim. Evidence of his guilt was overwhelming, and Shafer was convicted. It was not a total loss for Ewing, Stanbery, and Beecher. They were able to persuade the jury to convict Shafer of a lesser charge of manslaughter. After all, many people in central and southern Ohio went about their business armed—without any intention of causing harm.[37]

At other times there was less drama and more fun. Ewing enjoyed "riding the court circuit" in Ohio with Sherman and Stanbery. As Ewing recalled, "There was no professional jealousy among us. We lodged at the same taverns, ate at the same tables, and often to the number of eight or ten slept in the same large chamber." Ewing's fellow lawyers loudly hooted whenever he was the first to leave a hotel bar to prepare a case for the next morning. The attorneys understood that victory in court earned Ewing further renown and subsequently attracted more clients. But they were less aware that Ewing's court wins translated into name recognition with legislators and the electorate. Charles Hammond, an attorney and editor of the *Cincinnati Gazette*, recognized Ewing's political ambition—an ambition that others may not have seen behind his Latin quips and the rounds of drinks he purchased.[38]

Ewing's political beliefs came in part from his father. George Ewing, who died in 1824, had been a staunch Federalist and had held public office as township clerk. Just how staunchly Federalist George Ewing was Thomas experienced firsthand. Only once had he ever seen his father act rudely toward a traveler in search of drink and food. George Ewing tersely gave the stranger what he requested but made no conversation. When the man departed, Ewing told his son that he recognized the traveler as former vice president Aaron Burr, who had recently killed Alexander Hamilton in a duel. George Ewing revered Hamilton as a political thinker and sound economist; there was no forgiveness in his heart for Burr.[39]

Thomas Ewing's experiences as a salt boiler and prosecutor taught him much about economics, human nature, and the importance of the rule of law in fostering social stability. Philosophically, Ewing was a disciple of Hamilton, committed to a strong federal government, sound currency, and a partnership between public and private interests to advance economic growth. Hamilton's followers did not idealize their fellow citizens, being convinced that most were envious of the more successful, harder-working minority. The Federalists were never able to conceal their disdain for the masses that they suspected of being one demagogic appeal away from turning into a lawless mob.[40]

George Ewing, though he never acquired wealth, did not envy the affluent and did not believe they should be punished with confiscatory taxes. His son had even less patience for politicians who spewed hatred of the successful. To Federalists, and then to the Whigs who followed them, the keys to success were self-discipline, self-improvement, and a legal framework that protected individual liberty and property rights. Public-private investment in education and internal transportation would promote economic expansion, thereby providing opportunity to those not afraid of honest labor. The Whigs learned from the disastrous example of the Federalists. In a democracy, a successful political party had to expend more energy celebrating the common man and less effort decrying the ignorant masses.[41]

Federalists and their Whig Party heirs in the Old Northwest of the early 1820s had few redoubts of strength. Most were, like Charles Sherman and Philemon Beecher, migrants from Connecticut or, in the cases of George Ewing and Henry Stanbery, had been born in either New Jersey or New York. In the lower portion of Old Northwest such partisans clustered around a few economically dynamic communities, notably Lancaster. Most of Ohio's Federalists and Whigs could be found in the Western Reserve—closer to Lake Erie than to the Ohio River. Underscoring their New England roots, Western Reserve settlers named their towns Andover, Bath, New Haven, and Plymouth. The Western Reserve, however, did not grow—and become politically influential—until after the Erie Canal went into operation in 1825, creating a more easily traversed route from Cleveland to the East.[42]

The dominant political partisans of the early West were Virginians—most notably Ohio governor and U.S. senator Thomas Worthington of Chillicothe. Worthington followed the lead of the anti-Hamilton Thomas Jefferson—though he was ambivalent about the Northwest Ordinance's prohibition of slavery. He brought his slaves to Ohio from Virginia in 1796 but called them "indentured servants." Through legislation, Worthington made it impossible for black servants to leave his employ without first posting a $500 bond that two white men had to sign. Not coincidentally, Virginians dominated the 1802 Ohio Constitutional Convention, defeating the efforts of New Englanders to grant citizenship to blacks. (Indiana fought the same battle with similar results.) Also not coincidentally, Chillicothe in the early nineteenth century claimed the second-largest population of "free" blacks in the Old Northwest.[43]

Jeffersonians such as Worthington regarded the federal government with suspicion and wanted to keep it as weak as possible. Those who sought to create a more powerful central government were, to Worthington's Virginian allies, "despots" and "plotters" seeking to destroy "liberty." They also questioned government expenditure on internal improvements, viewing such endeavors as under-the-table bribes to corrupt businessmen. (Ohio Democrats consistently opposed improvements to Zane's Trace.) To them, the worst people in America were lawyer-entrepreneurs who saw public office as the vehicle to promote state-subsidized commercial development. Ohio Democrats merely disliked Philemon Beecher; they would passionately hate Thomas Ewing.[44]

The opening of the Erie Canal in 1825 had set off a political scramble in the Old Northwest. Ohio's Virginian Democrats split. A faction grouped around Worthington sought to get in on the commercial boom they expected to accompany linkage to Lake Erie on the way to the Erie Canal and New York City. As matters stood in the Lower Northwest, a farmer living thirty-five miles from the Ohio River required two horses and four days to move his surplus produce to a water transport point. Merchants who paid Lake Erie-rim farmers $15 for a barrel of flour gave southern Ohio flour producers $6 a barrel—or bartered goods instead of cash.[45]

Overland transportation was not a viable alternative. The National Road did not link up to Zane's Trace, now known as the Ohio State Road, until 1830. Moreover, even if the National Road was thirty feet wide and paved with three inches of broken stone, the best speed was seven miles per hour, making it better suited for passenger than commercial travel.[46]

The Democrats' divisions gave Whigs the political opening they needed to begin construction of a state-owned, 308-mile-long canal linking the Ohio River to Lake Erie. Western Reserve settlers were enthusiastic, a feeling that Lancaster's commercial and political leaders shared. Lancaster merchant Samuel MacCracken, a Scots-Irish Presbyterian from Pennsylvania, became a state canal commissioner and contractor. Thomas Ewing, a business associate of MacCracken, served as a featured speaker for the July 4, 1825, kickoff for construction of the Ohio Canal. An audience numbering in the thousands, his largest draw to date, gathered in Newark, outside Columbus, to hear his Independence Day oration.[47]

Ewing's speech intertwined praise for the United States as an inspiration for democratic revolution in Greece and Latin America, with calls for public investment in transportation in order to promote economic opportunity for the common man. "Vast supplies of the prime necessities of life, the wealth of the land," Ewing sadly observed, "are wasting in our barns, or sacrificed in search of a precarious market." Once the Ohio Canal and other such projects were completed, Ewing argued, Americans would achieve financial, in addition to political, freedom.[48]

As Ewing had hoped, the Ohio Canal, completed in 1833 with an initial state bond offering in New York of $13.2 million, stimulated economic growth in the communities it cut through. Even if it did take eighty hours for goods to travel between Portsmouth on the Ohio River and Cleveland on Lake Erie, road transport by horse-drawn cart would have required thirty days to cover the same distance in the best of weather conditions. The Ohio Canal, and its many siblings, however, had an unforeseen economic impact. Trading patterns in the Lower Northwest, which for years had been oriented south down the Ohio and Mississippi Rivers, shifted north. In 1830, 70 percent of western flour and nearly all western corn had gone to New Orleans. Within ten years most such traffic went mainly to New York City. Lower Ohio and the Old Northwest had become tied, at least commercially, to the East.[49]

Canal construction also reshaped state and regional politics, touching off a population boom that doubled the size of the Ohio electorate by 1840. Prosperous, growing communities along Ohio's new transportation routes increasingly voted for Whigs. The decision of the Ohio legislature to select Ewing as a U.S. senator in 1830 was an apparent precursor of the good times to come for the Whigs. His appointment as senator was also recognition that Ewing had the perfect face to place on the Ohio Whig Party. He was the humble "Salt Boiler" who, by dint of honest work, earned enough money to settle his father on a farm in Indiana and build a brick mansion in Lancaster. Rugged, intelligent, successful, and generous—such were the traits that Ohio Whigs showcased with Ewing.[50]

Having been admitted to practice law before the U.S. Supreme Court in 1828, Ewing was no stranger to Washington's social and political scene. He had met former President John Q. Adams and assessed him to be a most awkward, distracted, and intelligent man. Ewing also, at the invitation of one of General William Henry Harrison's sons, had attended a party at the residence of the British minister to the United States. He knew the Harrisons from his frequent stops in Cincinnati to try cases, as well as by way of the general's prominence in Ohio Whig politics. Whether out of devotion or out of concern for possible marital discord, Ewing hastened to write Maria that the women attending the British minister's affair were "as ugly as you ever saw, and the fashion of the day which they follow most punctiliously renders them hideous."[51]

Attorneys who appeared regularly before the U.S. Supreme Court needed to possess the mental agility to handle criminal, commercial, and constitutional cases. It also helped if they had some political savvy. These requirements restricted the size of the Supreme Court Bar and, as some charged, fostered a sense among its attorneys of belonging to a selective social club. Meeting in such intimate venues as taverns and the poorly lit basement of the Capitol Building enhanced their feeling of kinship. Especially strong friendships developed among Ewing, Massachusetts senator Daniel Webster, Illinois senator Orville Browning, Kentucky senator John Crittenden, Maryland senator Reverdy Johnson, North Carolina senator George Badger, and Georgia-born justice John Campbell.[52]

When Ewing arrived in the Senate in 1831, his relationship with Webster deepened. Like Charles Sherman, who had unexpectedly died two years earlier, Webster was a Dartmouth man, New England bred. Seven years older than Ewing, Webster built a reputation as a formidable constitutional lawyer and had already made two marks on national politics. In 1824, as a member of the U.S. House of Representatives, Webster had sharply attacked Henry Clay's protective tariff bill, which he believed was detrimental to Massachusetts. The irascible Kentuckian developed a dislike for Webster that worsened when they entered the Senate. It did not help Webster's and Clay's working relationship that both regarded themselves as leaders of the Whig Party.[53]

Webster's other achievement, beyond enraging Clay, was to deliver an oration on the Senate floor in 1830 that became an American classic. South Carolina senator Robert Hayne, upset over tariff legislation that many southerners believed discriminated against their region, advocated the nullification of "unconstitutional" federal laws. Hayne appealed to the West for support against the eastern commercial interests. Webster replied that the South, by dint of slavery and a lack of infrastructure investment, had isolated itself from the nation, forfeiting any claim to lead. After praising the West for its prohibition of slavery and commitment to canal construction, Webster extolled the virtues of union. His concluding sentence would become a rallying cry in the North thirty years later when South Carolina embraced secession: "Liberty and Union, now and forever, one and inseparable!"[54]

The seating arrangements of the Senate placed Ewing immediately behind Webster and next to Clay. The "Salt Boiler," as his Senate colleagues also called him, was literally caught in the middle of Clay's and Webster's feuds. Ewing urged both men to blunt the barbed comments they made on the Senate floor. He further encouraged Webster to vent privately to him in Latin. Webster appreciated Ewing's Latin quips and admired his storehouse of knowledge. He also had at least one occasion for astonishment. When he was traveling in Ohio with Ewing a fallen tree blocked the path of their buggy. The "Salt Boiler" grabbed an ax, effortlessly chopping up the tree so they could pass. Webster, like Philemon Beecher, expressed wonderment at Ewing's incongruities. He also had to express some chagrin. While he was attempting a turn at wielding the ax, his efforts were so feeble that some passersby mercilessly mocked him.[55]

Ewing and Clay's relationship bore little resemblance to Ewing's and Webster's camaraderie. Like Ewing, the Virginia-born Clay had started life with few advantages, ultimately achieving success by reading law—and by marrying a socially connected Kentucky woman. Bright though he was, Clay lacked the passion of Ewing and Webster for intellectual discussion. Ewing had Clay as a guest in Lancaster many times, but the cigars and bottles of Madeira sacrificed were in pursuit of winning electoral strategies, rather than passing time pleasantly with philosophical musings on the U.S. Constitution. Clay was a political intriguer with presidential ambitions—although Webster was no innocent on that score. Indeed, one of the reasons Webster and Clay enjoyed conversing with Ewing was his ability to predict how other politicians would react on any given issue. Ewing knew how to read people— a skill he had honed in the courtroom.[56]

In addition to Clay and Webster, another player in Washington proved enormously helpful to the "Salt Boiler." In 1827, the Pennsylvania Society for the Promotion of Manufactures and the Mechanic Arts held a national convention in Harrisburg. Bankers, merchants, and industrialists came together to endorse a protective tariff for manufacturing. Ewing, who had helped establish a bank in Lancaster a decade before, served as one of Ohio's representatives to the convention. Gideon Welles of Connecticut and Abbott Lawrence of Massachusetts also attended. Ewing met both men and left a strong impression.[57]

Abbott Lawrence was a driving force behind a group of industrialists and financiers known as "the Boston Associates." Webster, both as an attorney and as a senator, represented the interests of the Boston businessmen. In 1828, Lawrence had shown up in Washington to instruct Webster on how to vote on pending tariff legislation. When he returned to the nation's capital as a member of the House, Webster continued to defer to Lawrence, who was his junior in both office and age. Politically, the alliance with Lawrence was helpful to Webster but not essential. Webster's national stature as an orator was such that it would take a lot of bad faith for the Massachusetts legislature to throw him out of the Senate. It was in the financial rather than the political realm, however, where Webster was beholden to Lawrence. Because of poor choices in investments throughout his life, Webster needed Lawrence to keep him afloat—and had to be on his best behavior in the 1830s.[58]

Through Webster, Ewing became a member of Lawrence's inner circle. Introductions to investors in Boston, New York, and Philadelphia followed. Senator Ewing's courtship of eastern money men was necessarily ardent. He needed financial backing to build a short connector from Lancaster to the Ohio Canal. As matters stood, the Ohio Canal bypassed Lancaster—which would have spelled the eventual decline of the community. After completing the connector, known locally as the Lancaster Lateral, he wanted to extend the canal down the Hocking Valley to Athens. The fifty-six-mile-long project Ewing envisioned had a price tag of $947,000 and required the construction of thirty-four culverts, thirty-one locks, eight dams, and one aqueduct. When the Hocking Valley Canal finally reached Chauncey, near Athens, in 1842, Ewing's salt-boiling interests in southeastern Ohio became more commercially viable. The canal also encouraged him to speculate in coal mining once the fuel could be readily hauled to market.[59]

Ewing entered the Senate just as the political environment in Washington became toxic. Clay had sought the presidency in 1824 but, having come up short against John Q. Adams and Andrew Jackson, threw his support to the former in exchange for a cabinet post—and the tacit understanding that he was the Whig heir apparent. Jackson decried Clay's "corrupt bargain." His anger with the Whigs deepened when, in the 1828 election, Ohio lawyer and journalist Charles Hammond spread the first significant allegations that Jackson's wife, Rachel, was an adulterer. The charge was true, but the situation had been the result of a mistake made with the dissolution of her first marriage. Rachel died after Jackson's electoral victory, deepening his bitterness. If that was not bad enough, South Carolinian extremists would make their presence known once again.[60]

The second round of the dispute between Webster and Hayne over the protective tariff played out in 1832 and 1833. South Carolina's political leaders, led by Senator John C. Calhoun, threatened to disregard federal laws they disliked. After President Jackson demanded a "Force Bill" from Congress that would authorize him to use the military to collect tariff duties in South Carolina, Ewing and Webster crossed the aisle to lend their support.[61]

Prior to the introduction of the Force Bill, Ewing defended the tariff and then prosecuted the South Carolinians in the court of northern public opinion. He reviewed the history of the issue, observing that Massachusetts had been critical of the 1824 tariff. Massachusetts, however, accepted what "she had dreaded as an evil," finding that it instead "proved to be a blessing." Manufacturing boomed in New England, Ewing continued, in part because of the protective tariff that so many in Massachusetts had initially feared. The sturdy character of New Englanders, Ewing added, provided "the germ of prosperity" that was "inherent in the habits and genius of this people" and could never be destroyed.[62]

Why was the protective tariff necessary in the first place? Ewing asked. The answer was simple: Britain, groaning under the weight of overproduction, sought to dump its manufactured goods on American shores. Newborn industries in the United States could not compete against artificially underpriced British products. For American business, Ewing argued, "ruin and destruction would be the inevitable consequence," since "our manufacturers have not sufficient capital to stand the shock of this competition." All of America, not just New England and Pennsylvania, benefited from the protection of domestic industry from the desperate British.[63]

Turning to the South, Ewing asserted that the fluctuating market for such agricultural products as cotton had nothing to do with the tariff and everything to do with overproduction. Even allowing "that South Carolina is plunged as deeply into the abyss of misery and despair" as its leaders asserted, Ewing identified another cause other than the protective tariff for their woes: "The southern planter does not, like the hardy farmer of the North and West, lay his own hand to the plough; he neither holds nor drives; the culture of the fields is left to the overseer and the slaves, and their cultivation is without skill and without care."[64]

Once the fields and paddies of the South are "worn down by excessive cultivation" of a single crop, without effort "to renew or reinvigorate the soil," Ewing observed, "the bold and enterprising freeman" went West as an economic exile. The slaves remained behind. To Ewing, "the curse of slavery," not the tariff, brought blight to the South. At issue was not the treatment of slaves, Ewing insisted, since his own observations in Virginia and Kentucky had persuaded him that the masters felt "kindness and affection" toward their black workforce. The problem was that the slaves acquired no commercial and mechanical skills, making them economic drags on the South in the long run—even if they were a source of cheap labor.[65]

While Jackson appreciated Ewing's support in his showdown with South Carolina, and plied him with Madeira and champagne at the White House, their political differences precluded a lasting alliance. Ewing, Webster, Clay, and Lawrence regarded Jackson's allies as "collar men"—meaning they were slavish dogs led on a leash held by their master. Nowhere did this appear to be truer than the U.S. Post Office. Clay and Webster, appreciating Ewing's skills as a prosecutor, tasked him with investigating Postmaster General William Barry—a Jackson ally and crony of Vice President Martin Van Buren.[66]

Ewing's 1834 report to the Senate uncovered a post office deficit of just over $800,000, rampant misappropriation of funds, and the awarding of mail delivery contracts to Jackson's and Van Buren's friends. Senate Democrats and their advocates in the press denounced Ewing, with the Jacksonian *Washington Globe* calling him "degraded in the moral sense." While a few House Democrats concurred with Ewing on the need for reform of the post office, their senatorial counterparts followed Jackson's lead—denying that there was a problem and accusing the Whigs of being irresponsible partisans. Jackson finally, and reluctantly, appointed a new postmaster general. The Democratic practice of using government jobs and contracts to reward friends and punish enemies, however, was destined to become a bipartisan phenomenon.[67]

Congressional Whigs also clashed with Jackson over the disposition of public lands and the appropriation of federal funding for the construction of canals and roads. The two issues were linked, since Whigs desired to use the revenue from the sale of public land to finance roads and schools. Jackson did not believe that the federal government had the constitutional right to compel states to improve transportation networks and advance education. The president's thinking was in keeping with the Democratic Party's philosophy of limited government and reflected the values of the South, which lagged far behind Massachusetts and Ohio in road and school construction. To Whigs like Ewing and Webster, Democrats were complicit in rendering the South economically unviable and increasingly separated from the mainstream of American life.[68]

There was one dispute between Jackson and the congressional Whigs that dwarfed all others: the fate of the Second Bank of the United States. As U.S. secretary of the Treasury, Hamilton had desired a national bank that, among other functions, would provide credit to entrepreneurs. The Treasury could issue notes to investors, providing the funds the federal government needed—including money for war-related expenditures. Hamilton's Whig heirs understood that there was not enough gold available to provide the credit for internal transportation improvements, so paper notes were a necessary substitute.[69]

Local banks were not reliably solvent and could not, therefore, be counted on to provide credit. Ohio illustrated the financial limitations of working outside the U.S. Bank. Between 1811 and 1830, eighteen of twenty-nine Ohio banks failed, eliminating nearly $2 million in capital. The First and Second Bank of the United States more than made up the difference, providing Ohio and the Old Northwest with millions of dollars in credit between 1825 and 1832. Senator Ewing lauded the National Bank, observing that while the nation's finance capital might be based in the East, it was the West that reaped enormous benefits.[70]

Given the importance of the National Bank to the Whigs, the party's Senate leadership appointed Ewing to serve on a select committee. His mission was to examine the records of the bank and meet with New York and Philadelphia financiers. (It was not as if they were strangers.) Clay and Webster expected Ewing to make the case for an early renewal of the bank's charter. Given his own ideological predilections, on top of the need to finance his Ohio projects, Ewing could hardly disappoint. At the same time, though, he would not endorse the bank if it had failed in its purpose of generating credit and promoting commercial development. If bank president Nicholas Biddle was incompetent, then Ewing would have found a politically acceptable way of sending him packing. Ewing threw good money after bad only if it involved kin.[71]

Clay and Webster had moved up the date for rechartering the bank, calculating that Jackson would not oppose, let alone veto, their initiative in an election year. They were mistaken. Jackson seized the opportunity not only to deny the early recharter of the bank but to seek its destruction. After the 1832 election, the president appointed Roger Taney of Maryland as secretary of the Treasury and gave him his orders: withdraw federal deposits from the bank.[72]

Ewing made a strong case for the bank, highlighting its role in sustaining a growing economy. He denied Jackson's assertions that the bank served an entrenched elite, emphasizing that it was upwardly mobile, enterprising youths in search of capital who needed Biddle's services. Ewing also contended that Jackson did not have the constitutional authority to remove the Treasury's deposits. Not only did his arguments fail to carry the day, but Ewing made himself a political target nationally and in Ohio.[73]

Whigs in the Ohio legislature supported Ewing's battle over the bank. Democrats ordered him to support Jackson. After Ewing refused to change his position on the bank, the Democrats declared in a resolution that he had "disgraced the state of Ohio." They also positioned themselves to secure their majority so that they could deny Ewing reelection in 1836.[74]

The Ohio Constitution permitted the legislature to reapportion representation in districts every four years. Chillicothe Democrat William Allen purportedly came up with a cunning scheme for apportioning representation in advance of the 1836 election. The Ohio legislature created the designation of "floating representatives" and apportioned seats based upon county units rather than actual population. Under this scheme, a particular Democratic county might have two state representatives one year and a Whig county one representative. Then, in the next year, the ratio would be flipped and the Whigs would receive a second "floating" representative for a given county while the Democratic county would have one seat.[75]

Ohio Democrats made sure that the floating party ratio was in their favor during election years and ignored population growth outside their counties. In 1836, five counties in the Whig-dominated Western Reserve with a population of 30,205 received six Ohio House seats, while ten Democratic counties with a population of 30,504 claimed fourteen House seats. Democratic counties also contained the bulk of Ohio's black population, whom Virginian settlers had disenfranchised.[76]

In their defense, Ohio Democrats had a reasonable expectation that Ewing would obey his instructions from the legislature. Senators served at the sufferance of the state legislatures and invariably carried out their orders. Given presumed subordination to their respective legislatures, many who served in the U.S. Senate did not place much value on the office. Indeed, from 1790 to 1849, forty-eight senators resigned in order to accept state-level positions that they regarded as more powerful and prestigious. To Ohio Democrats, Ewing appeared exceptionally arrogant and deserved to be ejected from office—even if by chicanery.[77]

Charles Hammond had written to Ewing in 1834 that his reelection would be difficult: "[The bank] is a heavy weight to carry and keep with it popular sentiment. The right of the matter is one thing. But we know right has no peculiar claims or recommendation to public regard." It did not help the

Whigs—and Ewing back in Ohio—when a jobless house painter tried to assassinate Jackson in 1835. His "collar men" wasted no time making spurious links between Senate Whigs and the failed assassin. According to the *Washington Globe*, "disappointed and ambitious orators" on Capitol Hill had inspired the assassin. The *Globe* subsequently accused Ewing of obstructing an investigation of senators involved in the purported conspiracy.[78]

William Allen, the Democrats' choice to replace Ewing, was a native of North Carolina who had settled in Ohio's Virginia Military District. Like most of Jackson's loyalists, Allen distrusted bankers and regarded paper money with horror. Where Ewing championed a partnership with the federal government to provide credit and build transportation links, Allen recoiled. It would have been misleading, however, to characterize him as a consistent proponent of limited government. Allen looked forward to the day when the United States would declare war on Mexico and Great Britain in order to extend slavery to Texas and Oregon.[79]

Ewing knew his only hope for reelection in 1836 was to challenge the Democrats in every legislative district in Ohio. If he could help elect enough Whigs, Democratic gerrymandering would not matter. Ewing, however, had to first counteract Ohio Democrats' depiction of him as a champion of the privileged. On the campaign stump Ewing emphasized that he was a self-made man who came from ranks of the common folk: "With my mental and physical powers as my only inheritance, I was brought up a working man, or, rather, a working boy—among the people, truly one of them." Ewing nearly drew enough Whig votes to receive a second Senate term, falling three votes short. The Whigs won the governorship and gave the state's electoral votes to William Henry Harrison—who lost the presidential election to Martin Van Buren.[80]

Allen held an enormous victory celebration in Lancaster, where he read a letter from Jackson rejoicing at Ewing's defeat. Thousands roared with approval, their cheers and jeers advancing up Main Hill to the Ewing mansion. In his nearly three-hour oration, Allen identified Ewing and the Whigs as enemies of democracy. Fortunately, against "the stupid, the selfish and the base in spirit," whose true goals were "despotism," the heirs of the American Revolution had triumphed.[81]

The vindictiveness of Ewing's foes was not surprising. Although Lancaster owed its continued prosperity to Ewing, the bulk of the area's electorate was Democratic and traced its origins to the South. Fairfield County after all, had communities named Baltimore and (Canal) Winchester. To the Maryland and Virginia Democrats who lived in and near Lancaster, the Ewings, Shermans, and Stanberys were representatives of an alien culture that threatened to destroy their way of life with banks, canals, and manufacturing. Moreover, Democratic voters believed that constant Whig criticism of the southern economy sowed sectional discord. Ohio Democrats were also convinced that the Whigs undermined democracy through their embrace of the National Bank and the protective tariff. Men such as Ewing could only be considered traitors.[82]

Ewing's loss demoralized Clay, and he contemplated leaving the Senate "with the same pleasure that one would fly from a charnel-house." Without Ewing, Clay understood that he no longer had a key member of his team who could develop legislative strategies and serve as a lightning rod for outraged Democrats. As Clay concluded in a letter to a southern confidant, "What good can I do, what mischief avert, by remaining [in the Senate]?"[83]

Unfortunately for President Van Buren, a depression began in 1837. Ewing and his friends squarely placed blame for the economic downturn on the Democrats' war against the National Bank. Abbott Lawrence predicted that 1840 would be a Whig year. He recognized, however, that certain Whig politicians could not hold center stage, since their polarizing presence guaranteed a mobilized Democratic base. Lawrence first told Webster to stand down. Clay, who desired the support of Lawrence and Ewing, found both men, along with a reluctant Webster, backing Harrison for a second White House run. Although Webster's relationship with Lawrence was strained, he joined his fellow Supreme Court Club members in campaigning for Harrison. Webster, John Crittenden, George Badger, and Ewing subsequently received appointments in President Harrison's cabinet.[84]

Ewing had delivered speeches for Harrison across Ohio, as well as in Wheeling and New York. His relationship with Harrison was one of mutual trust, and they freely discussed the qualities of various Whig politicians. Ewing preferred to have Webster head the State Department rather than Treasury, since "with all Mr. Webster's gigantic intellect he is not a man of the labor and detail and supervisory care, which the complicated Treasury Department requires."[85]

Lawrence concurred with Ewing. He expressed to Harrison and Crittenden his desire to see Ewing as secretary of the Treasury rather than Webster. "Ewing," Lawrence insisted, "is with and of the people . . . [while] the monied interest of the country have confidence in him." For their part, Harrison and Ewing were relieved when Clay refused to serve as secretary of state, leaving the position to Webster. Neither Ohio politician wanted to be caught in a Massachusetts feud between Lawrence and Webster. Whatever Webster's limitations as an administrator, compared to Clay he was a more amiable and accomplished conversationalist—perfect prerequisites for a diplomat.[86]

Once Ewing gained access to the Treasury's ledgers, he was appalled. The Treasury was empty and the federal government had amassed a deficit of $11 million. One reason for the federal government's financial mess could be traced to the goings-on at the New York Custom House. For the previous twelve years under Jackson and Van Buren, the New York Custom House had been shielded from legislative—particularly Whig—oversight. Much of America's tariff duties were collected in New York and then should have been sent to the Treasury. That money, however, often disappeared into the Democrats' patronage coffers. The New York Custom House itself boasted the largest staff (five hundred) and payroll ($489,000) of any government operation. Ewing appreciated that patronage had become an inevitable feature of governance, but still there was a point at which it became criminal and left the United States unable to fund its constitutionally mandated obligations.[87]

The "Salt Boiler" hoped to clean up Van Buren's patronage morass and straighten out America's finances—the latter by rebuilding the Bank of the United States. He was destined to be disappointed in both endeavors. Many rank-and-file Whigs, though perfectly happy to advocate criminal prosecution of Democratic patronage abusers, were first in line for government jobs. Ohio's Whig governor, Thomas Corwin, who had been a close friend of Charles Sherman, tried to run interference for Ewing. Corwin's efforts to mollify Ohio office seekers, however, proved ineffective. Democrats, for their part, did not appreciate having the New York Custom House exposed and were looking for an opportunity to undermine Ewing. Their chance came soon and from an unexpected quarter.[88]

Within a month of taking the oath of office, the sixty-eight-year-old Harrison died—most likely from pneumonia. After a brief tussle between Ohio senator William Allen and Webster over what the Constitution said about presidential succession, Vice President John Tyler became president. Some Democrats wanted another presidential election in 1841, which, with Harrison gone, they might win. Clay himself did not want Tyler elevated to the presidency, anticipating that he would fill the power vacuum in Washington from the Senate. Given Webster's hatred for Clay, he bound himself to Tyler, leaving Ewing and the rest of the cabinet in an awkward position. Ewing decided to work with Tyler, but something about the Virginian's manner led him to start a secret diary so he could document his conversations with the president. His instincts served him well.[89]

Ewing had urged Harrison to call for a special session of Congress to deal with the nation's finances. With Harrison out of the picture, Clay asserted his authority, which only angered Tyler. At the center of their dispute was Ewing's proposal to establish a new U.S. Bank. Although Tyler had been listed on the Whig ticket in 1840, he was a recent, and only partial, convert from the Democratic Party. He had recoiled against Van Buren's excesses but largely agreed with the position Jackson had taken against the Second Bank. At his core, Tyler was a southern Democrat who reflexively opposed initiatives to enhance federal power. He vetoed the bank bill Clay submitted, branding it unconstitutional and a usurpation of states' rights.[90]

The "Salt Boiler" understood Tyler's concerns and sought to bring about a compromise with Clay. Like the accomplished contract lawyer he was, Ewing sat down with Tyler and reviewed all his objections. He pinned Tyler down on the precise language he would support and then made sure that all parties agreed on the definition of terms. Once Tyler's concerns were addressed, the Ewing version of the bank bill, which still retained some of Clay's handiwork, went to Congress. Once passed, the bank bill came back to the White House. Tyler vetoed Ewing's bill.[91]

Never before had Ewing felt so betrayed. He had spent weeks negotiating with the White House and Congress. Ewing had endured Clay's unpleasant posturing and tirades. Tyler had frequently summoned Ewing to the White House and then made him wait idly for hours before speaking to him. His frustration mounting daily, he had recited passages from Dante's *Inferno* to Badger and Crittenden—keeping the respective navy secretary and attorney general posted on which circle of hell he had just entered. Badger had responded with quotes from Milton's *Paradise Lost*.[92]

After Tyler's second veto, Ewing and all but one cabinet member resigned in protest. As he recorded in his diary: "I parted with a determination never to meet him [Tyler] again as a member of his cabinet. Indeed I could not feel that my reputation as a man of truth and candor was safe, while I attempted to represent him." Webster, who had allied with Tyler against Clay—in defiance of Abbott Lawrence—pleaded with Ewing to remain with him in the cabinet. Ewing refused. The Democrats rejoiced and joined Tyler in calling Ewing a liar when he publicly gave his version of the events leading to his resignation.[93]

Home in Lancaster, Ewing devoted more attention to his commercial enterprises. The opening of the Hocking Canal in 1843 did not generate sufficient income for Ewing to cover $5,000 in business obligations. Lawrence confessed that the Boston Associates were strapped. Lawrence and Ewing believed that the unwillingness of Tyler to deal with the federal deficit, and the failure to revive the National Bank, had dried up domestic and international sources of credit. There were other Americans far worse off than Lawrence and Ewing. The depression that commenced in 1837 had still not run its course. Ewing lacked ready cash; unemployed workers in Boston, New York, and Philadelphia were going hungry.[94]

Ewing hunkered down and weathered the credit crisis. A year later, in 1844, he stepped up his coal-mining operations. Soon Ewing was investing in the construction of a telegraph line between Lancaster and Columbus—at a cost of $120 a mile for a total of $3,600. A successful legal case involving land titles in St. Louis gave him entry into real estate speculation outside Ohio. Ewing's one business setback was his inability to persuade southern Ohioans to invest in a railroad line between Athens and Columbus.[95]

Even as his law practice in Ohio and Washington became one of America's most financially rewarding, Ewing could not avoid some entanglement with politics. Ohio Whigs finally overcame the Democrats in 1844 to capture the legislature and send Thomas Corwin to the Senate. The Whig victory in Ohio, however, owed much to the continued population growth in the Western Reserve—a hotbed of antisouthern, abolitionist sentiment. No less a figure than Daniel Webster, a stalwart critic of southern slave society, described the Western Reserve as "a laboratory of abolitionism, libel, and treason." The contrasting cultures and ideologies of the Western Reserve and the Virginian Military District were destined to clash.[96]

In response to rumblings in the Ohio legislature that Whigs wanted to repeal the state's 1807 "Black Laws," the Democrats erupted. The Democratic *Cincinnati Enquirer* in 1846 warned that if Ohio gave blacks citizenship rights the state would be invaded by "an ignorant and depraved class, who's color, and the prejudice existing against it, make an amalgamation of the races or a social equality of condition impossible." (Two years earlier, the *Enquirer* had speculated that Henry Clay's Whigs were plotting to enslave whites since they could not settle blacks in the North.) More bluntly, Samuel Medary, editor of the state Democratic Party's organ, the *Ohio Statesman*, wrote in 1845: "Are you ready to be on a level with the niggers in the political rights for which your fathers contended?" For such Democrats, whose forebears had migrated from the South, blacks were thieves, rapists, and competitors for jobs. They could never be social equals.[97]

The legislative battle over black rights in Ohio heated up as the United States went to war with Mexico. Most northern Whigs viewed the Mexican War as a ploy by Democrats to extend slavery westward. Senator Allen said nothing that would have led Whigs to a different conclusion. In contrast to Allen, Ohio's Thomas Corwin attracted national attention when, on the Senate floor, he called for Congress to shut off supplies to the U.S. Army in Mexico. A few southern Whigs, notably Ewing's sometime Supreme Court co-counsel, George Badger, stood up to their legislatures and denounced the war, but they were the exception. When the war ended triumphantly for the United States in 1848, being a peace advocate endangered more than a few politicians' careers in the South and the Lower Northwest, though Badger managed—by a single vote—to retain his Senate seat. (Antiwar congressman Abraham Lincoln of Illinois chose not to run for reelection, since he anticipated defeat.)[98]

Ewing believed that even if the president and Congress had followed the strictures of the Constitution in going to war, the annexation of Texas and California was an unconstitutional act. As he later contended to Oran Follett, a Whig publisher and businessman from the Western Reserve: "The Constitution of the United States did not contemplate the extension of our Republic over any new territory, and . . . Congress had no more right to acquire new territory and annex it to the Union, than they would have had to relinquish a portion of our actual territory."[99]

The problem the nation now faced, Ewing continued, was twofold. First, the western territories were in American hands, and, politically, that fact could not be undone. Second, the South would impose its slave culture on the West and paint its critics as radical abolitionists: "I know the southern tactics well, their union, their energy, and the various arts by which they make an impression upon our northern statesmen, and through them upon a portion of our people and hence I fear them even when they are wholly in the wrong, but let them have one point out of five and they will beat us almost uniformly and throwing all together beat us on the points on which we are right as well as that on which we are wrong."[100]

Ewing had a solution that would diminish the effectiveness of the Democrats' abolitionist and race-baiting tactics, prevent the expansion of slavery westward, and perhaps even save the South from itself: purchase slaves and then send them to Liberia in Africa. When an organizer of the American Colonization Society (ACS) had come to Lancaster in 1830, Ewing and Stanbery established a local chapter and served as its officers. Since blacks could not hope to live with southern—or northern—whites on a basis of equality, Ewing believed, the best course of action was repatriation—even if they had been born in America. Although Ewing regarded blacks as inferior, he still considered them human. Democrats like Allen and Medary viewed slaves as property and free blacks as "niggers."[101]

Given the fallout from the Mexican War, the 1848 presidential election was destined to be divisive. The "Salt Boiler" could not resist joining the political battle. Appalled by Thomas Corwin's alliance with abolitionists, Ewing persuaded the Ohio delegation at the Whig National Convention to support Zachary Taylor instead of their senator. Ewing knew that Taylor, as a southerner, a former slave owner, and a victorious general in the war with Mexico, would be a bitter pill for many Whigs to swallow. He was not initially enthusiastic about Taylor himself and warned his friend John Crittenden of "a secession from our party in Ohio and a powerful one which may utterly destroy us." On the other hand, there were no other Whig candidates who could win in the fall.[102]

Some deeply alienated Whigs, including Congressman Joshua Giddings of the Western Reserve, defected to the abolitionist Free Soil Party after Ewing's allies thwarted Corwin, though Corwin himself reluctantly chose to campaign for Taylor. Prior to the 1848 election, Giddings had stated on the House floor that "if [the slaves] cannot regain their God-given rights by peaceful measures, I nevertheless hope they will regain them; and if blood be shed, I should certainly hope that it might be the blood of those who stand between them and freedom, and not the blood of those who have long been robbed of their wives and children and all they hold dear in life." When Webster and Ewing referred to Western Reserve abolitionists as violent seditionists, they were thinking of Giddings.[103]

Thomas Ewing discovered that Taylor was not the only Whig with enemies in his own party. Ewing's friends had sought to nominate him for vice president. Anti-Catholic forces, led by Whig publisher and congressional candidate Lewis Campbell, maneuvered the nomination to New York's Millard Fillmore. Protestant mob assaults on Catholic churches, convents, and neighborhoods in Boston, Cincinnati, and Philadelphia had commenced a decade earlier. Lyman Beecher, a Presbyterian minister from the very same Connecticut family to which Philemon Beecher belonged, incited anti-Catholic violence in Boston and Cincinnati. The worst religious rioting prior to 1848 had taken place in Philadelphia. In 1844, Scots-Irish Protestants and Irish Catholics gleefully killed each other.[104]

Although Ewing had not converted to Catholicism, nativists regarded him as one in all but name. He made no secret of his marriage in the church, his support for Catholic schools, and his respect for Catholic clergy. By marrying into the Boyle and Gillespie families he had bridged the tribal divide separating Scots-Irish from Irish Catholic. Many others back east refused to end their historic feud. Philemon Beecher had welcomed him as a partner in his law practice; Lyman Beecher, both in Massachusetts and in Ohio, spewed anti-Catholic hatred with such sermons as "The Devil and the Pope in Rome." In his own backyard, the *Lancaster Gazette*, a Whig newspaper established in 1826, joined the anti-Catholic crusade in the 1840s. The *Gazette* later alerted readers to a "plot" to build a larger Catholic church in Lancaster and editorialized against "the social influence of a few Catholic families."[105]

As Ewing predicted, Ohio went Democratic, though by a tight margin of sixteen thousand votes. Thirty-five thousand angry Whigs defected to the

President Zachary Taylor and Cabinet. Interior Secretary Thomas Ewing is seated second from the right, while U.S. attorney general and Ewing ally Reverdy Johnson is seated on the left. (Courtesy of the Library of Congress.)

much-loathed Martin Van Buren on the Free Soil ticket. That cost Taylor the Buckeye State's electoral votes but not the general election. Most of the Free Soil support was concentrated in the Western Reserve, especially among Protestant clergy, teachers, and intellectuals. There was also much overlap between those professing abolitionist and anti-Catholic sentiments. To such voters, southern slave owners and drunken Irish Catholic immigrants were joined in the Democratic Party to destroy America. In turn, the *Cleveland Plain Dealer*, a Democratic newspaper, castigated Western Reserve reformers as "those old blue law, blue bellied Presbyterians that hung witches and banished Quakers, [who] are determined to convert the people of this region into a race of psalm singers, using the degenerate dregs of the old Puritans remaining here to drive the Democracy out."[106]

Opportunistic politicians saw in the Ohio Whig Party's divisions their chance to vie for the support of Free Soilers and Democrats. Ewing had decided not to make a bid for the Senate in 1848. Salmon Chase stepped in with a pledge to Free Soilers to support the abolitionist cause. To Ohio Democrats, Chase promised that he would champion their state Supreme Court candidates and that they would receive all the federal patronage he could deliver. Confronted with the possibility that Ewing might be politically resurrected if the Whigs made amends with the Free Soilers, the state's Democrats threw a stunned William Allen overboard in favor of Chase. Whigs of Ewing's generation never again trusted Chase, since it was apparent that power meant more than principle to him. When they were feeling less charitable, the Whig elders called Chase "a political vampire."[107]

Ewing's friend Crittenden could vouch for Taylor. Thirteen years earlier, Taylor had warned Crittenden that the army, given its preponderance of southerners, could not be relied upon to defend the Constitution against Carolinian secessionists. Although a native of Orange County, Virginia, Taylor distrusted many of his fellow southern officers—going so far as to recommend to Crittenden that the army be reduced in size. To do otherwise, he glumly predicted, would give future insurrectionists—namely southern Democrats—the tools to wage and win a civil war against the Constitution.[108]

Another Ewing confidant, Reverdy Johnson, backed Taylor. The "Salt Boiler" knew from Johnson, Crittenden, and other friends that the general opposed the extension of slavery to the territories acquired from Mexico. He shared that piece of intelligence only among his closest associates, since it would have hurt the Whig ticket in the South. In exchange for their support, Ewing became the secretary of the newly created Department of the Interior—also known as the Home Department—and Johnson assumed the office of U.S. attorney general. Boston's *Liberator*, the flagship newspaper of the abolitionist movement, harshly characterized the new administration as "four southern slaveholders to three northern doughfaces [proslavery Whigs], besides a slaveholding President! What has the cause of liberty to hope or expect from such an administration? Alas! For this corrupting alliance with the enslavers of men! It necessarily saps the virtue and manhood of the North."[109]

Ewing brushed aside such criticism. Serving in the Interior Department appealed to him, since its focus would be on disposing western lands, rather than dealing with the East and its "cities which contained [sundry] abominations." Ewing still smarted from his earlier clashes with New York Democrats. He also discovered that he enjoyed Taylor's company, finding him to be "a man of naturally vigorous intellect, sound judgment, inflexible integrity, and high sense of honor . . . calm in council, just and wise in decision and firm in purpose." When not discussing politics, Taylor regaled Ewing with the story of the 1847 Battle of Buena Vista. Outnumbered three to one, most American troops held firm—with a glaring exception. As Taylor recounted, a West Point-educated officer from North Carolina panicked at the approaching wave of Mexican infantry. He wanted to spike his battery and throw the cannon into a ravine. Taylor acted quickly to provide Captain Braxton Bragg with a backbone.[110]

Far less entertaining to Ewing were the incessant demands from Whig politicians for patronage. Having endured much invective as senator and as Treasury secretary when he went up against Democratic patronage abuse, Ewing decided to give as good as he received. Rather than fight for reform, Ewing advocated the "swift and extensive decapitations of Democrats" across all federal departments. Although this should have made him immensely popular among his Whig brethren, Ewing's problems were twofold. First, he insisted that while Whigs received preference, they still had to be qualified. Second, for every job opening in the Interior Department, for instance, there were fifty Whig applicants.[111]

One of the first in line was Daniel Webster, who sought a U.S. attorney position for his unaccomplished son Fletcher. Ewing had earlier observed to Clay that "the Whigs have much to forgive Mr. Webster. More I apprehend than they will readily forgive him." Still, he fondly characterized Webster as "the finest table companion" he ever knew—even if alcohol, ambition, and bitterness got the best of him. Ewing found a low-level position for Fletcher Webster in Boston. The senior Webster was hardly cheered when Abbott Lawrence turned down a position in Taylor's cabinet in favor of becoming the American minister to Great Britain.[112]

There were numerous Whig supplicants whose qualifications for federal employment were as weak as those of Fletcher Webster. Ewing patiently explained to one applicant that he lacked administrative experience relative to another candidate. The former congressman then claimed that when Ewing returned his application there were missing recommendation letters. Ewing replied that it was not the practice to share confidential letters with applicants—especially if references discussed more than one candidate. Enlisting the assistance of friends in Illinois, the applicant targeted Ewing with more entreaties and attacked the character of the successful candidate. Hoping to buy off the persistent office seeker, Ewing offered him the territorial governorship of Oregon. The job seeker replied that he preferred to live in Washington, D.C. Ewing found minor postings for the man's friends, which finally quieted him. This would not be Ewing's last encounter with Abraham Lincoln.[113]

Overseeing the operation of the Interior Department once again placed Ewing in conflict with southerners who, simultaneously, loathed enhancing the executive authority of the central government and desired the federal imposition of slavery in the West. Senator James Mason of Virginia and South Carolina's irrepressible John Calhoun led the opposition to the creation of the Interior Department. President Taylor expressed the hope that Ewing could prepare the newly acquired western territories for admission to the Union without slavery. Taylor also envisioned the day when a transcontinental railroad could be built. There were, however, two challenges. First, the native tribes might not appreciate having a railroad running through their hunting grounds and bringing in settlers. Second, the construction of a transcontinental railroad would hasten the settlement of the West, thereby arousing the ire of southerners if slavery were prohibited.[114]

Since the 1820 Missouri Compromise, southerners had counted on maintaining their sectional political clout by a balance of power in the Senate. Population trends favored the North in the apportionment of House seats and Electoral College votes. Admitting one free state for every slave state to the Union had worked—until the Mexican War, when the United States acquired a great number of potentially free states above the Missouri Compromise line. Southern proponents of the Mexican War had banked on annexing Texas and gaining two Senate allies; they had not anticipated the 1849 gold rush and likely admission of California into the Union as a free state—let alone the admission of territories between the Pacific Coast and Iowa.

As Interior secretary, Ewing was establishing territorial governments that were not welcoming of slavery. Ewing and Taylor wanted farmers and merchants settling the West—not planters and slaves. Neither the Interior secretary nor the president, however, was quite that forthcoming with fellow Whigs such as New York senator William Seward. Instead, they emphasized the need in California "to substitute the rule of law and order there for bowie-knife and revolvers."[115]

Not surprisingly, Ewing immediately ran afoul of Democrats. Lame-duck president James Polk had sent John Weller to California as the first U.S. boundary commissioner with Mexico. Weller, the unsuccessful 1848 Democratic candidate for Ohio governor, recruited a number of his cronies for the trip west—including several "Virginia" Democrats from Lancaster. In numerous letters written to male siblings, one Lancaster pilgrim recounted tales of New Orleans' fighting cock pits, "Niggers talking French," alcohol-fueled vomiting, and bronzed Central American women bathing nude. For his part, Weller racked up enormous expenses but failed to provide legitimate receipts. Ewing fired Weller in 1850 and refused to reimburse his expenses. Democrats cried that the Interior secretary had stranded the bankrupt Weller in California so he could not make another run for governor of Ohio. (Three years later, Weller returned east at public expense when the California legislature elected him to the U.S. Senate.)[116]

Although Ewing rented Francis Blair's spacious home on Pennsylvania Avenue across from the White House, the two were long-standing political enemies. As editor of the Democrats' *Washington Globe*, Blair had repeatedly attacked Ewing and rejoiced when Tyler had vetoed his bank bill. Writing to Martin Van Buren in 1849, Blair complained that President Taylor was under the Interior secretary's control: "The Salt Boiler Ewing seems to be the embodiment which gives momentum to everything—is looked upon as the wheel horse of the team." (The tensions between the Blairs and Ewings would continue into the next generation, when both families vied for political influence in Missouri and Kansas.)[117]

Congressional Democrats launched an investigation of the Interior Department, alleging nepotism and corruption. They also charged Ewing with personally profiting from the sale of public lands and cheating the widows and orphans of army veterans. While Democrats never found any evidence of criminal acts, that did not stop them from asserting in their report that there had been incidents of illegal reimbursements by the Interior Department. Ewing prepared a lengthy accounting of his conduct, but congressional Democrats were not about to permit him to defend himself on Capitol Hill so long as he led the Interior Department. All this was too much for Democratic House member Thomas Bayley of Virginia, who characterized the Ewing investigation as unconstitutional and motivated by partisan politics.[118]

William Marcy, Polk's secretary of war and an operative of New York's Tammany Hall Democratic organization, loathed Ewing and Taylor. Taylor's record of military success, Marcy asserted, was "accidental," while "his real character was surrounded by a halo of glory which prevented it from being seen in its true proportions." But Taylor was only a tool of the sinister Ewing: "He is a well-trained politician of the genuine Whig stamp; one who pushes forward to his ends unscrupulous of the means, more bold than sagacious; all partisan and no patriot. The features of his character are hard. By the proscriptive course he pursued for the short time he was a member of the Harrison Cabinet he acquired the sobriquet of the Butcher."[119]

After celebrating Independence Day with Taylor, Ewing had seen the president grow weary. To Ewing's shock, Taylor died five days later—on July 9, 1850. Once again, Ewing had lost a friend in the White House and faced a vice president with whom he was not on good terms. He resigned his cabinet post, only to be rewarded by the governor of Ohio with a short-term appointment to the Senate after Thomas Corwin became Fillmore's Treasury secretary. As was the story of Ewing's political career to date, his tenure in the Senate would steep him in controversy.[120]

As a senator, Ewing could defend his conduct as Interior secretary on Capitol Hill, though congressional rules on courtesy limited his freedom to attack members of the House. Choosing to address the dismissal of John Weller, Ewing insisted that, given the evidence, even if he had been a Whig instead of a Democrat, "I would have unhesitatingly advised his removal." Ewing then proceeded to run through the account ledgers, reviewing Weller's expenditures. Twisting the knife, "Butcher Ewing" acknowledged it was the practice of Washington Democrats to give their failed gubernatorial candidates federal jobs—and he was not opposed to that policy. The problem was the Democrats should have recognized that Weller was "wholly without qualifications, not trustworthy, [and] not fit for the office" of boundary commissioner. It would have been more prudent to send Weller overseas on a diplomatic post—which was what Democrats typically did with their weak links.[121]

Ewing's defense on the Senate floor was, as he well knew, his likely swan song for both elective and appointed political office. But before that moment arrived he had one more role to play. Ewing was going to stand up against the congressional appeasers of southern fire-eaters. There were three closely intertwined issues at stake in 1850: the continuation of the slave trade in the District of Columbia, the admission of California and the western territories as slave or free states, and a far-reaching revision of the 1793 Fugitive Slave Law.

The 1850 Fugitive Slave Law made aiding runaway slaves a federal crime—a dramatic extension of the authority of the central government over communities that prohibited human bondage and one that, paradoxically, was championed by the southern advocates of states' rights. Many Ohioans supported the revised Fugitive Slave Law and welcomed the removal of blacks—slave or free. Cincinnati, with a black population of two thousand in 1840, experienced racially motivated rioting in 1826 and 1841. Protestant clergy along the Ohio River, according to Buckeye abolitionists, defended slavery as readily as they "embraced baptism." When southern slave catchers descended upon the Ohio capital in 1846 and snatched a black man they claimed had fled Kentucky twenty years earlier, there were few local protests. Most working-class whites in the Lower Northwest and the Kanawha Valley would have heartily endorsed the stance of a Philadelphia labor organizer in 1832 who argued "that children born in slavery do not work one half the hours, nor perform one quarter of the labor that the white children do in the cotton mills in free New England."[122]

Abolitionists in the Western Reserve sought to punish the Whigs at the polls until the party took a more vigorous stand against slavery. The 1848 election had demonstrated that a small third-party movement could harm Whigs and persuade some Democrats to cut political side deals. Ewing knew that this state of affairs would only worsen and likely spread from Ohio to Indiana and Illinois, which shared the Buckeye State's demographics and ideological divisions. If that happened, the Whig Party would die.

Throughout 1850, Ewing received detailed political reports from William Dennison, an energetic thirty-five-year-old attorney who had caught his eye. Although born in the proslavery community of Cincinnati, Dennison's father was a New Jersey man—like George Ewing—while his mother was a Massachusetts native. Dennison had settled in Columbus to practice law and became an eager proponent of Ewing's proposed Hocking Valley Railroad. Unable to persuade Franklin County authorities to prosecute slave catchers for kidnapping, Dennison ran for the state senate in 1848. As a representative of Franklin and Delaware Counties, Dennison worked to repeal the state's Black Laws. (Delaware County contained a number of towns settled by antislavery partisans from New Jersey and Pennsylvania. Because of its political leanings and small black population, southern Ohioans contemptuously referred to the Delaware village of East Orange as "Africa.")[123]

The crux of Dennison's missives to Ewing was that Ohio Whigs had to move toward the Free Soilers' position on the Fugitive Slave Law—and on the slavery question in general. He also warned that Democratic Party activist and journalist Samuel Medary was succeeding in forging alliances of convenience with abolitionist Free Soilers and, at the same time, race-baiting antislavery Whigs. Ewing urged Dennison to organize a meeting in Columbus between Whigs and Free Soilers "to bring about the desired conciliation." As he ruefully noted, "we can do nothing in this state unless we reunite." Such a reunion, Ewing, concluded, required "influential Whigs" to "meet [abolitionists] at least halfway and be alike generous and conciliatory." From the Senate, and before that in the Interior Department, Ewing tried his best to bring the abolitionists back to their political home.[124]

Ewing, however, found it impossible to stop the momentum behind the 1850 Fugitive Slave Law. Even Daniel Webster, a few months before Taylor's death, had gone so far as to accuse abolitionists of being less interested in ending slavery than in using the issue to raise funds: "I know many abolitionists in my own neighborhood, very honest, good people, misled, I think, by strange enthusiasm; but they wish to do something, and they are called on to contribute, and they do contribute; and it is my firm opinion this day, that within the last twenty years as much money has been collected and paid to abolition societies, abolition presses, and abolition lectures, as would

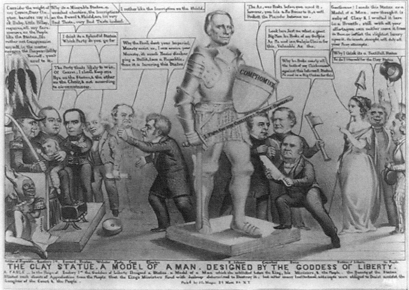

"The Clay Statue, A Model of a Man, Designed by the Goddess of Liberty," by John L. Magee, 1850. The Whig critics of Senator Henry Clay's 1850 Compromise, including Supreme Court Club members Thomas Ewing and Reverdy Johnson, espouse their views. Reverdy Johnson, wielding an ax, contends : "The Ax, was Broke before you used it, however, you Lie & I'll Swear to it, & we'll Pockett the Plunder between us," while Thomas Ewing, a saw in hand, rejoins: "Why I've Broke nearly all the teeth of my Chickensaw against this Infernall Statue. I'le send in a Big Claim for this." (Courtesy of the Library of Congress.)

purchase the freedom of every slave, man, woman, and child, in the State of Maryland, and send them to Liberia."[125]

If the Fugitive Slave Law was off the table, then battling over the abolition of the slave trade and slavery itself in the District of Columbia might serve to salvage Whig political fortunes in Ohio. Ewing championed legislation that would have not only abolished slavery in the District but resulted in setting free any slave who set foot in Washington. Further, Ewing argued, such a bill would have thereafter secured a slave's freedom even if he or she subsequently went to a southern state.[126]

Ewing further insisted that if a free black encouraged a spouse or child who remained in bondage to flee to the District, then there should be no prosecution under the Fugitive Slave Law. Going beyond his usual economic-based criticisms of slavery, Ewing simply stated that "it offends the moral sense of men" to punish anyone for wishing to reunite their family. "What is the offense which is committed?" Ewing asked. Certainly, he continued, it was "not larceny, for it does not rank in that class of crimes at all. Those trespasses are committed for purposes of gain or money." Although there was political calculation behind Ewing's position, he understood that there was a logical inconsistency to regarding humans as property—even without conceding the issue of social equality. Henry Clay and President Fillmore ensured that the slave trade in Washington came to an end—at least legally, if not in actual practice. Neither politician, however, accepted Ewing's interpretation of the legislation.[127]

Abolition of the slave trade in Washington and revisions to the Fugitive Slave Law were components of the grand compromise Clay was working out to deal with California and Texas. Clay had earlier complained that Taylor froze him out and, indeed, "Instead of any disposition to oblige me, I feel that a contrary disposition has been sometimes manifested." With Taylor gone, Clay asserted his primacy, especially when it came to the disposition of the western territories.[128]

Clay felt that southerners might be more accommodating about admitting California as a free state if the federal government assumed the debts of the former Republic of Texas. When he was leading the Interior Department, Ewing learned that Clay's interest in providing Texas debt relief went far beyond greasing the wheels of political accommodation.[129]

During the 1830s and 1840s, a number of individuals had purchased some $10 million in Texas bonds. Ewing knew that many of Clay's Kentucky friends had invested in Republic of Texas securities—which were now virtually worthless unless the federal government redeemed them. Other investors included Drexel & Company of Philadelphia, the Pennsylvania politician Simon Cameron, Daniel Webster, and Democratic senator James Bayard of Delaware. Clay successfully schemed to have the U.S. Treasury redeem the Texas bonds at nearly four times their face value. President Taylor had been appalled at the bipartisan shamelessness of Congress.[130]

Ewing worked until the point of physical collapse to thwart passage of Clay's handiwork. Supporters of the Compromise warned Ewing and his congressional allies that if Texas did not receive admission into the Union as a slave state, and if its debts were not assumed by the Treasury, then there would be civil war. Clay himself approached Ewing in the Senate Chamber and warned, "You must not make another pass at my omnibus [legislation] or I shall be down upon you." Meanwhile the small band of congressional abolitionists challenged the legitimacy of governmental institutions that, they charged, were tainted by the presence of southerners. Responding to an abolitionist assault led by Salmon Chase on the integrity of the U.S. Supreme Court, a deeply offended Ewing fired back: "I look upon that Bench as above all political influence, above influence of every kind except the main object—right, justice, and truth."[131]

To Ewing, at issue was not the alleged southern, proslavery bias of the U.S. Supreme Court. Rather, the central problem was Clay's initiative to bring about a flawed settlement. Instead of seeking to create a logical and constitutional framework to address the western territories, Congress was slapping together contradictory initiatives in some instances and not addressing specific matters in other places. Worse, there was so much ambiguity in the legislation that, while it satisfied senators' desire for participation, the results would stir up more grief further down the road. "What I desire," Ewing argued, "is distinct and unquestionable legislation. My opinion of this bill, from the first to the last, is that it lacks distinctness and certainty. It has never had proper distinctness. Different opinions are expressed of its effects upon different sides of this Chamber. There is no uniformity of interpretation." Inevitably, Ewing predicted, Clay's compromise would fail.[132]

Clay won, but victory proved temporary. Others would have to shoulder the consequences of the failure of Ewing's peers to halt the expansion of slavery and curb growing sectional tensions. The "Salt Boiler" left Congress for good, and Clay himself was dead within two years. Treasury Secretary Thomas Corwin realized he had made a horrible mistake allying with Fillmore and Clay. The Ohio legislature, with many of its Whigs radicalized by the debate over the Fugitive Slave Law and the 1850 Compromise, chose Benjamin Wade to take Ewing's seat. A law partner of Joshua Giddings in the Western Reserve, the fifty-year-old Wade had won statewide notoriety as a circuit judge when he announced that he would not enforce the Fugitive Slave Law. He cursed Ohio Democrats and moderate Whigs alike and brandished pistols with which he vowed to kill southerners. A new generation, and a new politics, had arrived in America in 1850.[133]

2

"Reaching Up into the Blue Ether ... Sinking Down into the Abyss"

The Next Generation Comes of Age

The Royal Road, or King's Highway, that leads from Durango to the sea at Mazatlan begins the ascent of the Cordillera, on leaving Durango, and, after a sinuous course of two hundred and eighty miles, descends to the coast almost in sight of the latter city. It was laid out, or rather traced, by the conquistadores three hundred years ago and, though in name a royal road, is in fact a mule path. It passes at one point over a mountain of obsidian, which furnished spear and arrow-heads to the armies of Montezuma and his predecessors. At another, it looks down a thousand feet upon a summit of mountains piled upon each other without order and without end, animated alone by flocks of parrots that scream and tumble somersaults in the air as they fly from peak to peak across the chasm. At times, it leads along the edge of a sheer precipice, with a perpendicular wall on the one hand reaching up into the blue ether, and on the other sinking down into the abyss, with only width enough for the careful mountain mule to make his footing sure.
—Hugh Ewing, 1893

If Henry Clay viewed the Lancaster home of Thomas and Maria Ewing as a hospitable locale for political scheming, then children trekked up Main Hill in expectation of adventure. In addition to the Ewing's six surviving children, two girls and a boy belonging to Thomas Ewing's sister, Sarah Clark, lived in the Main Hill mansion. While Cousin Hampton "Hamp" Denman did not live with the Ewings, he might as well have given how often he was there. (Hamp was the son of Maria's sister, Susan, who had married a successful merchant originally from Pennsylvania.) Charles Sherman's large brood, who resided nearby in their more humble abode on Lower Main Hill, joined in play with the Ewings, as did Henry Stanbery's five children. The Hunter boys—Henry, John, and Tom—were also likely to be found at the Ewing home.[1]

In tribute to their law partner and mentor, both Ewing and Stanbery named sons after Philemon Beecher. The two cousins could not have been less alike. Philemon Beecher Ewing, born in 1820, was reserved and studious. Although more interested in reading than playing war games with his

Ellen Ewing Sherman (1824–88). The devoted daughter of Thomas and Maria Ewing, Ellen Ewing Sherman was a stalwart Catholic and Unionist, as well as the wife of William T. Sherman. (Courtesy of the University of Notre Dame Archives.)

brothers, Phil Ewing enjoyed camping with his best friend, Tecumseh Sherman. (Since most children could not pronounce the Shawnee name "Tecumseh," Phil Ewing's best friend became known as "Cump.") Mature beyond his years, Phil Ewing idolized his father and wanted to be a member of the family law firm. He would be the only Ewing son to receive an undergraduate education at an Ohio college—Miami University, which was thirty-five miles from Cincinnati. Phil Ewing married his second cousin, Mary Rebecca Gillespie.[2]

Twelve years younger than Phil Ewing, Philemon Beecher Stanbery liked to have a good time. Five years after his mother's death in 1840, his father shipped him off to a military school in New York. Phil Stanbery returned to Ohio to attend Kenyon College—a strict Episcopalian school in Gambier. For reasons that have remained obscure, he graduated from Ohio University. Whatever the cause for Phil Stanbery's transfer, it could not be disputed that Athens had more taverns than could be found in the sober hamlet of Gambier. Phil Stanbery's subsequent saloon crawls in Leavenworth, Kansas, astonished his Ewing cousins. It would take far more than his father's admonishments to make young Stanbery grow up.[3]

The premature death of the Ewing's second-born child, George, was followed by the births of Eleanor (Ellen) in 1824 and Hugh in 1826. Although girls did not join boys in their rowdier games, Ellen loved sleigh rides around town with Cump Sherman. On one occasion, Cump lost control of the horse and the speeding sleigh tipped over. Hugh landed on the street and then slid for some distance. When the frantic Ellen and Cump caught up with the toddler, he was squealing excitedly.[4]

Named for his maternal grandfather, Hugh Boyle Ewing had a fascination with history and geography. For Hugh, the Hocking River became the Boyne as he and his friends dressed in Scottish tartan and wielded wooden swords. When they were not serving in William of Orange's army, then the Battle of Fallen Timbers beckoned. (Hugh's choice of sides in the Battle of the Boyne reflected his appreciation for Ewing family history, rather than representing his religious preference.) On other occasions Hugh was off with Hamp Denman tracking partridges and rabbits.[5]

With so many boys congregating on Main Hill, there were plenty of recruits for the Ewings' platoons. Cump and his younger brother John Sherman, who was born in 1823, joined the Ewing boys as they flanked enemies through Lancaster's dense woods. Since Cump was six years his senior, Hugh looked up to him. At the same time, however, it was Hugh who gave Cump a nickname that stuck with him for life: the Red-Haired Woodpecker. The name derived mostly from Cump's bright red hair. In part, though, Cump's

James Gillespie Blaine (1830–93). Ally and cousin of the Ewing family, Jimmy Blaine served as a Republican member of the U.S. House of Representatives and Senate and became the 1884 Republican presidential nominee. (Courtesy of the Library of Congress.)

Hugh Boyle Ewing (1826–1905). Expelled from West Point, Hugh Ewing became a California gold prospector, an attorney, a regimental and brigade colonel in the Kanawha Division, a Union general, a diplomat, and, finally, a novelist. Battles: Kanawha Valley, South Mountain, Antietam, Vicksburg, and Missionary Ridge. (Courtesy of the Library of Congress.)

Tom Ewing Jr. (1829–96). A graduate of Brown University, Tom Ewing tried his hand as an attorney, real estate developer, Union general, defense attorney for Samuel Mudd, policy advisor to President Andrew Johnson, and Democratic member of the U.S. House of Representatives. Battles: Prairie Grove, Kansas-Missouri Guerrilla Insurgency, and Pilot Knob. (Courtesy of the Library of Congress.)

restless energy reminded children of a woodpecker pounding his head against a tree. Cump embraced the nickname and later drew finely detailed pictures of woodpeckers.[6]

Tom Ewing, who was born three years after Hugh, organized a squad of "Highland archers" to beat back the forces of the vile King James II. Like Hugh, Tom had an instinct for mounting a successful ambush and was not fearful of the copperhead nests the boys often disturbed when racing through the woods. On the surface, he appeared more serious than Hugh—which helped him get away with playing pranks on siblings and adults. When travelers dismounted outside Lancaster hotels and taverns, Tom generously offered to take their horses to the stable—at no charge. Once the owners were out of sight, Tom and his friends "borrowed" the horses, eventually arriving at the stable after numerous detours.[7]

Whenever Cousin James Gillespie Blaine visited Lancaster, or the Ewings went to Pennsylvania, Tom had the perfect playmate. A year younger than Tom, Jimmy Blaine possessed an outward sobriety that belied his age and personality. Cousin Jimmy was further blessed with a "silver tongue" that he used to talk his way out of trouble. At their reenactments of Fallen Timbers, Jimmy took the Shawnee side, his theatrical sensibilities no doubt attracted to gaudy paint and feathers.[8]

Once, during the 1840 presidential election, Hugh was driving a buggy to Columbus. When he went by the home of a prominent Democrat, Tom and Jimmy issued loud catcalls and held their noses. Not wishing to have word of this brought back to Thomas Ewing, Hugh warned them that if they did that again he would make them walk back to Lancaster. Later, on the way home, while Tom reluctantly made a tactical retreat, Jimmy repeated his earlier performance. True to his word, Hugh stopped the buggy, but before he could toss him out Jimmy fled on his own accord.[9]

As Hugh watched Jimmy run across the farm fields, it dawned on him that his cousin was going to their aunt's house. Hugh knew that if Jimmy got there first with his version of events, Mary Miers Gillespie would thrash Hugh for picking on the defenseless, yet so eloquent, boy. He raced the buggy with little regard for Tom's comfort, arriving before Jimmy. Catching his wits, Hugh realized that if he told his tale, then all three would likely get whipped, so Hugh and Tom decided not to say anything. When Jimmy came upon the scene, he correctly surmised the situation and then invited himself to lunch.[10]

Even though he was the second-youngest Ewing child, Charley refused to be a tagalong—a mere follower of his older siblings' lead. Like his father, Charley had a spirited, gregarious nature. Charley, Cousin Phil Stanbery, and friend John Hunter banded together to play pranks on the older boys and

Charles Ewing (1835–83). A graduate of the University of Virginia, the youngest Ewing son was a Union general, patent attorney, and recipient of the Knight of the Order of Saint Gregory the Great from Pope Pius IX. Battles: Vicksburg, Missionary Ridge, and Sherman's March to the Sea. (Courtesy of the Library of Congress.)

mount their own ambushes. Unfortunately for Charley, while his enthusiasm was great, his ability to avoid exposure was not quite as good. It almost seemed as if all Ellen had to do was to give Charley a quick appraisal, after which she would send him to stand in the corner of their home's library.[11]

His grandfather, Hugh "Pap" Boyle, shared Ellen's instincts regarding Charley. On one occasion Pap Boyle had ordered Charley not to climb the black cherry trees around the Main Hill mansion lest he break an arm or leg. Though Charley assured his grandfather that he would behave better in the future, it was not long until Pap found the boy again swinging from the trees. The remarkably spry grandfather chased and cornered Charley, preparing to whack him with his cane. Desperation led to inspiration, and Charley told Pap that he should not hit his own uncle. The elderly and increasingly befuddled Pap hesitated in his swing just long enough for Charley to escape. Charley continued to climb and fall out of trees, finally succeeding in fracturing a few bones and earning Cump's bemused respect as "a hard case."[12]

Rambunctious as they were, the boys who played on Main Hill embraced an exacting standard of justice. A particularly nasty neighbor kept confiscating their homemade balls when they flew into his yard. He happily informed the children that he threw their toys into his cook stove for a thorough burning. Cump, who was as creative as he was spiteful, came up with a solution. He constructed a special new ball that contained a small charge of gunpowder. When their neighbor took zthis ball, the boys waited outside for the resulting discharge—and then scampered away as black smoke and curses billowed from his house.[13]

On another occasion, Hamp and Hugh were selling homemade ice cream from the Main Hill house. Tom Hunter paid for his treat with counterfeit money and then fled. As Hunter had earlier set up Charley Ewing for a whipping—which led to Hugh being thrashed when he placed himself between his unjustly accused little brother and the schoolmaster—he already had racked up one violation of the boys' honor code. Hugh and the others raced after Hunter, finally trapping him in a storage shed. The errant boy defiantly raised his fists. Hugh, spying a can of green paint, doused him. Unfortunately for Hunter, the paint turned out to be of unusually good quality. Unable to wash the paint away, Hunter's mother ended up shaving his head. The other boys envied his new look and begged their mothers to shave their heads.[14]

So far as his fatherly duties were concerned, Thomas Ewing had vowed not to be like Ohio's Virginian founder, Thomas Worthington. Although Worthington had been "a man of vigorous intellect, great industry, and force of character," Ewing observed, his sons "were ruined by the austerity and distance of his bearing towards them." In sum, Ewing believed, Worthington

William T. Sherman (1820–91). Raised by the Ewing Family, "Cump" Sherman graduated from West Point, married Ellen Ewing Sherman, and achieved fame as a Union general. Battles: First Bull Run, Shiloh, Vicksburg, Missionary Ridge, and the March to the Sea. (Courtesy of the Library of Congress.)

had been his sons' "monitor, but not their companion and confidential friend." Ewing approached his parental role much differently than Worthington, devoting more attention to his sons and daughters than might have been expected given his frequent absences on the court circuit in Ohio and time spent in Washington. He also exhibited a great deal of trust in his children, freely giving them blank checks to cover expenses. Henry Clay told Ewing that he would never consider giving a blank check to his own offspring.[15]

As might be expected in light of his history, the senior Ewing placed enormous value on education. Along with Philemon Beecher and Charles Sherman, Ewing established an academy for the children, and each took turns providing instruction. Education also occurred outside the school. The Ewing, Sherman, Stanbery, and Hunter children never knew when the senator might confront them in Lancaster's streets with a Latin grammar or multiplication question. The boys soon learned that if they could not take evasive action then they had better be prepared to have their minds stretched.[16]

In 1830, Ewing found two full-time teachers for the academy, the brothers Samuel and Mark Howe. Few enjoyed their educational experience at the Howes' Academy. After Charles Sherman died in 1829, Ewing helped pay the tuition for his friend's children and covered the taxes on the Sherman home for the next twenty years. John Sherman, who resisted the Ewings' efforts to show him affection, became ill-tempered and defiant. One day in 1836—being disgusted with Sam Howe's strict discipline—the thirteen-year-old John Sherman landed a heavy glass inkwell on his teacher's chest. The outraged—and ink-soaked—Howe whipped John Sherman as Hugh watched in horror. (Hugh likened the Howes to a "calamitous narcotic experience.") After several minutes, Howe collapsed in exhaustion and John Sherman triumphantly attended a dance that night in high spirits.[17]

John Sherman subsequently dropped out of school and landed a job as a surveyor on the Muskingum River thanks to his family's political connections. When the Democrats regained control of the legislature from the Whigs in 1838, however, they fired Sherman. His return to Lancaster saw him earn a less than desirable reputation. His mother, wearied by Sherman's daily tavern brawls and drunken climbs up Main Hill, encouraged him to live with relatives in northern Ohio.[18]

If Thomas Ewing felt he had failed John Sherman in some way, he remained determined to be a major presence in the lives of his children. When Ewing received an invitation to be the featured speaker at the launching of the Ohio Canal on Independence Day in 1825, he brought along the five-year-old Phil and Ellen—the latter still in diapers. Ewing wanted his brood to be at ease in crowds numbering in the thousands. Of course, Phil and Ellen were not yet

John Sherman (1823–1900). A friend of the Ewing family and relative by marriage, John Sherman defended his brother William T. Sherman, served as a Republican member of the U.S. House of Representatives and Senate, and criticized President Abraham Lincoln during much of the Civil War. (Courtesy of the Library of Congress.)

old enough to understand that their father's lofty praise for democratic revolution in the United States, Greece, and Latin America was also a challenge
directed at them: "The rising generation, the sons of her present race were
born in the midst of battles—they have learned on the knees, nay, even at the
breasts of their mothers, imbibed the spirit of bold and unyielding defiance—
the clangor of arms and the wild song of freedom have been the lullaby of
their cradle. Men who are nurtured and reared amidst scenes like these, are
not formed for a base and abject submission—each auspicious moment for
the assertion of their rights, will be watched for with impatience and seized
with avidity. Some champion of freedom, a Washington, a Bolivar, shall arise
and lead them to victory and emancipation."[19]

In his first Senate term, Ewing made a point of taking at least one child
with him to Washington. Phil dined at President Jackson's table and made
such a favorable impression that the crusty Democrat gave him a basket
of peaches. Hugh, at the age of five, took his turn in Washington. Unlike
Phil, Hugh was determined to see the sights of the city on his own. Seizing an opportunity when his father was engaged with guests, Hugh made
the rounds of Washington for several hours before finding the perfect play-
ground. Ewing, who would not have relished the prospect of explaining to
Maria how he had misplaced Hugh, finally located his wandering son. He
calmly explained to the child that the White House lawn was not intended
for his personal amusement.[20]

Phil, at the age of twenty, joined his father on the presidential campaign
trail in 1840, traveling through Ohio, Virginia, and New York on behalf of
William Henry Harrison. Massive rallies of more than ten thousand excited
Phil. The Ewing children, however, were also exposed to the less savory
aspects of American politics. It was common in campaigns, especially those
in the Lower Northwest, for candidates to denounce each other as assassins and tyrants. The more inventive accused rivals of having sexual intercourse with livestock. Throwing rotten vegetables at politicians and gouging
the eyes of their supporters were regular occurrences. Whether or not, as
contemporary New England commentators claimed, elections in the Lower
Northwest were notoriously violent because of the region's southern culture,
no one would have mistaken Cincinnati for Boston.[21]

Phil served as his father's secretary when Ewing led the Treasury Department in 1841. Tom Ewing held a similar position during his father's tenure as
secretary of the Interior. Phil and Tom spent hours on the U.S. Senate floor
and in the gallery observing formal speeches and quiet side negotiations. In
the early 1830s, when his father was in his first Senate term, it was a rare session in which Phil did not see South Carolina's John Calhoun pull Thomas

Ewing aside so they continue their debate over the Constitution. Calhoun, who disagreed with Ewing on every issue of the day, was respectful and genuinely interested in what the "Salt Boiler" had to say. The same could not be said of Henry Clay, as Tom Ewing personally witnessed in 1850. Clay did not tolerate dissent—especially among old allies.[22]

Where Thomas Ewing viewed his parental role as that of mentor to his children, Maria was the enforcer of discipline, propagator of the Catholic faith, and manager of the household. It was Maria who directed Thomas Ewing to erect a mansion on Lancaster's high ground, being convinced that her infant son George had died because of foul air in the lower part of town. (In all likelihood George's death could be attributed either to contaminated water or to malaria—both found in low-lying areas where human waste and mosquitoes collected.) Maria insisted that her husband purchase a piano so their children would acquire an appreciation of music. She also expected Ewing to fill the mansion with fine furniture. After all, if she was to entertain the accomplished men her husband drew to his side, she needed durable, yet attractive, furnishings. Ewing more than delivered. At an auction in Washington he purchased much of the estate of Anna Marie Haurte de Iturbide, the exiled Empress of Mexico.[23]

Although Maria took little interest in politics, she had strong views on the topic of patriotism. When her close friend Mary Sherman told her that her husband wanted to name a boy after Tecumseh, Maria was appalled. Tecumseh, after all, had allied with the British against the United States in the War of 1812. Ewing, in replying to Maria's objections, observed that Tecumseh "had a real power of organization, eloquence, and self-control." To Maria, however, using those gifts against his country proved Tecumseh's treason. That Tecumseh did not consider himself subject to American law was irrelevant to Maria. The fact that many native-born Protestants did not regard Catholics as any more patriotic than Native Americans was an irony lost on Maria.[24]

With nine children in the Ewing household—ten, once Cump moved up Main Hill following his father's death—Maria had her hands full. If the additional twenty or so young friends and cousins who came by were included, the Ewing house could have easily become chaotic. It did not. Many of Maria's disciplinary efforts were directed at Hugh and Charley—though the latter was such a handful that she outsourced a great deal of responsibility for him to Ellen. Phil was seldom a problem, Tom usually eluded detection, and Maria made allowances for Cump since she had also lost a parent at an early age. Cump later confided to Ellen that he would never be able "to repay the many kindnesses and favors" Maria bestowed upon him.[25]

If Hugh's choice was between going to school and fishing in the Hocking River, there was no debate. As Hugh observed, "I think I was sent [to school] without any expectation that I would make any progress in polite letters, but rather to make sure of my whereabouts for some portion of the day." Playing truant, Hugh often went fishing. Invariably, he would jump into the river to pursue his catch, emerging mud-splattered and unable to deny that he had skipped school. After one such fishing expedition, he came home prepared for the worst: "I glanced anxiously at mother, and awaited the expected cross-examination; it did not come, but in its stead, prevailed exceptional cheerfulness, which to an older soldier would have boded no good." Thinking he had gotten away with his truancy, Hugh was crushed when his smiling mother told him at the end of dinner that his father had returned from Washington with gifts. His presents, however, had been "sequestered" by the highest executive authority in the house.[26]

Maria Ewing expected her boys to be obedient *and* independent. Once, on a return trip from their Gillespie and Blaine kin in Pennsylvania, Hugh was behaving badly. When he continued to ignore her requests for peace, Maria Ewing halted the wagon, ejected Hugh, and continued on her way. Hugh walked for a while until Maria, who had grown weary of Ellen's protests, relented and let him ride. Five years later, when Hugh was fourteen, Maria permitted him to take the eleven-year-old Tom on visits to distant Ohio relations. It was just the two boys on horseback, traveling close to two hundred miles round trip. Although they entered the wrong farmhouse on one occasion and made themselves at home, Hugh and Tom otherwise navigated quite well.[27]

The Ewing matriarch insisted that her children encourage and support one another. She expected them to be loyal to one another and to their extended family. Where other prominent families have had their share of sibling rivalry, the Ewing children, even as adults, did not try to undercut each other, whether in politics, business, or military service. Ellen, who had her share of spats with her brothers, especially with Tom, tried to heed her mother's injunction that family came above all. On more than one occasion, however, Ellen placed her husband ahead of her brothers, although never ahead of her parents.

There was no doubt that the Ewing household was Roman Catholic, in spite of the church's sparse institutional presence in the early Ohio country. The Catholic diocese for Ohio was then headquartered in Bardstown, Kentucky—272 miles from Lancaster. Bardstown's Dominicans established St. Joseph's Parish in Somerset, Ohio, in 1818. Although it was little more than a village, Somerset was on Zane's Trace, served as a midpoint of sorts between

Bardstown and Pittsburgh, and had attracted a number of immigrant Irish construction workers. Lancaster was not assigned a priest until 1839.[28]

Lancaster's Catholics either traveled to Somerset for Mass or waited for Father Dominic Young of St. Joseph to make his monthly visit to Lancaster. Father Young typically said Mass in the Ewing mansion, in the home of another Catholic family, or in a small building erected for that purpose in 1822. Maria recited the Rosary with her children and made Alban Butler's eighteenth-century work *The Lives of the Fathers, Martyrs, and Principal Saints* a major feature of their religious instruction. When Cump became part of the Ewings' extended family, it was Father Young who baptized him and gave the boy the saint name of William. Although subsequently known by the rather grandiose name of William Tecumseh Sherman, he remained Cump to everyone in Lancaster.[29]

Cousin Maria Gillespie Blaine and her husband Ephraim had decided to raise their sons Protestant and their daughters Catholic. Cousin Jimmy Blaine, who moved from the Presbyterian to the Congregational Church with ease, was entirely comfortable among the Catholic Ewings. To make interfaith religious matters even more complex, Jimmy's cousins, Eliza "Angela" Gillespie and Neal Henry Gillespie, joined Catholic religious orders. Their mother, Mary Miers Gillespie, had herself been a convert to Catholicism. Phil Ewing married "Mother Angela's" sister.[30]

For his part, Tom Ewing, like his father, found sectarianism unappealing. To a large extent, Tom and Cump followed Senator Ewing's lead. Their devotion to the preservation of the United States went hand in glove with their belief in a nondenominational God. Given their origins in war-scarred Ulster, sectarian battles—and civil wars—were anathema to the Ewing-Blaine-Gillespie families. The Shermans and Stanberys, though not of Ulster, appreciated their cousins' perspective.[31]

While Hugh, Tom, and Cump attended the secular Howe academy in Lancaster, Ellen and cousin Eliza Gillespie took up residence at the Somerset convent school run by the Dominican sisters. Just as their religious faith became more pronounced than was true for Tom and Cump, Ellen and Eliza also developed a stronger attachment to the service ethos of "good works." In that, Maria Ewing was their role model. Maria took to heart the Catholic injunction to help "the least of my people." Certainly, there was no shortage of poor, hardworking Irish in Somerset whose children would not have been educated—or might have even gone hungry—without the Ewings' financial assistance to Father Young and such Dominican teachers as Sister Catherine Mudd.[32]

Among Ellen's and Eliza's classmates were the Sheridan children; their immigrant father was a laborer on the National Road. When the Ewings attended Mass at St. Joseph, Phil Sheridan watched his humble mother and the refined Maria Ewing take communion together and later converse as equals. The success of the Ewings in business, law, and politics served as an inspiration to St. Joseph's parishioners. Even Cump, who entered West Point in 1836, impressed Somerset's Irish boys on the occasion he appeared in his cadet uniform while on furlough, despite his being visibly ill at ease with Catholic rituals (in contrast to the more flexible Jimmy Blaine).[33]

From the Dominican convent in Somerset, Maria Ewing sent Ellen and Eliza to the convent of the Sisters of Visitation in Georgetown. Maria and Thomas Ewing paid for Eliza's tuition and board, as they did for their niece, Abby Clark. Thomas Ewing was subsequently able to spend more time with Ellen and Eliza. (When not visiting with Thomas Ewing, Eliza defied local law and custom to teach black children to read and write. For Eliza, teaching black children was part of the Catholic ethos of good works.) It was during those years in Washington that Ellen began to follow national politics— a pursuit that appealed neither to her mother nor to Cump. Indeed, Cump accurately observed that Ellen regarded Washington as a second home.[34]

At the Georgetown convent, Ellen became close to Mary and Emily Mudd, who were related to Somerset's Catherine Mudd. Emily Mudd's brother, John Henry Clay Mudd, later became clerk to the U.S. House of Representatives when Tom Ewing worked for his father in the Interior Department and the Ewings' youngest child, Maria Theresa, attended the Sisters of Visitation. Over the 1840s, both generations of Ewings came to know John Mudd and his many relations. Emily Mudd's cousin, Samuel Mudd, for instance, was, like John Mudd, a devout Catholic who graduated from Georgetown College. Samuel Mudd was destined to achieve notoriety in the practice of medicine and to value his connection to the Ewings.[35]

Ellen occasionally contemplated taking religious vows; Hugh set his sights on West Point. From the military academy, Cump had informed Ellen in 1839 that Hugh was "nearer my beau-ideal of a perfect boy" and "would make an excellent soldier—a captain already—why there are some men in our army with grey hairs who have scarcely attained that rank." A few years later, while stationed at Fort Moultrie in South Carolina, Cump warned his "perfect boy" not to waste his time reading abolitionist literature. After Hugh had sent him an antislavery pamphlet, Cump observed that it was authored by a "crazy fool" and of little use except for the entertainment "of our Negro servants."[36]

Thomas Ewing had initially refused to support Hugh in his ambition to become a member of the West Point class of 1848. He bluntly told Hugh, "It is not worthwhile. You have quarreled with all your tutors, and you will do the same there." Hugh assured his father that this would not be the case. As it turned out, the senior Ewing proved correct, though he could not have predicted the cause for Hugh's first quarrel. Moreover, considering Maria's religious principles, Thomas Ewing was in no position to express disapproval of his son's actions.[37]

West Point required cadets to attend weekly chapel—which meant going to Episcopalian services on the campus grounds. Hugh declined to go to chapel and wrote out an explanation, observing that he was Catholic and therefore should be permitted to attend Mass in town. He received his first warning. Next week, Hugh again refused to attend chapel and was notified that if he missed services the following week he would be expelled. The third Sunday came and Hugh did not go to chapel.[38]

Superintendent Richard Delafield summoned Hugh to his office and informed him that he was processing his expulsion papers. The superintendent also told Hugh that the academy had enrolled Catholics for years and that none of them had ever insisted on attending Mass. Hugh replied that while he could not speak for the religious commitment of other Catholic cadets, his conscience required that he be true to his church's teachings. He also subtly, and very politely, implied that West Point, the U.S. military, and the federal government apparently thought nothing of intimidating Catholics into religious conformity. Taken aback, Delafield relented. The following Sunday, as Hugh prepared to attend Mass outside the academy's gates, a dozen Catholic cadets voluntarily lined up behind him.[39]

Hugh's assertion of Catholic rights caught the eye of West Point instructor William Rosecrans, a native of Delaware, Ohio. Lieutenant Rosecrans had left the Episcopal Church to become Roman Catholic. He loved theological discussions, inviting Hugh to spend time with him and his brother, Sylvester, who had just graduated from Kenyon College. Hugh enjoyed his visit with the Rosecrans brothers and learned that Sylvester was contemplating his own religious conversion. (Sylvester Rosecrans did more than convert; he became first bishop of the Catholic Diocese of Columbus following its establishment after the Civil War.)[40]

Among the cadets, Hugh earned fame early in his stay at West Point. One evening, a barracks mate woke Hugh and told him that trouble was headed their way in the person of the inspector of cadets. The authorities were making late-night rounds to see who had sneaked off campus to carouse at Benny Haven's tavern, which was a few miles away. Hugh looked around and did not see the problem until his friend began pulling back the sheets on half the beds to reveal dummies.[41]

Unwilling to see so many boys expelled, Hugh had his mates quickly make a bedsheet ladder and then lowered him out the second-story window.

He eluded the detection of the guards and burst into Benny Haven's to spread the alarm. Hugh then successfully led a party of cadets past the guards and the inspector. After this incident, Hugh did not have to worry about paying for drinks at Benny Haven's. On the other hand, notice of his adventures reached Ellen Ewing. As she reminded Hugh, "Consider that each moment of the year that has past has *borne some report to Heaven of you.*" (In this instance, when Ellen wrote "Heaven" she meant God; however, there were also mere mortals receiving the Word.)[42]

Hugh loved the library at West Point and devoured works on military history, geography, and classical literature. He soon acquired the nickname of "the Monk" in recognition of his Catholic faith and fondness for Latin works. The nickname, though, was also meant ironically, since, as his sister fretted, he did sneak off campus and freely pursued the temptations of drinking, smoking, and shooting billiards. All in all, Hugh enjoyed West Point but for two irritants: engineering mathematics and bullies. He could not (or would not) do much about the former but was determined to deal with the latter.[43]

Superintendent Delafield, who was then followed by Henry Brewerton, proved incapable of curbing the culture of brutality that infected West Point in the 1840s. It was not clear to cadets if Brewerton took notice or cared. The physically strongest cadets, particularly those with political connections and wealth, assaulted their classmates with little fear of expulsion. William Crittenden, the nephew of Thomas Ewing's Whig comrade, Senator John Crittenden, was one of the worst bullies. On one occasion, he used his sword to beat and stab a good-natured cadet whose superior intelligence and humor annoyed Crittenden. Since the cadet in question lacked political protection, Crittenden considered him to be fair game.[44]

Crittenden was often joined in his patrols by Ambrose "Bully Burns" Burnside, who took sadistic pleasure in sneaking up behind smaller cadets and assaulting them. Hugh believed it was unjust for privileged cadets like Crittenden and Burnside to prey upon the less fortunate. He was disgusted that the Point's superintendents did not expel Crittenden and Burnside for their vicious, cowardly conduct. (Crittenden, who graduated with the class of 1845, became a mercenary soldier, or "filibuster," in Cuba. He was subsequently executed by a Spanish firing squad.)[45]

Because Hugh had so often defended fellow cadets from assault, Burnside's cronies ambushed him on several occasions. Though his foes seldom came at him frontally, Hugh usually won the fights. Wearied of Burnside's bullying and placing on report anyone who allegedly defied his authority as "captain" of his cadet company, Hugh had it out with him. As Hugh recounted, he knew he could not defeat the powerful Burnside even in a fair fight. He was, however, determined to inflict sufficient damage on Burnside to make him think twice about bullying others. Eventually, the army realized it had a discipline problem and recruited Robert E. Lee to be superintendent in 1852. Lee, who regarded West Point as a political "snake pit," reluctantly accepted the position.[46]

Cump's accounts of West Point camaraderie had not prepared Hugh for the reality that there would be abusive, incompetent, and petty men some day serving as army officers. Indeed, Sherman had been less than forthcoming with Hugh about his experiences, perhaps viewing West Point—warts and all—as the only avenue open to Cump to assert his independence from Thomas Ewing. Hugh became depressed, though he confided this only to Ellen. Her frequent, morally pointed letters did not cheer him up: "Have you heard yet of the awful death of poor Mr. Ainsworth? He went east about three months ago and commenced dissipating, wandered about the cities sometimes without hat, coat or shoes, and after spending some weeks in the brutal indulgence of his appetite, he started home, but poor unfortunate man, he died of delirium tremens before he reached Zanesville."[47]

Hugh began neglecting mathematics and astronomy, passing his time reading *Don Quixote*, the *Inferno*, and *Tristram Shandy*. When called to work out an astronomy equation on the chalkboard, he angered his instructor by arriving at the correct answer the wrong way. It was obvious to his instructors that he was not reading his texts, while to Hugh it was becoming obvious that the army liked officers who got the wrong answer so long as they embraced the right way—the army way. For the first time in the history of West Point up to 1848, Hugh was among three seniors to be flunked out, allegedly for failing grades. The practice had been to give seniors leeway since they had made it that far. Hugh and the other two cadets, however, for whatever actual reason, were cast off—much to the regret of their class. Although embarrassed, Hugh was also relieved.[48]

Hugh's departure from West Point presented an opportunity to Father Young. The Somerset priest approached Thomas and Maria Ewing and asked them to help a deserving young parishioner, Phil Sheridan, gain entrance into the military academy. Phil Sheridan either did not know, or refused to reveal, that his father had approached the priest. According to Phil Sheridan, his Whig congressman had been solicited by several prominent families who wanted their sons to go to West Point. Afraid that if he favored one candidate from this applicant pool he would offend the others, the congressmen passed all them over to support the poor Irish boy. It was an improbable story made even more fantastic by Sheridan omitting the names of the two Ohioans whose expulsion from West Point opened a slot for him. This latter act suggested that Sheridan knew if he made mention of Hugh Ewing then others would figure it out that his path to West Point was not as he described.[49]

The only opposition to Sheridan's choice of vocation came from Father Joshua Young, the resident priest at St. Mary's in Lancaster. As Dominic Young told Hugh, Joshua Young frequently visited Somerset and knew the Sheridans well. Learning that John Sheridan was considering sending his son to West Point, Joshua Young warned him that the boy would lose his religion by going to the academy. As the brutally blunt Dominican said to the elder Sheridan, "Rather than send him to West Point, take him out into the backyard behind the chicken coop and cut his throat." (Joshua Young's concerns were misplaced. Sheridan married in the Catholic Church, his bride an alumnus of the Sisters of Visitation—the same school attended by the Ewings and Mudds.)[50]

Hugh passed the summer of 1848 in Lancaster, reading law with his father and joining his cousin Hamp Denman on hunting trips. He remained restless and without direction. Hugh also felt he had disappointed his father by not completing what he had set out to do when he entered West Point. Then word of the discovery of gold in California reached Ohio. As Hugh later, and ruefully, recalled: "The amount of gold picked up by the few men as yet on the ground, was said to be beyond belief; two or three days were enough to transform a beggar into a millionaire. Lumps of enormous size were reported to have been found, and as to the gold-dust itself, it was everywhere; they walked on it, cooked over it, slept on it; it glittered from every point of the compass in the rays of the noon-day sun."[51]

California's population boomed, increasing from 15,000 in 1848 to 90,000 by 1849—and continued without abatement through 1852, when the new state claimed 220,000 people. Two dozen or so young men from Lancaster and Somerset caught gold fever, among them Hugh and Hamp. There would be two Lancaster parties leaving from Cincinnati down the Mississippi River: the Democrats such as Robert Effinger, who would be traveling at federal government expense with boundary commissioner John Weller, and the Whigs with Thomas Ewing's son and nephew.[52]

Like many who prospected in California, the Ohioans were socially connected men in their twenties, unmarried, and thus far without achievement in any field of endeavor. They wanted independence but often fell back on their family for funds to outfit their journey. Hugh and Hamp were no exception. Thomas Ewing reconciled himself to his son's newest adventure. Maria Ewing assured her husband that Hugh had made a religious retreat in Somerset and was of a proper Catholic frame of mind for the next stage in his life.

Indeed, Maria continued, Hugh had "made reconciliation with his God and returned a new man!" Ellen echoed her mother, writing to the senior Ewing that Hugh had "armed himself with the best resolutions" and had pledged to send her "a gold rosary." Tom Ewing, on the other hand, did not appear to share his sister's and mother's confidence and seemed taken aback when his elder brother hit him up for a loan. As Tom stiffly informed Hugh, "I have scarcely a single dollar that I could lend you." Tom loved his brother, but still Hugh needed to stand on his own feet.[53]

Hugh's correspondence with his family diminished the further he traveled from Ohio. He stopped in Vicksburg, Mississippi, to mail a letter home and look around, but the river port did not make much of an impression. New Orleans was livelier than Vicksburg, though Hugh did not join Effinger and Weller in their seamy explorations of the Crescent City. He did, however, witness his first slave auction: "They [the slaves] were clean, well dressed, and mounted the block, one after the other, apparently satisfied with the situation, and especially interested in the bidding, which they watched keenly, scrutinizing the persons of the bidders, and delighted to see the price go up to a high sum. Our party were not scandalized by this exhibition, as the mass of the people of Ohio at that day were proslavery, and looked with scorn upon an abolitionist."[54]

The adventurers parted company at New Orleans, taking separate steamers into the Gulf of Mexico. Hugh's ship began sinking and had to make haste for land. Weller's party, despite seeing the distress of their fellow Ohioans, refused repeated hails for assistance. Having barely made it to shore, Hugh's companions decided to journey across Mexico rather than attempt another voyage to the Central American isthmus. There was some trepidation, since the United States had recently been at war with Mexico. Their concerns, however, were largely misplaced. Indeed, Hugh came to like Mexicans. Texans, on the other hand, were trustworthy only when you held a gun to their heads.[55]

While stopping in Brownsville, Texas, Hugh purchased a horse. As he and his friends were about to depart, a posse appeared with an arrest warrant for Hugh. The posse, with guns drawn, accused Hugh of being a horse thief and demanded his surrender. Brandishing their own guns, the Ohioans faced down the surprised Texans. Hugh calmly told the sheriff, "We have been advised that it is a custom on the border to rob travelers in the name of the law; and believing this to be an attempt at robbery, we decline to be victimized, and will, in preference, defend our property to the last."[56]

Angered, the posse's leader said he was advancing, but halted when Hugh's party trained their weapons on him. Realizing he had a potentially bloody fight on his hands, the sheriff changed his tactics. He ordered Hugh to disarm and appear in court. The Ohioans agreed to go to court but would not surrender their weapons. Once in court, the judge threatened Hugh and ignored his bill of sale. One of the Lancaster youths, who had become thoroughly vexed with Brownsville law enforcement, informed the judge that the man they were threatening was the son of Thomas Ewing. Hugh, not sure if that bit of intelligence would help or hang him, cringed, but the judge did become more temperate. After identifying and locating the man who had sold Hugh the horse, Hugh's party gladly left Texas jurisdiction.[57]

Hugh loved Mexico. The food was so different and, to Hugh's palate, better than what could be found in Ohio. His party feasted on delicious corn tortillas and succulent armadillo meat. Nearly all the Mexicans they encountered were friendly, and many invited them to dine in their haciendas. A few government officials attempted to extort bribes, threatening them with imprisonment if they did not pay. On those occasions Hugh's friends sneaked out of town under the cover of darkness.[58]

In his memoirs, and in a subsequent novel, Hugh expressed admiration for the architecture of the Mexican churches. He appreciated the pageantry and spiritual sensuality of Spanish-influenced Catholicism—so different from the austere Irish Church of his own upbringing. Less appealing, however, was the rampant cholera that felled Hugh and Hamp. Mexican folk medicine capriciously killed or cured the stricken.[59]

Nearly six months after their departure from Cincinnati, the Ohioans arrived at the American River near Sacramento. Hugh discovered that the rule of law existed no more in California than it had in Mexico or Texas. Junior army officers based in California, including Ulysses "Sam" Grant and Cump, had been appalled by the disorder they encountered. Grant believed that conditions in the goldfields turned hitherto decent men into "criminals and outcasts." Sherman reserved his distaste for unscrupulous lawyers. Cump saw American lawyers use the courts to throw out Spanish land titles and steal property. Among the most detestable lawyers was Henry Halleck, a West Pointer who had graduated a year before Sherman. Halleck, while still in the army, made a fortune by invalidating Mexican land claims in court. (He resigned his commission in 1854.)[60]

Ellen Ewing wrote to Hugh often and let him know that "everyday of my life I say the especial 'Ave Maria' for you." Hugh's responses were less frequent. Ellen had to learn from relatives of the other Lancaster men that though her brother was collecting experiences to fill several novels, Hugh had less luck panning for gold at his claim—"the Buckeye Bar." Sherman visited with Hugh and Hamp when circumstances allowed and in September

1849 obtained temporary employment for them as part of an army rescue of starving miners. They went with Major D. H. Rucker's party into the Sierra Nevada mountains carrying thirteen thousand rations.[61]

Rucker's men journeyed through vast areas of desolate lava beds and volcanic sandstone. There was little grass and water for mules and horses, let alone sustenance for the ill-equipped miners. Few of the prospectors seemed able to shoot even a rabbit for dinner. Scurvy and cholera were everywhere, and Major Rucker and Hamp nearly perished. Hugh had never seen such destitution and would never forget how dire the consequences were for those who were not prepared for contingencies. He also came away with a restored faith in the army. Even the profanely critical Rucker earned Hugh's admiration.[62]

Across the continent in Washington, Ellen, Tom, and Charley were settling into the Blair House with their mother and father. With four floors to furnish in their rented home, Ellen and her mother kept busy preparing for the crush of anticipated visitors. Thomas Ewing, meanwhile, diligently added to his wine collection. The Marine Band gave Saturday sunset performances on the White House lawn and Wednesday concerts at Capitol Hill. Tom, who was working for his father and President Taylor, frequently escorted Ellen to the public concerts. Ellen wrote to Hugh that she greatly enjoyed observing the city's power brokers, who seldom missed a concert. For Ellen, though, the most exciting development was Cump's impending return east for their marriage in Washington.[63]

The May 1, 1850, Ewing-Sherman marriage was *the* social event of Washington. President Taylor, his cabinet, Daniel Webster, Henry Clay, and Great Britain's envoy were in attendance. Ewing's fellow Supreme Court Club members, and, moreover, the justices themselves, were among the three hundred guests. Cump's marriage into the Ewing family gave him entrée to General Winfield Scott and President Taylor, neither of whom would have otherwise given him much notice.[64]

Cump had often expressed his gratitude to the Ewings, but there were tensions in his relationship with the family. The wedding ceremony, though conducted by the president of Georgetown College, was not identifiably Catholic. Moreover, it was held at the Blair House, not in a Catholic church. Sherman did not become Catholic and only reluctantly agreed that any offspring they might have would be raised in the church.[65]

He also understood, though he groused about it, that maintaining Ellen in the manner in which she was accustomed was going to cost more than his salary as a junior officer could provide. Then again, if Cump complained to his in-laws about Ellen's expensive tastes, he did not return his John J. Fraser and Brooks Brothers tailored uniforms. Amid red clay dust and flying bul-lets, Sherman would always be the best-dressed soldier on any battlefield.[66]

President Taylor's death, followed by Ewing's appointment to the Senate, gave Tom and Cump front-row seats to the punishing debates over the 1850 Compromise. In a letter to Phil, Tom recounted how Henry Clay "used all means at his disposal first to conciliate and then, if possible, intimidate" their father. Tom expected the senior Ewing would "teach Mr. Clay a useful les-son to beware how he again pits himself against his old friends." Where Tom relished political combat, his brother-in-law recoiled. As Cump wrote to his reformed brother John, "I hope the political history of the past year will make a strong impression on your mind not to seek honors or distinction" by running for public office. Cump gladly returned to active duty and Tom headed to Brown University.[67]

Even though only Charley and Maria Theresa were still at home—when not enrolled at Catholic schools in Somerset or Washington—the Main Hill mansion remained a lively place. Maria helped with the dozen grand-children ultimately sired by Phil and Mary Rebecca. After Henry Stanbery became attorney general of Ohio in 1846, he sold his Lancaster mansion to Phil Ewing. While it might have been expected that Thomas Ewing would retire—he had already surpassed the typical life expectancy for men of that era—just the opposite occurred. Ewing's business ventures, Washington legal practice, and political mentoring grew.[68]

The expansion of rail track in Ohio, from 323 miles to 2,635 between 1850 and 1860, fueled Ewing's coal operations in the Hocking Valley. Railroad construction also generated lucrative lawsuits from communities tied to steamship transportation. Rutherford Hayes, a graduate of Kenyon College, had received Thomas Ewing's notice while making an appeal to the Ohio Supreme Court in a controversial criminal case. Hayes appreciated Ewing's praise, as well as his legal acumen. When litigation arose in 1853 concerning the erection of a railroad bridge that would have obstructed steamer naviga-tion into Lake Erie, Hayes enlisted Ewing. Although he was a rising criminal and contract attorney, Hayes knew his limitations. The thirty-one-year-old attorney was not about to appear before the U.S. Supreme Court without the senator. Ewing assured Hayes that his preparation was excellent, even if legal precedent worked against their case. (They did not win but did extract suf-ficient concessions from the railroad to satisfy their clients.)[69]

In 1852, Thomas Ewing and Henry Stanbery took opposite sides before the U.S. Circuit Court in the "Martha Washington" case, which involved a steamship purportedly set fire in an insurance scam. The ultimate winners of the "Martha Washington" arson, fraud, and wrongful death litigation were the attorneys. More ominous, at least from a national political perspective, was the "Swormstedt" affair. As part of the fallout over the growing antislavery movement, the Methodist Church in 1844 had split into northern and southern branches. In 1849, the southern separatists commenced litigation against Leroy Swormstedt in Cincinnati over the control of Methodist business interests in Ohio. The case went to the U.S. Supreme Court in 1853, with Stanbery pleading on behalf of the southerners and Ewing and his old friend George Badger working for the northerners.[70]

It was disconcerting to observers that even Christians from the same religious tradition could not overcome the rancor between abolitionists and the apologists of slavery. Then again, one of the initial attorneys for the northerners had picked up Daniel Webster's cry, "Union now and forever!," which did not soothe southern feelings. It was also ironic that Badger himself had fallen victim to the very forces of sectionalism that had torn apart the Methodists. His 1852 nomination to the U.S. Supreme Court had been wrecked in an increasingly dysfunctional Senate. Northern senators—mainly antislavery Whigs—did not want to place another southerner on the Court, while many southern Democrats perceived Badger—North Carolinian though he was—to be too much in harmony with northerners like Thomas Ewing. At the end of the day, Badger did not get his Supreme Court seat and the northern Methodists lost their case.[71]

Democrat Stephen Douglas of Illinois contributed to the rancorous atmosphere in the U.S. Senate. In 1854, Douglas proposed to set aside the 1820 Missouri Compromise and allow people in the West to vote on whether they wanted slavery. Thomas Ewing opposed the Kansas-Nebraska Act and publicly decried Douglas's handiwork as "a great wrong and great evil." Hayes, as an abolitionist, went further than his mentor, which was not unexpected, since he had already rejected both the Whig and Democratic Parties as "useless."[72]

Prior to the introduction of the Kansas-Nebraska Act, Democrats had been doing well in the Old Northwest. Ohio Democrats racked up impressive victories in the 1851 races for state and legislative offices. In 1852, Ohio Whigs held only seven of the twenty-three U.S. House of Representative seats. Just as disheartening, abolitionist dissidents in the Free Soil Party siphoned sufficient votes from the Whigs to throw Ohio's Electoral College votes to Franklin Pierce. Meanwhile, proslavery mobs operated with the tacit approval of Democratic sheriffs in southern and central Ohio. They frequently stoned abolitionist speakers and brandished "hanging" rope.[73]

Douglas's initiative, which led to Missouri Democrats flooding into the Kansas territory to support slavery, engendered an electoral backlash in

Ohio. Sensing impending doom, all but four of Ohio's congressional Democrats voted against the Kansas-Nebraska Act. Not surprisingly, Edson Olds, one of the few outspoken congressional supporters of the Kansas-Nebraska Act outside the South, lived in the Virginia Military District.[74]

Aroused, John Sherman declared himself a candidate for Congress and worked with Thomas Ewing and Senator Ben Wade to organize a mass protest rally in Columbus. (Ewing recognized that there was little choice but to work with Wade, even if he thought he was an irresponsible radical.) In the aftermath of the 1854 midterm elections, Ohio Democrats were reduced to four U.S. House seats. John Sherman went to Congress, representing a district that included two abolitionist Western Reserve counties. The Whigs collapsed in Ohio and nationally, unable to survive growing sectionalism and defections to the Free Soil Party.[75]

Thomas Ewing, as well as Tom and Phil, watched the evolving political scene intently. The political upheaval of 1854 potentially made room for a new party that could fuse Whig economic principles with a more moderate version of Free Soil abolitionism. John Sherman certainly saw such an opportunity and in 1855 presided at a Columbus convention that established the Ohio Republican Party. Ewing and his sons, however, were unwilling as yet to embrace the Republicans. They had ample cause: the new party was animated by a nativist, anti-Catholic spirit. Ohio's nativist voters, who had supported the so-called Know-Nothing—or American—Party, had grown from 50,000 in 1854 to 120,000 by early 1855. To nativists, Ohio's Catholics were criminals and drunkards from birth.[76]

Salmon Chase, a long-standing enemy of Thomas Ewing, welcomed support from the Know-Nothings in his 1855 gubernatorial race. If Chase deftly moved in such a way as to gain anti-Catholic support without directly denigrating Rome, the rest of the Republican Party's state candidates were more open in their religious and ethnic hatred. Lewis Campbell, who had helped deny Ewing the Whig Party's 1848 vice presidential nomination, built his record as a Dayton congressman on his opposition to the Kansas-Nebraska Act and the Catholic Church. Former Senator Thomas Corwin, who had also tussled with Thomas Ewing, welcomed the prospect of an explicitly anti-Catholic presidential candidate in the 1856 election. Republicans' tacit declaration of a cultural war on Catholics set the stage for a Protestant-led election-day riot in Cincinnati in 1855.[77]

The association of Ohio Republicans with religious intolerance gave Democrats their opening in 1856, making it possible for Clement Vallandigham to claim Campbell's House seat—though that contest was so close it ended up being resolved by the Democratic-controlled U.S. House of Representatives.

Samuel Cox also aroused the Democratic base to secure the "capital" congressional district of Franklin and Licking Counties in central Ohio. Samuel
Medary, the editor of the Democratic Party's newspaper, the *Ohio Statesman*,
rallied immigrants against nativists and abolitionists. Democrats regained
control of the Ohio legislature in 1856. Rutherford Hayes had futilely urged
his allies in the antislavery movement to disavow support from the Know-
Nothing "rowdies."[78]

For the Ewing family, religious and ethnic intolerance hit close to home.
Thomas Ewing had long been protective of his children and sensitive to
any religious slights they received. One of the rare occasions in which he
expressed open anger came about after some of Tom's playmates had ridiculed him for not eating meat on Fridays. Ewing directed Phil to shield his
little brother from those neighbors, "for it is cruel to subject so young a child
to the ordeal of seeing that which he holds sacred ridiculed, and he might be
tempted to be ashamed of his faith—a thing from which you must guard him
until he is older and stronger."[79]

Many of Lancaster's social elites disdained Catholics. Robert Effinger, on
his way across the isthmus to California in 1849, had observed: "In this place
one can form an opinion of a country governed by the Catholic persuasion.
Why there is no set of heathens in Christ's kingdom who are guiltier of wor-
shipping images than the people of this country. Their churches are filled
with them, and they bow down and worship those just as the Hindu does his
idol god." It was little wonder that the Ewings lent their political and financial support to Cincinnati archbishop John Purcell in his confrontations with
Protestant foes. As Ewing said of America's nativists, "I know nothing that is
good [about them], and much that is evil."[80]

Tom Ewing had no intention of becoming caught up in Ohio's religious
wars; he had other priorities. His four years at Brown University were idyllic.
He read Harriet Beecher's Stowe's best-selling novel, *Uncle Tom's Cabin*, but
viewed it less as an antislavery tract than as a work of satirical fiction com-
parable to *Don Quixote* and *Gulliver's Travels*. (Mrs. Stowe would have been
appalled.) When not discussing literature and philosophy with his profes-
sors, Tom rowed regularly on Narragansett Bay. Leaving Brown in 1854, Tom
attended the Cincinnati College of Law. He also read law with Henry Stanbery, who had established a practice in that city. Cousins Henry and Tom
worked well together and established a lifelong professional connection.[81]

In 1856, Tom married Ellen Cox, a Presbyterian minister's daughter. Maria
Ewing welcomed her new daughter-in-law into the family but worried that
Tom might succumb to "the danger of heresy and error." Tom also surprised
his father by giving up his Cincinnati law practice to head for Kansas. "The

fever of adventure seized him," Ewing wrote to his elder daughter and confidante, "and he must go." Hugh and Hamp, who had returned to Ohio in 1852, decided to go with Tom. Hugh, as his father lamented, possessed "a restless spirit." Although Hugh was not yet prepared to help administer the family's growing business concerns in Ohio, he had at least been looking after Thomas Ewing's St. Louis properties.[82]

Charley Ewing, to his regret, could not move to Kansas with his brothers and cousin Hamp. He was frustrated and had earlier complained to Hugh that their mother had arranged with the Dominican priests in Somerset to make sure he did not leave the grounds of the St. Joseph preparatory school. Somerset may have been small, but Finch's tavern on the town square was a fine place for Irish lads to study blasphemy. Charley Ewing, however, would have no such opportunity.[83]

By the time the Ewing kin arrived in Kansas the territory was at war with Missouri and politically unstable. (Ten men served as territorial governors of Kansas over a six-year period—including Ohio's proslavery editor, Samuel Medary.) Well before Senator Douglas had sponsored the Kansas-Nebraska Act, Missouri slave owners had taken a keen interest in their western neighbor. Of the southern states, Missouri was the most exposed to free territory, providing enormous temptation for slaves to escape to Illinois or Iowa. The last thing Missouri planters desired was yet another refuge on their borders for runaway slaves. This was no small concern since there were over fifty thousand slaves valued at $30 million along the Missouri River.[84]

The Missouri River was the best natural road across the state and extended into Kansas, linking Leavenworth to Kansas City and St. Louis. Even if sandbars and tree snags typically delayed passage of steamers for three or four hours, there was no better alternative. Indeed, most of the rivers in western Missouri and Kansas were more mud than water. The roads were just as bad. Tobacco and hemp planters clustered along the banks of Missouri River saw their natural domain extending westward without regard to an invisible state boundary.[85]

Senator David Atchison of Missouri sought to extend slavery into Kansas, working with President Pierce and fellow Democrats to pass the Kansas-Nebraska Act. Atchison went beyond rhetorical advocacy of slavery to organize bands of Missouri citizens to enter Kansas. His Missouri followers stuffed ballot boxes, elected their own territorial delegate to Congress, and drafted the proslavery "Lecompton" state constitution. The Missourians also levied harsher penalties for violation of the Fugitive Slave Law than what the federal government had provided. Kansans who sheltered runaway slaves would receive ten years' imprisonment, while those merely criticizing the "peculiar institution" could expect at least two years in jail.[86]

Missouri legislator Claiborne Jackson expressed the fury of proslavery partisans, warning in 1854 that if Kansas were allowed to become "free-nigger territory" then their own state would follow suit. Jackson's and Atchison's disciples acted on their leaders' exhortations. Outside Leavenworth in 1854, Isaac Cody, although not an abolitionist, had expressed reservations about the actions of the Missouri bands roaming Kansas. A mob slashed Cody in front of his eight-year old son Bill, leaving him barely alive. The rioters then stole Cody's horses, took his family's food, and burned his hay. Missouri newspapers reporting on the incident expressed regret that Cody had not been killed outright. (He never fully recovered from his knife wounds and died three years later, likely from pneumonia.)[87]

Most residents of Missouri, while supporting slavery less out of economic self-interest than out of the need to regard themselves as superior to at least one group, took little interest in Kansas. Many New Englanders, however, regarded all Missourians as bloodthirsty members of a "partially civilized race." Amos Lawrence, brother of Thomas Ewing's friend and business associate Abbott, exhorted abolitionists to defend Kansas. The New England Emigrant Aid Company went into operation in 1854, assisting hundreds of abolitionists in their relocation to Kansas. Agents of the New England Emigrant Aid Company also named a Kansas settlement after its key Boston benefactor. Lawrence, Kansas, became a hotbed of radical abolitionist political sentiment, and its eight hundred residents took to calling Missourians "white trash." Given how outnumbered they were, antislavery partisans in Lawrence might have been more cautious.[88]

The random incidents of violence in 1854 between the Missouri "Border Ruffians," as Lawrence residents branded them, and the northerners became more regular. Atchison, Jackson, and 1,500 armed Missourians arrived in Lawrence in 1855. Senator Atchison announced that "we've come to vote, and will vote, or kill every God Damned abolitionist in the territory." He made sure that everyone in Lawrence knew he had two cannons to enforce his words. Jackson's men, meanwhile, searched out locally prominent abolitionists and beat them without mercy. Not only had the U.S. Army failed to stop Atchison's and Jackson's band at the Missouri border, but southern sympathizers in the military were allegedly arresting and shooting antislavery activists. More than a few northerners suspected that Secretary of War Jefferson Davis sided with his fellow southerners against the abolitionists.[89]

In response to Atchison's actions, Rev. Henry Ward Beecher, brother of Harriet Beecher Stowe and son of the virulent nativist Lyman Beecher, smuggled Sharps rifles into Kansas under the noses of U.S. Army troops. Since the rifles were stashed in the false bottom of crates containing Protestant tracts, westerners began calling guns "Beecher's Bibles." So many armed abolitionists flocked into Kansas from the Western Reserve that armed proslavery partisans looked especially hard at Ohio settlers—"damned nigger stealers" one and all, they contended. Among the first wave of Western Reserve radicals was John Brown, imbued with the knowledge that he was God's instrument of justice on the earth. He also would soon be armed with a letter of commendation from Ohio governor Salmon Chase.[90]

John Sherman went to Kansas in the spring of 1856 as part of a congressional delegation to investigate the escalating border war. The delegation itself was sharply divided, with Mordecai Oliver of Missouri taking a break from the hearings to join a partisan band in an assault on abolitionists. During an early May 1856 hearing in Lawrence, a proslavery sheriff, with the support of Congressman Oliver, tried to arrest abolitionist witnesses. Sherman helped some of the witnesses escape. When the committee went to Leavenworth, Sherman and Michigan congressman William Howard found a note advising them "to leave Kansas 'upon penalty of death.'" Far from being intimidated, Sherman became more scornful of the proslavery forces.[91]

Paradoxically, even while Oliver denied that there were any assaults on abolitionists taking place in Kansas, Atchison returned to Lawrence, purportedly proclaiming to his band, "If one man or woman dare stand before you, blow them to hell with a chunk of cold lead." Although Atchison's men announced they were seeking revenge on the residents of Lawrence for having earlier wounded a proslavery sheriff, they also wanted to punish townspeople for testifying before Sherman's committee. Atchison personally fired his cannon into Lawrence buildings, while his troops destroyed houses and printing presses. The Missourians also burned books, looted anything they thought of value, and planted a South Carolinian flag as a symbol of their defiance of Yankee dictatorship.[92]

Sherman warned Congress and the White House that:

the worst evil that could befall our country is civil war, but the outrages in Kansas cannot be continued much longer without producing it. To our southern brethren I especially appeal. In the name of southern rights, crimes have been committed, and are being committed, which I know you cannot and do not approve. These have excited a feeling in the northern states that is deepening and strengthening daily. It may produce acts of retaliation. You are in a minority and, from the nature of your institutions, your relative power is yearly decreasing. In excusing this invasion from Missouri—in attempting to hold on to an advantage obtained by force and fraud—you are setting an example which, in its ultimate consequences, may trample your rights under foot.

President Pierce, however, would not reconsider his endorsement of slavery in Kansas, and Congressman Oliver insisted that the stories of atrocities committed by Missourians were lies.[93]

The seeming unwillingness of federal authorities to stop Atchison's rampages provided a political opening to the more bloody-minded foes of slavery. In retaliation for the sacking of Lawrence, John Brown executed five men in Osawatomie, Kansas, whom he believed were sympathetic to the Missouri slave owners. Jim Lane, a Democratic politician who had left Indiana for Kansas, threw in with the abolitionists. In Congress, Lane had supported the Kansas-Nebraska Act and had subsequently lost reelection. Lane reinvented himself in Kansas, becoming the embodiment of Radical Republicanism. With the connivance of the antislavery governor of Iowa, Lane took weapons from the Iowa City arsenal. He soon created his own paramilitary force outside the authority of the U.S. Army and the proslavery territorial government.[94]

Lane's rise to power in Kansas was unlikely. His own allies conceded that not only was he physically unattractive, but he often appeared wild-eyed and disheveled. Detractors described his speeches as "the broken screams of a maniac." Yet it was the power of Lane's orations that brought men to his side. By the summer and fall of 1856, Lane commanded at least 250 troops. They were not the kind to tolerate political moderates, especially "goddamned white-livered lawyers." More than a few of Lane's soldiers recommended shooting army troops if they got in their way. In a raid on the proslavery community of Franklin, Kansas, Lane set fire to a post office where residents had sought shelter. On this occasion Lane took prisoners; that practice, however, became progressively rarer.[95]

Tom Ewing had interrupted his studies at Brown in 1854 to watch the Senate debate the Kansas-Nebraska Act. In Cincinnati, he closely read newspaper accounts of "Bleeding Kansas" and made it a point to learn everything he could about the political players. Tom also followed trends in the Kansas real estate market. His motivations for moving to Kansas were many, but joining the abolitionists was not one of them. Tom regarded John Brown as insane and thought little better of Jim Lane. Temperamentally, Tom had no use for extremists, whether they were southern fire-eaters or moralizing Western Reserve Yankees.[96]

Although he did not admit publicly what really had attracted him to Kansas, the answer was not difficult to ascertain. For Tom Ewing, Leavenworth would be his own Lancaster, a frontier town in which he would leave his mark in business and politics. His father had shown him the way, and of the Ewing children he was the most politically ambitious. At loose ends, Hugh and Hamp accompanied Tom. They were looking for adventure and willing to serve as additional eyes and ears for the empire Tom planned to build. Tom also appreciated the fact that while Hugh was restless he was also intelligent, loyal, and brave.

Tom, Hugh, and Hamp were among the sixty thousand settlers—90 percent of whom were under the age of forty—who came to Kansas in the 1850s. While the clash between the New England Emigrant Aid Company and David Atchison riveted national attention, the reality was that most settlers were from the Old Northwest. Ohio had the distinction of providing Kansas with nearly twelve thousand settlers, including the territory's most violent abolitionist, John Brown, and the man who became the most vicious proslavery guerrilla in the West, William Quantrill. As was true in the Buckeye State, the Ewings would be the moderates situated between the ideological extremists of Kansas and Missouri.[97]

Lawrence was too radical for Tom's taste and, worse, had become a base of operations for Lane. In any event, Lawrence lacked adequate transportation links vital for successful real estate development. Tom chose to settle in Leavenworth, which had served as an army post since 1827 and was tied to St. Louis via the Missouri River. Leavenworth at the time was the only Kansas settlement in direct telegraph communication with points east. It was a rough frontier settlement of nearly five thousand people, making it the largest town west of St. Louis and east of San Francisco. Brothels and saloons outnumbered churches. Politically, Leavenworth had been proslavery in 1854, as the hapless Isaac Cody learned. More antislavery people had since moved to Leavenworth, including Daniel Anthony, editor of the misleadingly named newspaper the *Daily Conservative* and brother of women's rights activist Susan B. Anthony.[98]

Drawing upon his own funds and the greater resources of his father, Tom Ewing ranked among the top ten investors in Kansas. (The New England Emigrant Aid Company led the list with investments of $64,000—which were largely tied up with the Lawrence settlement.) The Ewing family invested at least $11,000, purchased 5,400 acres, and made a significant commitment to Leavenworth. Ewing, Denman and Company, however, also sought out land that the family believed would someday be linked by rail. As Tom wrote to his father, "I do not care about any investment in these lands as lands." Their chief value was as transport routes, not farms.[99]

Cousin Hamp, sometime between reading law with Thomas Ewing and prospecting in California, had learned to survey land. Hamp and Hugh diligently scoured the countryside, looking for the most likely routes of future railroads. Then, drawing upon the combined legal acumen of Hamp, Hugh, and Tom, the Ewings filed claims for those lands that they thought would soar in value. It would not be many years before westerners asserted that "a good fee, and Thomas Ewing, Jr., on one's side, is all that is necessary to secure almost anything in the line of Indian contracts or government lands from the Department of the Interior."[100]

Just as Thomas Ewing had gotten in on the ground floor of the Ohio and Hocking Valley Canals, Tom became a major booster of western transport lines. Tom, Hugh, and Hamp were partners in the Leavenworth, Pawnee & Western Railroad Company, which the territorial government had chartered in 1855. They ardently sought out investors and negotiated with the Delaware Indians for leasing or purchasing rights for one thousand acres of their land. (The Delaware were an oft-displaced tribe that had spent time in Ohio. At $3 an acre, Tom Ewing held out a better deal than his predecessors had offered—which was nothing.) They also cajoled investors as far away as London and lobbied friends in Washington to assist with land negotiations.[101]

John Sherman and Tom Ewing were frequent correspondents. On one occasion Tom asked Sherman, who was a prospective Speaker of the House, to do everything within his power to ensure that Pennsylvania representative William Montgomery did not receive a coveted seat on the Public Lands Committee. Since Montgomery had earlier rigged Kansas land legislation to further his own railroad speculation, Tom did not hesitate to respond in kind. The fact that Montgomery, as a loyal Democrat, had endorsed the proslavery Lecompton constitution for Kansas made Tom's action appear almost principled.[102]

Tom Ewing had other business ventures in Kansas beyond real estate and railroad speculation. In Leavenworth, he assisted with a stone-quarrying venture, looking to construct river piers and macadamize city streets and a levee. Having purchased a stone breaker, Tom rented it out to contractors in Independence, Missouri. (Tom celebrated when "a fine large stone brewery" went up near his Leavenworth lots, substantially increasing their value.) Tom and Hamp also erected a two-story brick building, reserving the second floor for their law office. The ground floor was to be rented out as a store and the basement as a saloon. While the Denman building looked impressive when compared to the haphazard wooden structures dotting Leavenworth, the rickety outside staircase to the Ewing law office caused visitors to wish they had first gone to the basement saloon.[103]

Unfortunately for the Ewings, profit was harder to come by in Kansas than it had been in frontier Ohio. Although the 1859 fire that gutted the Denman building was a demoralizing setback, most of Tom's difficulty stemmed from the regional climate. Tom soon learned that Kansas weather patterns were far more unforgiving than those of southern Ohio. Kansas seemed prone to dry summers and, indeed, went into extreme drought in the latter part of the decade. Settlers described Kansas summer air as "the very breath of hell." Crops withered and muddy streams became dust beds.[104]

If the Kansas summers were hell, in the winter hell froze over. The Missouri River choked with ice, preventing steamer shipments to Leavenworth. Tom struggled financially but resolved not to impose further upon his father. He also revealed himself to be a tough-minded pragmatist:

> My extravagance has been chiefly in traveling too much, and in contributing too freely to public and private demands on my friendship or public spirit. None of these calls shall be answered more until I am able to answer them.
>
> On fully considering the state of my affairs I have determined to ask you to make no effort to aid me further at present. I believe that I can get through unaided—perhaps with little or no property left—but still I feel sure that my good management whether matters grow much better they now are or not, I can get through. If I fail, it will be because the town comes to a dead halt and other towns take its place; and in that case almost everybody here will break, and whatever aid you might give me would be lost.[105]

Tom and his partners had more immediate success in Kansas politics. Hamp and Hugh, acting as his eyes and ears, attended territorial meetings of the Democratic Party. Denman's gregarious nature was such that he could not remain a mere bystander—he got himself elected mayor of Leavenworth on the Democratic ticket. He criticized the proslavery Missouri partisans while refusing to embrace the abolitionist New Englanders—making him a perfect moderate. (After more New England abolitionists settled Leavenworth, Hamp surrendered the mayor's office to the dour ideologue Daniel Anthony. Unlike Democrats, Kansas Republicans did not tend to lubricate voters with beer.) Meanwhile, Dan McCook, a fellow Ohioan who had joined Tom's law practice, became a probate judge. McCook brought a desperately needed annual salary of $1,000 to the firm.[106]

In the words of Kansas politician and New England scion John Ingalls, most lawyers in the territory were an "ignorant, detestable set of addle-headed numbskulls and blackguards." Tom Ewing was an exception to Ingalls's rule. Friend and foe alike described him as a "very prince in appearance," well-spoken, logical, and brave. While he was observing an election in Kickapoo, Kansas, which stood opposite of Weston, Missouri, a proslavery mob gathered. Recognizing that his thirty armed companions were so badly outnumbered that they would most likely be massacred, Tom handed off his pistol and sent most of them back to Leavenworth.[107]

Tom confronted the drunken mob, forcefully explaining his intentions and letting it be known that if violence erupted he "would burn Kickapoo and Weston to the subsoil before morning." Having watched his father on the raucous northwestern campaign trail for twenty years, Tom knew how to speak with erudition and to pose like a roughneck. The mob fired shots into the air and hurled rotten eggs at the polling place but left Ewing and the antislavery voters unmolested. His father, duly impressed, wrote Tom that "you have done more to give yourself a desirable reputation than, under other circumstances, you might have been able to do in a well spent life." The Kickapoo affair, followed by Tom's careful documentation of electoral fraud in Kansas, gave him his first national political exposure.[108]

Through 1857 and 1858, Tom built a political network of Kansas allies, including future state governor Charles Robinson and Emporia newspaperman and attorney Preston Plumb. Although Plumb had initially enlisted in Jim Lane's paramilitary force, he came to see Tom as the more logical and emotionally stable politician. Plumb also gave every indication that he was ready to follow Tom to hell if the occasion ever arose.[109]

Lane resented the men who defected to Ewing, but he could not complain too loudly after he was indicted for killing a neighbor in a property dispute. Not wishing to swing from a rope, Lane had no choice but to solicit the best attorney in Kansas—Tom Ewing. Tom persuaded a jury that Lane had acted in self-defense and thereby secured his acquittal. Lane did not become a Ewing friend, but he was a somewhat less effective political rival for the next few years. Tom carefully sidestepped questions as to whether he would support sending Lane to the U.S. Senate once Kansas was admitted to the Union.[110]

Acting in concert with Robinson and Plumb, Tom Ewing pushed for the electoral repudiation of the Lecompton constitution. In addition to spending $1,100 on campaign fliers—money that his law firm could ill afford to part with in 1858—Tom championed an alternative antislavery constitution. He half-jokingly predicted that "we shall have a penitentiary one of these days for the scoundrels who have been running riot" in Kansas—casting aspersion on both the Missouri Border Ruffians and Lane's so-called "Jayhawkers." So far as Tom was concerned, proslavery Democrats in Kansas were "political murderers," and abolitionist Republicans could be written off as little more than a "football for the Free Soilers in the northern states."[111]

Seeking an audience outside Kansas, Tom wrote a public letter that attracted national media attention; even the *New York Times* ran a reprint. He ostensibly addressed the letter to Cousin Jimmy Blaine—who had long since left his Shawnee war paint behind to become a founder of the Republican Party in Maine. In addition to advancing Tom's agenda, publishing the letter helped raise Cousin Jimmy's political profile in his quest for election to the Maine legislature. Tom insisted that if the choice was between joining the Union under the terms of the "base and treacherous" Lecompton constitution, and remaining a territory without slavery, the majority of Kansans would not "beleaguer the doors of Congress for admission." He also fired a shot at Senator Douglas and the Democrats, warning them that admitting Kansas into the Union as a slave state would increase Republican ranks by 50 percent in the West.[112]

Tom's family affairs were no less complicated than his Kansas political and business ventures. Phil Stanbery ended up in Leavenworth looking to speculate in real estate. Henry Stanbery, Hugh believed, was not inclined to throw any more money after his prodigal son. Tom and Hugh agreed to stake Cousin Phil. Within a year, however, Tom had become rather dubious about his cousin, and even the more forgiving Hugh described him as "seedy." As Tom wrote to the senior Ewing, "[Phil Stanbery] is given to dissipation, takes weekly sprees, and needs the influence of friends and encouragement and employment, more than could be given him here, to reform him. He is naturally a fine fellow and might be made a good and useful lawyer." None of this would have surprised Thomas Ewing. He had seen Henry Stanbery in his younger days spend hours indulging himself at the Eagle Tavern in Columbus—a fact that his onetime law partner conveniently forgot when it came to dealing with Phil.[113]

More troubling than Cousin Phil's "dissipation" was the erratic behavior of Cump, who seemed to swing from deep depression to arrogant bravado without missing a beat. Cump, having not advanced in the military—which was not an uncommon experience in peacetime—tried his hand at business. He was no more successful in his commercial pursuits than Charles Sherman had been—in spite of the political and financial clout that Thomas Ewing directly and indirectly exerted on his behalf. It did not help Cump's business prospects that San Francisco, and the nation in general, experienced many bank failures in the late 1850s. Ellen came up with numerous excuses not to follow her husband on his nomadic quests and sought to keep her growing brood in Lancaster. Her reaction to arriving in the boisterous settlement of San Francisco had been biting: "Is this what they call the Promised Land of Eldorado?"[114]

Tom came to Cump's rescue in 1858, inviting him to join his Leavenworth law firm. He even offered to share his home so that Ellen and her children could accompany Sherman. Their daughter, Minnie Sherman, threw such a fit at the prospect of leaving that her grandparents pleaded with Ellen that she be permitted to remain in Lancaster. Ellen agreed, much to Cump's distress. Thomas Ewing also gave his son-in-law lots in Leavenworth so that he could build his own home.[115]

In spite of the new opportunity handed to him by his in-laws, Cump's outlook darkened. Trying to stir his soul, Ellen forced him to accompany her to Mass—"marched him off under arrest," she related to Hugh. Cump took out his anger on the wife of one of the Ewing's Kansas employees, denigrating her job performance. Tom wrote to his father that Cump's negative characterization of the woman in question was unfair; indeed, she had continued working through a severe illness. (The Ewings were more considerate of their servants. On one occasion, Tom assisted an Irish Catholic servant whose boyfriend had impregnated and then abandoned her.) At other times, Cump was jovial—amusing his sister-in-law Ellen Cox Ewing by insisting to a group of Presbyterian ministers that cursing advanced the cause of clear communication.[116]

Cump quickly demonstrated that he was just as out of his depth in law as he had been in business. To compensate for his shortcomings, Cump informed Tom and Dan McCook that practicing law required no special mental acumen. Wearying of Cump's bravado, Tom and Dan pulled a prank on him. They arranged for a vexing client to come by the office while they were out. With no time to prepare, and with his partners nowhere in sight, Cump had to scurry off to court. The attorney he faced was as aggressively obnoxious as humanly possible. Cump lost his composure, vowing to thrash the attorney. The judge sternly admonished Cump. This was the last time Cump appeared in a Kansas court. His swan song, however, had not been in vain. Cump had given Tom and Dan much cause for merriment at his expense. Several months later he left Leavenworth to become the director of the Louisiana Military Seminary. Cump complained to Ellen that the problem with Kansas was it "has been settled by lawyers and politicians instead of farmers and mechanics."[117]

More surprising to Tom than Cump's implosion was Hugh's decision to get married in 1858. At the age of thirty-two Hugh had seemed on his way to a life of bachelorhood. To his family, Hugh had always been a romantic, unwilling to settle for anything less than a perfect soul mate. He had earlier cut off a relationship with one of Henry Stanbery's daughters, as he was reluctant to wed a second cousin—unlike Phil Ewing. Recently, Hugh had met Henrietta Young. In some ways she was already part of the Ewing family. Her great-uncle was Father Young of Somerset, and she had been schooled at Georgetown's Sisters of Visitation Convent, where she had met Maria Theresa and Ellen. While lobbying in Washington on behalf of the Leavenworth, Pawnee & Western Railroad, Hugh had renewed his acquaintance with the Youngs.[118]

Henrietta's father, George Washington Young, was a wealthy tobacco planter from Prince George's County, Maryland. Her family had been among the original Catholic settlers of Maryland in the service of Lord Baltimore. Thomas Ewing regarded George Young as "a true fine specimen of the Maryland gentlemen" and admired Henrietta's sweet disposition. It appeared that Thomas Ewing was more pleased when his restless boy finally decided to be married than when Hugh was admitted to practice law before the U.S. Supreme Court. As for Maria Ewing, she rejoiced at acquiring yet another daughter. She knew that an "old adage" she had heard since childhood would never apply to her boys: "A son is a son, until he gets a wife, but a daughter is a daughter all the days of her life."[119]

Father Young performed the ceremony at his kinsman's plantation. Charley and Maria Theresa were members of their brother's wedding party, and Cousin Jimmy Blaine turned up to enliven the affair. Notably absent were Cump and Tom. Cump claimed pressing business elsewhere. Tom apparently was afraid his presence might cause an embarrassing scene. The Youngs, after all, were among the largest slave owners in Maryland; their neighbors might have confronted Tom given his growing notoriety.[120]

After a European honeymoon, Hugh and Henrietta divided their time between Washington and Ohio. Hugh managed his father's saltworks and handled the family's St. Louis interests. He gave up on Tom's dream of a Kansas empire. With Henrietta at his side, Hugh accompanied Mother Xavier Ross on a Missouri River steamer bound for Leavenworth. In 1854, Bishop Jean Baptiste Miege had designated Leavenworth as the diocese for Kansas. Four years later, Bishop Miege directed Mother Xavier to establish a Sisters of Charity convent in that city. Hugh donated his town lots and house—the latter of which became a convent school. (Tom also donated land and money to the Leavenworth Diocese, which was rather generous considering that the city's Irish Catholic Democrats had branded him a religious "traitor" and "nigger stealer.")[121]

Hugh was not the only son to return to Ohio as the decade of the 1850s came to a close. Charley had not told Thomas and Maria Ewing much about his time at the University of Virginia. He had written that he enjoyed studying mathematics and made a point of informing his father that he had attended William McGuffey's stimulating lectures on grammar and rhetoric. (McGuffey had been president of Ohio University.) Whatever else Charley had learned in Virginia he did not tell his parents, though he subsequently took to carrying a pistol and bowie knife. Charley dutifully followed the path set by Tom and went to the Cincinnati College of Law.[122]

After Charlottesville and Cincinnati, returning to Lancaster to work the family's farm and launch a cornstarch factory was a severe letdown to Charley. Thomas Ewing provided detailed instructions to Charley on how to operate a new mechanical thresher and expected thorough reports on the progress of their starch-making enterprise. Charley dutifully informed his father that he had succeeded in burning his wrist while failing to manufacture commercially viable starch. He did let the senior Ewing know, however, that he had manure to spare for the fields. To Ellen, Charley read extended passages from their father's farming advice, groaning at the parts where Thomas Ewing set forth the proper width of the harrows. Having attained the age of twenty-four, Charley gave every indication he could not escape Lancaster fast enough—understanding Cump's feelings on that subject better than Ellen.[123]

Charley was the least politically inclined of the Ewing children. Even the youngest, Maria Theresa, knew how to keep a Washington scorecard. If Charley had been paying attention to politics, he would have known that something had been going horribly wrong in Congress since the Kansas-Nebraska Act. After his fact-finding mission to Kansas, John Sherman had become highly vocal in his criticism of the South. In 1857, following a heated argument with Tennessee representative John Wright, Sherman became so incensed that he landed a cup of heavy wax sealing wafers on the Democrat's chest. Wright attempted to draw a pistol and Sherman reached for his own gun. Only the intervention of several other congressmen prevented a shootout on the U.S. House floor.[124]

That same year Thomas Ewing's old friend Reverdy Johnson appeared before the U.S. Supreme Court to argue that a slave named Dred Scott should not be freed simply because he had once lived in free territory. Chief Justice Roger Taney, a Maryland slave owner and Jackson appointee, rendered a verdict far more sweeping than Johnson had anticipated. Taney, with the backing of a Democratic Court, ruled that no state or territory had the right to prohibit slavery. In essence, the Northwest Ordinance of 1787 went out the door, along with the 1820 Missouri Compromise and the Kansas-Nebraska Act. If Taney thought he was settling the controversy over slavery once and for all, he was tragically mistaken.[125]

The Ohio Supreme Court repudiated the *Dred Scott* decision, decreeing that any slave brought into the Buckeye State would be free. Republican legislators in Columbus concurred with the Ohio justices and denounced Taney's ruling as "incompatible with [the] states' rights" that the jurist and his fellow southerners claimed to hold so dear. Democrats in the Ohio legislature countered that blacks, even free blacks in the state, could never become citizens. They also charged Republicans with illegally helping blacks vote against Democratic candidates. Indeed, the *Dayton Daily Express*, a press organ of congressman Clement Vallandigham, had earlier gone on record against black voting in Ohio, contending that "the nigger has crawled out of the wood pile and slipped into a place, where, under the Constitution, he has no business."[126]

Southerners and law enforcement agents who attempted to capture slaves in the Western Reserve were mobbed and their prisoners freed. Both Rutherford Hayes and Thomas Ewing lent their legal talents to the violators of the Fugitive Slave Law. Even if Ewing did not, like his protégé, embrace the radical antislavery partisans, he would not stand aside and see the Northwest Ordinance summarily dismissed. Addressing an overflow crowd at a Marietta, Ohio, Congregational church in 1858, Ewing warned that those who brought "terrific anarchy" to Kansas were now menacing the Old Northwest. While he had no intention of eradicating slavery in the South, southerners, Ewing argued, ought not to advocate its extension into the North.[127]

Carried along by the wave of revulsion many Ohioans felt after the *Dred Scott* ruling, William Dennison—his political tutorial with Ewing having been completed—won the 1859 gubernatorial election. During the campaign, Dennison had vowed in the Democratic stronghold of Cincinnati, "I will oppose the recapture of a slave with a bayonet, so help me God!" No sooner than Dennison had assumed his duties than Kentucky governor Beriah Magoffin demanded the extradition of Willis Lago, a free black man who had helped a slave escape. Dennison refused and the case subsequently wended its way to the U.S. Supreme Court. The justices unanimously ruled that Dennison had a legal obligation to send Lago to Kentucky. Dennison did not oblige.[128]

Even as Dennison was fighting southerners in court, a former Western Reserve resident sought to launch a civil war in Virginia. In 1859, John Brown and a small band tried to seize a U.S. arsenal at Harper's Ferry, Virginia. His plan was to arm slaves and then exterminate as much of the white southern population as possible. He failed miserably. His capture by Robert E. Lee and his trial and execution in Charlestown, Virginia, riveted the nation. Congressman Vallandigham went to Charleston to interrogate Brown. U.S. Senator Ben Wade—one of the Ohioans Vallandigham wished to expose as a coconspirator—hailed Brown as a "sublime hero."[129]

After two of Brown's men fled to Ohio, Virginia governor Henry Wise demanded that Dennison return them for trial. Dennison refused. Echoing former governor Salmon Chase, Dennison also warned Wise, and his successor, John Letcher, that should Virginia militia cross the Ohio River he would go to war. If Charley Ewing had not been paying attention to this last development, others in Lancaster were less heedless. After Brown's execution, a few dozen men formed the Lancaster Guards and commenced drilling at the fairgrounds. They would be renamed Company A of the First Ohio Volunteer Infantry. No one could have predicted that eight of the Lancaster boys who had restaged the Battle of the Boyne years earlier, soon would be playing in deadly earnest.[130]

3

"Argument Is Exhausted"

An Election, an Insurrection, and an Invasion, 1860–61

Argument is exhausted, and the appeal to arms at last is made. If
the border states shall remain passive, all will work out to a successful issue for the Union—but if they go with the Confederate
States, the fight will end I think in a final disruption of the Government. In either event, we are in for a long war, during which there
will be little use for lawyers, judges, and town lot speculators.
—Thomas Ewing Jr., 1861

Tom Ewing's finances were in wretched shape at the beginning of 1860. He
owed nearly $73,000 to one New York creditor and lesser amounts to oth-
ers. The long drought had driven off thousands of settlers, making Kansas
real estate speculation a futile exercise. Indeed, Tom lamented, "There is
in fact no market for property at any price whatever." Worse, the unsettled
political situation, both in Kansas and nationally, delayed rail construction.
Tom informed his Washington business representative that he had little
expectation of Congress moving forward with transportation projects for
the West.[1]

Cump's and Hugh's departure from Kansas had left Tom in the company
of similarly distressed friends. His law practice kept him occupied, though it
seemed as if all Kansas lawyers did was to prosecute thieves, sue each other,
and charge 50 percent interest rates on loans secured by land no one wanted.
Amid the financial ruins, Tom wrote to his father that "there has been more
general embarrassment and depression here than I have seen before, but the
general belief is that we have touched bottom."[2]

James Lane (1814–66). An antagonist of Tom Ewing, James Lane was a Republican radical, Kansas paramilitary leader, and member of the U.S. Senate. (Courtesy of the Library of Congress.)

The Kansas branch of the Ewing family also suffered its share of political frustration. Cousin Hamp had gone to Washington seeking appointment as register of the Land Office at Lecompton. Although Denman remained a Democrat, he was, Tom observed, not in good standing with southerners, who resented his opposition to the westward expansion of slavery. President James Buchanan, heeding the demands of his southern Democratic advisers, turned Hamp down. Tom's reaction to Hamp's news was vivid: "I sincerely regret your failure. By rejecting you, however, Buchanan has paid you the only compliment in his power to bestow—the damned old scoundrel! Like a toad, he grows more ugly and venomous with increasing age. If the devil don't get him, then there's no use keeping a devil."[3]

Tom made no secret of his ambition to be selected for the U.S. Senate once Kansas received admission into the Union. However, he knew that Lane would do everything he could to thwart his political plans. Tom regarded Lane as "a decidedly bad man," but given how few moderate Republicans there were in Kansas he saw little prospect of stopping him. He also anticipated that Lane would promote his dutiful shadow, Samuel Pomeroy, for the other Senate seat.[4]

Pomeroy had arrived in Kansas as an associate of the New England Emigrant Aid Company. Tom's allies had little use for Pomeroy, calling him "Pom the Pompous." His ultimate selection, however, owed much to Lane's support, as well as to the charitable contributions he collected in New England and then distributed to destitute Kansas farmers. It was a slick move. Pomeroy appeared to be the devout abolitionist warrior back east as he exhorted New Englanders to succor those fighting in the front lines against southern aggression. In Kansas, Pomeroy seemed to be aiding the poor without any expectation of earthly reward—other than a U.S. Senate seat. Tom had to settle for the consolation prize of chief justice of the Kansas Supreme Court.[5]

So far as presidential politics were concerned, Tom expressed the hope that the Republican Party "will give us a leader . . . at least as moderate in his views as Abraham Lincoln." The last thing the American people needed, Tom believed, was another John Brown "preaching the irrepressible conflict." Tom wrote to Lincoln assuring him of his support, though warning that most Kansas Republicans were of a "zealous" bent. Their preferred candidate was New York senator William Henry Seward—a man of so little discretion that the senior Ewing had not apprised him of President Taylor's position on slavery in the territories. (Ewing had not been alone in believing that Seward's brain and tongue were separated at birth.) Tom informed Lincoln that if he could hold on to his supporters in the early stages of the convention, then the Kansas delegation would switch its allegiance to him.[6]

While Tom cast his lot with Lincoln, Hugh and Henrietta Ewing availed themselves of the opportunity to attend the Democratic presidential convention in Charleston. Writing from South Carolina, Hugh reported to his father that the Democrats "were much divided" and regarded Illinois senator Stephen Douglas as an unpalatable nominee given his criticism of the *Dred Scott* decision. Once the southern Democrats rejected Douglas and split into various factions, Tom rejoiced. He welcomed "the destruction of the Democratic Party which ought to have quietly and gracefully died when the old Whig Party gave up the ghost."[7]

Thomas Ewing did not share his son's enthusiasm for Lincoln, even though he viewed Douglas as "inconsiderate and reckless," not to mention "politically answerable for all the terrible atrocities" committed in Kansas "consequent upon the repeal of the Missouri Compromise." Remarkably circumspect in public, the elder Ewing did not speak of Lincoln's petty behavior when he had sought a patronage job from him a dozen years earlier. On the other hand, it had not been the kind of affair that could be easily forgotten, and from the Ewing family point of view it had revealed some unsavory aspects of Lincoln's character.[8]

So too, Ewing and Lincoln were very different people, in spite of the similarities in their backgrounds as poor frontier boys who made good in legal practice. Ewing "the Salt Boiler" may have moved on from his humble origins, but he never forgot his obligations to a large extended family. Lincoln "the Rail Splitter," in contrast, was self-conscious about his modest beginnings and acceded to his wife's relentless social climbing. He had not invited his parents to his wedding and had not attended his father's funeral because he was simultaneously embarrassed by and estranged from his family. Whereas George and Thomas Ewing had a close relationship, Lincoln's father was physically abusive. According to some observers, he felt threatened by his son's quick intelligence. Tellingly, Lincoln adopted the title of "Rail Splitter" as a calculated campaign ploy in 1860; it was not a sobriquet he had earned, or sought after, earlier in life.[9]

There was also a difference in style between Lincoln and Ewing. In court and on the campaign stump, Lincoln had often acted the buffoon so as to lull his opponents into letting their guard down. Ewing played roughneck by throwing axes over the county courthouse, but he would do so while quoting passages from Homer and Virgil. When Lincoln was running for office he joked but seldom drank alcohol. Moreover, he confided in very few. Ewing shared confidences with many friends, imbibed moderately with the boys, and was self-assured enough to order Madeira rather than corn liquor—not being concerned with the elitist impression he might be creating. "The Salt

Boiler" had not gone into politics to seek public acclaim; in that regard, he had been a successful officeholder.[10]

Troubled that the nation might be on the verge of civil war, Thomas Ewing girded for action. Taking to the Ohio campaign stump in the fall of 1860—a state critical to Lincoln's electoral fortunes—Ewing gave "the Rail Splitter" a lukewarm endorsement. He began one speech by noting, "I come not to arouse your enthusiasm in behalf of any man or any party." Ewing was true to his word. He first praised the presidential candidacy of former Tennessee senator John Bell, a longtime Whig friend. Bell desired to find a midpoint between Republican abolitionists and southern secessionists, a goal that Ewing endorsed. Unfortunately, Ewing observed, though Bell was the more experienced and politically "safe choice," he could not win.[11]

Given Bell's dismal electoral prospects, another option was Vice President John Breckinridge of Kentucky, the candidate of southern Democrats who despised Douglas. Although Ewing thought Breckinridge was "a gentleman, and as such I esteem him and believe him stainless," he served "as the representative of an extreme sectional party, whose opinions and policy tend strongly to disunion." Douglas, of course, was despicable, so voting for him was also out of the question. Lincoln, Ewing tepidly concluded, was the only practical choice, in spite of his support from vicious radicals. Ewing then issued a warning to all the candidates: "We are of a noble race, possessed in a high degree of vigor and energy and courage; but once freed from the restraints of law and social order, as fierce and cruel as lions' whelps that have tasted blood. And if disunion should come, it would not be peaceful, but bloody, and all that is fierce and cruel in the land would meet in mutual vengeance and rapine on the line of conflict."[12]

Abolitionists were outraged. Ohio congressman Joshua Giddings, speaking for Republicans who regarded John Brown as a heroic martyr, penned a widely circulated letter denouncing Ewing. Giddings charged that Ewing was trying to maneuver Lincoln toward a policy of moderation. Lincoln, Giddings asserted, belonged in the abolitionist camp, along with all true believers in liberty. Senior politicians such as Ewing, Giddings sneered, had long recommended "subserviency to the slave-power." The Western Reserve politician also informed Ewing that "you evince an arrogance, seldom united with great moral worth."[13]

Ewing paid no heed to Giddings. Three weeks before he took to the campaign trail Ewing had been flung from his carriage when a mounted rider collided into his team during an ill-advised attempt to pass along a narrow road. Ewing fell twenty-five feet down a steep embankment. The bruised and bleeding seventy-one-year-old had painfully clawed his way up the hill and back to the road. Any man of that advanced age who, in spite of extensive injury, would subsequently go out and campaign was not going to be silenced.[14]

Although Lincoln carried Ohio by a popular vote margin greater than his national tally, 52 percent as opposed to 40 percent, the election had been hard fought. Lincoln had performed poorly in the Virginia Military District and those sections of Ohio settled by southerners. Such voters regarded the Republicans as enemies of states' rights and proponents of elevating blacks above whites. For its part, the *Chillicothe Advertiser*, a house organ of former Democratic senator and Ewing enemy William Allen, championed the extension of slavery to Kansas. Allen's friends warned fellow Democrats that they must never contemplate working with Lincoln and his abolitionist minions.[15]

Meanwhile Democratic congressman Samuel Cox of Columbus went into John Sherman's district to campaign against him. Sherman had been engaged in an unsuccessful struggle to become Speaker of the U.S. House of Representatives, further arousing the ire of southern Democrats. It was not common practice for a fellow congressman, even if from a different party, to try to unseat a colleague, but Democrats wanted revenge for Sherman's role in seeking the admission of Kansas into the Union as a free state.[16]

If Cox's gracious demeanor persuaded Sherman that political expediency, rather than animosity, dictated his actions, the same could not be said for many other northwestern Democrats in their fight against the Republicans. *Chicago Tribune* publisher Joseph Medill, an Ohio native and Republican Party founder, apprised Lincoln that the Buckeye State had more than a few Democrats who would support southern secession rather than live with his presidency. Among the worst, Medill wrote, was Clement Vallandigham of Dayton.[17]

Medill knew his region. Dayton and Cincinnati, as well as the Virginia Military District, exhibited strong southern and proslavery sentiments. While the elites of Cincinnati were Republican, the bulk of the common people supported Democrats and believed the South had the right to leave the Union. Further, even if the Old Northwest's trading patterns had shifted east since the completion of the canal and railroad transport network, Cincinnati still sent the bulk of its locally produced goods to the South. During the 1860 presidential campaign, Alabama Democrat William Yancy rallied three thousand in Cincinnati, urging Ohio's secession from the Union if Lincoln won. It would not be long before a U.S. Army official, with some exaggeration, characterized Cincinnati as "the South Carolina of the North."[18]

The 1860 election results starkly exposed America's sectional divisions. Most of the South went to Breckinridge. Bell picked up sufficient support among moderate southerners to capture Kentucky, Tennessee, and Virginia. Lincoln was a cipher at best in the South even when his name appeared on the ballot. In the five southern states in which Lincoln vied for support, his entire vote total came to around twenty-six thousand. In contrast, Lincoln carried New England, the Old Northwest, and the Mid-Atlantic—except for Delaware, a slave state that Breckinridge captured. The Republicans' bastion was New England, with Maine delivering 62 percent of the state's vote to Lincoln. Cousin Jimmy Blaine first cajoled Maine Republicans to shift their support from Seward to Lincoln and then rallied the electorate in the fall. Douglas, the standard-bearer of the Democratic Party, took only Missouri.[19]

Missouri's presidential, gubernatorial, and legislative votes were of concern to the Ewings given their investments in St. Louis and the fact that Charley Ewing and his childhood friend John Hunter were building a law practice in the city. Douglas and Bell had virtually tied in Missouri, and Breckinridge claimed a respectable third place. Lincoln received a little more than seventeen thousand votes, with the bulk coming from German Lutheran immigrants in St. Louis. Republican politicians had ardently courted St. Louis's sixty thousand Germans, and they became their chief constituency.[20]

Claiborne Jackson, who had joined Senator Atchison in assaulting Kansas abolitionists, became governor. Democrats also exercised overwhelming domination of the Missouri state house and senate. Missouri's legislative leadership could be located firmly in the proslavery camp and was inclined to leaving the Union. Acting in concert, the legislature and Governor Jackson organized a state convention to debate secession. Jackson insisted that "the destiny of the slave-holding states of this Union is one and the same."[21]

Passions in both the South and the North erupted after the election. Tom Ewing warned Lane's jubilant followers in December 1860 that "they must stop shooting and hanging men by mob law, henceforth; or they will be condemned by every Republican in Kansas, who loves peace better than riot, and who dares speak his mind." While the South Carolina legislature met to discuss secession from the Union, abolitionists urged Lincoln to ignore entreaties from Thomas Ewing and men of his ilk. Ewing, attorney and author Worthington Snethen warned, wanted Lincoln to provide public assurances that the Republicans were not an abolitionist party. This, Snethen fumed, would not be acceptable to Lincoln's loyal abolitionist supporters.[22]

South Carolina voted itself out of the Union in mid-December 1860, followed in January by Mississippi, Florida, Alabama, Georgia, and Louisiana. Texas joined her southern sisters in February 1861. Frustrated with

Buchanan's political paralysis, and not persuaded that Lincoln would be up to the task once he assumed office in March, some congressmen and state legislators tried to head off a civil war. Senator John Crittenden of Kentucky offered a proposal in December that, through constitutional amendment, would have set aside the *Dred Scott* decision. Crittenden wanted to restore the Missouri Compromise line and permit residents in the western territories to vote on whether they wanted slavery. Although Crittenden's initiative stalled because of Senate opposition from abolitionist Republicans and intransigent southern Democrats, it inspired the Virginia legislature in January to call for a national peace conference. Virginia chose a delegation and requested that former president John Tyler preside at the convention.[23]

New Jersey, New York, Pennsylvania, and Rhode Island legislators embraced Virginia's effort at reconciliation, though abolitionist publisher Horace Greeley warned that it was "a trap" designed to divide the Republican Party. Maine and Vermont Republicans disliked the idea of a peace conference but chose to attend in order to thwart any apologists for slavery. Massachusetts senator Henry Wilson, who had identified himself with the nativist wing of the Republican Party, derided the idea of a peace convention and attacked its participants. In spite of Wilson's objections, Massachusetts sent a delegation.[24]

Governor Jackson urged Missouri to send delegates to both the Washington peace conference and the secessionist convention meeting in Montgomery, Alabama. Missouri's legislature opted for Washington over Montgomery but also warned Republicans "that the people of Missouri will instantly rally on the side of their southern brethren, to resist the invaders at all hazards and to the last extremity." North Carolina's governor contended that secession, not mediation, was the only answer. His legislature, however, did not yet concur, and North Carolina sent a delegation—unlike the southern states that had already left the Union. Republicans in the upper portion of the Old Northwest declined participation on the grounds—as Michigan legislators resolved—"that concession and compromise are not to be entertained or offered to traitors."[25]

Republican governors Oliver Morton of Indiana, Richard Yates of Illinois, and William Dennison of Ohio were leery of the peace conference lest its outcome limit Lincoln's room for maneuver once he became president. Ohio legislator Jacob Cox—a close friend of Dennison—had observed right after Lincoln's election, "There is no compromise possible in the nature of things. For us to do it after our victory would be to confess ourselves dastards unworthy of the name of freemen." Senator Ben Wade, whom Congressman Samuel Cox characterized "as a man after the Cromwellian type"—meaning that the

Jacob Cox (1828–1900). An ally of the Ewing family, Jacob Cox served as a member of the Ohio legislature, became general of the Kanawha Division, and later was Republican governor of Ohio. (Courtesy of the Library of Congress.)

Ohio Republican was a puritanical tyrant—was adamant in his opposition to further discussion. (Samuel Cox was not related to Jacob Cox.) To Wade, initiatives such as the one proposed by the Virginia legislature embodied the values of "fossil Whigs" like John Bell and Thomas Ewing. Such dinosaurs had to be laid to rest.[26]

In spite of their misgivings, Dennison, Morton, and Yates recognized the strength of northwestern Democratic support for southern independence. Indeed, Clement Vallandigham could be heard in Congress advocating the division of the United States into four independent "confederacies" and decrying "Black Republican traitors and disunionists." Further complicating matters, president-elect Lincoln, or at least his young, opinionated secretary, John Hay, contemptuously dismissed the Border State supporters of the Washington conference as "southern pseudo-Unionists." Hoping to make the best of a thorny situation, Dennison chose the most venerable dinosaur he knew to be a member of Ohio's peace delegation. Thomas Ewing would be joined in Washington by Tom who represented Kansas.[27]

The editors of the *Charleston Mercury* quickly denounced the peace convention as a "cut and dried" plot by Thomas Ewing, Reverdy Johnson, and their friends to undermine the southern independence movement. South Carolina's political elite had never forgiven Ewing for his efforts to prevent the expansion of slavery. Ewing and the detestable Daniel Webster, after all, had conspired in 1836 to permit the U.S. Post Office to deliver abolitionist literature to southern homes. Ewing had even employed free blacks in the Interior Department.[28]

Peace delegates met for a good part of February 1861 at Willard's—the grandest hotel in Washington. (Willard's lobby overflowed with people seeking political favors, allegedly giving rise to the term *lobbyist*.) Behind closed doors 132 delegates from twenty-one states debated heatedly for long hours. No news reporters were admitted. Delegate and former Massachusetts governor George Boutwell believed that convention president John Tyler was an out-and-out secessionist, while many of the eastern Republicans "had no faith that anything could be done by which the Union could be saved, except through war." Thomas Ewing and the good-faith moderates were, Boutwell perceived, hopelessly outnumbered. One of the Ohio delegates wrote glumly to his brother—a Republican state legislator—that "poor Lincoln is to have a sorry time—I hope he may be man enough for the times, but if he is, he is a giant. The prospect of the country is gloomy, but I hope for the best."[29]

Ewing attempted to act as a moderator and made a point of being especially generous to Tyler—even if he had been convinced years earlier that Dante and Milton could have drawn upon the former president for literary inspiration. He reminded delegates that he had never lectured the South on the morality of slavery, focusing instead on the ways in which the peculiar institution hampered business development. It was out of concern for the economic future of the western territories that he opposed the expansion of slavery.[30]

As he spoke to this very select audience—which included a half-dozen former cabinet officers and nineteen who had served as governors—Ewing turned his attention to the abolitionists. He asserted that whites and blacks "cannot occupy the same country" as equals. Ewing noted that he did not wish to abolish slavery in the South lest blacks move to the North: "As one northern man, I do not want the Negroes distributed through the North. We have got enough of them now. I have watched the operation of this emigration of slaves to the North. Ten Negroes will commit more petty thefts than one thousand white men. We cannot permit them to come into Ohio. Wherever they have been permitted to come, it has almost cost us a rebellion. Before we begin to preach abolition I think we had better see what is to be done with the Negroes."[31]

Although Ewing's words appeared to have irritated New England's abolitionist delegates, they could not say what would happen to African Americans after emancipation. Instead, many abolitionists fell back into a defensive posture, hurling charges of disloyalty at the southern delegates.[32]

When president-elect Lincoln turned up at Willard's—despite his private opposition to holding the conference in the first place—he stood awkwardly alone. Delegates from Vermont recognized his visible discomfort and took it upon themselves to introduce him to the conference participants. A Virginia delegate held nothing back in his description of Lincoln: "a cross between a sandhill crane and an Andalusian jackass . . . vain, weak, puerile, hypocritical, without manners, without moral grace." The peace convention broke up afterward, with Congress unwilling to take up its recommendations—which were largely along the lines of what Crittenden had originally proposed.[33]

Tom, like his father, had "great faith that a pacific settlement will be effected." However, he warned Thomas Ewing that "a terrible civil war seems to be the inevitable consequent of an adherence to the *status quo*." Just before he turned up at Willard's, Tom wrote to Jim Lane not to bury the hatchet but rather to plan the deployment of Kansas troops along portions of the Missouri border. Tom praised the Kansas volunteers as good men but observed that one company had already earned the nickname "the Invincibles—Invincible in peace, invisible in war." To Hugh, Tom concluded, "I want to see the dominant party extend to the South the olive branch—and if that is refused, draw the sword."[34]

Washington in 1860 and 1861 had become, incredibly, even more of a national theater for political posturing and intrigue. Maria Theresa, the youngest of the Ewing children, related to her father how she had seen Virginia senator James Mason and Virginia representative William "Extra Billy" Smith parade before their constituents in simple suits spun by southern hands. Both Mason and Smith claimed that they were demonstrating that the South did not need Yankee textile mills to make their clothes. However, Maria Theresa archly went on, "I saw both those gentlemen at the Levee Tuesday evening dressed in black broadcloth. I presume the homespun is only the official suit."[35]

By the time Lincoln met with the peace convention delegates, rumors of treasonous plots filled the air. Supreme Court Justice John Archibald Campbell of Alabama grew worried by what he was observing. Although he had endorsed the *Dred Scott* decision, Campbell agreed with Thomas Ewing, his friend and mentor, that slavery hindered southern commercial progress. Slavery, as an institution, Campbell assured Stephen Douglas, was doomed to extinction. Despite being a Democrat, Campbell had approached one of Lincoln's associates to urge Ewing's appointment to the cabinet. Ewing, Campbell insisted, had "the most elephantine mental proportions of any man now living in the United States."[36]

Campbell went to Buchanan and charged that former secretary of war John Floyd of Virginia had deliberately deployed Regular Army troops in such a manner as to make it nearly impossible to protect Washington Unionists—let alone the president-elect. (Floyd had resigned as war secretary a few days after South Carolina left the Union.) Buchanan dismissed Campbell's concerns. Alarmed, Campbell met on a secret basis with Ewing, who passed on to Lincoln's advisers whatever intelligence the Supreme Court justice had on violent secessionists in Washington. Although Campbell regarded Lincoln as "a conceited man" who sought "to set the country in a blaze," he did not wish to see him harmed. Ewing credited Campbell with saving the city—and Lincoln—from rebel capture or worse.[37]

After his inauguration, President Lincoln had to prevent secessionists in Charleston from starving out the federal garrison at Fort Sumter. If the rebels were successful in their endeavor this would amount to a tacit recognition of South Carolina's independence. At the same time, Lincoln knew that if he made a show of force, northern states possessing strong southern sentiments—namely Ohio and Indiana—might not rally to the Union. He had to maneuver South Carolina into firing the first shot, which, he hoped, would unite the North and boost Unionist support in the border states of Kentucky, Maryland, and Missouri. After he announced that he was sending nonmilitary supplies to Fort Sumter, thereby undercutting the secessionists, South Carolina commenced firing on April 12, 1861. Lincoln's April 15th call for seventy-five thousand troops to put down the rebellion prompted Virginia to leave the Union on April 17, followed by Arkansas, North Carolina, and Tennessee.

Thomas Ewing, born in the year George Washington assumed the presidency, had lived to see the United States at the point of extinction. Some of his dear friends in the Supreme Court Club declared their allegiance to the Confederate government. Sometime co-counsel and fellow cabinet confidant George Badger had not wanted to see North Carolina opt for secession, but he sorrowfully went with his state. Campbell, with the weight of his Dixie origins bearing down on him, was the only southern-born Supreme Court justice to resign his seat. He ultimately joined the Confederate government in Richmond as assistant secretary of war. (Chief Justice Roger Taney had more than a little sympathy for the secessionists but felt he could do more to protect states' rights by remaining on the Court. Taney quickly became a thorn in Lincoln's side.)[38]

Reverdy Johnson was nearly alone among Ewing's southern friends to stay with the Union. Johnson had organized a large Unionist rally in Maryland and joined Ewing as a delegate to the Washington peace convention. His stance was not popular in Maryland's plantation-dominated Eastern Shore, but Johnson had as little desire for public acclaim as Ewing. Years earlier, in 1835, a mob of Jacksonian Democrats, angered with his support for the Bank of the United States, had stormed his Baltimore home. They burned every book in his extensive library before stealing whatever furniture they could drag out of his house. Then in the 1850s he had stood up to Baltimore's riotous nativists. To Johnson, secessionists were just another group of cowards who hid behind the anonymity of the mob; it made no difference if they voted Democratic or Republican.[39]

Ewing expressed relief to John Crittenden when the Kentuckian swore his allegiance to the Union. Corresponding with his onetime Senate and cabinet colleague, Ewing wrote, "There can be no truce or compromise till the opposites have met in force and measured strength, and the sooner this occurs the better." Crittenden may have agreed with his friend's assessment of the political situation in early 1861, but it could have brought him no joy. One of his sons, George Crittenden, joined the Confederate service, while another, Thomas Crittenden, would fight for the Union.[40]

Tom's reaction to the bombardment of Fort Sumter was bellicose. Writing to Hugh, Tom declared: "Now that the South has tendered the wager of battle, on the issue of Union or Disunion, I want to see the issue accepted and fought out. If we are to lose the Government, I had rather lose it by action than by inaction. And I had rather see the old ship go down with the flag flying, amid the roar of its own and the enemies' cannon, than to see her grow into disuse and contempt while rotting idly at the wharf."

Tom then joined Jim Lane as part of a company of Kansas "Frontier Guards" that took up residence in the White House. Lincoln expressed immense gratitude to his well-armed houseguests. *Harper's Weekly*, whose politics were staunchly Republican, subsequently enthused that Lane "has an expression of great good humor and enjoyment that wins one irresistibly to the conclusion that he is the best fellow in the world."[41]

Cump and Ellen had been watching the events of early 1861 unfold with a mixture of dismay and anger. Before her father left for the peace convention Ellen had concluded, "I used to dislike the abolitionists but their folly sinks to insignificance when compared with the treason of the South." Having obtained a job without falling back on his father-in-law's political and business connections, Cump felt much discomfort when his new home of Louisiana left the Union. Cump now had to rely once again on Thomas Ewing's assistance, landing in St. Louis as a street railway president. He and Ellen shared a house with newly minted law partners Charley Ewing and John Hunter. Cump might not be living in Lancaster, which was of some consolation to him, but Lancaster was living with Cump.[42]

Cump's friend from West Point and California days, Edward Ord, had contacted Lincoln days after South Carolina left the Union to recommend Cump for appointment as secretary of war. Ord observed that Cump had the respect of many army officers and, as a bonus, was a member of a powerful family. Instead, Lincoln chose Pennsylvania senator Simeon Cameron as secretary of war. Though corrupt, incompetent, and not respected by the officer corps, Cameron had made an enormous contribution toward Lincoln's election—unlike Thomas Ewing. Not deterred by Ord's lack of success, Cump half-jokingly confided to Tom's wife, "I'm praying for war, pestilence, and famine." Ellen Cox Ewing was taken aback as he continued, "I'm praying for war so that I can get back into the army; pestilence and famine naturally follow."[43]

Knowing of his brother's wish for a Regular Army command, John Sherman, who had replaced Salmon Chase in the Senate when Ewing's "political vampire" became secretary of the Treasury, arranged for Cump to meet Lincoln. After he explained to Lincoln that calling up seventy-five thousand volunteers for a three-month term of service was a militarily inadequate response, Lincoln casually replied, "Oh well! I guess we'll manage to keep house." Cump fumed to his brother afterward: "You have got things in a hell of a fix, and you may get them out as you best can." Concurring with Tom and his father-in-law, Cump told his wife, "You might as well try to put out a fire with a squirt gun as put down this rebellion in three months' time." He returned to St. Louis.[44]

Cump was not destined to sit out the war. Governor Jackson had refused Lincoln's request for volunteers, denouncing the call as "inhuman and diabolical." While Lieutenant Governor Thomas Reynolds formed "the Minute Men," a pro-Confederate paramilitary organization, Jackson plotted to take Missouri out of the Union. Charley Ewing, in a nod to St. Louis's breweries, apprised Hugh that the Minute Men "are as thick as hops in this town." Although the delegates elected to discuss secession had insisted that Missouri remain in the Union, Jackson was not deterred. He requested weapons from Confederate president Jefferson Davis, who ordered two cannon to be smuggled into St. Louis. Jackson also took the initiative on April 20 to seize 1,500 muskets at a federal arsenal in Liberty, Missouri.[45]

Jackson relied heavily on Sterling Price, his brother-in-law, for military advice. Price, a tobacco planter, Mexican War veteran, and former Missouri governor, had earlier supported Senator Atchison's military excursions into Kansas. He had also presided over the February state convention that, to the dismay of his allies, had failed to embrace secession. Now in early 1861, the secessionists established a military base outside St. Louis—Camp Jackson. Price intended to clean out the Unionists in St. Louis, which was a necessary step before Missouri could join the Confederacy.[46]

Taking the lead against Jackson were Francis Blair and his ambitious sons, Frank Jr. and Montgomery. Francis Blair had grown disenchanted with the Democrats in the 1850s and moved toward the moderate wing of the Republican Party. Ironically, Francis Blair and Thomas Ewing, long political archfoes, found themselves being cursed by the same radical abolitionists. Even more peculiar was that although Montgomery Blair had served as legal counsel for Dred Scott, Republican radicals questioned his commitment to abolition and did not welcome his appointment as U.S. postmaster general. Meanwhile, Congressman Frank Blair raised a militia composed mainly of German immigrants—the only reliably Unionist population in St. Louis. Since the Missouri legislature and Jackson had wrested control of the St. Louis police force from the city's Republican leaders, Frank Blair decided he needed his own army.[47]

Inevitably, the Blairs and the Ewings, both having extensive business affairs in St. Louis and both exercising political influence on the national stage, kept bumping into each other in 1861. As Cump wrote to Tom Ewing, he found Frank Blair too zealous for his tastes: "I know Frank Blair declares war on slavery. I see him daily, and yesterday had a long talk with him. I say the time is not yet come to destroy slavery, but it may be [time] to circumscribe it." Frank Blair, however, was not inclined toward moderation, at least not in 1861, and certainly not in the face of successive assassination attempts.[48]

While his German-immigrant troops displayed martial airs worthy of Hessian mercenaries, at least according to proslavery Missourians, Frank Blair needed a commander with military experience. Blair found what he was looking for in Captain Nathaniel Lyon. To say that Lyon possessed a messianic streak would be an understatement. Having witnessed firsthand the sorrows of "Bleeding Kansas," Lyon, like John Brown, regarded himself as God's angel of destruction. To friend and foe alike, Lyon appeared to be a lit fuse in search of a powder keg.[49]

Whatever the problems that might come as a result of recruiting Lyon, Frank Blair exercised superb strategic thinking by sneaking sixty thousand muskets and 1.5 million rounds of ammunition out of the St. Louis arsenal and delivering them to the Illinois governor. He retained sufficient weapons and ammunition to equip his "Home Guards." Missouri Unionists were convinced that Buchanan's war secretary had stockpiled so many weapons in St. Louis in anticipation that these arms would fall into Governor Jackson's hands. Blair, however, had put one over Jackson, who was outraged when he learned of his cunning.[50]

On May 10, Blair sent Lyon and Lieutenant John Schofield, a West Pointer and St. Louis college professor, to capture Camp Jackson. The move caught Jackson and Price off guard, even though anyone who recognized the importance of St. Louis as a river port and railroad hub for the Union would have expected such a move. Lyon and Schofield stormed the rebel base with a few thousand troops and quickly took 1,500 prisoners. The assault had been virtually bloodless, the aftermath was not.[51]

Whether out of military ignorance or the desire to mount a Roman-style victory procession, Blair's Praetorian Guard marched their prisoners through the streets of St. Louis. Charley Ewing and John Hunter, having gone to St. Louis to experience adventure, went to gawk at the captured rebels. Hugh, who was in town visiting prior to his deployment with the Ohio Volunteers, joined the pair. Cump felt some apprehension but nonetheless also joined Hugh and brought along his young son Willie. The gathering crowd of spectators included the sullen, the cheerful, and the irreconcilable—the latter bringing forth calls of "Hurrah for Jeff Davis!" Sherman did not realize that an old West Point acquaintance, Ulysses Grant, and a Confederate Army recruiter, Joe Shelby, had joined the assembly. (There were seven future Union generals and two who became Confederate generals among the troops and spectators.)[52]

Without warning, rocks began hitting Blair's Germans. Suddenly, a shot rang out and a trooper fell mortally wounded. The enraged Home Guards fired indiscriminately into the crowd. Thinking quickly, Charley threw his nephew to the ground and shielded him from the musket balls. Hunter's first instinct was to run for cover while Hugh and Cump dropped to the ground. In the pause when Blair's troops reloaded before letting loose another volley of bullets, Cump crawled over to Charley and helped cover Willie. In all, twenty-eight were killed, including one child and two women, with many more wounded. Rioting erupted and lasted into the night. Ellen quickly wrote to her father, assuring him that the family had escaped unharmed. Hugh, however, was upset that he had been caught in such a fix without a weapon and from then on went about St. Louis with several loaded pistols. Whether or not Hugh intended to shoot Price's or Blair's soldiers, or both, was unclear.[53]

The St. Louis shootings had been the bloodiest day of the Civil War to date, even worse than the April 19 clash in Baltimore between Union troops and civilians. Politically, Lyon's lit fuse had met the powder keg. Missouri's legislature, which had been held back from secession by the earlier state convention vote, now authorized Jackson and Price to put an end to the Unionists.[54]

In Ohio, Governor Dennison had swung into action following South Carolina's attack on Fort Sumter. He concurred with Thomas Ewing and the other Buckeyes that Lincoln's request for seventy-five thousand soldiers was woefully inadequate. In the first days after Lincoln requested troops, enough Ohio men volunteered to fill the call for every loyal state in the Union. The Lancaster Guards, who were incorporated into the First Ohio Volunteer Infantry, quickly went to Washington with the Second Ohio Volunteers. While Lieutenant Tom Hunter and his Lancaster mates might have been long on enthusiasm, they were short on weapons. Their train had to halt in Harrisburg so Pennsylvania governor Andrew Curtin could give the Ohioans arms and ammunition.[55]

Although defending Washington from possible rebel assault had been a priority for Dennison, he had other pressing concerns. When Dennison looked at a map of Ohio, he saw a state flanked by enemies and a river that could not serve as a barrier to Confederate invasion. Dennison regarded Kentucky governor Beriah Magoffin as a traitor after he had informed Lincoln that his state would not join with him "for the wicked purpose of subduing her Sister Southern States." His opinion of Magoffin was also formed by the fact that they had been fighting each other in the courts over the extradition of an African American charged with helping slaves escape to Ohio. When Magoffin declared Kentucky's neutrality and, at the same time, ignored Confederate Army recruitment, Dennison called for an invasion. The governors of Indiana and Illinois, whose states also shared a border with Kentucky, backed Dennison. Lincoln, having been born in Kentucky, clung to the hope that the state would remain loyal. He feared that an advance into Kentucky by Ohio, Illinois, and Indiana volunteers would cause that state officially to join the Confederacy.[56]

Virginia worried Dennison no less than Kentucky. Confederate president Jefferson Davis regarded the Ohio River as the natural boundary of his new nation—a stance that Dennison and the governor of Pennsylvania found intolerable. Concurring with Davis, Virginia governor John Letcher deployed troops toward Grafton, which was the point where the Baltimore & Ohio Railroad split off to Wheeling and Parkersburg. From Parkersburg, Virginia troops could cross the Ohio River and advance to Columbus through the Hocking Valley. Taking Wheeling would also give Virginia a launch point from which to attack Pittsburgh. Anticipating the arrival of Confederate troops, secessionists raided Point Pleasant, Virginia, where the Kanawha River met the Ohio River, and arrested all the Unionists they could find. Outraged, a posse from the river town of Gallipolis, Ohio, crossed into Virginia and took thirty hostages and then demanded the release of the Point Pleasant prisoners.[57]

While Lincoln eventually gave in to Dennison's and Curtin's demands that they be permitted to deal with Virginia, neither governor could expect much in the way of federal military assistance. On the other hand, Dennison, Curtin, Morton, and Yates soon learned they could expect a great deal of federal political interference. Simon Cameron, Lincoln's war secretary, insisted that he, not the governors, had the right to appoint senior officers in the states' militias. Cameron wanted his own loyalists in place. Both Curtin and Dennison suspected that Cameron would receive kickbacks for those commissions. Dennison ignored the War Department's appointments, leading U.S. Army General Don Carlos Buell to fume that the governor "evidently looks upon all Ohio troops as his army."[58]

Dennison needed officers for his Ohio volunteers who had not garnered their commissions through the War Department. He had been impressed with the defensive measures undertaken by Cincinnati mayor George Hatch and railroad executive George McClellan. Though neither Hatch nor McClellan liked Lincoln, they had rallied to defend the Union. McClellan, a graduate of West Point, had shown much bravery during the Mexican-American War

Rutherford B. Hayes (1822–93). Befriended by Thomas Ewing, Rutherford Hayes served as a regimental colonel in the Kanawha Division, became a member of the U.S. House of Representatives, was elected Republican governor of Ohio, and then was elected president of the United States. (Courtesy of the Library of Congress.)

William S. Rosecrans (1819–98). A West Point instructor and friend of Hugh Ewing, William Rosecrans was an Ohio native and Catholic convert. As a Union general, Rosecrans served as the commanding officer of Hugh Ewing, Rutherford Hayes, and Jacob Cox (western Virginia), as well as Tom Ewing (Missouri). (Courtesy of the Library of Congress.)

and, in Cincinnati, displayed fine organizational skills. Dennison appointed McClellan as major general of the Ohio Volunteers. Soon, however, Dennison came to see that McClellan's alleged military genius was undercut by a deep streak of arrogance and condescension.[59]

Ohio's governor believed that residents who had earned distinction in academia, business, law, and politics would be able to transfer their success to military command. William Rosecrans, Hugh Ewing's mentor at West Point, had done well as a civilian engineer in Cincinnati, so he became McClellan's aide-de-camp. Rutherford Hayes, sometime-co-counsel with Thomas Ewing, received the rank of major in the Twenty-Third Ohio. Dennison made Republican state senator James Garfield a lieutenant colonel in the Forty-Second Ohio and ordered him to collect as many weapons from the governor of Illinois as he could transport. (These were the same muskets that Blair had whisked away from St. Louis.) Lorin Andrews, the president of Kenyon College and a classmate of Hayes, became colonel of the Fourth Ohio. Dennison gave Republican state senator Jacob Cox the rank of brigadier general and command of a division that included the Third and Eleventh Ohio.[60]

Returning to Lancaster following the St. Louis massacre, Ellen Sherman witnessed Dennison's rapid, and often chaotic, mobilization. Tom Hunter— her brothers' playmate and occasional tormentor—enlisted, and John Hunter became a lieutenant in the Thirteenth Ohio while Henry Hunter mustered into the Sixty-First Ohio as a lieutenant colonel. Fairfield County men made up most of the Sixty-First Ohio and were well represented in the Seventeenth Ohio. Thomas Ewing's grandchildren excitedly watched the troops drill at the county fairgrounds and play their drums and fifes. Maria Ewing exalted Fairfield County's men when they left for Washington "to defend the stars and stripes of her country, and defeat the rebels, the traitors of their country." In her role as matriarch, Maria told her sons that she expected them to do their duty and give their lives if necessary.[61]

Soon the recruits departed and Lancaster heard fewer cries of "Hurrah for Union!" Lincoln had received only 39 percent of the vote in the county and was not a popular figure. Nearly all of Lincoln's military-aged voters in the area had volunteered for service. Tellingly, most of the men who enlisted in the Sixty-First Ohio were German Protestant immigrants or their children. Those who declined Dennison's invitation to go to war were largely Democrats whose Scots-Irish grandparents had migrated from the Upland South. They formed the majority of the county's population and embraced the view of the *Lancaster Eagle*: "The [Democrats] of old Fairfield believe this is an unholy war, fruitless for good, certain in its results to add to the estrangement and bitter hatred of the [two] sections." With the able-bodied Unionists sent east, assaults on outspoken African American Unionists in southern Ohio escalated.[62]

Most of the Ewings' extended family had wasted no time volunteer-ing, though Tom believed he needed to pay off his most burdensome debts before enlisting. (Tom's conversations with Lincoln concerning rail construction in the West gave him much encouragement about his future financial prospects.) Dennison made Hugh a major in Ohio's Third Bri-gade, whose ranks included the Twelfth and Thirteenth Ohio. Thanks to the efforts of John Sherman and Thomas Ewing, Cump had received a Regu-lar Army commission—becoming colonel of the Thirteenth U.S. Infantry. Charley joined him as a company captain. Cump, however, soon left the Thirteenth U.S. Infantry, heading to Washington as a colonel in the Third Brigade, First Division.[63]

As April passed into May, the situation of the Unionists in western Vir-ginia became desperate. Rebels, seizing the opportunity to settle old feuds, murdered Unionists and burned their homes. Acts of sabotage against tele-graph lines and the Baltimore & Ohio tracks also mounted. Although Lin-coln had received just 4 percent of the vote in western Virginia, many of its citizens—especially those clustered along the banks of the Ohio River—opposed secession. They wanted nothing to do with Richmond's "nigger traders." The editor of the *Wheeling Intelligencer* privately implored Dennison to rescue the Unionists: "The sooner your state and Pennsylvania occupies a position on our borders the better. Secession is creeping up. I am afraid that the Union men in western Virginia will shortly all be slaughtered."[64]

Unionists in Wheeling moved to establish a provisional government and army, while Dennison encouraged Ohioans to assist in their endeavors. At least one company of the First West Virginia, organized in May, was made up of volunteers from Steubenville, Ohio. The other nine companies of the First West Virginia hailed from Wheeling and Pittsburgh. The Fourth West Virginia, organized shortly afterward, recruited in the southern Ohio coun-ties of Athens, Gallia, and Meigs. Among its lieutenants was none other than Cousin Phil Stanbery. Having hit bottom in Kansas, and with no prospect of being bailed out by his father, Phil Stanbery returned to Ohio to practice law. As was true of Charley Ewing, Phil was not yet inclined to settle down. When the recruiters for the Fourth West Virginia came through Meigs County he enlisted. Some of Phil's neighbors were unimpressed, observing, "If a dozen old women were to come along with broomsticks in their hands they could make the whole kit of you run."[65]

Both Dennison and McClellan waited anxiously for Lincoln to approve the movement of troops into western Virginia. While Chase had used his influence to give McClellan the rank of major general in the Regular Army, little else had gone forward. McClellan lamented to Dennison on May 13 that "the apathy in Washington is very singular and very discouraging." Lincoln finally assented, though matters had reached the point where Dennison seemed poised to invade with or without the president on board. As Dennison said, "I will defend Ohio where it costs least and accomplishes most . . . beyond rather than on her border!"[66]

The vote of the Virginia legislature to leave the Union in April had been subsequently ratified by the electorate, with secession officially announced on May 23. In response, McClellan addressed a proclamation to his command, which, in addition to Ohio's sixteen regiments, included nine regiments from Indiana and two from western Virginia. McClellan revealed that he had a flair for the dramatic:

> Soldiers!
>
> You are ordered to cross the frontier, and enter upon the soil of Virginia. Your mission is to restore peace and confidence, to protect the majesty of the law, and to rescue our brethren from the grasp of armed traitors. . . . Preserve the strictest discipline; remember that each one of you holds in his keeping the honor of Ohio and the Union. If you are called upon to overcome armed opposition, I know that your courage is equal to the task; but remember that your only foes are armed traitors—and show mercy to them when they are in your power, for many of them are misguided. When, under your protection, the loyal men of Western Virginia have been enabled to organize and arm, they can protect themselves, and you can then return to your homes, with the proud satisfaction of having saved a gallant people from destruction.[67]

While the First and Second West Virginia moved out of Wheeling southward along the Baltimore & Ohio tracks, other Union regiments marched across the Ohio River into Parkersburg on May 27. Nearly all of Parkersburg's citizens heartily greeted the thousand men of the Thirteenth Ohio as liberators. Several days later the Thirteenth Ohio and First West Virginia converged at Philippi outside Grafton. The overly confident rebels had expected to hold the Wheeling-Parkersburg junction of the Baltimore & Ohio. Indeed, the village of Philippi had raised volunteers for Virginia's secessionist government and they were looking for a fight. The contest for Philippi, however, became less of a fight than a footrace. Rebel forces panicked in the face of the superior Union forces, discarding their equipment and running. Some rebels retained enough of their wits to torch a few Baltimore & Ohio bridges, but their efforts were for naught.[68]

Despite their initial flush of bloodless victory, the soldiers of the Thirteenth Ohio were on edge. With the exception of officers like Lancaster's John Hunter, few enlisted men had ever been more than a day's ride from home. Virtually none, including the officers, had formal military training. They believed that the enemy lurked behind every tree. Most disconcerting, at least for the Unionist troops from Circleville, a town rooted in the Virginia Military District, was the poverty they encountered. They saw firsthand what their Upland South grandparents had fled.[69]

Pushing deeper into Virginia, the Thirteenth began to encounter slaves. Far from sympathizing with their plight, many of the southern Ohio troops concluded that the slaves enjoyed a better material standard of living than poor whites. Whether being enslaved mitigated whatever possible material benefit African Americans may have enjoyed in their bondage did not often become a topic of conversation. As had been true in Thomas Ewing's youth, slaves were too valuable to have their lives put at risk in the most dangerous jobs—those were reserved for whites. In every sense of the word, as Ohio troops wrote home, western Virginia was "foreign." Old Ewing may have been right that slavery kept most white southerners in a state of poverty, illiteracy, and resentment.[70]

The embarrassing defeat at Philippi galvanized Virginian rebels. This should have come as no surprise. After all, twenty-six of western Virginia's fifty counties had voted for secession. Possessing 40 percent of western Virginia's 350,000 whites, the rebel counties had an admittedly smaller recruiting pool than the Unionists did. On the other hand, the western Virginian secessionists claimed a few advantages. First, the rebels had a mountainous terrain that they could use to their advantage in ambushing their enemies. Second, they had aggressive leadership at the local level, including Captain George S. Patton and the twenty Charleston lawyers who formed the backbone of the Kanawha Rifles, Twenty-Second Virginia.[71]

Secessionists also asserted one more advantage over the Unionists. Numerous officers at the higher ranks had varying degrees of acquaintance with the military. John McCausland, the colonel of the Twenty-Second Virginia, was a graduate of the Virginia Military Institute (VMI). Colonel William Jackson of the Thirty-First Virginia, a regiment that recruited heavily in western Virginia's Pocahontas County, could look to his cousin, Major Thomas Jackson, a West Pointer and VMI instructor, for advice. General

Robert E. Lee had been a Mexican War veteran and superintendent of West Point. His chief of staff, Robert Garnett, had been commandant of cadets at West Point when Lee served as superintendent. Joining Lee in command of the several thousand rebel troops in western Virginia were General John Floyd, the onetime war secretary, and General Henry Wise, who as governor claimed credit for capturing John Brown at Harper's Ferry.[72]

In response to the increasing influx of rebel soldiers, Dennison dispatched more troops to western Virginia. Phil Stanbery, Hugh Ewing, Jacob Cox, and Rutherford Hayes joined the Virginian campaign. Hayes was apprehensive given that the Twenty-Third Ohio was armed with obsolete flintlock muskets. The regiment's colonel, West Point alum Eliakim Scammon, waved aside Hayes's complaint. As someone who had never previously operated under a military chain of command, Hayes thought little of bypassing his superior officer. He informed Salmon Chase that Lincoln had better get Ohio modern arms. To Hayes's relief, the Virginians they encountered in Clarksburg greeted the Twenty-Third Ohio with cheers rather than bullets. As he wrote to his wife: "It was pleasant to see we were not invading an enemy's country but defending the people among whom we came. Our men enjoyed it beyond measure. Many had never seen a mountain; none had ever seen such a reception."[73]

Unlike the Twenty-Third Ohio, Hugh and the Third Brigade quickly ran into opposition. At Rich Mountain on July 11, General McClellan mauled a portion of General Garnett's army. Much credit for the Union victory, however, should have gone to General Rosecrans. Thanks to a helpful Unionist youth, Rosecrans learned of a mountain pass through which to flank the 1,200 Virginians. In spite of rain, mud, and thick underbrush, Ohio and Indiana troops closed on the Confederate position. In a three-hour fight, Union forces lost twelve, compared to one-third of the Virginian command who were killed, injured, or captured. When Hugh and his men entered the hastily abandoned rebel encampment, they found, beyond discarded equipment and cannon, a peculiar sight: "[The rebels] also abandoned an inn keeper from Richmond, weighing over three hundred pounds, captain of a company of foot, who had come to the wars in a sulky. When discovered in the abandoned camp he was in great bodily fear, being evidently apprehensive that we would call upon him for some of his flesh. In his joy at not being immolated he voluntarily pledged himself never to make war again, but henceforth to take his ease in his inn at Richmond."[74]

Prior to the fighting at Rich Mountain, Hugh had spent rain-drenched evenings instructing individual soldiers in the manual of arms. The preparation had paid off at Rich Mountain, and Hugh proudly reported to Henrietta that Ohio's boys charged with fixed bayonets, "not a man flinching." Determined to maintain momentum even as McClellan counseled greater caution, Rosecrans pushed on to the Cheat River Valley. Garnett died in action on July 13, leaving General Lee with a command staff of three. Just before his death, Garnett had complained to Richmond that the ungrateful natives of western Virginia were "thoroughly imbued with an ignorant and bigoted Union sentiment."[75]

While Hugh and his soldiers were on a scouting mission on July 16, the Pocahontas Rifles, Thirty-First Virginia, ambushed the Buckeyes, wounding several of them. The Third Brigade's reconnaissance force, which included John Hunter and forty men from the Thirteenth Ohio, had entered a strongly secessionist region. These western Virginians had no intention of being liberated by Ohio. That fact, however, did not matter. The area was home to one of the strategic mountain passes Governor Dennison wished to occupy.[76]

Hugh withdrew his pickets and then studied the mountain terrain and the dense forest covering its slopes. He soon located a narrow trail. Under the cover of darkness and pouring rain, Hugh deployed a company to get around and then attack the Pocahontas Rifles. His assault force suffered no injuries while killing several of the rebels and scattering the rest. Colonel Jackson's Thirty-First Virginia had not believed that Yankees could humiliate them on their own soil, in their own neighborhood. Having spent years in southern Ohio forests hunting quail, Hugh knew how to read ground—and to hit moving targets with one shot. The same was true for many of his Ohio soldiers, whom he praised without reservation.[77]

Although his father's influence, in addition to a rekindled friendship with Rosecrans, gave Hugh a leg up on the promotion ladder, he had impressed a number of soldiers in western Virginia. John Beatty, a Cincinnati businessman before becoming lieutenant colonel of the Third Ohio, thought Hugh was "a man of excellent natural capacity"—as well as a heroic drinker. Beatty did not know that because of the chilling rains of western Virginia and injuries sustained years earlier in California, Hugh was experiencing joint pain. Drinking was Hugh's way of self-medicating; he would not contemplate a medical discharge.[78]

Both Beatty and Hugh perceived that McClellan, his favorable publicity notwithstanding, was a poor commander. The *New York Times* might have persuaded readers back east that rebels were overcome with fear whenever McClellan approached, but Ohio's officers knew better. Beatty was appalled that McClellan "should know so little about the character of the country, the number of the enemy, and the extent of his fortifications." Hugh told Beatty that McClellan and the generals in Washington were "too damn slow," thus giving the rebels time to regroup. After the Confederate defeat of General Irvin McDowell on July 21 at Manassas, McClellan left western Virginia to take command of the Army of the Potomac. The Ohioans anticipated more disasters to come for the easterners.[79]

While Hugh and the Third Brigade pushed aside rebel forces at Rich Mountain, General Jacob Cox's regiments advanced from Gallipolis, Ohio, to Charleston. Henry Wise, who arrived in Charleston on July 6, sought to hold the city with a force that ranged between 2,800 and 5,000—depending upon whether the volunteers felt like reporting on any given day. Although Charleston's salt wells were in an advanced stage of neglect, and its coal operations barely developed, the city was strategically important. As the route through the Kanawha Valley, Charleston was a gateway to Richmond. Given its strategic importance, General Lee was hoping that Wise might hold the Kanawha Valley—even if the former governor was not inclined to take orders from a mere soldier.[80]

At the peculiarly named Scary Creek outside Charleston on July 17, Wise declared victory after the Twelfth Ohio spent its ammunition and withdrew. The onetime Virginia governor, however, proved no match against the former Ohio state legislator. Cox simply worked the Eleventh and Twelfth Ohio, along with the First and Second Kentucky, around Wise's forces. The rebels, among them Captain Patton and the highly perturbed Kanawha Rifles, evacuated Charleston on July 25. Cousin Phil Stanbery and the Fourth West Virginia moved in as an occupying force.[81]

Wise established camp headquarters to the rear in the resort community of White Sulphur Springs. He could relax at a fine spa and consume an abundant supply of delicious strawberries. His troops, however, were not so fortunate. They began to succumb to dysentery and bad liquor—one Confederate regiment alone consumed ninety quarts of locally distilled whiskey weekly. In mounting a political defense for his failure, Wise fumed that "the Kanawha Valley is wholly disaffected and traitorous."[82]

General Floyd arrived at White Sulpher Springs on August 6 to demonstrate that not only had he been a better governor than Wise but he was the superior military commander as well. Wise complained to Jefferson Davis that Floyd wanted "to destroy my command." Floyd ambushed a few of Cox's men at Gauley River in the vicinity of Carnifex Ferry on August 26. Having successfully interrupted the Seventh Ohio's breakfast, Floyd reported to Richmond that he had won a great victory. A jealous Wise dismissed Floyd as a liar, but the reality was worse: Floyd thought he really had defeated Cox's army. As Cox observed, while he had "hare-brained" officers in his command, "Wise showed a capacity for keeping a command in hot water which was unique. If he had been half as troublesome to me as he was to Floyd, I should, indeed, have had a hot time of it."[83]

With the three-month terms of service expiring for a number of Union volunteers, new regiments, signed for three-year enlistments, appeared. Governor Dennison made Hugh a colonel and gave him command of the Thirtieth Ohio. Hugh wrote to Henrietta that his officers were "very pleasant gentlemen." Major George Hildt, for instance, had, like Hugh and Tom, tried to make a living in Kansas—leaving Canal Dover, Ohio, with his childhood friend William Quantrill. (Hildt and Quantrill parted company in the vicious political environment of Kansas.) The enlisted ranks of the Thirtieth Ohio were filled with eager but untrained volunteers largely hailing from Harrison County, one hundred miles east and north of Columbus.[84]

Hugh's regiment took the Baltimore & Ohio from Wheeling to Clarksburg on August 30. From there, they marched to join Rosecrans and Cox at Carnifex Ferry. His men were not used to steep mountain slopes, let alone navigating them in the dark. At one point, the troops at the bottom of a slope mistook the soldiers on the crest for the enemy and prepared to fire. Hugh had to move quickly among the Thirtieth, shouting at them to stand down. A little later, outside Bulltown on the Weston and Gauley Turnpike, Hugh halted his companies, which were preparing to cross a narrow suspension bridge. After examining the bridge and finding its support system wanting, Hugh ordered the troops to cross in smaller numbers. He also warned them not to march in unison—Hugh was afraid the vibrations would shake the bridge apart and send his boys falling to their deaths.[85]

Hayes and the Twenty-Third Ohio met up with Hugh and his regiment for one of the final major offensive operations of 1861 in their combat theater. Since their initial, welcoming, reception in western Virginia, the Twenty-Third Ohio had been subjected to frequent guerrilla sniper fire. Hayes asserted that "the secessionists in this region are the wealthy and educated, who do nothing openly, and the vagabonds, criminals, and ignorant barbarians of the country; while the Union men are in the middle classes—the law-and-order, well-behaved folks. Persecutions are common, killings not rare, robberies an every-day occurrence."[86]

Nearly as bad as the "bushwhackers," Hayes observed, was his own colonel. Eliakim Scammon, Hayes confided to relatives, was "impatient and fault-finding," with a "nervous system out of order." His promotion to Third Brigade commander, which gave him authority over the Twenty-Third and Thirtieth Ohio, did not improve Scammon's temperament. In contrast to Scammon, according to Hayes, Hugh Ewing was "kind to a fault." Further, even if Hugh was a stickler for keen discipline and training, it was clear he wanted his soldiers to fight bravely and not die needlessly.[87]

Rosecrans and Cox attacked the five thousand rebels at Carnifex Ferry on September 10. General Lee had demanded a resolute defense, but Floyd and Wise would not follow his orders. Wise refused to send his 2,500 troops to reinforce Floyd, claiming that many of his troops either had deserted or were stricken with measles. Lee appeared helpless to resolve the conflict of egos. He also felt persecuted by the critical reporters employed by the *Richmond Enquirer*, a newspaper whose major investor was none other than Wise.[88]

Cox's forces welcomed a fight in the open, having grown weary of rebel sniping. Indeed, just a couple of weeks earlier, rebels had ambushed Lieutenant Colonel Joseph Frizell and the Eleventh Ohio. An enraged Frizell shouted that the rebel commander was a coward, prompting the boisterous Confederate officer to mock the Buckeyes. Frizell then asked one of his soldiers if he could borrow an Enfield rifle, one of the newer and more accurate weapons recently distributed to the troops. Since the concealed Confederate officer continued to hurl insults, Frizell located his position. A native of rural, southwestern Ohio, Frizell dispatched the rebel with the ease of an experienced hunter.[89]

The Ninth, Tenth, Twelfth, and Thirteenth Ohio assaulted Floyd's entrenchments while the Twenty-Third and Thirtieth Ohio moved in as reserves. Hayes and the Twenty-Third spent most of the afternoon crawling through dense thickets. He admitted to his wife that at one point he looked around and realized he had only three men with him, the other few hundred of his command being dispersed and nearly consumed by the underbrush. If bewildered, Hayes's men were highly motivated. Private William McKinley had written in his diary prior to the battle, "If it be my lot to fall, I want to fall at my post and have it said that I fell in defense of my country in honor of the glorious stars and stripes. Not only do I want it said that I fell a valiant soldier of my country, but a soldier for my Redeemer."[90]

Cox's attacking regiments lost 17 men with an additional 141 wounded. They failed to dislodge the rebels. Floyd, demonstrating the same caliber of tactical thinking that Wise had earlier exhibited, withdrew to the opposite side of the Gauley River, destroying the bridge after crossing. He had received a minor wound that, critics alleged, rendered him hysterical and senseless. The Kanawha volunteers in the Twenty-Second Virginia had now been all but driven from their homes through a combined effort of Union forces and their own Richmond commanders.[91]

On the morning of September 11 Hugh encountered a runaway slave who informed him that the Confederates had withdrawn. Rosecrans gave

permission for Hugh to take a company from the Thirtieth with him to ver-
ify the report. He rode into the line of entrenchments ahead of his troops to
scout out the situation. There fifteen Confederates met him. They did not
know that Floyd had left them behind. The rebels appeared to be in need
of guidance, so Hugh suggested that they surrender—as they promptly did.
As he looked around, Hugh discovered that Floyd, in his hasty retreat, had
forgotten his headquarters flag. Floyd's banner bore his name, as well as the
inscription, "The Price of Liberty is the Blood of the Brave." Rosecrans, wishing to add further tarnish to Floyd's reputation, promised Hugh that the flag
would be displayed in Washington as a war trophy.[92]

General Lee had taken a defensive posture at Valley Mountain, a few days'
march south of the positions held by Rosecrans and Cox. Rain and, most dis-
concertingly to the Tidewater Virginians, *snow* had began to fall on Lee's few
thousand troops in mid-August. Regiments operated at half-strength as men
collapsed with typhoid fever and measles. Desertions mounted to as high as
75 percent in some of the rebel brigades.[93]

By October, Lee had grown frustrated that Rosecrans had not made a
mistake he could exploit. With his command ill, and his fellow theater generals spending more time feuding with each other than fighting the enemy, Lee
went back to Richmond a frustrated, weary man. Floyd issued a proclamation that was as stirring as it was disconnected from reality. The *New York
Times* could not resist republishing it for northern readers:

> Soldiers of the Army of the Kanawha: The campaign in the western por-
> tion of this State is now, as far as you are concerned, ended. At its close
> you can review it with pride and satisfaction. . . . Hard-contested battles
> and skirmishes were matters of almost daily occurrence. Nor is it to be
> forgotten that laborious and arduous march by day and by night were nec-
> essary, not only as furnishing you the opportunity of fighting there, but
> of baffling the foe at different points upon the march of invasion. And it
> is a fact which entitles you to the warm congratulations of your General,
> and to the thanks and gratitude of your country, that in the midst of the
> trying scenes through which you have passed, you have proved yourselves
> men and patriots, who, undaunted by superior numbers, have engaged the
> foe, beaten him in the field, and baffled and frustrated him in his plans to
> surprise you.[94]

Aside from skirmishes, the newly named Kanawha Division went into
occupation mode. General Cox could be seen in his downtime reading
Charles Dickens's *Great Expectations*—a book whose title was funnier in

the context of the western Virginia theater than its plot. Rosecrans, to Cox's wonderment, was so insistent on maintaining military fitness and discipline that he would seek out lax privates and give them heated lectures. As Cox observed: "If Rosecrans's method was not an ideal one, it was at least vigorous, and every week showed that the little army was improving in discipline and in knowledge of duty." Meanwhile, Eliakim Scammon, Cox's irascible brigade commander, all but disappeared from sight. This would have been fine with Hayes and Hugh, except that as a colonel with more service in the field than most others, Hugh had to perform Scammon's job in all but title.[95]

Whatever new leadership skills Hugh acquired doing the work Scammon avoided—and his superiors did make note—were balanced by the trouble Hayes's Twenty-Third Ohio generated. Hayes knew that his soldiers were summarily executing captured guerrilla fighters but could not summon up much desire to halt the practice. When Hugh could document an offense by the Twenty-Third against unarmed Virginian civilians, he acted swiftly. On one occasion, when no one in the Twenty-Third would own up to destroying a civilian's property, Hugh lined up the regiment in the cold, pouring rain. He sternly informed them that he could wait as long as they could until the guilty parties came forward. Hugh wore them down. The offending soldiers agreed to have their pay docked for the damages they had caused.[96]

Both Hugh and Hayes found western Virginia to be a depressing place in the fall of 1861. Colonel Lorin Andrews of the Fourth Ohio, Hayes's old friend and the president of Kenyon College, died of typhoid fever. In late August, Hayes had exuberantly written to his wife: "These marches and campaigns in the hills of western Virginia will always be among the pleasantest things I can remember. I know we are in frequent perils, that we may never return and all that, but the feeling that I am where I ought to be is a full compensation for all that is sinister, leaving me free to enjoy as if on a pleasure tour." A month later, his letters led off more darkly: "It is a cold, drizzly, suicidal morning."[97]

As Hugh wrote to Henrietta in October, "I have, all my life, entertained the opinion that the health of mountainous countries was uniformly good; but my march through these 'high hills,' has disabused my mind, and I find them quite subject to fevers which are quite fatal, as well as to other diseases." Having been to the Sonora and Sierra mountains, Hugh found western Virginia's scenery to be comparably dreary. Cousin Jimmy Blaine, far away in Maine and still a civilian, extolled the beauty of western Virginia, impressing anyone who had not actually been in the combat theater: "[The western Virginians] enjoyed a climate as genial as that of the Italians who dwell on the slopes of the Apennines."[98]

After his pickets surprised a rebel lieutenant and mortally wounded him, Hugh recovered a blood-stained photograph of a woman who, to his horror, looked much like Henrietta. He subsequently promised Henrietta, whose own recently taken picture seemed to be so full of sadness: "We will get together some day and it will be all right and we will have a very happy time—and it will be all sunshine; and none of the children will ever get sick, and the servants will not need scolding, and the money bay will have no bottom—and we will glide away, down the tide of time, meeting no rocks, or cascades, or falls; or anything to knock a hole in our boat—and we will go down, down, down, stopping once in a while to take in a few grandchildren, to the end of the chapter."[99]

If western Virginia depressed Hugh, the news from Ohio was at least diverting. Cousin Eliza Gillespie, now known as Sister Mary of St. Angela, had "enlisted" that very fall. Addressing Gillespie and the Congregation of the Sisters of the Holy Cross in South Bend, Indiana, Notre Dame college founder Edward Sorin saw an opportunity to serve the Union and demonstrate the patriotism of American Catholics: "A little band of devoted Sisters, ministering like angels among the soldiery, will do away with prejudices and show the beauty and resources of the Catholic faith to support man in all possible trials much more forcibly than volumes of argument and evidence."[100]

Sorin had another unspoken reason for offering the nuns to the Union cause. The War Department, fearful that the nurses it recruited might be objects of sexual temptation to the soldiers, had insisted that they be over the age of thirty and not particularly good looking. As "Brides of Christ" adorned in religious garb, the nuns would, theoretically, have less cause to worry about sexual advances. Gillespie subsequently reported to Illinois brigadier general Ulysses Grant that the Sisters of the Holy Cross were ready to establish a military hospital. Grant gratefully accepted her offer.[101]

Ellen Ewing wrote to Hugh often and sent him woolen socks and cigars. In one letter to Hugh, she contended that "the crime of these rebels [is] second only to that of Lucifer and the Jews." (It was not uncommon for nineteenth-century Catholics to view Jews as "Christ Killers" in league with Satan.) Ellen also informed Hugh that she was "anxious to secure a pistol somewhere and learn to load and fire briskly so that I may not feel too helpless when the marauders come our way."[102]

Ellen reported that as the secretary of the Ladies Society in Lancaster she had helped collect or manufacture four hundred blankets for the hometown heroes of the Sixty-First Ohio. Newton Schleich, the commander of the Sixty-First Ohio, Ellen related with disgust, had refused to contribute any money for the support of his own soldiers. This would have come as no surprise to Hugh, since Lancaster's former legislator—and Governor Dennison's worst appointment to military command—had earned a miserable reputation in western Virginia. Hugh's new friend, Colonel Beatty of the Third Ohio, had earlier gotten into a heated argument with the "rampant demagogue." When Schleich contended that any slaves they encountered should be sold to the Cubans to help finance the Union war effort, Beatty expressed revulsion.[103]

There were other newsworthy developments from Ohio for Hugh to digest. Politically, much of the Ohio Valley was in a state of flux. The pro-southern faction of the Ohio Democratic Party had revealed its strategy in May. Far from rallying to the Union, Democratic legislators sponsored a bill to prohibit marriages between blacks and whites. Democrats hoped to distract the public from the Fort Sumter attack and brand the Republicans as advocates of interracial sex. For his part, Samuel Medary, the editor of the Democratic Party's *Columbus Crisis*, warned that Lincoln was encouraging slaves to flee the South and overrun Ohio.[104]

Working in concert with their state legislative and journalist counterparts were six of the eight members of Ohio's Democratic congressional delegation, most notably Samuel Cox. (The other two Ohio Democrats chose to maintain a lower profile on the secession crisis than their colleagues.) They appealed to Thomas Ewing and Reverdy Johnson to bypass Lincoln and negotiate a peace settlement directly with the South. Congressman Vallandigham went so far as to go among the Ohio troops outside Washington informing them that they were going to die to free blacks. He got into at least one fistfight with several Western Reserve soldiers before being rescued by friends.[105]

Determined to thwart Samuel Cox, who was emerging as a leader of the congressional opposition to Lincoln, John Sherman and Thomas Ewing launched their counterstroke. Along with moderate Republicans and the faction of Democrats who supported a war for the preservation of the Union, Ewing presided at a special convention held in Columbus on September 5. Their goal was to launch a "unity ticket" which would sideline prosouthern Democrats and temper Radical Republicans. Ewing made his case logically and forcefully, with eloquence he had not summoned for years:

> The Ship of State is among the breakers now. I do not propose to inquire what Lincoln has done or what Buchanan has done; let all that pass. Let all past differences among us be laid aside; our duty is to save the country. Since 1854 I had had no political home; have belonged to no party; but now give adherence to the party of the people. Let Democrats and Republicans balance their accounts and begin anew. Ever since 1833, South Carolina has been educating her sons in the heresy of rebellion. That State will never return to the Union of her own accord. . . . She, along with the others, must be brought back by the strong arm of the law.[106]

Ohio's unity slate chose not to reelect Governor Dennison, in part because he had become a lightning rod for criticism regarding all the inevitable glitches that sprang from overnight military mobilization. His friendship with Colonel James Garfield, whose strident rhetoric made no distinction between prowar and antiwar Democrats, also hurt Dennison. Instead, the unity ticket offered up David Tod, a pro-Union Democrat who had campaigned against Lincoln. Tod defeated the Democratic gubernatorial candidate by a comfortable margin of fifty-five thousand votes. The Union coalition also took 100 of the 131 seats in the Ohio legislature.[107]

Ewing and Sherman would have liked to have thrown Senator Ben Wade overboard. Their distaste for him was understandable. To begin with, Wade had exhorted Dennison not to appoint Sherman to Chase's Senate seat. Sherman, Wade contended, lacked the abolitionist principles of a real Republican. Then, at the Manassas battlefield, where Wade had gone to picnic, he had stormed about threatening to execute retreating Union soldiers. Wade further enhanced his reputation among moderates by contending that Lincoln's opposition to emancipation could be attributed to his "poor white trash" background. Unfortunately, Ewing and Sherman concluded, Wade was so popular in the vote-rich Western Reserve that they could not remove him without political repercussions.[108]

The alliance between moderate Republicans and pro-Union Democrats in Ohio appealed to Border State politicians, including Tennessee senator Andrew Johnson. Having little use for slave-owning southern aristocrats, Johnson had proclaimed his loyalty to the Union. Through the summer and fall of 1861 Johnson had traveled about Kentucky and Ohio seeking political and military support for eastern Tennessee Unionists. He delivered an impassioned three-and-half-hour speech in Lancaster. Ellen Sherman wrote to Hugh that Johnson spoke in "bursts of eloquence and patriotism" that "brought shouts of applause" and "induced tears of the sincerest sympathy."[109]

Thomas Ewing, who had introduced Johnson to his audience in Lancaster, was enormously impressed with him. He insisted that Johnson spend the night at the Main Hill mansion. In Johnson, a principled politician who had worked his way up from illiteracy and poverty, Ewing saw a kindred spirit. Johnson's speeches, moreover, were of the old Whig style that harkened back to Clay, Webster, and Ewing himself—lengthy and loaded with historical and literary allusions. After the fall of 1861, Johnson became a valued member of the Ewing political circle. Thomas Ewing and his children championed Johnson, and he in turn supported the family. No one anticipated that the first member of the Ewing family in need of political assistance would be Cump.[110]

At the outbreak of the war everything finally had appeared to go Cump's way. He held a commission in the Regular Army. Hugh and Hayes, in contrast, served with the less prestigious Ohio Volunteers. The fact that both had practiced law before the U.S. Supreme Court mattered not at all in the hour of the professional soldier. Cump wore a colonel's eagles in service to an army led by fellow Ohioan Irvin McDowell. Then everything became more complicated. Cump could hardly be blamed when Union troops became disorganized at Manassas. Colonel Sherman kept his wits, earning promotion to brigadier general. He soon received a transfer to Kentucky. His position as second in command, and subsequent elevation to overall commander in October when his superior resigned, required a disciplined tongue and calm forbearance—neither of which Cump possessed.[111]

The Kentucky military theater was one where political shadowboxing initially substituted for open combat. Governor Magoffin maintained a position of hostile neutrality toward the Union. His divided legislature acquiesced to neutrality while contributing funds and sons to Confederate and Union Army recruiters. When Confederate general Leonidas Polk took the western rail and river hub of Columbus, Kentucky, in September 1861, Unionist legislators declared the state's fictitious neutrality to be over. Others did not agree. Lincoln, though having won just 1,364 votes in his native state, believed that Kentucky would remain loyal, since the secessionist wing of the Democratic Party had not carried the state in 1860.[112]

Cump provoked growing ridicule from his military superiors in Washington as he fretted about Confederate recruiting and the readiness of his own troops. As Ellen reported to Hugh, Cump believed "that the Kentuckians are not so ready to fight for the Union as they were to vote for it." She also speculated that the Union might need a dictator to "hang all the [newspaper] editors for they have been the agents of all the ruin that is threatening us now." Governor Morton of Indiana understood Cump's concerns and wrote to Lincoln in September. Morton insisted that Cump faced superior numbers and informed Lincoln that Indiana was prepared to send him three thousand troops. Andrew Johnson penned a warm letter to Cump in October, observing that he shared the same concerns about Confederate political and military strength in Kentucky.[113]

Cump argued that he did not have sufficient troops to drive out Polk's forces. Further, as he informed Simon Cameron, if they were serious about holding Kentucky and the general area, then the Union needed to commit sixty thousand troops. Offensive operations in Kentucky and Tennessee would require two hundred thousand soldiers. Cameron thought that Cump's constant appeals to the War Department were the product of an overly agitated man. A military-oriented War Department secretary might have evaluated Cump's points in light of the facts on the ground. Then Cameron could have concluded that while Cump might have been overestimating the strength of the Confederates, there was little enthusiasm among most Kentuckians for joining the Union Army. Cameron's War Department, of course, viewed all matters through a political lens. Cump's pleas for reinforcements were inevitably interpreted as rebukes to Cameron. In Cameron's defense, there was no shortage of Regular Army officers who took Cump's restless energy and blunt language as evidence of insubordination or mental instability.[114]

Though Cump resigned as commander of the Department of the Cumberland and transferred to St. Louis in the late fall of 1861, the attacks on him intensified. His superior in the Department of Missouri, Major General Henry Halleck, seemed—to the Ewing family—to be less than enthusiastic in the defense of his subordinate. Having known Halleck since their service in California, Cump mistakenly thought he could trust his commanding officer. Cump did not understand that an officer who would cheat California's Mexicans out of their land holdings could be equally dishonorable with his own people. Now in 1861, Halleck thoughtfully urged Cump to go home to Lancaster to rest. He then pulled out the knives and informed George McClellan that Cump's "physical and mental system is so completely broken by labor and care as to render him for the present completely unfit for duty."[115]

Personnel in the War Department leaked their derogatory impressions of Cump to reporters. Both Democratic and Republican newspapers in Ohio led the offensive, unable to resist the temptation to increase circulation by luridly attacking a close relation of Thomas Ewing and John Sherman. The *Cincinnati Commercial* reported that "General W. T. Sherman, late commander of the Department of the Cumberland, is insane. It appears that he was at time, when commanding in Kentucky, stark mad." Although Cump had grown progressively more tense and tired, his critics preferred to hurl charges of insanity at him rather than objectively looking at the concerns he raised.[116]

The wrath of the Ewing family fell upon the news media, Cameron, Halleck, and Lincoln. When the president ignored Ellen Sherman's request for a meeting to discuss Cump, her father, brothers, and brother-in-law John Sherman threw their combined weight against White House and War Department. The news media would be part of the collateral damage. As for George McClellan, Ellen Sherman vowed to Hugh, the American people would "wreck their vengeance upon" him for not giving Cump the weapons and troops he needed.[117]

Phil Ewing went on a multifront offensive to defend his brother-in-law. He tersely informed Halleck that Cump was rested and would soon be reporting to duty—and he had already informed the press of that fact. Indeed, Phil issued a long, detailed letter to the *Cincinnati Commercial* and sent a copy to Halleck. After refuting line by line every accusation made against Cump, Phil expressed the hope that the editor would repent of his "libelous" and "malignant" ways and see fit to publish his rebuttal. (As an attorney, Halleck would have recognized Phil's deliberate choice of words.) Phil assured the *Cincinnati Commercial* that the military intelligence he was sharing in the letter would "give no aid and comfort to the enemy." By invoking that particular phrase, he was implying that the newspaper itself had a history of treasonous behavior. Phil Ewing, the most reserved of the boys, proved to be a ferocious lawyer. His next stop was the White House, though there were other family members in line ahead of him.[118]

Hugh received a brief leave from western Virginia so that he could corner personnel in the War Department and force them to produce their evidence against Cump or recant. He then talked his way into the White House and met with Lincoln. John Sherman, who coordinated his defense of Cump with Phil and Hugh, also went to the White House. Sherman conceded to Lincoln that though Cump might have overstated Confederate strength in the Kentucky-Tennessee theater it was a mistake to then underestimate the difficulty of the military task facing the Union. Lincoln appeared noncommittal, leading Sherman to become disaffected with the president. He soon questioned whether Lincoln was insane himself or merely an incompetent "fool and baboon."[119]

Thomas Ewing then landed on Lincoln. Their past history up through the 1860 election had not created the basis for a warm relationship. Since the South Carolinian capture of Fort Sumter, Ewing had taken Lincoln to task for appointing John Fremont commander of the Department of Missouri. Fremont's credentials consisted of being the son-in-law of a former Missouri senator, making an electoral run as the 1856 Republican presidential candidate, and having an abolitionist philosophy hearty enough for Ben Wade's tastes. Fremont soon embarrassed Lincoln by ordering the immediate emancipation of slaves held by Missouri rebels.[120]

Ewing warned Lincoln in September that Fremont was a "pompous absurdity" with "imperfect military education and no military experience and habitually jealous of those who possess these qualifications which he has not." The Blairs, who had initially supported Fremont, came to the same conclusion Ewing had reached. Halleck took Fremont's command. Ironically, on the very day Lincoln removed Fremont, Ewing had written to Hugh observing that the president had a habit of acting on bad advice and making bad judgment calls. (To Thomas Ewing's disgust, Fremont ended up in western Virginia.)[121]

Most recently, in November, Ewing had taken Lincoln to task when the *U.S.S. San Jacinto* seized two Confederate commissioners aboard the British ship *Trent*. Confederate commissioner James Mason, who had selectively worn the homespun suit Maria Theresa Ewing had found so amusingly hypocritical, was in an agitated state. Britain regarded the capture of the Confederate commissioners as intolerable. Secretary of State Seward, who had months earlier speculated with Lincoln that a foreign war might reunite the nation, did not want to release Mason and the other commissioner, John Slidell, a former Louisiana senator.[122]

Ewing, concerned that Britain had just cause to declare war on the United States, offered blunt, unsolicited advice to Lincoln. The president ultimately accepted Ewing's rationale, which his secretary, John Hay, snidely referred to as a "dissertation on neutral rights":

> England will no doubt demand redress and in my opinion you ought to give it at once and in all frankness—without question and without controversy. It is not yet *in fact* the wrong of the U.S., but of the commanding officer, for the boarding and arrest under the British flag was not ordered by you—and now the Law of Nations requires that you disavow the act—if England requires it. This is her right. She has no right, however, to prescribe the censure which shall be passed on your officer. *He* acted under the mistaken opinion of duty and having done no willful wrong his censure should be light.
>
> Then as to the further redress which England has a right to demand— Mason & Slidell have no right in the matter. They were traitors wherever found and deserved to be treated accordingly, and the British Government has no right in them or over them except in this: It may be justly claimed that in the persons of these men the immunity secured by the British flag has been violated and in order to repair this wrong and cause that immunity *to have been*, and still to be absolute, England may rightfully demand that the prisoners be placed as nearly as possible in status quo. That is to say, that they be placed on board a British ship and suffered to pursue their voyage without interruption.[123]

Lincoln could hardly refuse Ewing an accommodation after he had given him the legal cover to free the Confederate commissioners and consequently avert further conflict with Britain. He also could not say much in response when Ewing insisted that Cump's trouble was that he "saw too far and too accurately into the future." Ellen, who had insisted on being with her father when he met Lincoln, put the president on the spot. She forced Lincoln to say that he did not believe Cump was insane. Paradoxically, Ellen had her own doubts about Cump's mental stability when he felt stressed; Leavenworth had been in some ways a prelude to Kentucky. Prior to their meeting with Lincoln, Halleck had welcomed Cump back with open arms and, as the Ewing family believed, with clenched fists. A contrite Cump promised his father-in-law that he would be more careful with his public words and behavior.[124]

By the end of 1861 it was clear that for the Union the war effort had met with some success and much failure. Thomas Ewing and John Sherman were disgusted with Lincoln's team of incompetents and with the president himself. Then again, there were some signs of encouragement in that Cameron would be departing from the War Department. It also appeared that Lincoln intended to keep Seward—"a low, vulgar, vain demagogue," according to Ewing—on a shorter leash. Moreover, many northern Democrats had rallied to defend the Union, and western Virginia had been separated from the Confederacy.[125]

Still, there remained serious challenges. Richmond might have withdrawn its troops from western Virginia, but a guerrilla insurgency had developed. In Ohio, a state that provided critical manpower and economic resources to the Union, the alliance between moderate Republicans and "War Democrats" was tenuous. As was true throughout the Ohio Valley and Border States, pro-Union Democrats in 1861 would fight to save the Union, not to abolish slavery—the latter being the goal of the abolitionist Republicans. Ohio was in the peculiar political position by the close of 1861 of providing the Union with the most vociferous Republican radicals and strident antiwar Democrats. How long the center could hold in such a political environment was an open question.

For the Ewings, the war had become a family affair. Thomas Ewing and Tom had not wanted war and had tried unsuccessfully at the Washington peace conference to reach a compromise. The Patriarch had roused himself to champion his country even as friends of many years chose the Confederacy. Meanwhile, the Matriarch, far from recoiling at the prospect of her sons' dying in combat, sent them to battle. For Maria Ewing, her sons were no better than anyone else's in God's eyes, and, indeed, their having been so hugely blessed made their obligation to lead greater.

Hugh Ewing appeared to have found his calling. He no longer sought adventure for its own sake. It was Henrietta and his growing brood that occupied his thoughts in western Virginia. But Hugh also knew that years spent at West Point, and through Mexico, California, and Kansas, had taught him valuable survival lessons that he could share with his troops. The stakes, of course, were much higher than they had been when he prospected for California gold. Still, Hugh had not entirely settled down. If adventure came of its own accord, Hugh would not pass it up. Along the Ohio River, in the days when Thomas Ewing was but a boy, there was a folk saying. When a restless spirit went looking for fun, he was bound to "see the varmint." Hugh could not resist looking for the "varmint."[126]

Cump's war, in contrast, had not been as gratifying. Indeed, Cump could have been forgiven if he regarded himself as the "cave-dwelling varmint" everyone wanted to poke. No matter how often he tried to assert his independence, Cump needed the Ewing family and his little brother to rescue him. He may have always seen himself as a professional soldier above politics, but Cump did not understand that many of his fellow officers were as politically calculating as Thomas Ewing, Tom, and John Sherman. Even those officers who had not been politically inclined before the war, like George McClellan, became prima donnas.

Ultimately, whether Cump prospered militarily as well as Hugh mattered little. If 1862 went as badly as 1861, the Union might well be lost.

4

"Render to Caesar"

Shiloh, Antietam, and Prairie Grove, 1862

I intend to remain in the Army until the rebellion is utterly subdued. The future happiness of our children, and children's children, depend upon their overthrow and the triumph of our Government. We will have many wars otherwise, as they have for a thousand years in Europe. After God, every man's duty is due his Government: and it has a right to demand his life, if it needs it—in obedience to the divine command I will "render to Caesar what belongs to Caesar."
—Hugh Ewing, 1862

The Ewings had waged a no-holds-barred campaign to salvage Cump's military career. Whatever small prospect they might have had for warmer relations with President Lincoln was considerably diminished as a result. Thomas Ewing and Lincoln had found it difficult to interact with each other on a comfortable footing even before the "Kentucky Affair." Now the estrangement between Cump's kin and Lincoln had worsened. Senator John Sherman so openly disdained Lincoln that the president commented on it to visitors.[1]

For her part, Ellen had been upset with Lincoln when he initially ignored her pleas. "As malice cannot prevail, where justice rules," Ellen wrote to Lincoln, "I look for speedy relief from the sorrow that has afflicted me, in this trial to my husband." Ellen's father, who was at her side, forcefully intervened. Lincoln, Ewing insisted, would meet his daughter in the White House and explain his administration's treatment of Cump. As Ellen reassured Cump, "It is not in the power of your enemies to lower you in the estimation of those who know you and time will prove the falsity of their charges to the world."[2]

Cump's redemption came early in April 1862, though, as seemed to be his lot, it was not without controversy. General Ulysses Grant, who had also married into a prominent family and subsequently failed in business, mounted a combined naval and infantry assault on Fort Henry and Fort Donelson. The February 1862 campaign gave the Union command of the Cumberland and Tennessee Rivers, forcing Confederate general Albert Sidney Johnston to redeploy from Kentucky and western Tennessee to Corinth, Mississippi.

Determined to regain the initiative, Johnston and General P. T. Beauregard attacked Grant on April 6, 1862, at Pittsburg Landing, Tennessee. Cump held up well under the onslaught and assisted Grant in a successful counterstroke the next day. Grant scored the Union's first major battlefield victory, but at the cost of thirteen thousand casualties out of a force of forty thousand. Confederate casualties totaled eleven thousand. General Johnston was killed, leaving Beauregard to organize the Confederate withdrawal. As soldiers from both sides observed with gallows humor, many men had spent their last Sunday on earth at the Shiloh Meeting House near Pittsburg Landing. So many soldiers had died near the church that the battle also became known as "Shiloh."

Grant felt stung by newspaper accusations that Johnston had caught him unprepared because he was drunk to the point of incapacitation. General Henry Halleck seemingly concurred with the reporters, which came as no surprise to Ellen. She had earlier warned Cump that Halleck could not be trusted. Cump, who had bucked up Grant's morale during the battle, leapt to his defense. He informed Ewing that Halleck and Lincoln should have anticipated that there would be considerable bloodshed in taking the war to enemy territory. "The attempt to throw blame on Grant," Cump continued, "is villainous." Cump also observed that if he had to choose between serving a government dictated to by slanderous newspaper reporters and one led by General Beauregard, then he knew where he would stand. Cump wisely expressed that thought in confidence.[3]

Whitelaw Reid of the *Cincinnati Gazette* not only condemned Grant but disparaged the performance of Ohio soldiers at Pittsburg Landing. Other newspapers echoed Reid's charges, as did Ohio's Democratic lieutenant governor, Benjamin Stanton. The Ewings reacted harshly to these attacks—and not just because of pride in Cump and in their state. There had been friends and other family members associated with the Tennessee battle and its aftermath.[4]

Lancaster's Tom Hunter had mustered into the Seventeenth Ohio as a captain and had subsequently arrived at Pittsburg Landing just after combat ceased. Captain Dan McCook, Tom Ewing's law partner in Leavenworth, fought in the battle with the Second Division, Army of the Ohio. Cousin Eliza "Mother Angela" Gillespie and the Sisters of the Holy Cross were awash in blood as they cared for the wounded. Since her mobilization, Mother Angela had lost two members of her order to camp-spawned disease and had seen one of the hospitals she built destroyed by flood. After Pittsburg Landing, she had to separate the Union and Confederate wounded, since the soldiers continued in their efforts to kill each other. A grateful Grant gave Cousin Eliza two cannon, which she took back to Indiana. St. Mary's College, the "home" of the Sisters of the Holy Cross, would be the only female Catholic school in the United States to have its own war trophies.[5]

Thomas Ewing edited a public letter Cump had composed that refuted the newspaper allegations against Grant. He warned his son-in-law "to write with greater care" and to use less colorful language. Ewing himself published a twenty-four-page rebuttal to Lieutenant Governor Stanton. He reviewed the accounts of every combatant who had spoken to the Democrat, noting inconsistencies and separating opinion from fact. Ewing informed Stanton that there were times when a commander had to make the best of less than perfect circumstances: "You object—and this is fair criticism—to General Sherman placing raw troops *in front, in the very key of his position.* The answer to this is that he had none other—there was not in his whole Division a single regiment that had ever seen the face of an enemy."[6]

Less legalistic and more impassioned, John Sherman took to the floor of the Senate to defend Ohio's honor. Senator Sherman, somewhat gratuitously, observed that in 1861 Lincoln had made an inadequate request for troops. In response to Lincoln's call, so many Ohio volunteers stepped forward that the president had unwisely turned them away. Fortunately, Sherman continued, Governor Dennison had been smart enough to keep raising new regiments, which he used to liberate western Virginia. When the Confederates attacked Grant at Pittsburg Landing, Ohio troops had performed heroically. Sherman sharply criticized the "innuendo" and "indiscriminate imputation" coming from Democratic politicians and newspapermen whom he regarded as traitors.[7]

From his vantage point in the backwater theater of western Virginia, Hugh Ewing wished he could be reunited with Cump. Ellen had enthused in letters to Hugh that Cump had had two horses shot out from under him at Pittsburg Landing. She also rejoiced "at Cump's deliverance from vile slanderers and envious men." After months of occupation duty in the Virginian mountains, Hugh would have been grateful for his own deliverance.[8]

Rutherford Hayes was a conscientious commander, albeit lax on discipline. There were other officers in the Kanawha Division, however, whose behavior fell short of Hugh's expectations. After Colonel Augustus Moor of the Twenty-Eighth Ohio beat one of Hugh's soldiers with the flat of his sword because he had not moved quickly enough out of his way, he went to rebuke him. Once Hugh arrived at Moor's encampment he immediately understood the problem. Moor was a Prussian, and the Cincinnati German immigrants in his command expected to be beaten—or to be stoked with beer. Hugh explained to Moor that other Ohioans, not sharing the Twenty-Eighth's Teutonic culture, took offense at being assaulted—even if by an officer.[9]

Since Hugh had practiced law before the U.S. Supreme Court and held senior rank, he received the unenviable task of presiding at the courts-martial of derelict officers. The Kanawha Division's own Charles de Villiers, colonel of the Eleventh Ohio, was court-martialed in Charleston in the winter of 1862. Serving as the presiding officer, Hugh learned that Colonel de Villiers, a veteran of the French Army, had been seizing cattle from allegedly disloyal Virginians. De Villiers then arranged for the army to purchase the cattle from him. He soon branched out from livestock, taking several slaves hostage until their owners paid him a ransom. De Villiers received no support from his officers. Instead, they testified to his vindictiveness and corruption. Hugh had no reservation in finding him guilty, which resulted in de Villiers's dismissal from military service.[10]

In the winter of 1862 Hugh had to confront a problem even more exasperating than some of his fellow colonels—the Virginian guerrillas. Francis Peirpoint, the provisional governor of Unionist Virginia and a former Baltimore & Ohio Railroad attorney, repeatedly pleaded with General William Rosecrans and Lincoln for increased military aid. Loyal western Virginians, Peirpoint had informed Lincoln in 1861, needed better arms with which "to defend themselves from vile men infesting neighborhoods and sections who are burning and plundering."[11]

Since Robert E. Lee's humiliating departure from western Virginia, rebel regiments had broken into platoon-sized bands of "bushwhackers." Hayes had earlier written to an uncle that the guerrillas were "cowardly, cunning, and lazy. The height of their ambition is to shoot a Yankee from some place of safety." General Robert Milroy, formerly of the Ninth Indiana, received orders to mount a campaign against the bushwhackers. He had limited success, reporting that even with forty thousand soldiers he could not "catch guerrillas in the mountains anymore than a cow can catch fleas." Milroy recommended to his superiors that Washington "inaugurate a system of Union guerrillas to put down the rebel guerrillas."[12]

The barbaric behavior of Virginia's guerrillas in 1862 stunned the soldiers of the Kanawha Division. Virginian bushwhackers dug up the bodies of dead

Benjamin F. Wade (1800–1878). A Radical Republican who embodied the abolitionist values of Ohio's Western Reserve, U.S. Senator Wade regarded the Ewing family and its allies as disloyal and described President Lincoln as "white trash." (Courtesy of the Library of Congress.)

Union troops and chopped off their heads, which they took as prizes. They then removed the intestines of the decapitated Yankee corpses, scattering their guts about where federal troops were sure to find them. On the occasions when they could get their hands on live Yankee soldiers or pro-Union civilians, the Confederates tied them to trees and then engaged in an orgy of disembowelment and decapitation. Despite guerrilla atrocities and freezing temperatures, a private in the Thirtieth Ohio maintained a generally positive perspective when writing home: "I think a soldier's life is much better than digging coal, although Uncle Sam has forgot to pay us anything."[13]

As the insurgency worsened, Hayes and Hugh gained a greater understanding of their foes. One key to the guerrillas' success was that they operated with the clandestine support of neighbors and, most importantly, kin. Hugh told Ellen and his father that the guerrillas used their mothers, sisters, and wives to pose as women in distress in order to get his patrols to lower their guard. Once Union troops halted to provide assistance, the guerrillas opened fire. Ellen exhorted Hugh to execute such treacherous women. After all, his sister asserted, "What perdition can be too deep for such inhuman wretches?" Hayes concurred. In the winter of 1862, the Twenty-Third Ohio commenced burning the homes of suspected guerrillas, calculating that if they turned the rebels' families into refugees the insurgency would collapse.[14]

In April 1862, General Rosecrans received reassignment to the Army of the Tennessee. Ohio senator Ben Wade made sure that his favorite abolitionist general, John Fremont, became head of the newly created Mountain Department. Fortunately for Hugh and Hayes, the militarily inept Fremont left Jacob Cox in command of the Kanawha Division. Cox's regiments would form the spine of a spring offensive directed at taking Princeton and Lewisburg, Virginia. Most importantly, Ohio and western Virginian troops were to secure Flat Top Mountain, whose heights gave them an enormous tactical advantage against the 3,500 rebels in the area. While it proved difficult for Cox to move supplies and troops along western Virginia's muddy roads, at least the Confederates suffered as well.[15]

As the Kanawha Division moved toward Princeton in the spring of 1862, patrols from the Thirtieth Ohio probed more aggressively into the guerrilla sanctuaries. Captain Elijah Warner reported to Hugh that previously frightened Unionists felt confident enough to identify rebel families. Warner's company subsequently captured several rebels, including a "rabid secessionist" who had pillaged Unionist farms. Warner assured Hugh that Company E had administered an oath of allegiance to all but the worst and then set them free. Unlike the Thirtieth Ohio, the Twenty-Third Ohio did not have a catch-and-release policy. Hayes's men had been disinclined to take prisoners since the fall of 1861.[16]

Second Lieutenant Ezra McConnell of Company B delivered a more harrowing report to Hugh. McConnell had taken seven men on a reconnaissance patrol a few miles across the New River where it met the mouth of the East River. While they were moving through a ravine, a guerrilla band of twenty-five fired on them. The Ohioans advanced quickly through the underbrush in an effort to flank their foes but were instead met with more fire. McConnell then retreated toward New River, leading his men up a steep hill and across an open field. Reaching a cabin, McConnell formed a defensive line and called out for the attackers to identify themselves. They did: "Kanawha Rifles—you Yankee sons of bitches." It was the remnant of George Patton's band of lawyers—exiled from Charleston and reduced to hit-and-run assaults.[17]

While McConnell could not see his foes in the dense forest, the flashes from their muzzles clearly indicated that the Kanawha Rifles were closing on the cabin. McConnell ordered his men to leap over a stone wall—which provided cover to their backsides—and make a final dash for the banks of the New River. Fortunately for McConnell's outnumbered soldiers, Patton's men were horrible shots. A Union cavalry troop, drawn to the sound of gunfire, arrived on the scene. The Kanawha Rifles immediately broke off their attack and fled. McConnell's patrol had suffered not a single casualty Patton's Virginians were not so fortunate. Every scream that came from the forest after McConnell's men targeted a muzzle flash meant that a Yankee musket ball had found its mark.[18]

The momentum of Cox's campaign had slowed considerably by the time McConnell's patrol had their run through the woods. Major George Hildt of the Thirtieth Ohio reassured his parents that the serious fighting in his theater had ceased in mid-May. Hugh Ewing's regiment, Hildt observed, had to worry about only the "shots [that were] fired across the [East River] continually and the howitzers [that] open out frequently." More threatening to the Union troops than the Confederates was the locally produced corn liquor. "Bloats," Hildt insisted, "die first in the army, and whiskey is our greatest trouble, which all army officers will attest." However, what else the men of the Kanawha Division could safely drink in western Virginia remained a mystery. Hildt observed that the stream water often sickened thirsty soldiers.[19]

Hugh wrote frequently to Henrietta, who was staying in Washington. She had chosen not to remain with her Maryland relations, whose loyalties were divided between Washington and Richmond. He appreciated that his wife had become estranged from much of her family after Hugh had enlisted with

Henrietta Young Ewing (1834–1927). As the wife of Hugh Ewing and the daughter of a Maryland plantation owner, Henrietta Ewing grappled with her husband over the emancipation of slaves. (Courtesy of the University of Notre Dame Archives.)

the Ohio Volunteers. Indeed, several of Henrietta's kin served in the rebel forces. Hugh enclosed mountain flowers and tree blossoms with his letters and confided that he dreamed of her every night.[20]

Although Hugh understood the inner turmoil Henrietta experienced with the war, there was one political topic that he could not avoid raising with her: the abolition of slavery. A year earlier, Hugh would have identified himself as a Democrat committed to the preservation of the Union. Taking a position that was embraced by Lincoln and Thomas Ewing, Hugh had been willing to tolerate slavery so long as it remained contained in the South.

Fighting Confederate guerrillas in western Virginia, seeing the wretched living conditions of slaves, and serving with courageous abolitionists changed Hugh's attitude toward the peculiar institution. Hayes had been sending escaped slaves to Ohio for months. Hugh followed suit, requesting that his father find them jobs in Lancaster. Ironically, Thomas Ewing, who had proclaimed a year earlier at the Washington Peace Conference that Ohio did not want southern blacks coming into the state, now assisted his son in their relocation. In spite of his misgivings, Thomas Ewing had never been able to say "no" to his most idealistic son. He did, however, urge Hugh not to reveal his abolitionist sentiments outside the family.[21]

Hugh insisted that Henrietta come to terms with the immorality of slavery and the role many in the American Catholic Church had played in defending the institution. For instance, Charleston, South Carolina, bishop John England had insisted that when Pope Gregory XVI condemned the slave trade in 1839 he was not criticizing American slavery. Both Bishop England and New York Archbishop John Hughes exhorted American Catholics to shun the abolitionist movement. Abolitionists, American Catholic clergy and newspaper editors contended, were Protestant religious bigots intent upon plunging the nation into civil war. Savannah, Georgia, Bishop Augustin Verot concurred with his northern counterparts and then went further, defending slavery as a humane and necessary institution given the uncivilized nature of Africans.[22]

As Hugh contended with Henrietta, the Catholic Church in Europe had been more forthright than its American branch in opposing enslavement. Outside Europe, particularly in Latin America, Catholic colonizers had embraced African slavery, leaving it to Protestant Britain to suppress the trade in human lives. Meanwhile the United States passed up an opportunity to abolish slavery after the Revolutionary War. Too many Protestants and Catholics feared tearing their new nation apart over the issue of abolishing slavery. And now, thanks to that earlier political expediency and cowardice,

"[Southern slave owners] have convulsed the entire nation. The only reason why slavery was even allowed a day's life by the Church was to avoid convulsion. But slavery has brought in a convulsion and is shattering the whole continent in its horrible struggles. Now, I say, in the name of Almighty God who abhors it let it die and disturb the world no more."[23]

Ultimately, Hugh concluded, though he loved Henrietta and his children, if "the choice is between abolition and a widowed wife and orphan children, I will choose abolition." Hugh, like many other northern soldiers, had ranked the stability and preservation of the nation as a matter of first importance. His wife and children, Hugh believed, had to live with the possible sacrifice of his life. A divided and half-free America, he had concluded, would condemn their children to a future of endless strife. After much anguish, Henrietta reluctantly accepted her husband's stance. Her father also took Hugh's abolitionist arguments to heart by voluntarily freeing his slaves and paying them wages for their labor.[24]

It was easier for Hugh to discuss such matters with Ellen; after all, politics had been the Ewing family business for forty years. After hearing Hugh's stories of guerrilla atrocities and, being simultaneously proud of Cump's military performance—while fearful that she would lose him—Ellen became militant. Ellen informed Cump in the spring of 1862 that when she learned of southern complaints about Union soldiers assisting runaway slaves:

> I think too it is a gross outrage to prevent the Negroes in their efforts to escape. The rebels—inhuman blood thirsty wretches who have brought all this suffering upon us, their women as well as their men—ought not to be protected in their property, especially that property which enables them to keep up the means of carrying on this warfare. They have been treated every where with too much kindness, their bushwhackers, wire cutters and bridge burners, when among pretended peaceful citizens ought to be shot without preliminaries of the law. I, for one, shall be sorry to see the South received into the Union again until her slaves are free and she is humbled in that which has led to her pride and wickedness. Miserable people. I feel no compassion for them.[25]

Ellen and Hugh also shared, along with their father, grave reservations about Union commander George McClellan. By the spring of 1862 Thomas Ewing believed that McClellan was a Confederate sympathizer. Ellen concurred, informing Hugh and Cump that McClellan was a member of the subversive Knights of the Golden Circle. Indeed, Ellen asserted, McClellan was "sworn to Jeff Davis without a doubt." The senior Ewing did not hesitate to lecture Lincoln on McClellan's defects—whether the president was inclined to listen or not.[26]

Hugh did not believe McClellan was a rebel sympathizer, being more inclined to view him merely as "a jackass." In correspondence with friends, Hugh speculated on why Lincoln had drawn so many military incompetents to him in Washington: "I forgive Abraham for this reason—military men, like the medical 'licensed assassin,' blacken each other with such malignity and their political friends whiten them with such devotion, that Father Abraham cannot penetrate the double cloud and distinguish the true from the false. A man's military friends tell him that the black hole is too good for him and his political friends represent him as a touch about Julius [Caesar]—one to whom Frederick [the Great] was a fool—and the Iron Duke [Wellington] a dummy—in short a 'Small Corporal [Napoleon].'"[27]

A deep sense of foreboding had taken hold of the Ewing family after the Pittsburg Landing bloodbath. McClellan's failed "Peninsula Campaign" between June 25 and July 1 outside Richmond, followed by John Pope's spectacular defeat at the "Second Manassas" in late August, further darkened the Ewings' mood. Hugh confessed to Henrietta, "I fully hoped and believed until lately that this summer would end the war: but I now will cease fixing a time for that hoped for event and our own meeting." Grimly, Cump asked Ellen to pass along a proposition to Hugh: "If he [Cump] should be killed he wants you to take care of his children and if you killed he will take care of yours."[28]

To the surprise of her children, Maria Ewing, who had stoically borne the loss of a child so many years ago, appeared to be faltering. She sought refuge in her bed, citing exhaustion, chills, and jangled nerves. Maria expressed trepidation when her youngest child, Maria Theresa, began a serious courtship with Clemens Steele, a onetime California gold prospector who had become lieutenant colonel of the Sixty-Second Ohio. The thought of another daughter possibly becoming a widow weighed heavily on Maria. Her patriotism did not slacken, but the price of maintaining the Union had risen sharply over the past year.[29]

Their increasingly emotional mother, Ellen confided to Hugh, cherished his letters, which she read and reread in her bedroom. Maria wrote Hugh as often as her strength would allow. "We must put our trust in God," Maria exhorted her son, "and in the intervention of the Blessed Virgin who has all power with her divine Son!" Faith notwithstanding, Maria confessed to Hugh that she was grateful that he and Charley had not yet experienced major combat: "Had [Charley] been in the battle of Shiloh, where he was most eager to be, and you, in that terrible slaughter before Richmond [Peninsula

Campaign], you might both be numbered among the dead! God in his mercy take care of you! May we strive, to deserve his holy protection throughout the dangers of this terrible war."[30]

Although Maria Ewing was grateful that her youngest son had seen less action than Hugh, Charley felt depressed. After Cump had left the Thirteenth U.S. Infantry to join the Army of the Potomac in 1861, Charley and his regiment had become prison guards. In December 1861, General Halleck had taken over the Illinois State Penitentiary in Alton. The newly renamed Alton Federal Military Prison officially opened for business on February 9, 1862. There was little in the way of amenities for either guards or Confederate prisoners, Halleck having spent less than $3,000 to upgrade the decrepit facility. Alton soon became a breeding ground for dysentery and smallpox, which ultimately killed hundreds of guards and prisoners.

Charley, who was not one to correspond beyond a few terse sentences, still managed to convey dismay over his assignment. Being killed heroically in combat was one thing; dying as a prison guard from dysentery was another. He wrote Cump in February, reminding him that his former regiment continued to exist. Charley also informed his father that the Thirteenth U.S. seemed destined to deteriorate in "discipline, drill, and efficiency." Ellen reassured her brother that he would have "many chances of distinction and honorable action." Before that could happen, however, Charley had "to put your pride in your pocket" and plead with Halleck to send his regiment into the field.[31]

Ellen made it her mission to boost Charley's morale, writing him lengthy letters and visiting him prior to touring one of Cousin Eliza Gillespie's hospitals near Memphis. If nothing else, Ellen pointed out to Charley, his assignment to Alton and fine behavior demonstrated that he had earned his rank; no one could charge that Thomas Ewing had done his youngest son any favors. To Charley's credit, Ellen wrote, "You are ready to offer your life a willing sacrifice to your country, you have proved yourself a soldier of discipline, and no one will ever doubt your bravery." Finally, no matter how much he despaired, "Let nothing on earth induce you to resign" your commission. If Charley resigned from the army, Ellen fretted, then "it would be a disgrace" to himself and his family.[32]

She met with Halleck in St. Louis to discuss the plight of the Thirteenth U.S. and persistently prodded Cump to rescue Charley from Alton, observing, "He must come from that vile pestilential prison and you must get him away quickly." Her father exerted what influence he could muster in the War Department. Thomas Ewing, however, had few promising contacts remaining there, having spent so much political capital in salvaging Cump's fortunes. Ellen insisted that the family would "not leave a stone unturned" to help Charley. Senator Sherman was also willing to help, but, as Ellen informed Charley, his relations with the Lincoln administration had grown so chilly that he was "ice and hail to anything that comes near him."[33]

While Charley chafed in Alton and Hugh hunted Virginian guerrillas, their brother Tom had been dividing his time between Kansas and Washington—attending to Kansas Supreme Court affairs and lobbying Congress to appropriate funds for railroad development. In an effort to win the support of abolitionist congressmen, Tom pointed out that slaves who escaped the South could be employed building a transcontinental railroad. Since Tom had joined Senator Jim Lane in the White House to guard Lincoln in the spring of 1861, the war in the Kansas-Missouri theater had gone through many tortuous turns.[34]

In the aftermath of the violent clash between Unionist troops and civilians in the streets of St. Louis on May 10, 1861, a short and uneasy truce held between Congressman Frank Blair and Missouri governor Claiborne Jackson. On June 11, Jackson and his brother-in-law, Sterling Price, held a bitter four-hour meeting with Blair and the newly minted General Nathaniel Lyon. His anger at the boiling point, Lyon vented to Jackson: "Better, sir, far better, that the blood of every man, woman, and child within the limits of the state should flow, than that she should defy the federal government. This means war."[35]

Although Governor Jackson exhorted Missouri volunteers to take swift action against the Unionists, it was Lyon who delivered the first blow by capturing the state capital of Jefferson City on June 15 and driving out its secessionist legislators. In flight, Jackson and former senator David Atchison went to Richmond to pledge their allegiance to Jefferson Davis. They then linked up in Tennessee with Confederate general Leonidas Polk, hoping he would coordinate a military offensive with Price.[36]

Lyon's victories came to an end on August 10. At Wilson's Creek, near Springfield, Lyon's five thousand troops suffered a shattering defeat at the hands of Price's ten thousand soldiers. The badly outnumbered Union forces suffered a 25 percent casualty rate—nearly twice that of the rebels. Lyon had the dubious distinction of being the first Union general killed in the Civil War. Prior to his death, he had proclaimed his willingness to be martyred for the abolitionist cause.[37]

The Confederates' victory at Wilson's Creek did not turn around their military situation in Missouri. Union forces regrouped. The new commander of the Department of the West, John Fremont, placed sufficient troops in the field to intimidate Price. Fremont, however, failed to pursue the

Confederates. He also sowed ill will among politically neutral whites when he issued an order freeing any slaves held by disloyal residents. The Blairs, who had embraced Fremont, turned on him. After Congressman Blair criticized Fremont in the press, the Union commander placed him under arrest. Unwilling to bear the wrath of the Blairs, Lincoln reversed Fremont's order and sent him to western Virginia. Thomas and Hugh Ewing were appalled with the transfer, regarding Fremont as militarily and politically inept.[38]

Before his death, Lyon had succeeded in disrupting the rebels' recruitment operations. Given his inability to recruit and train larger numbers of troops, Price believed there was no other option but to wage irregular warfare. He reorganized many of his soldiers into guerrilla bands, just as their western Virginian counterparts had done. Missouri outside the Union bastion of St. Louis provided numerous, highly vulnerable targets: railroad bridges, slow-moving Missouri River traffic, and, of course, Unionist civilians. Price all but baited his guerrillas to engage in a slaughter of the innocents, asking them if they were real men or "a timid, time-serving, craven race, fit only for subjection to a despot." From St. Louis, Halleck, who had replaced Fremont, initially argued that the war in the Missouri-Kansas theater was over.[39]

Cump had, without success, warned Halleck that the Missouri guerrillas posed both a military and political threat to Union interests. Thomas Ewing, driven by the reports Hugh had given him about guerrilla war in Virginia, as well as by a concern for the family's St. Louis properties, prodded Halleck to take more vigorous action in late 1861. Ewing was profoundly angered by the tactics of the Missouri guerrillas, which included weakening the supports of wooden railroad bridges. Unsuspecting trains would get halfway across a ravine before the bridge collapsed, sending scores of troops and civilians plunging to their deaths.[40]

Ewing exhorted Halleck to hang Missouri guerrillas who engaged in "the promiscuous massacre" of Unionist civilians. As for Missouri secessionists who fed, armed, or provided military intelligence to guerrillas, Ewing continued, they should be tried before a military court-martial and face the possibility of execution. Responding to the rising chorus of outrage against the bushwhackers, Halleck assured Ewing in January 1862 that he would "put down these insurgents and bridge-burners with a strong hand."[41]

Halleck was true to his word, at least on this score. He told his subordinates "that insurgents and marauders, predatory and guerilla bands," were not recognized "by the laws of war" as combatants. Confederate soldiers, though serving a treasonous cause, were still uniformed and operated under a military code of conduct; they could not be executed for betraying their country. Missouri guerrillas, however, should be court-martialed or sent

Jesse James (1847–82). A Confederate guerrilla and son of a Missouri planter and politician, Jesse James joined an insurgency that burned, raped, and plundered the Kansas borderlands during the Civil War. A number of these guerrillas, including Jesse's brother Frank James, and Cole Younger, continued to commit atrocities and banditry after the end of the war. (Courtesy of the Library of Congress.)

before a tribunal. Such tribunals, whether civilian or military, would investigate and punish guerrillas. Unlike normal court trials, these would leave no room for defendants to cite mitigating circumstances or claim self-defense. Under Halleck's formulation, the question for guerrilla leaders would not be if they were to be executed, but how quickly they would swing from a rope.[42]

The pillage and murder that had taken place along the Missouri-Kansas border since 1854 grew worse in 1861 and 1862. Senator Lane and his followers, whether called "Jayhawkers" or "Red Legs"—the latter name acquired by virtue of the red leggings worn over their boots—were now federally sanctioned killers. Lane, who received a general's commission at Lincoln's behest, organized the Third and Fourth Kansas Infantry, as well the Fifth Kansas Cavalry, in 1861. In his campaign against Price, Lane avoided Confederate troops and instead hit the Missouri civilians who had purportedly aided the rebels. In September 1861, Lane sacked the Missouri town of Osceola, which had served as one of Price's encampments. His troops executed nine reputed secessionists, burned the town, and carried off two hundred slaves—a number of whom subsequently joined Lane's regiments.[43]

Lane had pledged in October 1861 that "confiscation of slaves and other property which can be made useful to the Army should follow treason as the thunder peal follows the lightening flash." Going well beyond what Fremont had attempted to do in Missouri, Lane's Seventh Kansas Cavalry recruited black troopers. Lane ignored federal policy that barred enlistment of black soldiers. Outraged, many Missouri whites denounced the Jayhawkers and their "contraband niggers." Undeterred, Charles Jennison, the commander of the Seventh Kansas, paraded his interracial horse soldiers through the restive streets of Kansas City, Missouri.[44]

Secessionists charged that Jennison's souvenir-seeking troops sliced off the ears of Missouri planters. Whether or not these lurid allegations were true, the Seventh Kansas had no shortage of soldiers seeking to settle scores in Missouri. A teenaged Bill Cody, for instance, enlisted in the Seventh Kansas to avenge his father's death—as did a son of John Brown. In their wake, Jennison's cavalry left torched buildings and broken pianos, which, proving too heavy for the Seventh Kansas to lug back to Lawrence, were abandoned on the roadside.[45]

Apologists for the Missouri guerrillas asserted—during the war and thereafter—that the men who earned the greatest notoriety as butchers had taken their course because of Jayhawker brutality. Cole Younger, the son of a prominent Jackson County (western Missouri) slave owner, claimed that he had left Price's regulars to avenge the Jayhawker murder of his father. Frank James, who had also served with Price, similarly claimed that the Jayhawkers had executed his defenseless father. Of course, the fact that Younger and James had taken up arms against the Union *before* their fathers were killed by Lane's soldiers suggested that they were hardly pacifists. They also had the option of going to Arkansas and enlisting with regular Confederate forces, rather than killing unarmed civilians and dragging blacks who had taken refuge in Kansas back into slavery.[46]

Tom Ewing detested Jennison and Lane, convinced that their conduct harmed the Union cause in the West. Lincoln was not blameless either. The president had contributed to the lawlessness of the Kansas-Missouri border, first by making Lane a general and second by running all military appointments through him rather than the governor. In the Old Northwest and the East, state military commissions typically went out from the governor's office, rather than through a U.S. senator. Lane, not surprisingly, had recruited officers in his own image. Tom found a solution that he shared with his brother Phil. As chief justice of the Kansas Supreme Court, Tom was in a position to rule on the constitutionality of a senator simultaneously serving as a field general. Tom knew that if Lane was presented the choice of either retaining his patronage power and easy access to Lincoln in Washington or continuing to torch Missouri towns, he would return to the Senate.[47]

By the late summer of 1862, with Congress agreeing to subsidize railroad development in the West—and with Lane back in the Senate—Tom felt it was an opportune time to resign as chief justice and enlist. He became colonel of the Eleventh Kansas Infantry. Edmund Ross, another Ohio transplant to Kansas, joined the Eleventh Kansas as a captain of Company E. Ross and Tom were soon fast friends, both sharing an interest in politics and railroad construction. Tom's friend Preston Plumb, who had stood with him against the Missouri Border Ruffians a few years earlier, received a commission as a major. A number of officers and enlisted men from other Kansas regiments, wishing to escape the odium of being associated with the Jayhawkers, transferred to the Eleventh Kansas. Tom's regiment became a place of exile for Lane's enemies.[48]

Even while Tom prepared to go on a fall offensive against Confederate forces in the West, Lee assumed the initiative in the East. His victory against Pope at the Second Manassas convinced Lee that the North was demoralized and on the verge of political collapse. A decisive battle closely following on the heels of Pope's defeat—and just prior to the congressional midterm elections—might compel Lincoln to seek peace. To Lee, there was no question that his final great victory would take place in Maryland or perhaps even Pennsylvania. In some ways his decision made sense. Lee wanted to take the war out of Confederate territory and show the Yankees that their soil could be invaded as well. He also believed that the tens of thousands of Confederate loyalists in Maryland would rally to his banner, compelling the state to switch sides.[49]

Of course, there were other military considerations that led Lee to his course of action in September 1862. The Army of Northern Virginia had "eaten out" the countryside; Lee needed to find food for his fifty-five thousand men. Not only did his army suffer from hunger, but many of his troops possessed shoes, uniforms, and weapons only because they had captured these items from Union soldiers at the Manassas battlefield. In sum, an emaciated Confederate Army decided to advance far from its base—hoping that bravery would overcome its lack of logistical support. Then again, the dysfunction of the Army of the Potomac, which had yet to win a single battle, evened the odds.[50]

The opening of Lee's operations in August 1862 found Hugh suffering severe discomfort from chronic dysentery and writing to Henrietta, "I am extremely tired of this wretched country—and in bad health and worse spirits." Ordered to depart for Washington, the Kanawha Division went into motion. In three days Hugh and the Thirtieth Ohio made a one-hundred-mile march to Camp Piatt on the Kanawha River twelve miles below Charleston. They then took steamboats to Parkersburg on the Ohio River, arriving at their destination on August 20. The division would have made the trip more quickly, Cox lamented, but for its boats dragging bottom at several places because of seasonally low water. From Parkersburg, Hugh received orders to load the division's regiments on whatever Baltimore & Ohio trains were available. The first elements of the Kanawha Division rolled into Washington three days later to help defend the city.[51]

Her brother's redeployment to the Army of the Potomac put Ellen on edge. She wrote Cump that Hugh "was on the move—we feel uneasy about him. His regiment is in splendid order. I would rather have him killed than taken prisoner." At the end of August, hearing rumors that the Kanawha Division had engaged Lee at Manassas, Ellen poured out her fear and anger to Cump:

> It is said that Cox's Division has been cut up by the rebels and forced to retire. . . . I trust in God that they are safe but think of the poor fellows who went on but ten days ago full of hope and ardor to offer their lives for their country being slaughtered by base and diabolical rebels. I hope this may be not only a war of emancipation but of extermination and that all under the influence of the foul fiend may be driven like the Swine into the Sea. May we carry fire and sword into their states till not one habitation is left standing.

My boys shall go when strong enough to carry a musket—would they were all boys to offer their lives in exterminating and punishing foul treason.[52]

Ellen Sherman was hardly alone in listening to the rumor mill. Plenty of soldiers, journalists, and politicians in Washington were equally susceptible—though many lacked her resolve to carry on regardless of setbacks. According to McClellan, when he met Lincoln on September 2, the president was depressed and feared Washington would fall. McClellan also believed that Lincoln would execute him as a traitor if he did not stop Lee. Navy Secretary Gideon Welles confided in his diary, "The army is, I fear, much demoralized, and its demoralization is much of it to be attributed to the officers whose highest duty it is to prevent it."[53]

Cox's division encamped in Alexandria, Virginia, with two infantry brigades, as well as two light batteries and two cavalry companies. The First Brigade, commanded by the irascible Eliakim Scammon, included the Twelfth, Twenty-Third, and Thirtieth Ohio. Second Brigade, led by the imperious Augustus Moor, had the Eleventh, Twenty-Eighth, and Thirty-Sixth Ohio. Having largely operated independently since the outbreak of the war, the Kanawha Division became part of the Army of the Potomac's Ninth Corps. The overall commander of Ninth and First Corps was none other than Hugh's West Point nemesis, Ambrose "Bully" Burnside. It was a harbinger of worse things to come for the Kanawha Division.[54]

Hugh's reunion with Henrietta was more abbreviated than he had anticipated. Burnside's designated leader of Ninth Corps, General Jesse Reno, was determined that the Kanawha Division would assimilate the spit-and-polish culture of the Army of the Potomac. If the Army of the Potomac could not win a battle, at least it looked good on the parade ground—and that was more than enough for Jesse Reno, West Point class of 1846. In contrast, the Kanawha Division, having spent a year in the wilds of western Virginia, appeared primitive. When troops from the Thirtieth Ohio used some bagged sheaf oats from a farmer's barn for bedding, a cursing Reno made an entrance. He accused Hugh's men of being vandals and threatened to shoot them as thieves.[55]

It was no time at all before Hugh heard about the incident. Fuming, he found Reno in Washington and laid into him. (Whether Hugh and Reno had clashed years earlier at West Point was not clear.) Hugh, ignoring Reno's superior rank, demanded that he apologize to his men. Reno bristled, snidely replying, "I suppose you think your troops are better than those of the East." Hugh replied, "No, but they are good, and to keep them so, I must protect and care for them." Miffed, Reno informed Hugh that if he thought the

Thirtieth Ohio was so good, then his regiment would take point when Ninth Corps left Washington to find Lee.[56]

On September 4, the Confederates crossed the Potomac River at Leesburg, Virginia, forty miles northwest of Washington. Unionists informed a *Harper's Weekly* reporter that "the rebels are wretchedly clad, and generally destitute of shoes. The cavalry men are mostly barefooted, and the feet of the infantry are bound up in rags and pieces of rawhide." When Lee's men arrived in Frederick, Maryland, they had anticipated a heroes' welcome. Instead, the rebels received mostly silence, with the exception of a few citizens who speculated on how much vermin Lee's men carried underneath their filth. Most people in western Maryland raised wheat on their family farms; the state's slave-owning tobacco planters largely lived on the Eastern Shore. Lee had stumbled among a hostile population that would report his every move to the Union forces.[57]

The Kanawha Division and Ninth Corps marched through Georgetown on September 6, headed westward toward Lee. Cox saw, to his shock, how slowly the Army of the Potomac moved. His division, hardened by constant movements through mountainous terrain and knowing that slow-moving targets tempted guerrilla sniper fire, "had not *learned* to straggle." He could see no reason why the rest of McClellan's command could not keep up with his troops as they crossed the relatively flat "park-like landscape with alternations of groves and meadows which could not have been more beautifully composed by a master artist."[58]

Hayes was equally unimpressed with the eastern troops, confiding to his diary that "'the Grand Army of the Potomac' appeared to bad advantage by the side of our troops. Men were lost from their regiments; officers left their commands to rest in the shade, to feed on fruit; thousands were straggling—confusion and disorder everywhere." If Hayes thought the Twenty-Third Ohio would receive any credit for its stamina and good order, General Reno soon disabused him of that notion. As he had done with Hugh, Reno swooped down on Hayes, cursing the Twenty-Third Ohio: "You damned black sons of bitches!" (A native of Wheeling, Reno believed that calling someone black was the worst possible insult.) Hayes's troops had committed the unpardonable offense of resting on stacks of wheat just off the Leesboro Road. This, Reno roared, was an act of vandalism.[59]

Appalled by Reno's vicious outburst, Hayes defended his soldiers' conduct. He then rebuked Reno and concluded with a jab: "Well, I trust our generals will exhibit the same energy in dealing with our foes that they do in the treatment of their friends!" Reno rode off seething as Hayes's men cheered their colonel. An irate Reno then unloaded his bile on Hugh. Reno threatened to

The Battle of South Mountain, 1862. The Kanawha Division attacked Confederate positions, with Colonel Rutherford B. Hayes's Twenty-Third Ohio and Colonel Hugh Ewing's Thirtieth Ohio in the thick of the battle. (Courtesy of the Library of Congress.)

arrest all the colonels of the Kanawha Division as looters. At first, Hugh was, so he told Hayes, "cut to the quick" and angry with the Twenty-Third Ohio. From his own experiences, Hugh knew that Hayes's men required a firm hand. Hugh, however, quickly concluded that the Twenty-Third Ohio was blameless in this instance.[60]

Cox soon heard about Reno's verbal assault on Hayes—as did most of Ninth Corps. He vowed to obtain a transfer for the Kanawha Division to another corps, since, Hayes recounted, "General Reno has given such offense to the Ohio troops that they will serve under him with reluctance." Adding insult to injury, rumors circulated that the Kanawha Division was, so Cox fumed, "disposed to plunder and pillage." Cox observed that these slanders originated with eastern regiments. Most of the eastern soldiers, Cox contended, were straggling so far behind the Kanawha Division that they might as well not even have bothered to have left Washington. Massachusetts and New York troops, therefore, could not have witnessed the allegedly destructive path of Cox's Ohioans through Maryland.[61]

On September 12 the Kanawha Division skirmished outside Frederick with General Wade Hampton's cavalry brigade. To Cox's dismay, while the rest of Ninth Corps was nowhere to be found, one of Reno's junior staff offi-cers showed up and began issuing commands. After ascertaining that the young officer had no actual orders from Burnside, Cox told him to get lost. Undeterred, Reno's staffer found Colonel Moor and resumed giving military instructions. Moor, thinking the orders came from Cox, went to scout the position that Reno's staff officer was directing him toward. Within a matter of minutes, forty of Hampton's troopers took Moor prisoner. The less experi-enced George Crook had to assume command of the Second Brigade. Moor subsequently received a "parole" but had to pledge not to rejoin the fight.[62]

Driving Hampton's brigade out of Frederick eliminated a key Confederate chokepoint on the National Road. Lee now found himself confronting three interrelated problems. First, there were few strong positions from which to block the Union troops until the South Mountain range fourteen miles to the northwest of Frederick. That meant the quick-marching Kanawha Divi-sion would be on top of him in no time. Second—and the reason Lee did not want to see Cox any sooner than necessary—his troops were widely dis-persed. The narrow roads and mountainous terrain had compelled Lee to move his fifty-five thousand troops along different routes, anticipating that he would have plenty of time to regroup. He had even diverted troops to cap-ture the Union garrison at Harper's Ferry. Third, on September 13 a Union patrol discovered a copy of Lee's orders that had been carelessly discarded. Those orders revealed to McClellan that the Army of Northern Virginia was scattered and therefore highly vulnerable. Lee soon learned that McClellan had read his orders.[63]

South Mountain, whose crests loomed nearly 1,300 feet above the Union forces, possessed a few critical passages—notably Fox's Gap and Turner's Gap. The steeply ascending Sharpsburg Road crossed the former and the gentler rising National Road the latter. General D. H. Hill had to hold both passages against Union forces. The Kanawha Division brushed aside a small Confederate detachment at Middletown on September 13. Early the next day, with Hugh and the Thirtieth Ohio in the vanguard, Cox's soldiers reached the base of South Mountain and entered Fox's Gap. Artillery from the heights rained down on the Union infantry. For the next several hours the Kanawha Division, outnumbered two to one, was on its own.[64]

Fixing bayonets, the First Brigade charged into Confederate artillery and infantry, with the Twenty-Third Ohio on the left flank, the Twelfth Ohio in the center, and the Thirtieth Ohio on the right flank. Lacking cover as they crossed an open field, Hugh's regiment went straight into the woods and toward concealed rebel cannon. Colonel Carr White's Twelfth Ohio also swept over an open field, making easy targets for the Confederate infantry shielded behind a stone wall. Despite their superior cover, the Thirteenth North Carolina failed to hold off the Twelfth Ohio. During the next few hours the Twelfth Ohio, taking cover behind that very same stone wall, fought off repeated attacks and endured constant shelling. Carr's men were so exhausted that only one soldier moved out of the way when a rattlesnake slithered across the crouching infantry.[65]

Meanwhile, Hayes and the Twenty-Third Ohio pushed up a tree-covered slope toward the Fifth North Carolina. Coming under heavy fire that one soldier said "pattered about us like raindrops on the leaves," Hayes rallied his troops with a full-throated charge: "Give them Hell! Give the sons of bitches Hell!" He took a musket ball in his left arm, shattering bone and causing him to bleed so badly that he went in and out of consciousness. At first, Hayes refused to relinquish command, but he finally collapsed. One of the Twenty-Third Ohio's lieutenants dragged him out of the line of fire.[66]

The Thirtieth Ohio took its objective and then held it against numerous counterattacks. So much gunsmoke filled the air that Hugh had to order his men to cease firing on three occasions so that they could better see their targets. Each firing pause revealed more and more Confederates, dead, dying, or wishing they were dead, immediately to the front of Hugh's regiment. The Thirtieth Ohio stood its ground, expending nearly all its ammunition and losing twenty-one killed and sixty-five wounded. For the past year, many of his men had complained about Hugh's constant drilling. Now, as they faced their first serious combat, they finally understood that if their discipline faltered the rebels would shoot and bayonet them piecemeal.[67]

Hugh subsequently reported that "the officers and men, under an unceasing fire of eight hours of musketry, grape, and shell, obeyed all orders with alacrity, intelligence, and skill, and stood at the close under an excessive fire of musketry and grape with a hardihood which elicited the applause of all who saw them." Major Hildt gleefully wrote to his parents that the Confederate prisoners the Thirtieth Ohio took "report that they knew after our first fire that we were not eastern troops, and were either damned Irish or western men." On a more somber note, Hildt observed that both of the regiment's color, or flag, bearers were killed. There were so many Confederate dead in front of the Thirtieth Ohio that there was no open space between the bodies. "I do not," Hildt continued, "wish to get into as warm a place again."[68]

Even with Colonel Crook's Second Brigade joining the fight, the Kanawha Division lacked adequate numbers of heavy guns and troops. Instead, officers relied on good shooting and discipline, as well as the psychological terror inflicted on the Confederates when bayonets drew dangerously near while the rebels attempted to reload their single-shot muskets.

As the day progressed, D. H. Hill's five brigades were joined by troops from James Longstreet's and John Bell Hood's commands. The Confederates fought ferociously and used numerous ruses, even waving white flags of surrender. When the Ohio troops ceased firing and went to take the Confederates prisoner, the southerners opened fire. Because of such deception, many regiments followed the example long set by the Twenty-Third Ohio—refusing to take prisoners and executing the Confederate wounded.[69]

Appreciating how tenuous his position was, Cox had, since 7:30 a.m., been sending messages to Reno asking for assistance. He had not gone into Fox's Gap without first receiving assurance from Reno that the Kanawha Division "would be supported by the whole corps." Reno, however, who was six miles away in Middletown, only moved Ninth Corps toward Fox's Gap at 1 p.m. The bulk of Ninth Corps was not engaged in the fight until 4 p.m. General Joe Hooker, whom Burnside had delegated to lead First Corps, did not appear at Turner's Gap and relieve pressure on Cox's men until 1:30 p.m. To Cox's great disgust, Hooker boasted that the Kanawha Division had been defeated; only First Corps had saved the day at South Mountain. The *New York Times*'s correspondent hailed Hooker. Ironically, Longstreet was less biased than the *New York Times;* he praised the Kanawha Division and marveled at how slowly the bulk of the Army of the Potomac deployed.[70]

The Kanawha Division lost 106 troops, with another 336 wounded and 86 missing and presumed dead. Thirty-four percent of the Union casualties at South Mountain came from Cox's division, even though they accounted for less than 17 percent of the federal soldiers engaged. Hayes had lost a great deal of blood, and no one could be sure he would survive. The dazed troops of the Thirtieth Ohio walked silently over the battleground. Hugh recounted the ironic sight they came across: "We found an officer of a South Carolina regiment in a breast plate of hardened steel, thick and heavy, after the fashion of old, fitting close up to the neck and under the armpits, and reaching to the waist, with a bullet through his forehead."[71]

With the Confederates in retreat, Reno arrived at Fox's Gap toward sunset to claim his victory. Reno, however, did not have time to savor his triumph— he was shot dead in the saddle. *Harper's Weekly* hailed Reno as "the bravest of the brave," struck down by a Confederate sharpshooter. Cox, Hayes, and Hugh endorsed that version of Reno's death. There was, though, another version that did not receive much press. In this account, jittery troops from the Thirty-Fifth Massachusetts (Ninth Corps) mistook Reno for a Confederate cavalry troop and fired blindly. Still a third version—which circulated more widely than the second scenario—had the irate men of the Kanawha Division settling scores with Reno. The *New York Times* kept this last version alive for years. Perhaps such speculation was inevitable given that the Kanawha Division included two future presidents, a man who became a powerful Ohio governor, and the son of Thomas Ewing.[72]

With the rebel forces driven from the South Mountain passes, Lee, who was just eleven miles away in Sharpsburg, seemed on the verge of being annihilated. He had lost two thousand men—over 3 percent of his army—at South Mountain. All McClellan had to do was strike before Lee could bring his army together. He chose not to advance. Part of the reason McClellan hesitated had to do with Washington politics. In July 1862 Lincoln had promoted Halleck to "general-in-chief" as a reward for the victories he claimed at Forts Donelson and Henry, as well as Pittsburg Landing and Corinth, Mississippi. (His greatest victory had been in stealing credit from Grant and Cump.) Halleck was convinced that Lee intended to attack Washington. Lee's movements in western Maryland, therefore, were merely a diversion from his true objective. Given the constant barrage of nay-saying and second-guessing coming from Halleck, McClellan's cautious nature came to the fore.[73]

McClellan made matters worse for his army. He thought that Lee had as many as 120,000 troops when in fact he had less than half that number. Further, McClellan believed that the Army of the Potomac was exhausted from the fighting at South Mountain and required a respite. Certainly the Kanawha Division and a few regiments in First and Ninth Corps were near the limits of their endurance, but there were four corps that had not fought at South Mountain. They could have hit Sharpsburg before General Thomas "Stonewall" Jackson left Harper's Ferry to link up with Lee. If McClellan had advanced on September 15 he might have decimated Lee's twenty-five thousand soldiers.[74]

While McClellan hesitated, the 11,500 Union soldiers at Harper's Ferry surrendered on September 15, allowing the Army of Northern Virginia to capture seventy-three cannon, thirteen thousand guns, and two hundred wagons. Compared to the carnage of South Mountain, Jackson claimed just two hundred killed or wounded. The Union capitulation also freed Jackson's eleven thousand troops to reunite with Lee. The next day, September 16, McClellan still did not launch a full-out attack, giving more time for General A. P. Hill's soldiers to prepare for their departure from Harper's Ferry. Finally, on September 17, McClellan was ready for battle. Unfortunately for the Army of the Potomac, Lee had secured good ground opposite of Antietam Creek.[75]

To make matters worse for the Army of the Potomac, McClellan did not have firm control of his troops. Union losses at South Mountain had forced a reorganization of Ninth Corps. Burnside and Hooker despised each other, and the latter was not about to take orders from the former. Miffed, Burnside directed Ninth Corps haphazardly. Cox, who had moved into Reno's job, did not believe he had real authority to lead Ninth Corps and kept waiting for Burnside to show some creative thinking. (Hugh could have told him how unlikely a development that would have been.) Scammon became commander of the Kanawha Division—which would not have been such a bad assignment if McClellan had replenished their ammunition and food supplies after the South Mountain engagement. Hugh took over First Brigade, giving him combat responsibility for three infantry regiments rather than just one. As for the Twenty-Third Ohio, its men were at their breaking point.[76]

Not only did McClellan hold back twenty thousand troops from the battle, but he failed to coordinate attacks along his right, center, and left. Consequently, Lee had little difficulty in shifting troops to reinforce his defenses. McClellan advanced with his right, initially leaving his center and left idle. While Joe Hooker was vain and notoriously indiscreet—he allegedly lent his name to an illicit profession—no one could fault his courage. Mounted, and thus clearly visible to Confederate snipers, Hooker led First Corps into an engagement that would thereafter be known as "the Cornfield." Jackson's brigades tore into First Corps, but not without a cost: 82 percent of the troops in the First Texas were killed or wounded in the span of forty-five minutes. First Corps withdrew, leaving Twelfth Corps to take a bullet-harvested cornfield.[77]

The center of the Confederate line came under Union attack after the struggle for "the Cornfield" had commenced. Second Corps's brigades advanced against rebel troops that were sheltered behind a wooden fence situated alongside a below-grade roadbed. The protection afforded to the Confederates by the fence and embankment above "Bloody Lane" turned the ground to their front into a kill zone. Three hundred soldiers in the First Delaware (Second Corps) alone fell to cannon and gun shot. In spite of the Confederates' seemingly strong defensive position, Union troops inflicted casualty rates of up to 50 percent on a number of rebel regiments at "Bloody Lane." However, as had been true of "the Cornfield," McClellan failed to translate ground possession into battlefield victory.[78]

McClellan twice issued orders for Burnside to launch the Union left. For some reason those instructions did not reach Cox until 9 a.m., two hours after McClellan had sent his first order to attack. On the basis of their cursory survey of the terrain, Union engineers insisted that Antietam Creek was too deep to cross. Ninth Corps would have to use the Rohrbach Bridge, an arched and very long, but also narrow, stone structure. Since the Confederates occupied the heights on the western bank, they could blanket the bridge with little fear of accurate return fire. When the first attack failed at 10 a.m., Burnside sent more troops—expecting that the same effort would achieve a different result. The slaughter that befell Ninth Corps made the newly christened "Burnside Bridge" into *the* symbol of the Antietam battlefield. On the third attempt elements of Ninth Corps successfully crossed and gained the opposing heights.[79]

The officers and enlisted men of the Kanawha Division were appalled by the carnage inflicted upon Ninth Corps. For hours the First and Second Brigades held their positions below Burnside Bridge, listening helplessly to the screams of dying men as Kanawha Division came under merciless artillery fire. It simply did not make sense that there were no other possible crossings. Antietam Creek was no more imposing than Lancaster's Hocking River— a body of water that, in places, became a ditch in the dry months of late summer.

Hugh watched in horror as sixteen of his wounded troops, taken to a makeshift hospital on the line, were ripped to pieces by Confederate grapeshot. The Kanawha Division grew weary of taking fire and began aggressively probing the creek to locate shallow crossing points. The First and Second Brigades forced a crossing at 1 p.m. A few of the shorter men in the Eleventh Ohio (Second Brigade) had to be boosted above the water, but at least they did not drown. Lieutenant Colonel Augustus Coleman, commander of the Eleventh Ohio, however, had less luck. He fell mortally wounded. Hugh led the First Brigade across Antietam Creek in the face of what he described as "a shower of grape" and "trying fire." Two of his staff officers from the Thirtieth Ohio died from multiple hits, as did two of that regiment's color-bearers. Lieutenant Colonel Jonathan Hines, Twelfth Ohio (Second Brigade), also died.[80]

The Kanawha Division stood poised to prevent Lee from retreating along Boteler's Ford Road and escaping across the Potomac River. There was, though, a problem for Colonels Ewing and Crook. McClellan had never made up his mind as to whether Ninth Corps's attack was more than a diversion to cover Hooker's initial assault. Consequently, he had not resupplied the Kanawha Division. Its six infantry regiments, which could have advanced on Sharpsburg at 1 p.m., had little ammunition. To compound the division's problems, the Twenty-Third Ohio had reached a collective state of psychological collapse. Its men stared blankly into space, unable to move forward or backward. Sergeant William McKinley, braving Confederate cannon fire that homed in on him, delivered hot coffee to his shattered regiment. McKinley's initiative brought at least a few companies of the Twenty-Third Ohio back to their unpleasant reality.[81]

Two hours after their successful crossing of Antietam Creek, the Kanawha Division and other elements of Ninth Corps had received sufficient ammunition to continue their advance toward Sharpsburg. Confederate forces gave way, and by 4 p.m. it seemed as if Lee's troops were trapped in Sharpsburg. But then, as if the Kanawha Division were acting out scenes from the *Aeneid*, the fortunes of war shifted capriciously. A. P. Hill's brigades arrived from Harper's Ferry and sent the Ninth New York and the Sixteenth Connecticut to flight. One member of the Ninth New York defensively observed afterward that "when bullets are whacking against tree trunks and solid shot are cracking skulls like eggshells, the consuming passion in the breast of the average man is to get out of the way."[82]

The Sixteenth Connecticut ran through the lines of Hugh's disgusted First Brigade. When more blue-uniformed troops moved quickly toward First and Second Brigades, Ewing and Crook had their regiments hold their fire, even if some of the Ohio troops were sorely tempted to shoot. As events quickly developed, their instincts to fire had been correct. A. P. Hill's men had outfitted themselves in captured Yankee uniforms; only too late did the Kanawha Division realize their mistake. There was now a real threat that Hill's men would crack the Kanawha Division and turn McClellan's flank. To make matters worse, as First Brigade positioned itself to slow down the Confederate assault, elements of the Sixteenth Connecticut regrouped and opened fire on Hugh's men. Scared witless, the Sixteenth Connecticut could not distinguish between friend and foe. Hugh was too busy with the southerners on his front to deal with the New Englanders at his rear.[83]

Ninth Corps's batteries hurriedly withdrew, leaving the Kanawha Division to absorb the fire of forty rebel cannon. Cox pleaded for reinforcements from McClellan, noting later, with considerable frustration, that "a single strong division, marching beyond the left flank of Ninth Corps, would have so occupied A. P. Hill's division that our movement into Sharpsburg could not have been checked." Colonel Scammon, who had been typically parsimonious when it came to complimenting his men, hailed the skillful leadership that Ewing and Crook displayed. Both Scammon and Cox observed that the Kanawha Division retreated in good order, halting Hill's momentum and successfully covering McClellan's flank. Major Hildt, who had taken over the Thirtieth Ohio when Hugh became brigade commander, composed his own heartfelt after-action report: "Too much praise cannot be given the officers and men for their coolness, courage, and gallant conduct on the field, and, having scarcely recovered from the terrible contest on Hagerstown Heights [South Mountain], they stood up and bravely bore a fire upon their front and left, of which veterans might well be proud."[84]

The highest praise for the Kanawha Division came from the Confederates. General Longstreet was convinced that only the arrival of A. P. Hill had prevented Hugh Ewing and George Crook from routing the Army of Northern Virginia. Longstreet, however, was not celebrating Lee's luck; he had not wanted to engage at Sharpsburg in the first place. As the firing gradually ceased, the cost of the battle began to register with its survivors. On a battlefield of a thousand acres it was almost impossible to walk anywhere without stepping on a dead soldier or horse. Nearly twenty-three thousand Union and Confederate soldiers were dead, wounded, captured, or missing, leading Longstreet to write years later: "The little town of Sharpsburg—was destined to pass into history as the scene of the bloodiest single day of fighting in the war, and that 17th of September was to become memorable as the day of greatest carnage in the campaigns between the North and South."[85]

Four of McClellan's corps had absorbed most of the Union's losses, with the First, Second, Ninth, and Twelfth Corps each sustaining a casualty rate above 20 percent. Ninth Corps alone suffered 2,350 casualties. Taking advantage of the first quiet moment he had in weeks, Hugh composed a quick letter to Henrietta to let her know that he was alive:

> I have passed unhurt, thank God, through almost uninterrupted danger since our parting . . . .
>
>   I have lost very many of my best men and officers—on the 17th two of my aids were killed and the third had his horse shot under him. The night of the battle of South Mountain I was placed in command of the First Brigade and have turned over the regiment (I was about to say to Lieutenant Colonel [Theodore] Jones but he is gone) to Major Hildt. We have driven the enemy whenever we have met them, but our loss is heavy and we are worn almost to death. There is some fighting now on our right, but all quiet with us giving me a moment to send you my love.[86]

McClellan's botched fight at Antietam, followed by his failure to destroy Lee's army as it retreated to Virginia, brought forth howls of outrage. Hugh wrote his brother Phil that he was appalled by the "military imbecility" he had seen in the East and regarded McClellan as "a second-rate man." If Lincoln did not immediately remove McClellan from command, Hugh predicted, the president "will divide the country [the North]." Once she learned from Hugh what had happened at Antietam, Ellen informed Cump that her faith in West Point graduates was shattered. She allowed that Cump was an exception.[87]

Senator Wade and the Committee on the Conduct of the War held lengthy hearings on the Army of the Potomac, interviewing over two hundred witnesses and subsequently issuing a sixty-four-page report. The committee roasted McClellan and cheered Burnside and Hooker. Republican newspapers followed Wade's lead. The *New York Times* placed McClellan in the worst possible light—which was, admittedly, not a difficult task. Lincoln also came in for oblique criticism from Wade's committee. This development was not surprising given that Vice President Hannibal Hamlin, in helping to choose the Senate members of the committee, had stacked it with radical abolitionists who distrusted the president. Outside Congress, Reverdy Johnson, Thomas Ewing's old comrade from Maryland, was nearly alone among the North's Unionist politicians to insist that McClellan's failures were not the product of alleged prosouthern convictions.[88]

Since the outbreak of the war Lincoln had been moving toward a policy of freeing the slaves. Neither France nor Great Britain, Lincoln correctly believed, would be able to defend—at least publicly—their military assistance to the Confederacy if the objective of the war changed from preservation of the Union to the abolition of slavery. Further, restless abolitionists in the Republican coalition would be somewhat mollified by emancipation. The *New York Herald*, however, insisted upon a constitutional amendment to abolish slavery, warning that a subsequent president could easily rescind Lincoln's proclamation.[89]

As for pro-Union Democrats in Kentucky, Maryland, and Missouri, Lincoln framed emancipation as applicable only to states that had joined the rebellion. Abolitionists might not approve, but if the Union won the war, then the majority the slaves would be freed. In need of a battlefield victory in the East so that issuing the Preliminary Emancipation Proclamation would not appear to be the act of political desperation that it was, Lincoln decided that Antietam would be scored a win. Calling Antietam "victory," however, did not save McClellan's military career.

Postmaster General Montgomery Blair, representing his family's political interests, warned Lincoln that even if no slaves were freed in Missouri there would be an electoral backlash against the Republican Party and pro-Union Democrats. Emancipation, Blair continued, might even bring more recruits to Missouri's guerrilla forces. Illinois senator Orville Browning, who was one of the few people claiming a close friendship with both Lincoln and Thomas Ewing, thought that Indiana, Illinois, and Ohio, as well as the Border States, might go over to the Confederacy in reaction to emancipation. Among the U.S. Supreme Court justices and congressmen that dined in Washington with Browning and Ewing, all regarded Lincoln as a weak president and saw emancipation as a policy disaster.[90]

Ewing had previously written Lincoln to oppose Republican legislation that authorized the confiscation of slaves owned by Confederate loyalists. Once again, Ewing had felt it necessary to lecture Lincoln on constitutional law. Ewing was not alone in that endeavor. John Crittenden, Ewing's Kentucky friend of many years, joined over a dozen Border State congressmen in castigating Republican proposals to purchase the freedom of slaves. "The right to hold slaves," these Unionist congressmen wrote in July 1862, "is a right appertaining to all the States of this Union. They have the right to cherish or abolish the institution as their tastes or their interests may prompt, and no one is authorized to question the right, or limit its enjoyment."[91]

Now, in the aftermath of Antietam, Ewing branded the Emancipation Proclamation a "pernicious document" that was constitutionally questionable and politically suicidal. Ewing concurred with Browning and the Border State Unionists that Lincoln had succumbed to political pressure from radical abolitionists.[92]

Although Lincoln had no expectation that Ewing would support emancipation, Browning's polite, but firm, dissent strained their friendship. Despite having consoled the Lincolns over the recent death of their young son Willie, Browning became a target of Mary Todd Lincoln's wrath. She would not brook any criticism of her husband. Most disturbing, Browning confided to Ewing, Mary had become so irrational that she claimed Willie spoke to her from the grave. Willie Lincoln's ghost, Browning reported, had directed the president to purge all enemies—real and imagined—from the government. This was not the kind of political intelligence that inspired confidence in the White House among Ewing's circle of friends.[93]

Browning, Ewing, and the Border State Unionists were supportive of Lincoln's war in spite of emancipation. The same could not be said for many in the opposition party. Democratic newspapers such as the *Detroit Free Press* and the *Cincinnati Enquirer* predicted that the Emancipation Proclamation would lead to several hundred thousand blacks invading Michigan and Ohio. In the summer of 1862 race riots broke out in Chicago, Cincinnati, and Toledo, Ohio, when working-class whites claimed that blacks were charging less for their labor.[94]

Democratic state conventions in Illinois, Indiana, Iowa, Ohio, and Pennsylvania warned Lincoln not to even consider emancipation and demanded legislation to prohibit southern blacks from relocating to the North. By a tally of 70 percent to 30 percent, Illinois voters approved of a ballot measure in June 1862 to ban future black settlement. Indiana Democrats organized posses to round up blacks they suspected of being escaped slaves. At

Samuel S. Cox (1824–98). An Ohio journalist and attorney, Samuel Cox was the leader of the antiwar Democratic Party faction in the U.S. House of Representatives, as well as an outspoken foe of emancipation and President Lincoln. Defeated in 1864 election, Cox later returned Congress as a representative of New York City's Tammany Hall political machine. (Courtesy of the Library of Congress.)

least one Indiana regiment patrolled the Ohio River, shooting runaway slaves fleeing Kentucky. For their part, Pennsylvania Democrats charged Republicans with "degrading and insulting [the white laboring masses'] manhood by placing them on an equality with Negroes."[95]

Ohio Democrats assumed leadership roles in the northern effort to oppose emancipation. Antiwar Democrats in the Buckeye State had a clear message: Union soldiers bled so that southern blacks could steal their jobs and homes. But at the same time Ohio Democrats expressed concern for the troops, they opposed legislative efforts that would allow soldiers to vote in state elections. Ohio antiwar partisans, realizing that most of the men who volunteered in 1861 were either Republicans or prowar Democrats, wanted Union soldiers to remain disenfranchised. Democrats argued that soldiers, by joining federal service and deploying outside Ohio, had abandoned their legal residences and Buckeye citizenship claims.[96]

Democratic newspaper editors were just as vocal in their loathing of emancipation in 1862 as Ohio's legislators. Samuel Medary of the *Columbus Crisis* blamed the war on abolitionists and predicted that Ohio would be overrun by Africans. Archibald MacGregor, editor of the *Stark County Democrat*, decried emancipation as "another step in the nigger business." In Circleville, located in the Virginia Military District, editor John Kees of the *Watchman* ridiculed Lincoln's "nigger war."[97]

Three of Ohio's U.S. House members orchestrated congressional assaults on Lincoln: Samuel Cox (Columbus-Newark), George Pendleton (Cincinnati), and Clement Vallandigham (Dayton). Of the three congressional Democrats, Cox, a former editorialist for Medary, was the antiwar leader national and Ohio Republicans most feared. When it came to the issue of abolishing slavery, Cox was an eloquent racist who endeavored to seem reasonable when at his most partisan:

> Slavery may be an evil, it may be wrong for southern men to use unpaid labor, but what will be the condition of the people of Ohio when the free jubilee shall have come in its ripe and rotten maturity? If slavery is bad, the condition of the State of Ohio, with an unrestrained black population, only double what we now have partly subservient, partly slothful, partly criminal, and all disadvantageous and ruinous, will be far worse.
>
> I do not speak these things out of any unkindness to the Negro. It is not for the interest of the free Negroes of my State that that class of the population should be increased. I speak as their friend when I oppose such immigration.[98]

Ironically, it was not Lincoln who set the stage for Cox's best political performance. Ohio governor David Tod and several Union Army officers had
grown annoyed with antiwar Democrats, who, they contended, were hurting
efforts at conscripting and recruiting soldiers. In the summer and fall of 1862,
Republicans and prowar Democrats made their move, arresting John Kees,
Archibald MacGregor, and a few other newspaper editors. Incarcerating
journalists carried some political risk but not enough to give the governor
pause. Tod, however, went too far by arresting former Democratic congressman Edson Olds for denouncing emancipation and military recruitment.[99]

In his order to transport Olds from Lancaster to a prison in New York
City, Tod wrote: "I have most satisfactory evidence that Edson B. Olds, a former member of Congress, is doing all the mischief he can. He is a shrewd,
cunning man, with capacity for great mischief, and should at once be put
out of the way." Tod could have made a much stronger case against his own
Democratic lieutenant governor, Benjamin Stanton, who, in his continuing
feud with Thomas Ewing and Cump, stopped just short of exhorting men not
to fight for an incompetent president.[100]

Cox hailed Olds as a martyr to liberty and sponsored a sharply worded
House resolution that denounced "all such arrests as unwarranted by the
Constitution and laws of the United States; and as a usurpation of power
never given up by the people to their rulers" and demanded "that all such
arrests shall hereafter cease; and all persons so arrested and yet held should
have a prompt and public trail, according to the provisions of the Constitution." Senator Sherman felt he had little choice but to concur with Cox;
government officials should not incarcerate people for their political beliefs.
(Governor Tod and Secretary of War Stanton implausibly insisted that they
detained only disloyal individuals who interfered with military recruitment;
their political opinions did not lead to arrest.) Sherman also believed that
Congress had erred in not limiting governmental authority to suspend citizens' constitutional protections.[101]

While Senator Sherman declined to rebuke Lincoln on this occasion, his
critical attitude toward the president was well known. Sherman had earlier written Andrew Johnson, the Tennessee military governor and Thomas
Ewing protégé, that he desired "honesty—nerve and fidelity to friends in a
new leader not already stained with a disgraceful record."[102]

As Senator Sherman and Thomas Ewing feared, the arrest of Democratic
dissenters like Olds, the Antietam bloodbath, and Lincoln's emancipation
policy contributed to an electoral backlash against Unionists. Antiwar Democrats won control of the state legislatures of Indiana and Illinois—the latter
development ensuring the end of Orville Browning's stint in the Senate. The

Republican majority in the U.S. House was halved, from a seventy-seat margin to thirty-five. Many of the Republicans' losses were in the Old Northwest, in spite of Andrew Johnson's efforts to campaign for Unionist candidates. (He once again stayed with the Ewing family when he came to Lancaster.) Democrats claimed nine of fourteen House seats in Illinois, seven of eleven in Indiana, and fourteen of nineteen in Ohio. Two of the newly elected anti-war Democrats sent to Congress represented Cincinnati. Both had centered their campaigns on opposition to emancipation.[103]

Perhaps the most peculiar political development of 1862 occurred in Lancaster. Even as newly recruited Union regiments marched down Main Hill cheering as they passed the Ewing mansion, the overwhelming majority of residents opposed the war. From his prison cell in New York, Olds won election to the Ohio House. After the president consented to Olds's release, Lancaster's newest representative went to Fairfield County's court of common pleas to swear out an arrest warrant for Governor Tod on the charge of kidnapping. The sheriff's office executed the warrant and attempted to bring Tod back to Lancaster in shackles. Only the intervention of the Ohio Supreme Court kept the governor free.[104]

While Unionist political prospects plummeted and Hugh Ewing had seen enough dying men for several lifetimes, Colonel Tom Ewing eagerly headed off to his first combat engagement. Maria Ewing had, with Tom's enlistment, finally recoiled at the prospect of still another son facing death. From Maria's correspondence with her daughter-in-law Henrietta, it was evident that Antietam had shaken Maria to her core. As a mother Maria simultaneously expressed pride in Hugh's courage and fear that she would bury him. Not surprisingly, then, both Maria and Thomas Ewing pleaded with Tom not to enlist, as did Tom's wife. Tom responded with a word that he knew would shush his parents: "Duty."[105]

Since the Union victory against Confederate forces at Pea Ridge, Arkansas, near the Missouri border, in March 1862, the rebels had been in a process of rebuilding their forces. The Confederates were also providing a fallback position for guerrillas operating in western Missouri. Given these developments, Union general James Blunt decided to launch a fall offensive. Blunt fully lived up to his name—he was not known for either his military or his political subtlety. The thirty-five-year-old abolitionist had advanced in rank as one of Lane's Jayhawkers. His Kansas enemies, who included nearly everyone who disliked Lane, charged that syphilis had made Blunt an unhinged radical.[106]

In his rush to link up with Blunt in late September, Tom insisted that the Eleventh Kansas march thirty miles a day. His brother Hugh and the

Kanawha Division, after all, had covered that much ground in their scramble to reach Washington. Lieutenant Colonel Thomas Moonlight, an army veteran, demurred, successfully arguing that fifteen miles a day was a more realistic goal. The veteran Thirtieth Ohio, unlike the raw Eleventh Kansas, had a year of service by 1862. Moreover, moving through the mountainous terrain of western Virginia had built up leg muscles and created a vast reservoir of physical endurance among Hugh's troops. Pancake-flat Kansas had not similarly conditioned Tom's regiment. Moreover, many of the Kansas regiments—unlike the Eleventh—were mounted troopers, which may have given them iron butts but did little to toughen up their feet. Once dismounted, Kansas soldiers often found themselves severely tested by physically hardened rebels.[107]

With little time to equip prior to their departure, the Eleventh Kansas made do with weapons that General Fremont had earlier procured. Tom learned firsthand that Fremont exhibited as much good judgment in purchasing military equipment as he did in making political decisions. The Eleventh Kansas would be marching to Arkansas carrying extremely heavy, long-barreled muskets manufactured in Prussia. Tom's neophyte soldiers would have to learn how to load (quickly) a .72 caliber ball and three buckshot after each firing. Most muskets fired a single, smaller caliber ball. Major Plumb and the soldiers in the Eleventh Kansas speculated that their infantry regiment had been redesignated as an artillery unit.[108]

If Tom was a demanding officer and, as his Kansas friends admitted, "cold in temperament"—unable to stir passions with the same success Plumb and Lane enjoyed—he cared deeply about his men. It seemed that no sooner had the Eleventh Kansas reached Arkansas than Third Brigade commander William Cloud tore into Ewing's troops. He was a stern Methodist minister and abolitionist from Ohio, and his service in the Second Kansas Cavalry marked him as a Lane man. As such, he ranked causing grief for Ewing and the Eleventh Kansas a close second to killing slave owners.[109]

Colonel Cloud repeatedly charged Tom's troops with stealing apples and shooting pigs. Putting his legal training to good use, Tom mixed his accused soldiers among the innocent in order to confuse witnesses and make positive identification nearly impossible. He also argued that even if his troops had hunted Arkansas farmers' livestock, they had *bayoneted*, not shot, their prey. Ewing's soldiers had obeyed the letter of Cloud's "law" and could not be brought up on charges. Cloud fumed but allowed that Ewing was a fine lawyer—by which he meant that Tom was destined to burn in hell.[110]

On November 28, 1862, General Blunt surprised a Confederate force at Cane Hill, Arkansas, which was approximately fifty miles south of Pea

Ridge. Blunt's five thousand troops faced two thousand Confederates under the command of General John Marmaduke, a relative of General Sterling Price and Missouri's exiled secessionist governor, Claiborne Jackson. Blunt sent the Second and Eleventh Kansas, as well as the Third Indian (Cherokee tribe), headlong into the fight, reporting that "the resistance of the rebels was stubborn and determined. The storm of lead and iron hail that came down the side of the mountain, both from their small-arms and artillery, was terrific; yet most of it went over our heads without doings us much damage. The regiments [Second Kansas, Eleventh Kansas, Third Indian], with a wild shout rushed up the steep acclivity, contesting every inch of ground, and steadily pushing the enemy before them until the crest was reached, when the rebels again fled in disorder."[111]

Tom had unflinchingly led his men into the battle. With enormous pride, he observed that "although the regiment was never before under fire, there was no lack of spirit or courage evinced by any officer or private belonging to it." Remarkably, only four of Ewing's men had been wounded and none killed. Overall, Blunt's division had inflicted far more damage on Marmaduke than the Confederates had scored against Union forces. The only sour note Tom heard at Cane Hill came from Colonel Cloud, who, Ewing disgustedly wrote his wife, castigated the Eleventh Kansas's foot soldiers "for not outracing the cavalry."[112]

Major General Thomas Hindman, an Arkansas lawyer and Democratic politician, hoped to crush Blunt's three combined divisions at Prairie Grove on December 7. His five thousand troops managed to inflict nearly as much damage on Union forces as they themselves sustained—with both sides suffering 2,700 casualties. His self-confidence shattered by the Confederates' high casualties, Hindman chose not to fight on to victory, opting, instead, for retreat. Blunt singled out Ewing, Plumb, and Moonlight "as gallant officers who fought well." Prairie Grove, however, resulted in the Eleventh Kansas losing six men, including a private that Ewing hailed as extraordinarily dutiful. Tom subsequently wrote to his brother Phil that the motley Confederates at Prairie Grove looked as if they belonged to an inferior race. Most of the Arkansas troops, Tom concluded, were poor conscripts who fought only because of their "fear of being shot or cut down by the Texas cavalry posted in their rear."[113]

In recognition of his performance in Arkansas, Tom received promotion to brigadier general. Soon he would become commander of the District of the Border. Tom would be tasked with dealing with the guerrilla insurgency along eastern Kansas and western Missouri. There was little doubt that Tom Ewing partly owed his apparent good fortune to the political fallout from the 1862 state and congressional elections. Moderate Republicans, Lincoln included, did not wish to push Missouri any closer to the antiwar Democrats. That being the case, Blunt was too much of Republican radical to police the Kansas-Missouri border; a moderate Unionist was required.[114]

Other members of the Ewing family circle had some cause to celebrate as 1862 drew to a close. Rutherford Hayes was recovering from his wound, and the Kanawha Division returned to western Virginia, gratefully severed from the Army of the Potomac. Hugh Ewing became a brigadier general. Best of all, Hugh would be transferred west to join Cump's Fifteenth Corps as commander of the Third Brigade, Second Division. His immediate superior was none other than the combative Frank Blair Jr., who had left Congress to go to war.

Hugh took the Thirtieth Ohio with him, the regiment buoyed by his successful efforts to obtain passes so that his soldiers could visit their homes. He also brought the Fourth West Virginia into his new brigade, rescuing Cousin Phil Stanbery from boring occupation duty. Best of all, the Thirteenth U.S. Infantry and Charley Ewing left the Alton prison to join Cump. With Charley, Hugh, Cump, and Cousin Phil reunited, it would be as if they were children again playing war in Lancaster's forests.[115]

5

"Forlorn Hope"

Vicksburg, Lawrence, and Missionary Ridge, 1863

At nine o'clock, at the head of this road, where it is still covered by woods, lies Blair's division, with Tuttle's for a support; and, at half a mile to the left, Steele is massed, and directs his attack against a battery at the mouth of a creek which enters the Mississippi at the north-western angle of Vicksburg. But it is upon the storming party posted upon the road that our interest concentrates. It consists of a forlorn hope of a hundred and fifty men, furnished with poles and boards for crossing the dry ditch of the redoubt; and close in their rear are the brigades of [Hugh] Ewing, Kirby Smith, and Giles Smith. You cannot look at this detachment without a premonitory shudder. These are the bold men whom Sherman sends on an errand of death to-day.
—Colonel Henry Champion Deming, Twelfth Connecticut, 1868

Years earlier Hugh Ewing had walked the streets of Vicksburg, Mississippi. He had been unmolested—and unimpressed. Now, as the new year of 1863 approached, the port had become a navigation chokepoint on the Mississippi River. Vicksburg was also a militarily vital transfer point between rail lines headed east and west. Dense forests, alligator-infested swamps, and an extensive chain of high bluffs transformed sleepy Vicksburg into a seemingly impenetrable bastion. By October 1862, General Ulysses Grant had thousands of troops poised to assault Vicksburg. Although his forces outnumbered Confederate troops in Mississippi, Grant was stymied. Logistical support was a particular concern. Grant required 1,900 wagons and eleven thousand animals to help transport and distribute just three days' worth of supplies. Seeing Grant's vulnerability, rebel forces raided and destroyed Union supply depots with near impunity.[1]

In preparation for his deployment to Cump's Fifteenth Corps outside Vicksburg, Hugh asked Phil Ewing to liquidate his property holdings in Cincinnati. His brother was to direct most of the money from the sale to the

Frank Blair (1821–75). The son of Francis Blair Sr., the younger Blair also had mixed relations with the Ewings. As a Missouri politician with presidential ambitions, Frank Blair clashed with Tom Ewing over how to handle the guerrilla insurgency. As a Union general, Frank Blair lavished praise upon Hugh and Charley Ewing during the Vicksburg campaign. He served as a member of both the U.S. House of Representatives and the Senate. (Courtesy of the Library of Congress.)

support of Henrietta. Hugh also instructed Phil to make a substantial dona-tion to the Catholic Church. After Antietam, Hugh was making preparations, both financial and spiritual, in the event of his death. Additionally, he made arrangements to move Henrietta and their three "little brigadiers" to Lan-caster. His father-in-law gave Henrietta $5,000 to help with her relocation. (Such generous financial support was not typically extended by families in either North or South.) As Hugh wrote to Henrietta, there was a far greater prospect that he could take military leave to visit her in Lancaster than if she remained in Washington. Left unwritten was the fact that closer proximity to Vicksburg made possible funeral arrangements for Hugh easier.[2]

By moving to Lancaster Henrietta would also be able to assist Ellen Sher-man in caring for Maria Ewing during Thomas Ewing's stints in Washing-ton. Neither Ellen nor Maria was in the most serene of moods as 1862 came to a close. Ellen, of course, had always been high-strung. Maria's anxiety attacks, however, made their first public appearance in 1862. Her children had insisted that Maria go to a Columbus sanitarium and try to block out war news. Ellen, upset by her mother's mental and physical decline, became even more religiously fervent in her correspondence with Cump: "I will have a Mass of thanksgiving offered for your safety as well as constant and ear-nest prayers for your continued preservation until faith crowns your virtues and you pass from the pure-minded patriot—generous, unselfish, superior man—to the humble worshipper of an incarnate God who died to redeem us."[3]

Charley Ewing made plans as well. Unlike Hugh, however, Charley had debts, not assets, which required liquidation. He asked Phil to take care of his $600 in obligations, pledging that he would pay him back in eight monthly installments. Given that Charley had just $10 in his pocket at the time he wrote to his oldest brother, his repayment schedule was optimistic at best. In light of his financial circumstances, Charley understandably dropped the subject of money and commenced discussing combat preparations. He expressed full faith that "although not disciplined," Grant's army would fight on to victory. Charley assured Phil that Cump would "do quick work here." Yet again, Charley's optimism drew little from the facts on the ground. Cump had confided in his brother John that Vicksburg was "going to be a hard nut to crack."[4]

Ever the protective big sister, Ellen implored Cump to keep an eye on Charley since he would also be assigned to the Fifteenth Corps. She accepted the prospect that Charley might well die for the "just and holy" cause of sav-ing the Union, "but it is a terrible trial to those who have to sit quietly at home and wait the random reports that are often harrowing in the extreme."

Ellen would always regard Charley as her special charge, and even if he did not contemplate his own mortality, she did not hesitate to take up that chore for him.[5]

Hoping to throw rebel forces off balance, Grant had ordered Cump to make assaults at Chickasaw Bluffs in late December 1862. Although Cump had thirty-two thousand troops against the Confederates' twelve thousand, the Union probes failed. Nearly two thousand men in his command were killed, wounded, or missing in action—the latter most likely drowned. Cump ruefully reported to John Sherman, "I pushed the attack as far as prudence would justify, and . . . re-embarked my command in the nick of time, for a heavy rain set in which would have swamped us and made it impossible to withdraw artillery and stores."[6]

Since Shiloh, Cump and Grant had forged a bond that Hugh had not seen among ranking officers during his brief service in the Army of the Potomac. Cump understood that for military and political considerations Grant had to try desperate assaults such as the one at Chickasaw Bluffs before commencing a prolonged siege. In any event, Cump would brook no criticism of the man who had given him a chance at redemption. For his part, Cump had bucked up Grant after northern newspapers castigated his performance at Shiloh.[7]

Although the fighting at Vicksburg would be hard, the camaraderie among the Union forces was exceptional—mainly because of the collegial example set by Grant and Cump. Hugh, Charley, and Cump, along with other officers, would gather in the evenings to converse and drink bourbon and scotch. Even former St. Louis congressman Frank Blair, who became Hugh's and Charley's superior in the Second Division, Fifteenth Corps, proved a gracious host despite the years-long sniping between their families. Hugh, with no little awe, recounted that Blair's headquarters near Milliken's Bend was "the finest I have seen in the country; tokens all about it of great wealth and luxury." Unlike Hugh, Cump remained wary of Blair because of his propensity to cultivate journalists. As Ellen reminded Cump, currying favor with reporters was the politician's affliction; even his brother John indulged in the practice.[8]

Hugh's men appeared glad to be gone from the Kanawha Valley and in a buoyant mood when they reported to Fifteenth Corps. Sergeant Thomas White of the Thirtieth Ohio recounted to his sister that "it is a magnificent scenery to see the fleet floating on the waters of the Mississippi." George Hildt, now commanding the Thirtieth Ohio, wrote home in January 1863, "The weather is cool but pleasant, with a prospect of rain." The troops, Hildt continued, were kept busy digging a twenty-foot wide canal. While the notion that a new water route could be dug out to bypass Vicksburg appeared fantastic, Grant had given the command. Thus far, Hildt noted, the futile task went forward with little interference other than the Confederates firing "a shell about twice a day to let us know they are about and kicking." After Antietam, Hugh's troops regarded the occasional rebel shell as a peaceful respite.[9]

Charley's first combat experience occurred at Fort Hindman (also known as Arkansas Post), on January 11, 1863. Located 150 miles from Vicksburg on the Arkansas River—which branched off the Mississippi—Ford Hindman had limited strategic value. Rather, the Union's intention was to score an easy victory, thereby making up for the setback at Chickasaw Bluffs. Union gunboats blasted Fort Hindman while assault forces, among them the Thirteenth U.S. Infantry, went forward. Writing home to his mother after the engagement, Charley expressed concern that Cump had unnecessarily exposed himself to rebel fire. Ellen immediately shot off a letter chastising Cump. After conferring with Hugh and Charley, and apparently after a few sips of bourbon, Cump reassured Ellen that she was a strong woman who could endure his combat role with forbearance. Indeed, Cump wrote, Hugh and Charley "agree that you have bottom and in the race of life will hold out against many a nag of more speed."[10]

In a matter-of-fact tone, Charley conveyed to Maria his general feelings about the action: "I was about certain that before day would come again I would have my precious old head knocked off with a piece of shell or be froze to death. But I did survive it, and feel all the more comfortable now for having gone through it." Given his mother's fragile nerves, it was just as well that Charley did not tell Maria what else had happened at Fort Hindman. After the rebel garrison surrendered, Charley had held a severely wounded Confederate soldier in his arms and kept him company until he died. In spite of not knowing this last piece of information, Ellen confided to Cump that Maria had become greatly agitated after receiving Charley's letter.[11]

Back in the swamps outside Vicksburg, canal digging progressed to the point where Union troops had a mile-long, nine-foot-deep ditch. There were, however, two insurmountable problems. First, Confederate cannon covered the lower end of the canal so thickly that attempting to move supplies or troops was suicidal. Second, by March 8 torrential rainfall had led to massive flooding, which in turn all-but-obliterated the canal. Under these circumstances, Grant had Cump commence "the Bayou Expedition" on March 17 in an effort to find a navigable bypass. Hugh personally went about in a rowboat to study the aptly named "Muddy Bayou." Although the particulars of engineering mathematics had eluded him at West Point, Hugh recognized that the Union forces would have to build an extensive "road of bridges." He also deployed his brigade in cutting out the mass of tree snags that blocked navigation on the "Muddy."[12]

By March 22 enough snags and vines had been cleared to permit Hugh's Fourth West Virginia to link up with gunboats at the fork of Deer Creek. As Hugh subsequently reported, by the time the rest of his brigade regrouped on a plantation near the Yazoo River, their "boats were reduced to mere hulks, everything light having been carried away by the tops and limbs of trees, through which the upper works and sides forced their way." Having achieved little beyond destroying U.S. property, Hugh's brigade went back to their original encampment on March 27.[13]

Within a few days of their return, yet another round of flooding occurred. Hugh's troops had no choice but to throw up a levee as quickly as possible or be drowned. Once that immediate threat was over, Hugh directed construction of a raised patch of ground for a graveyard. Too many of the Union dead were rising to the surface as a result of the extensive flooding. Under the circumstances it was little wonder that Sergeant White of the Thirtieth Ohio wrote home that he had no patience for civilians who complained about wartime hardships and demanded an end to the conflict on Confederate terms. As White bluntly informed his mother: "We are down on all Copperheads and where there is one found hissing, I want them to cut his head off without any hesitation whatever. This is the sentiment of the soldiers in the field. If they will keep their heads shut we will settle the difficulty and settle it right. When I say right I mean to sweep every traitor from our land we live. 'Proverbs 2' for the upright shall dwell in the land and transgressors shall be rooted out of it. So say I."[14]

For the historically minded troops among the Union forces, Vicksburg was looking like a Magnolia-scented Troy. While Grant did not construct a Trojan horse, he came up with a successful ploy to thwart the Confederates. On April 16 Grant ordered transport ships to line their decks with cotton and hay bales in the hope that they would absorb Confederate gunfire meant for his soldiers. They would then run under Vicksburg's guns to a position from which they could flank the city. Hugh stepped forward with other volunteers to make the dangerous midnight maneuver on board the *Silver Wave*. As he recounted in his official reports—but not in as full of detail to Henrietta:

> In a few minutes the batteries of the enemy opened fiercely, replied to by the gunboats as they passed. The river in front of, above and below the city, was rendered bright as day by buildings fired by the enemy on both sides, the village of De Soto, on the peninsula, (surrounded by water and under their

guns,) being in their possession. The buildings, previously filled with combustibles, were set on fire as soon as the fleet was seen, and blazing up in a moment rendered the boats as good targets as they would have been by day.[15]

From the *Silver Wave*'s pilothouse, Hugh watched the transport boat *Forest Queen* receive disabling fire. As the *Forest Queen* drifted helplessly, another troop transport, the *Henry Clay*, took so many Confederate shells that it caught fire and subsequently disintegrated. Hugh's boat was able to rescue the *Henry Clay*'s chilled-to-the-bone pilot as they steamed by. Sadly, Hugh reported, the pilot "had lost his reason and was sent north to an asylum." Remarkably, the *Silver Wave* made it through without a single fatality. Hugh exalted in the "splendid spectacle." George Hildt came away from this experience with enormous respect for Grant and Cump. Little did Hildt and the Thirtieth Ohio know what Hugh knew; Cump had expressed strong reservations about Grant's plan and did not believe many of the Union troops would survive the gauntlet.[16]

More Union transports subsequently forced their way past Vicksburg, though, as Hildt wrote home, the Confederates' aim vastly improved. On May 3, Hugh took command of a tugboat that was to tow two other crafts loaded with three hundred thousand rations. He also had as company one of Lancaster's prominent doctors, Andrew Davidson, who had volunteered his medical services to the Forty-Seventh Ohio. Hugh praised Davidson's heroic conduct after a rebel artillery shell scored a direct hit on the tugboat's boilers. Davidson rushed about trying to treat the soldiers' burns from the spewing, scalding water. Unfortunately for the doctor, he was captured when he remained too long on one of the drifting supply craft as he tended the wounded. He ended up at the brutal Libby prison camp in Richmond, Virginia. Hugh made sure his superiors knew about Davidson's courage and sacrifice. (Davidson survived Libby and received the Medal of Honor for his actions at Vicksburg.)[17]

Faced with John Pemberton's estimated thirty thousand soldiers in Vicksburg, and a second rebel army of twenty-four thousand under General Joe Johnston forming in Alabama, Grant became even more audacious. He severed his supply lines in order to make a rapid forty-five-mile march to the Mississippi capital of Jackson. Hugh's brigade had participated in a diversionary assault on Haines' Bluff near the Yazoo River on April 29, leaving Grant to move swiftly toward Jackson. The capital city fell to Union forces on May 14, though the situation was so chaotic that many residents did not even know that the six thousand Confederates soldiers responsible for their defense had withdrawn.[18]

Having caught the Confederates off guard, Grant was poised to attack Vicksburg from its more vulnerable rear. After the failure of an initial assault on May 19, Union troops commenced a grueling forty-seven-day siege. Pemberton held a seven-mile-long line while Grant spread out over a distance of fifteen miles. Some 250 cannon, among them naval guns, fired nearly continuously into the city. Vicksburg's civilians, with dark humor, began to speak of "the iron storm" as part of the natural weather patterns. Cump's Fifteenth Corps occupied the right flank north of Vicksburg. As Sergeant White of the Thirtieth Ohio wrote his mother: "There is a constant roar, morning, noon, and night. At this time there is about forty pieces of cannon within about a hundred yards of me. As I am writing they all burst forth and it makes the whole earth shake apparently with fear." If it was any consolation to Hugh's brigade, there were worse places to be—namely, inside Vicksburg, where residents took to dwelling in crude dirt shelters and dining on rats.[19]

Charley and the Thirteenth U.S. Infantry were in the thick of Grant's May 19 attack. Cump candidly apprised Ellen that many of his regiments had been "swept away as chaff thrown from the hand on a windy day." Several of the Thirteenth U.S.'s standard-bearers fell, prompting Charley to grab the staff and rally his company. Confederate bullets immediately severed Charley's staff, along with one of his fingers. A reporter for *Harper's Weekly* recounted the scene:

> The charge of the battalion of the 13th Regulars, who were in the command of Colonel [Giles] Smith, is said to have never been surpassed in its desperate gallantry; Captain [Edward] Washington, the commanding officer, was killed, and but two or three officers escaped unwounded, five color-bearers were shot, one after the other, two being officers, Captains [Charley] Ewing and [L. B.] Yorke. The colors were being placed at the foot of the parapet by Captain Ewing as he was shot.
>
> I never have seen colors so torn as were these after this desperate charge; in one of the flags eighty shot-holes were to be counted.[20]

The *Harper's Weekly* reporter had not exaggerated the carnage. One of the Thirteenth U.S.'s noncommissioned officers sadly observed that "the next roll-call was a dirge." In a letter to Ellen, Cump hailed Charley as a courageous man, no longer regarding him as an amusing, sometimes pesky boy. Ellen's response to the news was euphoric: "My pride and pleasure on hearing of Charley's noble daring and successful bravery is unbounded." Aware that his actions had attracted a great deal of attention, Charley took the unprecedented (for him) step of writing a quick note to his parents. He assured Thomas and Maria that his wound was minor. Charley also focused on the heroics and sacrifice of the Thirteenth U.S., saying little about his role in the engagement and what he had seen on the battlefield. To Ellen's surprise, Thomas Ewing openly wept upon learning of Charley's heroics.[21]

Not only had the youngest Ewing son captured his first bit of national notice; along the way he had demonstrated immense courage and leadership skills. In a nighttime skirmish prior to its May 19 repulse, Charley had taken Company A of the Thirteenth U.S. out for an adventure. Ordered to capture a rebel battery, Charley led his company across open ground. The dark did nothing to conceal their approach. Charley could clearly hear the Confederate batteries loading grapeshot that would tear them into shreds as soon as the Thirteenth U.S. was in range. Just as the Charley heard the fuses lit, he ordered his men to hit the ground. The grapeshot flew thickly and closely over their heads but no one in Company A was hit. In a matter of seconds, Charley's company was up and running, crossing into rebel territory before the cannons could be reloaded. He took the battery with his company intact and sent the Confederates into surprised flight.[22]

General Frank Blair had nothing but praise for Charley, Hugh, and the troops in their commands. He observed that on May 19 the Thirtieth Ohio "went forward with equal impetuosity and gallantry." When the Thirty-Seventh Ohio froze in their tracks, Hugh rushed in among the regiment to move them forward, rather than allowing his troops to remain stationary targets for a Confederate cannonading. At a second Union assault on May 22, Blair singled out Charley Ewing and George Hildt's steadfastness and then recommended many of their enlisted men for Medals of Honor. Blair's pride, though, was tempered by the knowledge that in the space of four days the Second Division had suffered 890 casualties. His officers' ranks, in true Roman fashion, had been decimated.[23]

Unlike the contemporaneous and subsequent accounts Hugh wrote of his engagements prior to Vicksburg, his account of the May 22, 1863 assault would never be able to convey the full horror of what his brigade endured. The portion of the Confederate breastworks Hugh was to assault had an unusually deep depression in its front that could easily become a deathtrap for his troops. Knowing the odds against success, Hugh asked for 150 *volunteers*. He dubbed them "the Forlorn Hope"—a name once given to the Duke of Wellington's lead assault forces in the Napoleonic Wars. Hugh would not send these men forward unless he commanded them personally. Blair gave Hugh permission to lead "the Forlorn Hope." Trying to make the best of his poor tactical situation, Hugh directed his men to construct portable ladder-bridges in an effort to span the Confederates' wide "ditch." When the only decent lumber available for construction proved to be a house that Grant was sleeping in, Hugh roused his commander politely, but firmly. His troops then demolished the house, plank by plank.[24]

The Forlorn Hope ran briskly along the chillingly named "Graveyard Road." Each assault team carried homemade wooden ladders, most of which were anywhere from sixteen to twenty-two feet long. Thanks to Second Division's batteries, which forced the Confederates to keep their heads down, Hugh's men made it to the ditch. The subsequent engagement, however, did not go well for the Forlorn Hope. Its ladder-bridges proved too short. As the Union shelling ceased when Hugh arrived in front of the Confederate position, his men had to take shelter from rebel guns. This meant clinging to the sides of the ditch. For the next several hours, the Forlorn Hope attempted to claw its way out of the depression. A private in the Thirty-Seventh Ohio later observed that "to advance was almost sure death from the enemy's cross and concentrated fire." It was Hugh's "personal bravery," according to this soldier, that kept the Forlorn Hope in the fight.[25]

Hugh directed one of his officers to plant his headquarters' flag close to the Confederate parapet. The officer died in the attempt, but a subsequent effort proved successful. Upon placing the Union marker, the soldier defiantly shouted at the Confederates, "You sons of bitches surrender this fort." Hugh's plan was to rally his Forlorn Hope toward the flag and tempt the Confederates to come out into the open to seize it. Many of the rebel defenders took the bait and went to their eternal reward, but their actions did little to improve Hugh's prospects.[26]

For the next several hours, Confederates from *three regiments* kept up an intense fire. They also lit six- and twelve-pound shells and rolled them down the side of the ditch. Union troops reacted fast, using their bayonets to roll the shells out of harm's way. Although the fighting raged well beyond Hugh's immediate patch of woe, with the Fourth West Virginia and the Thirteenth U.S. Infantry trying to cover Hugh's assault force, soldiers from both sides stopped to watch the struggle. A mesmerized Grant, who was on horseback and clearly visible to Confederate sharpshooters, lost track of his whereabouts. He began to drift toward Hugh's position. The men of the Thirteenth U.S. shouted at their commander to turn back. Finally, Charley unceremoniously reined in Grant's horse and forced the general to take cover from rebel snipers and shells.[27]

After his men had spent the day fighting on their bellies, Hugh finally received permission to retreat. He insisted on retrieving his headquarters flag and carrying back the wounded and the dead as best they could under Confederate fire. One of Hugh's favorites from the Thirtieth Ohio,

Lieutenant George O'Neal, was sprawled on the ground with three bullets lodged in him. Weeks earlier, O'Neal had coolly piloted the *Silver Wave* past Vicksburg's batteries, earning Hugh's immense admiration. It was, therefore, with no little relief that Hugh, during a subsequent tour of his division's field hospital, found O'Neal sitting up in bed reading a novel and puffing on a cigar. The young officer had miraculously risen from the dead to enjoy a good smoke.[28]

Few soldiers in the Fifteenth Corps appeared willing to discuss the casualties sustained by the Forlorn Hope, invariably rolling those numbers into the overall count sustained by Grant's army. Over four thousand men, among them Cousin Phil Stanbery of the Fourth West Virginia, had been wounded or killed in the recent engagements. A bullet taken in the hand had nearly caused Stanbery to bleed to death and had resulted in his honorable discharge from service. Hugh reported that his brigade had suffered 140 casualties on May 22 but did not indicate how many of those men were from the Forlorn Hope. He commended his troops who "bore themselves throughout with gallantry and spirit." Hugh also informed his superiors that Captain Thomas Hayes of the Thirtieth Ohio had been "the model of a Christian soldier," falling "in the front rank of honor, where he lived and still lives." Captain Hayes—no direct relation to Rutherford Hayes—had gone through the battles of South Mountain and Antietam under Hugh's approving command.[29]

George Hildt made two observations in the aftermath of the Forlorn Hope's failed assault. First, and most remarkably, the "men are in better fighting order than the day of the battle." Troop morale remained high, sustained by Hugh's willingness to lead from the front and care to look after his troops' material and spiritual welfare. Hugh, with considerable bureaucratic effort and wire-pulling, had even obtained a Catholic priest to say Mass on a regular basis. And second, as Hildt wrote to his parents, "We do not intend to charge again upon their dirt piles and the men know it, but if [General Joe] Johnston should come up in the rear with anything less than 60,000 men, woe be unto him."[30]

Having failed in a succession of assaults to pry the Confederates loose from their earth and timber "forts" or redoubts, Grant and Cump opted to starve and shell Vicksburg into submission. Robert Norris, an enlisted man in the Thirtieth Ohio, wrote to his wife, "Our situation is very peculiar. We are camped about a mile behind Vicksburg in a hollow so that the bullets cannot hit us. Skirmishing is going on all of the time. . . . We have to go on guard every fourth day and stand six hours and shoot at the rebels whenever we see them stick up their heads. We are both in rifle pits or behind fortifications so there not much damage done on either side." Confederate deserters, Norris concluded, were demoralized and famished.[31]

Union troops bore the siege with general good cheer. Unlike the Confederates, they had meals that did not scurry about in the trenches before being killed and cooked. Still, regiments throughout Grant's army reported that "the men have been oppressed with the heat, and good water is very scarce." The northern soldiers closer to the mosquito-infested, brackish rivers expressed concern that the alligators seemed less and less standoffish. Sweat-drenched and mud-encrusted blue uniforms were also beginning to fall off the soldiers. There was little prospect of having fresh clothing issued, since Grant had to make ammunition and food his logistical priorities.[32]

There was also the problem of troop demoralization that followed whenever new issues of the *Chicago Times* and the *Cincinnati Commercial* circulated. None of the Union soldiers liked to read that they were losing the war, and they were very upset to see militarily sensitive information—including their deployments and numbers—published for the Confederates to read. The *Cincinnati Commercial* also helpfully characterized Grant as "a poor drunken imbecile." Hugh took it upon himself to intercept civilian vendors and then burn their newspapers. Not surprisingly, most of the Union Army had no problem when Cump had earlier sought to court-martial a critical reporter from the *New York Herald*. Cump wanted the reporter executed as a spy but had to settle for him being sent away from Vicksburg.[33]

One activity that Hugh's brigade pursued during the siege was to tunnel under the ground separating the two armies. Once the diggers reached the Confederate side, they would place explosives under a rebel redoubt and then blow it to pieces. Hugh's Fourth West Virginia did a lot of the tunneling, since so many of the southern Ohio and Wheeling-Kanawha Valley troops were coal miners. Realizing what Ewing had in store for them, the rebels ventured out at night with shovels in an attempt to undermine the Union tunnels. They did not, however, commit large numbers of skirmishers to attack the miners. Many of the Confederate defenders were not from Vicksburg, let alone Mississippi. Consequently, they were afraid of getting lost and captured in the dark. Trying to dig their own mines to intercept the Union diggers was not an option either, since few southerners had ever seen a mine shaft, let alone dug one. It was just one of the many times during 1863 that the South suffered from not joining the Industrial Revolution. Thomas Ewing had warned southerners thirty years earlier about remaining mired in the eighteenth century.[34]

At the beginning of June, Cump took an opportunity to inspect "Battery Sherman," located in what Hugh regarded as an extremely forward and exposed position. Hugh had come to accept that the shells fired by Union batteries to his rear would probably explode prematurely over his advanced gun and infantry deployments. There was nothing Hugh or his troops could do about their friends. Confederate snipers, however, were a different matter. While chatting with Hugh at Battery Sherman, Cump came to the attention of a rebel sharpshooter. Three times the Confederate fired at Cump, missing narrowly with each bullet. After the third shot, Cump lost patience. He directed the crew of a one of the heavy guns to resite their aim. The rebel shooter, apparently not understanding that snipers needed to relocate after firing since the gun smoke revealed their position, received an artillery shell down his throat.[35]

By the first week of July, Pemberton's troops and the civilian population of Vicksburg had reached the limit of their endurance. Nearly thirty-two thousand rebels surrendered to Grant on July 4, giving Lincoln the greatest Independence Day observance of his presidency. (By peculiar coincidence, that very same day Lee withdrew his bloodied army from Gettysburg, Pennsylvania.) Demonstrating a decided lack of contrition, Vicksburg's civilians complained that Grant had not given them sufficient rations from his provisions. Cump's anger was clearly visible as he responded to southern complaints: "I contend that after the firing on our steam-boats navigating our own rivers, after the long and desperate resistance to our armies at Vicksburg, on the Yazoo, and in Mississippi generally, we are justified in treating all inhabitants as combatants and would be perfectly justifiable in transporting you all beyond the seas if the United States deemed it to her interests." If Grant had left matters up to Cump, Vicksburg's citizens would still be eating rats.[36]

Grant's troops wasted little time in celebration. Thousands of Union soldiers, among them Hugh's brigade, moved out on July 5 headed toward Jackson. General Joe Johnston, having failed to relieve Pemberton, belatedly made threatening moves to the east of Vicksburg. Faced with a battle-hardened and well-equipped army, Johnston's troops withdrew after some fighting. They poisoned cisterns and ponds as they retreated. Most viciously, a detachment of the Third Texas Cavalry tortured Hugh's orderly, who had become separated from the brigade. The Texans were enraged when they found orders in the Yankee's pocket transferring him to a black regiment. They shot him in the stomach. Hugh listened to the orderly's account as he bled to death. Cump promised Hugh that he would execute a captured officer in the Third Texas in retaliation.[37]

Hugh ordered his troops to show some restraint when they entered Jackson. That resolve, however, flagged after some Union soldiers fatally tripped explosive booby traps, or "torpedoes," planted by the retreating Confederate army. Hugh decided not to inquire too closely about the activities of his souvenir-hunting soldiers. He did, however, post a guard at the State House, since there was a "good law library" inside that deserved preservation. Of course, as Hugh led from the front in battle, so he led in collecting Confederate "curiosities." As Cump subsequently boasted to his brother John, "Jackson will never again be a point where an enemy can assemble and threaten us." For that matter, Mississippi at large had been sacked, with Cump directing Blair to destroy five hundred thousand bushels of corn.[38]

Jefferson Davis took the looting of Jackson in stride and could even live with Cump hosting a large victory dinner at the governor's mansion. Davis, however, saw himself as a martyr for a holy cause when Union troops descended upon his plantation, as well as other estates belonging to his family. Hugh wrote to Henrietta that he had taken Jefferson Davis's checkers set as a war trophy and indeed was corresponding with her on the Confederate's president's personal stationery. He enclosed a "passion flower" with these letters and told Henrietta that the Jackson planters seemed spiritually broken and ready to end the war. Hugh gleefully reported to his superiors that he had Davis's 1824 letter of appointment to West Point, signed by Secretary of War John C. Calhoun of South Carolina. As Hugh argued, "Thus early linked, their names [Calhoun and Davis] will be handed down to posterity together as stirrers up of strife, and the future historian and poet will point to them to deter our descendants from entering upon the path of mad ambition."[39]

More disturbing to Davis than Yankee looting of the family's plantations was the news from a friend that Hugh Ewing—whom he identified by name—had taken his personal correspondence. There was little doubt as to what a Ewing would do with letters between Davis and nationally prominent northern Democrats. Former Democratic president Franklin Pierce, who had shared antiabolitionist sentiments with Davis, subsequently became a major political casualty of the Vicksburg campaign. Pierce might have been spared but for the fact that he decided to end his public silence in 1863 to condemn the war and the Lincoln administration. After the Ewings and their allies were finished with him, Pierce literally could not even be invited to a funeral in his home state of New Hampshire.[40]

The humiliation of Pierce, a president many Republicans held responsible for creating "Bleeding Kansas" in the 1850s, was merely the crowning touch to an enormously successful Union military campaign. Hugh crowed to his father, "The army is confident Cump can defeat anybody. His praise is on every tongue." For their actions at Vicksburg, Charley received promotion to the rank of lieutenant colonel and appointment as inspector general for Cump. In addition to his personal courage, Charley had demonstrated, as a captain in the Thirteenth U.S. Infantry, a keen analytical mind and attention to detail that resulted in the efficient organization of supplies and troops. Hugh, meanwhile, moved up from brigade leader to commander of the Fourth Division, Fifteenth Corps.[41]

In terms of human cost, Grant racked up 10,142 casualties to a Confederate count of 9,091. There was little doubt that Hugh's brigade had disproportionately borne the brunt of the Union campaign. Of the 141 Medals of Honor awarded for heroism at Vicksburg, Hugh's troops received thirty-four, or 24 percent. This was particularly noteworthy, since his command represented perhaps 5 percent of the total number of Union troops involved in the Vicksburg siege and related operations. Most of the Medal of Honor recipients in Hugh's brigade were recognized either for their valor while running the guns under Vicksburg or for their actions as members of the Forlorn Hope.[42]

Thomas Ewing was proud of his sons and impressed with Frank Blair. He wrote to Lincoln expressing his happy amazement that Blair had proved to be such a better man than his father: "I am most happy to say I have been agreeably disappointed in General Blair—he is a brave fellow and has intellect and energy." The senior Ewing, however, could not refrain from criticism in another letter to Lincoln. Ewing opined that a subdued Mississippi should not have the Emancipation Proclamation imposed, since such an action would lead to unrest throughout the Old Northwest and the western states. Although not privy to Ewing's correspondence with Lincoln, George Hildt of the Thirtieth Ohio informed a southern cousin that he wanted a reconciliation of the two sections. Whether "retaining the Old Union" meant that slavery might still exist in a postwar South Hildt left unanswered.[43]

While Hugh and Charley were experiencing the most grueling military campaign of the war to date, General Tom Ewing prepared to bring law and order to "the District of the Border." Tom could count on Edmund Ross and the Eleventh Kansas to fight cleanly and not target innocent civilians in Missouri—unlike Jim Lane's Red Legs. Friend and Eleventh Kansas alumnus Preston Plumb became Tom's chief of staff. Tom could also mark General John Schofield, who replaced Samuel Curtis as head of the Department of Missouri, as a likely ally. Schofield had navigated well among the Blair, Ewing, and Jackson-Price factions in St. Louis during the spring of 1861. He would not intentionally cross Tom. He also had the enthusiastic endorsement of the St. Louis-based *Daily Missouri Republican,* which all but proclaimed him to be Caesar incarnate in June 1863: "He is a most strict disciplinarian, loves nothing so much as to see his men acquiring the habits and demeanor of soldiers; has care, thoughtfulness, wisdom, and the most mature judgment and always in readiness for exercise. And if there is a quality that unites all manly qualities, he has it, and it is this; he is well balanced. . . . His courage never becomes rashness, nor his firmness, obstinacy, nor his prudence dilatory action. He has a large, well cultivated mind, in a large well proportioned body."[44]

As always, Tom could count on his father's political support. The senior Ewing reminded Lincoln that Tom faced danger not just from the guerrillas but also from the "Jayhawkers and Red Legs who rob and murder in behalf of the Union, as they profess, and they have had too much the countenance of the public authorities." Senator Lane, Thomas Ewing insisted, was by "nature made for a bandit" and "is not to be relied on as a safe and prudent counselor."[45]

Beyond his father, Schofield, Ross, and Plumb, however, Tom had few on his side. Given his experiences with the violent politics of the Kansas-Missouri borderlands in the 1850s, Tom knew that his Unionist peers were nearly as vicious as his Confederates foes. Samuel Crawford, a Kansas legislator and crony of Senator Lane's, waged a campaign of slander against Tom Ewing. Crawford contended that Ewing's Eleventh Kansas had behaved in a cowardly fashion at Cane Hill and Prairie Grove in 1862. Although Crawford was, like Tom, a politician and not a professional soldier—they had even attended the same law school—Crawford did not know when to step down from the campaign stump. Crawford divided his time between serving in the Second Kansas Cavalry and preparing for the 1864 gubernatorial race. Tom temporarily set aside his political ambitions when he enlisted, choosing to focus on the military struggle.[46]

If more willing than Crawford to recognize Tom's steadfastness in battle, General James Blunt still perceived the Ewing family as a political threat. Blunt alleged that both Tom and the senior Ewing had met in St. Louis in the winter of 1863 "to devise a program or plot to insure my discomfiture and destruction." In truth, the Ewings, as well as the Blairs, were troubled by Blunt's inability (or unwillingness) to restrain Lane's loyalists—including the marauding Second Kansas Calvary. There were also credible charges delivered to President Lincoln that Blunt had authorized the release of guerrilla suspects to Unionist lynch mobs. Melodramatically, Blunt predicted that when Tom Ewing took his place he would be sent to his death among hostile Indians. Blunt avoided this fate, though Lincoln did express the opinion to Lane that Blunt's successor should "not take persons charged with *civil* crimes, out of the hands of the courts, and turn them over to mobs to be hung."[47]

As the war in the West intensified in 1863, St. Louis and Leavenworth boomed. Army contractors, troops, and prostitutes crowded the streets of both cities. St. Louis played an important supporting role in Grant's

Vicksburg campaign, providing the Union with a seemingly secure provisioning base and transportation hub. The city was also a fine place for military prisons, with Unionists often converting "slave pens" into holding cells for Confederate soldiers. Leavenworth added even more saloons and brothels to its roster of businesses. Tom Ewing's stomping grounds, however, endeavored to elevate itself culturally. Shakespearean theater came to the Kansas outlands, featuring such nationally prominent actors as John Wilkes Booth. In one of his last formal stage performances, Booth went to Leavenworth in 1863 to perform *Richard III*—the tale of a vicious tyrant well-deserving of assassination.[48]

Military security for Unionists along the Missouri-Kansas border sharply deteriorated in 1863 when Ohio native William Quantrill stepped up guerrilla attacks. As Quantrill boasted in May 1863, "Ewing commands the district but I run the machine." Missouri's Confederate sympathizers spread unsubstantiated tales of black troops in the First Kansas Colored Volunteers gang-raping white women and then slicing off their ears. (The First Kansas Colored was one of newly organized black Union regiments and was largely made up of escaped slaves.) It was thus only in their own self-defense, Missourians claimed, that they targeted blacks for execution. Guerrilla bands blocked and then boarded steamboats on the Missouri River, hunting for blacks and white Unionists. The Confederate partisans also robbed stagecoaches, compiled death lists, and murdered Missouri's Union soldiers when they came home on furlough. Guerrilla bands made a practice of raping and torturing black women; those crimes were documented, unlike Missourians' allegations of black-on-white rape.[59]

The guerrillas claimed critical advantages over Schofield and Ewing's troops. They knew their home turf well and melted into the countryside. The only Union troops likely to know where the Confederates hid were escaped slaves. This was the actual reason, other than virulent racism, why the rebels targeted blacks. Further, the terrain of western Missouri, with its thick forests, ravines, and brush-covered hills, was ideal for sheltering guerrillas from Union patrols. Moreover, the guerrillas lived among their families, who provided them with food and military intelligence. Although Missouri women claimed to be innocent civilians, most likely if they lived along the Kansas border they were actively assisting in the killing of Unionists in both states. No real distinction could be made between combatants and noncombatants. Additionally, a number of political officeholders in Kansas City, Missouri, and the surrounding counties were secretly supportive of the Confederacy. They used their power to levy excessive taxes on Union sympathizers and reported Tom's troop deployments to the guerrillas.[50]

Guerrillas who rode with such leaders as Quantrill were excellent horsemen, each armed with several revolvers. They swooped down on Union patrols and unleashed a great deal of firepower at extremely close range. Tom's 2,500 or so men would have to ride as equally well and shoot revolvers as accurately. Unfortunately for Tom, the Union forces in the West were ill prepared for guerrilla war. He was horrified to learn in June 1863 that Union patrols, *knowing* that guerrillas were in the vicinity, "had their guns strapped to their saddles, and could not disengage them until the rebels had delivered two volleys and charged and thrown them into confusion." It did not help Tom, or John Schofield, that every time they built up a force sufficiently large and well trained to deal with the guerrillas, Grant arranged for their transfer to Vicksburg.[51]

Major Plumb found to his dismay that the guerrillas exercised pervasive influence throughout Kansas City and its region. The guerrillas, or "banditti," as Plumb preferred to call them, "lurked in every thicket and prowled around every outpost," leaving "a trail of blood and ruin." Nearly as bad, Plumb argued, were Lane's friends, whom Tom denounced in the summer of 1863 for "stealing themselves rich in the name of liberty." The worst of those men, Plumb and Tom concurred, was *Daily Conservative* editor and Leavenworth mayor Daniel Anthony. While Anthony's sister back east was crusading for women's voting rights, he was trafficking in stolen cattle—all the while justifying it on the grounds that he was punishing Missouri slave owners.[52]

On July 17, Tom had enough of Anthony's behavior. He proclaimed martial law in Leavenworth. As Tom informed Schofield in St. Louis, "I became perfectly satisfied that I could not get along with the mayor, who was bent on 'running the machine,' as he expressed it, in his own way, and whose interference with my officers was proclaimed as intention, and with the purpose of controlling arrests and seizures for robbery in Leavenworth." Anthony responded angrily, insisting that he had the right to arrest Ewing's representatives whenever they came to Leavenworth to investigate alleged criminal activities. Local civil authority, Anthony insisted, took precedence over military and, by extension, federal authority. It was ironic that an abolitionist Republican was essentially making the Democratic states' rights (or municipalities' rights) argument. Anthony, however, had no ear for irony.[53]

Publicly, Tom expressed great confidence, informing a meeting of citizens in Olathe, Kansas, "I can assure you there is little at present to fear on this side of the border from guerilla bands." Within military circles, however, Tom was becoming pessimistic and inclined toward harsh retaliation. When guerrillas ambushed troops in the Fourth Missouri near Sibley, Missouri, Tom defended the subsequent burning of the town. The Fourth Missouri, to its credit, at least moved the disloyal civilians out of harm's way before torching the settlement. By August 1863, Tom embraced General Order Number 10, which authorized the detention of civilians who provided supplies and military intelligence to the guerrillas. He had also expanded Union military posts along the border in Aubry, Olathe, Mound City, and Paola. Having been reassured by Ewing just weeks earlier that they had little to fear from guerrillas, the citizens of Olathe had to wonder why, then, they were now designated as an army outpost.[54]

Tom came to regard the Kansas-Missouri border as a "hornet's nest of a district." He also recognized that all around him there could be found "people who not only befriended and sympathized with the guerrillas, but furnished them with advantageous information as to the movements of the army or any detachment." Tom estimated that "about two-thirds of the families on the occupied farms of that region are kin to the guerrillas, and are actively and heartily engaged in feeding, clothing, and sustaining them." Among the worst of civilian supporters of the insurgency, Tom believed, were the wives, sisters, mothers, and girlfriends of the guerrillas. As Hugh had encountered in western Virginia, southern women aided the insurgency but insisted that because of their gender they could not be punished. Tom concluded, just as Hugh and their sister Ellen had, that rebel women, by their actions, had forfeited the right to be treated as defenseless ladies.[55]

Thanks to the reports from the besieged Unionist minority in western Missouri, Tom identified and subsequently took prisoner a number of women who had aided their relatives in the guerrilla bands. Their ranks included a cousin of Cole Younger and Jesse and Frank James's sister and mother, along with the wives and sisters of other insurgents. In spite of his decision to treat the women as more or less combatants, Tom tried to make them physically comfortable. His courtesy, however, did have an edge. Tom insisted on lodging Quantrill's personal prostitutes with the other, highly displeased, women. The patriarch of the Younger family, after all, had been a Jackson County legislator and judge.[56]

Tragically, the three-story brick building that Ewing used for the incarceration of the women proved to be structurally unsound. On August 13 it collapsed, killing five women, including the Younger cousin and the sister of guerrilla "Bloody" Bill Anderson. (Anderson had earned his nickname by scalping *white* women and raping young black girls.) Major Plumb and guards from the Ninth Kansas desperately hunted through the wreckage in an effort to rescue survivors. Hundreds of hostile Kansas City residents gathered to curse the Kansas soldiers, prompting Plumb to deploy troops—bayonets fixed—around the perimeter of the debris. Confederate sympathizers accused Tom of intentionally weakening the foundations of the structure to murder defenseless women. Meanwhile the owner of the building, Missouri state treasurer and portrait painter George Caleb Bingham, deflected blame and joined the anti-Ewing chorus. Bingham had earlier complained to Schofield about Tom's policy of detaining civilians suspected of aiding the insurgency. If anyone was predisposed to think the worst of Tom, it was Bingham.[57]

Quantrill viewed the events of August 13 as a pretext to carry forward a plan he already had been contemplating—a raid on Lawrence, Kansas, and the extermination of its male population. Once Quantrill learned that Senator Lane was in Lawrence, rather than Washington, he launched his raid on August 20. He had with him the largest band ever assembled on the frontier—a force of approximately four hundred guerrillas. Their plan was to make the fifty-mile ride from the Missouri border to Lawrence, taking captives as guides and then killing them when their usefulness ended. His plan was nearly wrecked, however, when the Union outpost at Aubry, Kansas, spotted Quantrill's troops. Although Captain Joshua Pike of the Ninth Kansas had two companies in his command, he chose not to intercept the guerrillas. Worse, he sent an alarm to other army outposts along the border but failed to warn civilians to the west.[58]

The guerrillas entered Lawrence in the early hours of August 21. Some of the rural Missourians were initially reluctant to continue their mission. They had never been in a city as large and imposing as Lawrence, with its 185 buildings and population of over two thousand. Quantrill, however, urged his men forward, with Cole Younger throwing himself into the fray. Jim Lane topped their "death list," but the senator managed to sneak out of town, leaving his wife behind to greet Quantrill's murder squad. One hundred and seventy-five other men and boys were not so fortunate. The southerners shot all the male children they could find, killing them in front of their mothers and sisters. Black males were highly valued targets and could expect a prolonged death rather than a quick bullet to the head.[59]

Since there were but twenty Union soldiers in Lawrence, Quantrill's men had little interference as they killed and burned over the course of four hours. Guerrillas lined up seventeen of the troops from the Fourteenth Kansas and trampled them under their horses. When they found that some of the Kansas soldiers and male civilians had survived their initial trampling and gunshot wounds, Quantrill's men threw them into burning buildings. *Harper's Weekly* subsequently described a scene that could have been copied from the pages of Exodus or Matthew: "Women distraught with anguish, sobbing children, homeless families; weeping mothers, wives, and sisters, kneeling beside

The ruins of Lawrence, Kansas, 1863. Confederate guerrillas, under the command of Ohio native William Quantrill, murdered 175 men and male children in the abolitionist stronghold of Lawrence. This infamous massacre provided one of the pretexts for General Tom Ewing to issue General Order Number 11 in an effort to crush the insurgency. (Courtesy of the Library of Congress.)

bleeding bodies. The sultry, heavy air, blue with smoke of burning buildings, resounded with lamentations."[60]

Belatedly learning of Quantrill's movement deep into Kansas, Major Plumb galloped out of Kansas City with two hundred cavalry troopers from the Ninth and Eleventh Kansas. Although Plumb caught up with some of Quantrill's men in Paola, Kansas, near the Missouri border, the guerrillas escaped with few casualties. Plumb had ridden hard in a futile effort to catch up with Quantrill; both his horses and troops fell under the August sun. Meanwhile, Tom, who had been in Leavenworth, on August 20, placed himself at the head of five companies of the Eleventh Ohio Cavalry and also pursued Quantrill. Tom, however, was no more successful than Plumb. To say that the Eleventh Ohio Cavalry was not ready for hard duty would have been an understatement. One of the company captains had thought it would be funny to see what would happen if he and his horse got drunk together. Neither man nor beast was up for chasing the best white guerrilla fighters in America.[61]

The political fallout from the "Lawrence Massacre" came hard and fast. Southern newspapers, among them the *Charleston Mercury* and the *Richmond Examiner*, celebrated Quantrill's victory. To Confederate partisans, the people of Lawrence were a "malignant" disease that had to be destroyed. It did not occur to such southerners that Quantrill, in committing the mass murder of unarmed men and children, had crossed a line between civilized warfare and barbarism. The Lawrence Massacre enraged Union commanders like Cump—and the Ewing family at large—who were already making fewer distinctions between combatants and noncombatants. Quantrill's actions, which were enthusiastically endorsed by important southern opinion leaders, gave license to the North to target entire communities and populations for collective punishment.[62]

Tom hurriedly sought to minimize the political damage to himself and Plumb. He rightly chastised Captain Pike for not apprising Kansas civilians of Quantrill's foray into the state. Of course, even Pike could receive some allowance, Tom continued. No one, including the residents of Lawrence, could have anticipated a bold attack that deep into Kansas and with such a murderous agenda. Tom also emphasized how vigorously he and Plumb had chased Quantrill, leaving an impression that the guerrillas had only just gotten away. In a ploy worthy of the defense attorney that he was, Tom argued that Grant's voracious appetite for troops had stripped the West of adequate defenses. Tom then went further and hinted that Grant's parole of Vicksburg's Confederates had added to the ranks of the guerrillas: "Great numbers of rebel soldiers, whose families live in Western Missouri, have returned, and being unable or unwilling to live at home, have joined the bands of guerrillas infesting the border. Companies which before this summer mustered but 20 or 23 have now grown to 50 or 100."[63]

General Schofield came to Tom's assistance. Schofield understood that if Tom was removed from command he would be next. Standing behind Tom, Schofield emphasized to superiors that blame for the Lawrence Massacre rested with Quantrill, not with the small number of greatly dispersed Union troops along the Kansas-Missouri border. "It is possible," Schofield allowed, "that General Ewing might have done more than he did do to guard against such a calamity as that at Lawrence; but I believe he is entitled to great credit for the energy, wisdom, and zeal displayed while in command of that district." Schofield also picked up Tom's theme of how few Union troops were available in their theater and pointed out that he had sent eight thousand men to Vicksburg. He noted as well that political factions in Kansas, chiefly the Red Legs, saw Quantrill's actions as justification for a war of extermination against Missouri. Tom Ewing, given his stature in Kansas, was one of the few people who could stand up to "unprincipled leaders" who planned "to fan the flame of popular excitement and goad the people to madness, in the hope of thereby accomplishing their own selfish ends."[64]

The "unprincipled leaders" Schofield had in mind—the same ones Tom pithily referred to as "political Quantrill's"—were, the *New York Times* reported, preparing for an invasion of Missouri. *Harper's Weekly* concurred with the *New York Times*'s assessment of the situation, writing, "Independence, the most important town in Jackson County, is to be plundered and reduced to ashes." Everything Lane said gave fuel to such news media speculation. In Leavenworth, Lane delivered a vivid—and somewhat prophetic—speech: "I will tell you what I want to see. I want to see every foot of ground in Jackson, Cass, and Bates counties [Missouri] burned over—everything laid waste. Then we shall have no further trouble. The bushwhackers cannot remain in the country, for they will have nobody to feed them—nobody to harbor them—nobody to provide them with transportation—no place to sleep in, and will have thirty-five miles further to march before they reach Kansas."[65]

Lane wrote to Lincoln demanding Tom's ouster in hopes of removing a key obstacle to his plans. He denounced Schofield as well, characterizing him as a man of "imbecility and incapacity." Schofield knew that Lane and Leavenworth's Red Leg mayor were raising an armed mob that would kill every man, woman, and child they could find in Missouri, regardless of whether they supported the Union or the Confederacy. He was not about to permit Lane and Anthony to have their way. As Schofield recorded in his diary, "The people of Missouri will not be reconciled to the idea of a total destruction of the State without regard to Loyalty." Both Ewing and Schofield met with Lane and provided reassurances that the guerrillas would pay for their deeds. At the same time, however, they deployed additional troops along the border with orders to shoot Red Leg marauders. One of Tom's investigators took Anthony into custody and transported him to Kansas City. Tom implausibly denied that he had ordered the well-timed detention and released Anthony after the mayor promised to embrace what Schofield described as "a correct understanding as to the relation between the Military and civil authorities" in Leavenworth.[66]

Lincoln gave Lane a brief, noncommittal response to his demand for the dismissal of Schofield and Ewing. To Schofield, Lincoln noted complaints "from two very influential citizens of Kansas, whose names I omit," and issued a short, vague directive: "Please do your utmost to give them future security and to punish their invaders." Their response to Lincoln's vague command was a very explicit plan to crush the guerrilla insurgency. Tom believed that General Order Number 11, which he and Schofield had drafted in a milder form before the Lawrence Massacre, did not violate American military law or the U.S. Constitution in a time of national emergency. Whether or not

Tom was correct, and he was not one to lose cases easily, there was little American historical precedent for their initiative. Perhaps President Andrew Jackson's removal of the "civilized Indian tribes" by U.S. Army troops could be claimed as a historical precedent, but Jackson had defied the U.S. Supreme Court in this instance—part of an overall pattern of behavior that the senior Ewing had roundly condemned in the 1830s.[67]

The thrust of General Order Number 11, which Tom issued on August 25, 1863, could be found in the first paragraph:

> All persons living in Jackson, Cass, and Bates Counties, Missouri, and in that part of Vernon included in this district, except those living within 1 mile of the limits of Independence, Hickman Mills, Pleasant Hill, and Harrisonville, and except those in that part of Kaw Township, Jackson County, north of Brush Creek and west of the Big Blue, are hereby ordered to remove from their present places of residence within fifteen days from the date hereof. Those who, within that time, establish their loyalty to the satisfaction of the commanding officer of the military station nearest their present places of residence will receive from him certificates stating the fact of their loyalty, and the names of the witnesses by whom it can be shown. All who receive such certificates will be permitted to remove to any military station in this district, or to any part of the State of Kansas, except the counties on the eastern border of the State. All others shall remove out of this district.[68]

Most Kansas and Missouri Unionists greeted General Order Number 11 with enthusiasm. As Schofield noted, many of the loyal residents of western Missouri were "warm in their support of General Ewing" and knew that he was "able, popular, and incorruptible." Missouri Unionists, Schofield insisted, regarded General Order Number 11 as "wise and just—in fact a necessity." Though it expelled ten thousand Missouri residents from their homes, there were, Schofield observed, Republican radicals who did not believe that General Order Number 11 had gone far enough; they wanted harsher penalties, perhaps even a wholesale execution of suspected supporters of the guerrillas. Letters from civilians flowed into Tom's Kansas City headquarters, warning him of the verbal attacks Lane continued to make against Ewing and Plumb. Cousin Hamp Denman, writing from Leavenworth, kept a close eye on Mayor Anthony and the other radicals.[69]

Charles Blair—no relation to the Missouri Blairs—also provided support and political intelligence to Tom. Though the son-in-law of Samuel Medary, Ohio's chief antiwar newspaper publisher, Charles Blair was a Unionist

Democrat and former colonel of the Second Kansas Infantry. Blair had even been born in the same southern Ohio, pro-Confederate town as Grant. He was adamant in his opposition to Lane's minions, whom he regarded as vicious purveyors of "terror." As Charles Blair subsequently wrote to Tom, General Order Number 11 "was as necessary for the protection of these very people [western Missouri residents], as it was for that of the border and of the people of Kansas. While beyond military lines, they were subject to contributions from all wandering bands, on both sides, and their houses were made feeding stations and places of rendezvous for the bushwhackers who were the curse and the pest of border warfare."[70]

Although Tom sincerely believed that he was saving the lives of western Missouri residents by removing the guerrilla supporters from the border, others did not agree. Presidential portrait painter George Bingham, already smarting from the deaths of several guerrilla women when his building had collapsed on them, embarked upon what would become a lifetime pursuit of destroying Tom's reputation. Bingham insisted that the Missouri residents Tom removed were innocent women and children, burned out of their homes and raped by Union soldiers. Confederate sympathizers picked up this line of attack, claiming that the roads were crowded with starving refugees cradling their crying babies as they began their exodus. One of guerrillas whose family had to leave western Missouri complained bitterly that "they were banished and robbed" by General Order Number 11. A young exile came away from this experience with a burning hatred of Yankees and armies of occupation—she later conveyed those sentiments to her grandson, Harry S. Truman.[71]

Concerned about his postwar political plans and the prospect of permanently alienating voters in western Missouri, General Frank Blair blasted Tom. Blair called General Order Number 11 "the subterfuge of an imbecile." Already embroiled in a bitter factional fight between Republican conservatives and radicals over Lincoln's policy of emancipation, Blair perceived Ewing's and Schofield's actions to be another threat to his march to the White House. Heeding the wails of protest from Blair and other Missouri Unionists, Lincoln sent Schofield a directive that tried to soften the blow of General Order Number 11. While Lincoln insisted that he did not want General Order Number 11 set aside, he ordered Ewing and Schofield to "only arrest individuals, and suppress assemblies, or newspapers, when they may be working *palpable* injury to the military in your charge; and in no other case will you interfere with the expression of opinion in any form, or allow it to be interfered with violently by others." Schofield urged Lincoln to stop listening to wild, unsubstantiated charges made against him and Tom.[72]

Ellen Cox Ewing (1833–1919). The daughter of an Ohio Presbyterian minister, Ellen Cox Ewing loyally followed her husband Tom to Kansas and stood by his side during most of the guerrilla warfare in the Missouri theater. Like her husband, she had good relations with William T. Sherman but found Ellen Sherman to be less tolerable. (Courtesy of the University of Notre Dame Archives.)

Even as Lincoln, Blair, and others debated the politics and military utility of General Order Number 11, Tom was able to suspend it by November 1863. General Order Number 11 had worked as he and Schofield anticipated. One guerrilla chief observed that "the country having been depopulated under General Ewing's Order Number Eleven, the men were sorely tried for food, apples being the only edible thing found in Missouri after leaving Lafayette County, and the boys nearly starved." Confederate general Joe Shelby, having relied upon the guerrillas to aid his western forces, lamented that General Order Number 11 "not only cut off a large amount of supplies, but it removed a large number of our friends and sympathizers." Major Wyllis Ransom of the Sixth Kansas Cavalry came to the same conclusion. Other commentators, contemporaneous and after the fact, also credited Tom and General Order Number 11 with preventing Lane and Anthony from taking a rage-filled revenge on all Missouri residents in the Kansas City vicinity.[73]

Tom could, and did, claim vindication, and saw Quantrill's unsuccessful October 6, 1863, raid on Baxter Springs, Kansas, as the last great gasp of the insurgency. Subsequent guerrilla attacks, which mainly occurred in central and eastern Missouri, rather than along the border with Kansas, tended not to be large and well planned. Guerrillas also could no longer operate as effectively as they once had in Missouri without the protection of regular Confederate forces. As an independent fighting force and instrument of political terror, the guerrillas were greatly diminished after Tom issued General Order Number 11.[74]

Whatever comfort Tom could take in his apparent success in the fall of 1863 was nearly outweighed by the mental toll the insurgency had inflicted upon him. Faced with an unrelenting chorus of criticism from Lane, Anthony, Blair, and Bingham, Tom saw himself as a human sacrifice for their ambitions: "My political enemies are fanning the flames, and wish me for a burnt offering to satisfy the just and terrible passion of the people." He also became more short-tempered with his wife. Most plainly visible were the large number of boils that appeared on his body as his nerves became frayed. The boils, along with stabbing pain in the areas of skin eruption, were the symptoms of what was most likely neuralgia—a nervous disorder. (Antidepressants are often used to treat neuralgia today.) His sister Ellen had been plagued by neuralgia for years. Until he had to deal the consequences of the Lawrence Massacre, Tom had always been able to control his emotions, maintain a calm repose, and avoid major skin eruptions.[75]

While Tom eventually regained his composure, Ellen Sherman sank into a depression from which she never fully recovered. In August 1863, Ellen and the children—Minnie, Lizzie, Willie, and Tommy—had joined Cump at

Vicksburg. They toured the battlefield and even compelled Cump to attend Mass. Willie and Tommy Sherman shared a tent with Charley—their most entertaining uncle. Like his father and Uncle Charley, Willie had a restless and curious nature. Tommy, in contrast, was as studious and reserved as his namesake uncle. It took no time at all for the troops in the Thirteenth U.S. Infantry to adopt Willie Sherman, giving him a uniform and "rank" of sergeant. Charley even taught Willie the U.S. Army's manual of arms—just as his great-grandfather George Ewing had learned its original incarnation at Valley Forge.[76]

Tragically, when Cump's family prepared their return to Lancaster, Willie fell fatally sick from typhoid fever. Hugh observed that Willie "suffered dreadfully before he died," burning with fever as he received the Last Rites. Just a couple of years earlier in St. Louis, Charley had thrown his body over Willie to shield him from flying bullets. Now Charley helped his inconsolable sister bring Willie home for burial. Ellen memorialized Cump's favorite son thus:

> A Christian hero, in death as in life, he bore his sharp illness with unmurmuring patience; and although distressed to leave his parents sorrowing, he offered his soul with living abandon to the will of his Heavenly Father, and in Christian faith and hope he passed the dark portal, and entered into everlasting life.
>
> . . . The morning sun shone in upon his birth—the evening sun shed luster about his dying head. The angel of morning brought him to the earth. The angel of night bore him to the living source of all life, and light and love.[77]

It was all too much for Maria Ewing to bear. In addition to Willie's death, Maria Theresa's fiancée, Clemens Steele, had been shot up in July 1863 while unsuccessfully assaulting Battery Wagner outside Charleston, South Carolina. Scores of men in the Sixty-Second Ohio and the Fifty-Fourth Massachusetts, an African American regiment, were either killed or wounded. Completely bedridden by the fall of 1863, the Ewing matriarch cradled her daughters and wept. Clemens recovered sufficiently enough to wed Maria Theresa—the ceremony performed by a Catholic priest in Maria Ewing's bedroom. Like Cousin Phil Stanbery, Steele had been disabled too severely to return to combat.[78]

After Willie's sudden demise, Cump became distracted, finding it difficult to focus on logistics, terrain, and deployments. Charley stepped forward to fill some of the void, but the timing of Cump's mental fog could not have been worse for his troops. A few hundred miles away, in the vicinity of Chattanooga, Tennessee, General William Rosecrans, Hugh's mentor from West Point and superior in the western Virginian campaign, had gotten his army into a desperate situation. Thrown into retreat by Confederate general Braxton Bragg, Rosecrans had fallen back on Chattanooga. Entrenched in the high ground above Chattanooga, Bragg and General James Longstreet—Lee's finest surviving corps commander—pinned down Union forces. Chattanooga was, like Vicksburg, a key river and rail hub, providing Union and Confederate forces with transportation links to Nashville and Atlanta. So long as Bragg occupied Lookout Mountain and Missionary Ridge, the Union would have difficulty pacifying Tennessee, let alone mounting an invasion of Georgia.[79]

Rosecrans had little in his favor beyond Bragg's intense jealousy of Longstreet, which demoralized the rebel army and hampered timely communication and coordination. Indeed, relations were so bad between Longstreet and Bragg that they avoided each other for two weeks during the crucial month of October. As Thomas Ewing had heard from Zachary Taylor years ago, Bragg was a fearful and petty man—personality flaws that enemies could exploit. Still, Rosecrans could not count on Bragg to make mistakes. Given the circumstances, Lincoln knew he needed Grant to salvage Union fortunes once again.[80]

Cump, Hugh, Charley, and a detachment of the Thirteenth U.S. Infantry boarded a train in advance of the rest of Fifteenth Corps. On October 11, twenty-six miles east of Memphis, the soldiers riding on top of Cump's train spotted a rebel force in front attempting to remove sections of rail. The train, which had just gone through Collierville, Tennessee, went into reverse to link up with the Sixty-Sixth Indiana, which garrisoned the station. Cump just managed to send a telegram requesting help before the wires were cut. He had an improvised force of 450 soldiers and 30 Unionist civilians facing 3,100 Confederate troops. The rebels also had five small cannons. Civilians sympathetic to the Confederacy had most likely passed along the information that a lightly protected Cump and his staff were passing through.[81]

When Confederate general James Chalmers of Mississippi demanded that the Yankees lay down their arms lest he kill them all, Cump gave a laconic reply: "The government pays me to fight, not to surrender." Chalmers immediately fired his artillery pieces, mostly overshooting, though one sergeant seeking cover had the heel of his boot torn off by shrapnel. Cump, who, as one soldier observed, "was mad as a march hare at being trapped in such a manner," came to life, helping to improvise a defense.[82]

While Cump held the center with a few infantry, Charley and Hugh engaged the enemy at the flanks. Charley and the Thirteenth U.S. battled along their train, moving in and out among the boxcars in a lethal game of hide-and-seek. Hugh, watching another band of rebels preparing to attack from the north, ordered the Sixty-Sixth Indiana to set fire to a house. The flames burned so intensely that the Confederates shifted their line westward—straight into the teeth of Hugh's firing lines. The fighting had lasted for four hours when a Union relief column finally arrived and Chalmers fled. A quarter of Cump's little command had been killed or wounded. He had been lucky. Many of the headquarters' troops were cooks and orderlies who had never seen action, while the Thirteenth U.S. was well represented by the members of its marching band. Indeed, the moment it became clear that Chalmers was withdrawing, many of the Thirteenth U.S. soldiers dropped their muskets, picked up their musical instruments, and played a rousing rendition of "The Battle Cry of Freedom."[83]

Unfortunately for his command, Cump's moment of clarity faded after the Collierville skirmish. Ellen's letters to Cump revealed a woman who had fallen into an emotional abyss: "My heart is now in heaven and the world is dark and dreary to me. Now I realize that this life is but a probation and that we really live only in our home above." Her depression worked to deepen Cump's and contributed to his own mental fog. Writing to Ellen, Cump confessed that "sleeping, walking, everywhere I see poor Willie." Cump, who had long wanted to separate Ellen from Lancaster and the influence of his in-laws, had insisted that his children join him at Vicksburg. He faulted himself for causing his cherished son's death.[84]

Grant organized his forces and by November 1863 had made a perilous link up with Rosecrans in Chattanooga. The Union supply and communication line into Chattanooga ran along a narrow and mostly washed-out road some sixty miles in length. Gazing up to the cloud-shrouded mountains, George Hildt was not alone among Hugh's troops to feel "despondent." If it was any consolation to Grant's sixty thousand soldiers, Confederate deserters reported that they were lucky to receive one meal a day. When President Jefferson Davis visited his old friend Bragg, the Confederates chanted, "Send us something to eat, Massa Jeff. I'm hungry! I'm hungry!" If the Confederates were starving, perhaps then they would susceptible to tactics designed to weaken their morale further. Hugh shrewdly ordered his men to light as many campfires at night as possible so that Bragg's army would think the Yankees' numbers were far larger. Maybe if Fifteenth Corps was lucky, the rebels would be sufficiently intimidated enough to flee without a Union assault.[85]

Until his arrival in Chattanooga, Grant had proven himself to be a fair-minded commander who was able to make swift tactical adjustments when necessary. There was little evidence of these strengths at Missionary Ridge. Grant, for some reason, neither respected nor trusted General George Thomas, even though his determined stand at Chickamauga had enabled Rosecrans to retreat safely to Chattanooga. Cump, who had known Thomas for years, did not come to his defense, seemingly regarding Thomas as a rival. Clearly playing favorites, Grant ordered Thomas to make a diversionary assault on the Confederate center, while Sherman directed the real attack against the rebel right flank. Cump, mired in his remorse over the death of Willie, failed to study the terrain where he would be sending Hugh. If he had, he would have realized that instead of ordering his brother-in-law to assault the base of Missionary Ridge, he was sending him into a gorge where Hugh's command would be the proverbial fish shot in the barrel.[86]

Prior to the morning assault on November 25, Hugh had written to Henrietta that he hoped Cump "will be well again." Hugh fretted as Cump refused food and withdrew from others. When Cump ordered the Fourth Division to prepare for Fifteenth Corps's attack, Hugh, who had studied the ground, expressed concern. Cump not only cut Hugh short but loudly mocked his brother-in-law. *New York Herald* reporter William Shanks heard Sherman tell Hugh, "I say, Ewing, don't call for help until you actually need it." Shanks expressed his disgust with Sherman. Hugh, after all, had spent hours with his outnumbered Forlorn Hope at Vicksburg absorbing Confederate shot without respite. Cump's admonishment, Shanks believed, was as undeserved as it was humiliating.[87]

As Hugh had anticipated, his division advanced through Billy Goat Hill and into a gorge near Tunnel Hill, where his troops became easy targets for Confederate artillery and muskets. A soldier in the Thirty-Seventh Ohio observed, "The fire was so murderous that it fairly plowed up the leaves and made the very ground seem alive."[88]

In their subsequent official reports, Hugh and his senior officers focused on the heroism of the Fourth Division, not writing a single word of reproach directed toward either Cump or Grant. Hugh's emotional tumult, however, came through. At four o'clock in the afternoon Hugh ordered a withdrawal, sending an aide to relay the command through the artillery storm. When the visibly terrified aide returned, Hugh exclaimed, "My God, I am glad to see you, I never expected to see you come back alive." His written report was a chronicle of horror:

> The loss in killed and wounded of the troops under my command in this battle was eight hundred; among them the gallant [Colonel Timothy] O'Meara, who, when the line wavered, seized a musket from the hands of

a fallen man, and pushing through to the front, was shot well in advance of his regiment [Ninetieth Illinois], urging them forward. He refused to be taken from the field, directing the party that came for him to take off his wounded men. He was not found until after midnight, nearly frozen, having received a second mortal wound as he lay, and died in the morning. I rode over the field at daybreak and found Captain [Daniel] O'Connor ten paces in advance of the skirmishers of the [Chicago] Irish Legion, kneeling upright on one knee, sword in hand, frozen to a statue. His men lay dead behind him, in line, well dressed, at their regular intervals of five paces.[89]

To Grant's chagrin, it was George Thomas's men who turned a Union defeat into a decisive victory for the North. It had become an open secret among the Union troops that Grant favored Cump over Thomas. Aroused at the perceived offense given to their commander—and, by extension, to themselves—Thomas's soldiers made more than a diversionary assault; they stormed the ridge. Both Grant and Sherman, in their official reports and memoirs, gave the impression that the plan all along had been for Thomas to assault Bragg's center. In their revisionist accounts, Cump's attack at Tunnel Hill was a diversion intended to lure Bragg into transferring troops to his flank and thereby weakening his center. Revealing a particularly unpleasant side of his personality to his relatives and friends, Cump criticized Thomas for not assaulting Bragg's center sooner. Hugh's losses, Cump insisted in a letter to his father-in-law, were not his fault.[90]

Regardless of Cump's and Grant's petty behavior toward Thomas, Bragg had suffered a major strategic loss and left the gate open to Atlanta. In terms of killed, wounded, and missing, however, Missionary Ridge seemed less like a victory and more like a bloodbath. Grant's casualties were 5,824, while Bragg's tallied to 6,687. Hugh Ewing's division accounted for 13 percent of Grant's casualties. The overall Union casualty rate had been 10 percent. Scores of Hugh's wounded subsequently died in the field hospital. When Hugh, despite his losses, urged Cump to pursue and destroy Bragg's retreating forces, Sherman and his other officers refused.[91]

While Hugh became more frustrated with Cump, and the cold Tennessee mountain weather worsened his joint pains, the Ewing family faced its worst crisis to date. All of the Ewing children had seen from their father's recent letters that his once steady hand was wavering. Ellen reported worriedly to Cump that Thomas Ewing frequently appeared exhausted. She did not recognize from his symptoms that the senior Ewing had been experiencing a series of heart attacks. Worse, Ellen informed Cump, was that according to the family's doctors Maria Ewing's condition was terminal. It finally came to light, during a surgical probing of her body, that Maria was cancerous. Hugh, Tom, and Charley were, if possible, to obtain leaves. Cump returned to Lancaster for a few days but then left to assume command of the Military Division of the Mississippi when Grant received promotion and prepared to depart for the eastern theater.[92]

Thomas Ewing's illness, coupled with Maria's dramatic physical deterioration, had reduced his political activities—both in Ohio and nationally. With Lincoln, he confined himself mainly to correspondence, rather than actual White House visits. Thomas Ewing advised the president not to provoke war with England by protesting too publicly the British production of ironclad raiding ships for the Confederate Navy. As Ewing argued, "England would now be delighted with the opportunity of pouncing down upon us unprepared—I trust in God we will one day be able to pay her up old scores and new and that the day of retribution is not distant—but I see nothing but mischief from assuming an absolute hostile position now."[93]

Within the Ewing inner circle, the Patriarch offered advice but did not take to the campaign trail. He continued, along with John Sherman and his old friend Orville Browning, to advance the career of Andrew Johnson. The Tennessee military governor spent much time in Ohio, addressing Unionist audiences in Cincinnati and delivering a speech to the Ohio legislature in Columbus. His Columbus address was a three-hour-long indictment of antiwar Democrats. Acting on behalf of his father and Johnson, Phil Ewing organized a Unionist rally in Lancaster in the fall of 1863 that drew twenty thousand participants. As Browning wrote to the elder Ewing, prowar Democrats and moderate Republicans had to unite against disloyal northern Democrats and Radical Republican extremists. John Sherman concurred with Browning and warned Cump that the Gettysburg and Vicksburg victories gave Unionists little political advantage so long as the war continued. Alarmingly, the senator continued, "[George] McClellan has succeeded in establishing the position of a [Democratic] Party leader, and now enjoys the bad honor of being cheered by a New York mob of thieves and scoundrels."[94]

Cousin Jimmy Blaine shared the Ewing family's fears for the success of the Union. As a first-term member of the U.S. House of Representatives from Maine he had spent much of 1863 clashing with antiwar Democrats. He found them defiant, confidant of victory, and viciously racist. When Blaine expressed some concern for wounded black Union soldiers, Ohio's irrepressible Democratic congressman, Samuel Cox, shot back that all wounded black troops should be returned to their masters. It did not seem to matter to Cox that there were thousands of black troops who had been born free in the North; he would send them south in chains. As Cox had proclaimed on the floors of Congress, Lincoln's pointless war had killed hundreds of thousands of white men for the benefit of racially inferior Africans. Taking a leaf from the Ten Commandments, Cox intoned, "Thou shalt not degrade the white race by such intermixtures as emancipation will bring."[95]

Encouraged by mounting Union casualties in 1863, more northern antiwar Democrats emulated Cox's example. Antiwar partisans shot or stoned Union Army recruiters in Indiana, Ohio, and Wisconsin. Irish Catholic rioters opposed to military conscription clashed with U.S. Army and police officers in Boston and New York City—the latter incident claiming the lives of at least 105 people. Some three thousand black residents were burned out of their homes. Middle-class Americans were shocked that working-class *women* had helped torch a black orphanage in New York. An assassin attempted to kill Indiana's Republican governor, Oliver Morton. Indeed, the political situation in Indiana was so intense that the Democratic legislature refused to authorize funding for the state's war effort. Morton decided not to call the legislature back into session and had to borrow funds from private individuals and the War Department. Prior to the battle at Gettysburg, Pennsylvania senator and moderate Republican Edgar Cowan warned Lincoln, "The sentiment of despondency is universal, indeed I think I may say that I have not met a single man who entertains a rational hope of ultimate success—under the present management of affairs." So far there was little available evidence that public opinion in Pennsylvania had turned around after Lee's repulse.[96]

When Confederate general John Hunt Morgan led a three-thousand-man cavalry raid across southern Indiana and Ohio, Confederate sympathizers directed them to loot and burn Unionist homes and businesses. Morgan's men subsequently set fire to Thomas Ewing's Hocking Valley canal boats in the coal-producing settlement of Nelsonville. Samuel Medary's *Columbus Crisis* decried Lincoln's "bastard government." Ohio's Democratic attorney general, Lyman Critchfield, exhorted antiwar partisans to engage in "armed resistance" against Republicans if Lincoln continued to have his critics detained. Lancaster's "Copperheads" grew so bold that they assaulted Union soldiers home on leave. They also ransacked the office of the Republican newspaper, the *Lancaster Gazette*.[97]

Wearied of heated antiwar speeches, General Ambrose Burnside, exiled to the Department of the Ohio after the disastrous battle of Fredericksburg, ordered the arrest of former Democratic congressman Clement Vallandigham. (Prior to his departure from Congress, Vallandigham had earned much praise among antiwar voters for refusing to vote for resolutions praising Union soldiers and increasing their pay.) Rioting broke out in Dayton,

Clement L. Vallandigham (1820–71), Ohio attorney and antiwar Democratic member of the U.S House of Representatives, arrested by military leaders in Ohio and exiled from the North. As the only member of Congress ever expelled from the United States (or at least the portion of the United States that had remained in the Union), Vallandigham mounted from Canada an unsuccessful campaign for Ohio governor in 1863. (Courtesy of the Library of Congress.)

with two hundred of Vallandigham's supporters setting fire to the city's Republican newspaper office. Burnside proclaimed martial law and shut down Dayton's Democratic newspaper.[98]

Lincoln did not want to see Vallandigham arrested, let alone tried before a military tribunal. Putting a former U.S. congressman and Lincoln critic in the docket carried enormous political risk. Even the reliably bellicose naval secretary Gideon Welles considered Vallandigham's arrest and trial to have been "arbitrary and injudicious." The political damage, however, could not be reversed. Vallandigham became a national political martyr. Cox rushed to Dayton to stand by Vallandigham. Lincoln decided it would be better to exile Vallandigham to the South than to hang him for treason. Far from being counted out, Vallandigham received Ohio's Democratic gubernatorial nomination. As Cousin Jimmy Blaine observed of Vallandigham, "if not the ablest" Democratic politician in the North, he "was the frankest and boldest member of his party."[99]

Confederate general P. T. Beauregard exulted at Vallandigham's nomination, hoping that his election would result in Ohio casting "off the yoke of the accursed Yankee nation." Equally enthusiastic Ohio Democrats turned out in droves for their candidate in exile. At campaign rallies, Vallandigham's supporters paraded in Union uniforms, their faces painted black. These mock black soldiers used their bayonets to poke Lincoln's innocent Democratic "prisoners" while the crowds roared in approval. Democrats also distributed banners to their wives and daughters that pleaded, "Save us from nigger husbands." None of this surprised John Sherman, who, after gauging public sentiment in Ohio, had gone on record as opposed to the enlistment of black soldiers. He pithily observed in 1863 that most of Ohio's white Democrats "will fight for the flag and country, but they hate niggers, and easily influenced by a party cry, stick to their party while its organization is controlled by the [worst] set of traitors in this country, North or South."[100]

Fearful that Governor Tod had, like Dennison before him, become a lightning rod for antiwar critics, moderate Republicans and Unionist Democrats chose a new candidate to face Vallandigham. The Western Reserve's Radical Republicans were enraged. John Brough was a longtime Democrat who effortlessly sidestepped questions about emancipation and the enlistment of black soldiers. As if to damn him further, Brough had been publisher of the Democratic Party's Lancaster Eagle before the war. In spite of his Lancaster connections, Brough's memories of the Ewing tribe were not fond. Since Brough's girth was enormous, Hugh and Tom had put Charley up to any number of "fat man" pranks. On one occasion, Hugh found a large, round pumpkin on which he drew a remarkable likeness of Brough. He and Tom then encouraged Charley to roll the pumpkin down Main Hill to Brough's house, knock on the publisher's door, and wait around long enough for the rotund gentlemen to see the pumpkin. Both brothers howled when Brough slowly trotted after Charley, puffing away and shouting but never quite able to catch their little brother as he fled up Main Hill.[101]

Vallandigham mobilized the old Virginia Military District and performed well in central Ohio, carrying the capital county of Franklin along with the Ewing's own Fairfield County. But in these elections, unlike the 1862 elections, Unionists won, with Vallandigham receiving 187,000 votes, or 39 percent. It helped considerably that the U.S. Army released Ohio troops to return home to vote, while other soldiers received absentee ballots. Ohio Democrats had failed to prevent passage of Unionist legislation in the spring of 1863 granting troops the right to vote. When confronted with soldier tallies that went 41,467 for Brough to 2,228 for Vallandigham, Democratic newspapers and politicians cried fraud. The truth was that if Ohio's Union troops had not been inclined to vote Republican earlier, putting their lives on the firing line while antiwar Democrats at home avoided the fight led them to support Unionists. General Rosecrans captured the dark, angry mood of his fellow Ohioans when he remarked, "Tell them [in Ohio] that this army would have given a stronger vote for Brough had not Vallandigham's friends over yonder [on Missionary Ridge] killed two or three thousand Ohio voters the other day at Chickamauga."[102]

When it became apparent that Brough's electoral coattails had enabled Unionists to capture twenty-nine of the thirty-four Ohio senate seats and seventy-three of the ninety-seven Ohio house seats, Secretary of War Edwin Stanton told the governor-elect, "Your election is a glorious victory, worthy of the rejoicing which will greet it." Gideon Welles confided to his diary that Lincoln had been watching Ohio's gubernatorial race with "more anxiety in regard to the election results of yesterday than he had in 1860 when he was chosen [for president]." Still, Lincoln thought that the considerable Vallandigham vote was "a discredit to the country."[103]

Whatever satisfaction the Ewings could take in Vallandigham's defeat was tempered by the knowledge that the antiwar Democrats could still make a resurgence in 1864, capture the White House, and recognize Confederate independence. Few in the family's circle of allies had any faith in Lincoln. All knew that emancipation had, as Thomas Ewing and Orville Brown predicted, alienated many northern Democrats who had been supportive of a war to preserve the Union. The Vicksburg and Gettysburg victories counted for little with the northern electorate so long as the war continued its bloody way at places such as Missionary Ridge.

The war, as Democrats like Vallandigham and Cox rightly said, had already shattered the lives of hundreds of thousands of Americans by the close of 1863. Even the Ewings, as stalwart in the defense of the Union as they were, had suffered. Both Cump and Ellen perceived their cherished Willie to have been a casualty of war. Cousin Phil Stanbery and Maria Theresa's husband had come home from war permanently crippled. The young Stanbery made a partial physical recovery, but his wild prewar spirit had been replaced with a sobriety he took to his grave.

Cousin Eliza Gillespie ("Mother Angela") had worn herself out nursing the legion of casualties, thwarting the attempted assassination of a wounded Confederate officer by Union troops, and contending with superiors in France who did not approve of the role her religious order was playing in the war. For their part, Hugh and Tom were at the point of mental exhaustion. Only Charley, slightly wounded, appeared in decent spirits as the family prepared for what would be Maria Ewing's last Christmas.

6

"War Is Cruelty"

Atlanta, Pilot Knob, and Washington, 1864

You cannot qualify war in harsher terms than I will. War is cruelty, and you cannot refine it; and those who brought war into our country deserve all the curses and maledictions a people can pour out. I know I had no hand in making this war, and I know I will make more sacrifices to-day than any of you to secure peace. But you cannot have peace and a division of our country. If the United States submits to a division now, it will not stop, but will go on until we reap the fate of Mexico, which is eternal war. The United States does and must assert its authority, wherever it once had power; for, if it relaxes one bit to pressure, it is gone, and I believe that such is the national feeling.
—William T. Sherman, 1864

As December 1863 slipped into the New Year, Cump had regained his footing. The fact that he and Grant had nearly destroyed their reputations—along with Hugh's Fourth Division—at Missionary Ridge may have shocked Cump out of his doldrums. He also had more time to grieve and then come to accept the loss of Willie as something beyond his control. When it came to religious matters, Cump's God had a capricious, vengeful side—unlike Ellen's wise, loving God whose Divine Plan was beyond her comprehension. Further lifting Cump's spirits was the fact that he had received his own army and a new, major military objective: Atlanta. At the end of 1863 Cump was more than his old self; he had become jubilant and eloquent. To Grant, Cump wrote that his chief would defeat Robert E. Lee in the East and then "heal and mend up the breaches made by war." It helped the Union cause immensely that Lincoln had pushed the militarily inept Henry Halleck aside and placed Grant in operational command of all the armies.[1]

Addressing a crowd that had gathered at the Main Hill mansion, Cump gave his first political speech. It was one part Thomas Ewing—paeans to western expansion and America's revolutionary heritage—and one part Daniel Webster—Union now and forever. The *New York Times* took notice:

> I did not believe that the men of this generation were so degenerate, so unworthy of their revolutionary fathers, as to allow this great country to be destroyed. Gentlemen, our country is an entirety—as a unit it came into our hands, from Washington and his compeers—one single grand domain, since stretched from one ocean on the east to another on the west, and capable of indefinite extension to the north and south—and *one* country it must remain to the latest generations. Such is the resolves of your armies in the field; and that this result will be worked out, you may take my word for it.[2]

Cump left Lancaster before Hugh, Tom, and Charley arrived. It would be up to Ellen, her brothers, and Hugh's and Tom's wives to maintain a death vigil for Maria Ewing. All the children took turns talking to their mother. During the periods when Maria was able to sleep through her pain, the brothers had individual and group photographs taken. It was the first time since the war had begun that they were together in uniform. Phil, looking out of place in his civilian dress, nonetheless joined his younger brothers, striking his best Napoleonic pose. Maria died a week later, in late February 1864. Cincinnati Archbishop John Baptist Purcell said the funeral Mass. Despite woefully swollen legs, likely due to his heart condition and resultant water retention, Thomas Ewing rallied. He buried Maria and then rededicated himself to saving the Union from rebels and Radical Republicans. He could not, however, stave off the civil war brewing within his family.[3]

Distraught over her mother's death, and once again feeling abandoned by Cump, Ellen lashed out at Tom and Hugh. Charley, as usual, escaped largely unscathed, since his sister regarded him as her first child who could do little wrong. It also helped that Charley studiously avoided arguments with his sister. Still, Ellen lamented, Charley was not "free from the faults and vices of men as I am." More charitably, Thomas Ewing later confided to Grant, "Among my sons Charles has perhaps more uncalculating chivalry than any other." Ewing, however, also observed that Charley had a "somewhat nervous temperament."[4]

Ellen mistook Tom's and Hugh's emotional detachment for indifference toward the deaths of Maria Ewing and Willie Sherman. She could not empathize with the mental and physical toll the war had taken on them. Cump, after all, was invigorated by the war, while Hugh and Tom, like the overwhelming majority of soldiers on both sides of the conflict, were wearied.

The Ewing brothers had a sad reunion in Lancaster, Ohio, in 1864 as their mother Maria, broken physically by cancer and distraught by the toll the war had taken upon her family, awaited death. (Courtesy of the University of Notre Dame Archives.)

Ellen denounced Tom as "a supremely selfish man [who] has failed in my affliction to treat me even as an ordinary friend." She ordered Cump to have nothing to do with Tom and his equally deplorable wife. As for Hugh, Ellen conceded that Cump had "often wounded his feelings by a want of courtesy of manner." Still, she continued, Hugh's wife Henrietta was a social climber who had kept Ellen at arm's length. Ellen also slyly faulted Hugh for drinking excessively, not acknowledging that his painful rheumatism had become so pronounced that there were times when he could not stand up without assistance. She did, however, observe that Grant was a worse drunk.[5]

The Ewing brothers shrugged off Ellen's attacks. They knew that Ellen had always possessed the most nervous temperament of the siblings. Contrary to what Ellen believed, Hugh and Tom did appreciate how deeply the loss of Willie and Maria weighed on their elder sister. Tom himself, as his experiences in Kansas demonstrated, had a nervous disorder just like Ellen. Unlike, Ellen, however, Tom disciplined himself and kept his feelings in tight check. His emotions only occasionally found expression. Hugh was an emotional man in his own right, a romantic and idealist who had seen so many horrors that he could not readily find the words to describe his combat experiences. Ellen, however, could not, or would not, try to understand what had been happening with Tom and Hugh. Only Charley appeared lively, but even he did not talk with his sisters about what he had endured. By the beginning of 1864, Ellen's circle of confidants had contracted to three: Mother Angela Gillespie, Thomas Ewing, and Cump. And at that, Cump had increasingly acted as if his true love was Grant—if not the war itself. This might have been why Grant received Ellen's barbs; her jealously and tartness sprang from her sense of abandonment.

Hugh requested and received reassignment from Grant, who appointed him commander of the Western Division of the Military District of Kentucky. (There was a separate Eastern Division.) With a few thousand troops Hugh would be responsible for dealing with guerrilla insurgents and Confederate raiders. Although Tom's toxic experiences with Missouri bushwhackers might have given Hugh cause to reconsider his decision, he liked the prospect of having his family with him in Louisville. The city had good theaters and restaurants, which were, as Ellen Sherman correctly surmised, major considerations for Henrietta.[6]

Cultural amenities aside, the fact remained that guerrillas were, as the New York Times reported, capturing and then burning express trains running out of Louisville. Worse, the raw Union troops assigned to protect the trains, even though outnumbering the guerrillas two to one, had a habit of surrendering without firing a shot. Never one to shirk from charging headlong into a challenge, Hugh wasted little time in organizing aggressive patrols and detaining civilians who aided the insurgents. He even detained Joshua Bullitt, the chief justice of the Kentucky Court of Appeals. Bullitt, Hugh charged, was a member of the pro-Confederate Order of American Knights. The judge's politically connected relatives complained to Lincoln and he received a parole. Bullitt, who had kin serving in the Confederate Army, subsequently fled to Canada, where he joined the company of other rebel exiles.[7]

Kentucky governor Thomas Bramlette demonstrated that he was more concerned about racial issues than with guerrilla assaults on Unionists. Although he had been a prowar Democrat, Bramlette rejected Lincoln following the Emancipation Proclamation and the enlistment of black soldiers. He vowed that no black Union soldiers would ever be allowed to live in Kentucky after the war. Those troops included the 122nd U.S. Colored Infantry, who were under Hugh's command. Bramlette expressed anger at Hugh's judicial and military pursuit of Confederate sympathizers. He was also upset because Hugh executed guerrilla prisoners in retaliation for the murder of Unionists. The irate governor ordered all state officials to refuse cooperation with the army. Hugh reported to his superiors that Bramlette reminded him of a child who "fell into the river at Louisville; a stranger caught him by the hair as he was sinking and brought him out; the boy, when sufficiently recovered, ran to a pile of brick, seized a bat and threw it as the stranger, exclaiming, 'Damn you, you pulled my hair!' The cases are analogous. The resentment of each arose from a like insult; but they differed in this: that Governor Bramlette, more hasty than the boy, resented the indignity before he got his head above water."[8]

While Hugh swatted Kentucky guerrillas and politicians, Cump and Charley prepared to launch an invasion of Georgia that was destined to cripple the South while bolstering Lincoln's reelection prospects. Cump's line of advance would be no secret to Confederate General Joe Johnston. The Western & Atlantic Railroad ran between Chattanooga and Atlanta, providing the best transport route into the interior of the Deep South. In 1862 a handful of Union volunteers, among them two residents of the Ewing's hometown, had stolen a train outside Atlanta. Their mission had been to disrupt the Western & Atlantic in the hope of preventing the Confederates from reinforcing Chattanooga while it came under Union assault. Many of those soldiers had been executed as Union spies, though others managed to escape. Six of the "Great Train Raiders" received the first Medals of Honor ever awarded.[9]

Cump's army numbered one hundred thousand men and included Hugh and Tom Ewing's erstwhile military commanders, Jacob Cox and John Schofield. Even their prewar law partner in Leavenworth, Dan McCook, filled a general's slot. The Union forces encompassed all sorts of specialists, from artillery gunners and engineers to combat infantry and cooks. Among the duties of Cump's engineers was to repair railroad line and bridges damaged by retreating Confederates. Fortunately for Cump's construction gangs, the limited know-how of the South to build railroads nearly matched their inability to destroy infrastructure beyond the point of quick repair. Not only were the seventy thousand Confederate troops inferior in numbers, but their limited technical skills placed them at a further disadvantage.[10]

Charley had begged Cump that, although a staff officer, he would have ample opportunity to be at the front lines. Cump obliged his youngest brother-in-law. In his role as inspector general, Charley was responsible for overseeing a myriad of tasks. Troops had to be fed, deployments had to be carried out, and law and order was to reign within the ranks. So far as military-civilian relations went, Charley, with Cump's approval, gave the men some latitude. It could not have been otherwise. As Cump had recently announced, "We claim the unmolested navigation of the Mississippi River, and we shall have it, if all the country within reach has to be laid waste." Cump also questioned why it was fine for rebels to burn the homes of Unionists in Kentucky and kidnap free blacks into slavery, "when I, poor innocent, would not let a soldier take a green apple, or a fence rail to [start a fire and] make a cup of coffee?"[11]

The bulk of Cump's soldiers were natives of the Old Northwest who had grown up on farms. A full quarter of the troops were Ohioans. Their numbers included Lancaster's own battle-scarred Sixty-First Ohio, which had been transferred from the Army of the Potomac. Cump's troops were literate but unpolished. So far as discipline went, they fought better than they marched on a parade ground. If, through the spring of 1864, they had not stolen so much as "a green apple"—Cump was less than truthful with that claim—his troops were repelled by Georgia's white population. One soldier, whose letter was reprinted in *Harper's Weekly*, described a populace that he implicitly hoped would die off and be replaced with better people:

> I wish those people in the North who have such queer notions of the exalted character of the Southern Chivalry could see the real people of the South as they really are. I suppose Georgia is the best of the Southern States, as we Northern men regard best; at least I have seen more churches, school-houses, and pretty villages than elsewhere in the same space in the South. But the people whom we meet almost without exception are ignorant, superstitious, bigoted, and uncouth; at least those who are left behind. The women chew [tobacco], smoke, and drink. The men are all off

General William T. Sherman, leaning on a cannon at the Gates of Atlanta, 1864. (Courtesy of the Library of Congress.)

in the war. By-and-by we shall see a new population here, and then it will be a country to which we can point with pride.[12]

Although the troops were unimpressed with the tobacco-stained women they encountered at Resaca and Dalton, Charley expressed enormous respect for Joe Johnston. He wrote to his father that Johnston took advantage of every feature of the north Georgia terrain to delay Cump's advance. Johnston had initially made one mistake in early May 1864, and Cump nearly trapped him at Resaca. Union troops did not deploy quickly enough, however, and Johnston made good his escape. This opportunity would not come again. Whenever Cump sought to outflank Johnston, the wily Confederate anticipated his move, retreated, and then fortified a new position.[13]

It did not help Cump that he depended upon the Western & Atlantic Railroad for supplies and so would not venture too far from it. Indeed, within a few months of the opening of his Atlanta campaign, Cump had to replace nearly one million socks, 574,000 underpants, and 290,000 blankets. Moreover, since Cump's military objective was glaringly obvious, it was not hard for Johnston to anticipate his opponent's moves. Despite their problems, Charley assured Thomas Ewing that Cump remained physically and mentally strong. Victory would come—eventually.[14]

Hugh's old regiment, the Thirtieth Ohio, was once again part of a key military campaign. The regiment's numbers, however, were far less than they had been at South Mountain in 1862. What the siege of Vicksburg had not taken from the Thirtieth Ohio's ranks, Missionary Ridge had. A regiment that had once mustered one thousand men might have had four hundred who had not been killed, captured, or discharged for the severity of their wounds. Despite a snowstorm that took them by surprise before the launch of the Atlanta campaign, the troops' morale remained high. On March 22, for instance, the Thirtieth Ohio's enlisted men ambushed their officers with snowballs. They respected their officers and would follow them without hesitation but still treated them roughly.[15]

Cump and Johnston's troops skirmished throughout May and June with no decisive result, though Union forces came closer and closer to Atlanta. On June 27, at Kennesaw Mountain, twenty-five miles from Atlanta, Cump initiated a full-scale battle. On the basis of reports from Union patrols, George Hildt of the Thirtieth Ohio believed that Johnston's position was far stronger than anything he had seen at Vicksburg. Cump's forces, in contrast, could not count on their trenches for much protection. Hildt ruefully observed that Johnston, in occupying the high ground eight hundred feet above the Union line, was effortlessly cannonading the Yankees with little fear of accurate return fire.[16]

Charley concurred with Hildt's assessment. He wrote to his father, "Johnston's position here was very strong and from the top of the mountain he
could see our whole line and every change that was made." Still, Cump felt
that he had little choice but to launch an assault. Going around Johnston's
position, Cump believed, would have placed him too far from the Western
& Atlantic line for comfort. Hildt recorded the subsequent carnage: "[We]
drove the rebels from their front line of rifle pits and advanced about 25 yards
beyond to the crest of the hill where we were within 150 yards of their main
lines of works and in direct range. We held the crest until we were enfiladed
by their batteries. Captain [Aaron] Chamberlain had his head blown off by
a percussion shell which exploded afterwards and tore off his arms, blowing
his brains over his first Sergeant and Captain [Emerson] Brooks."[17]

Cump took the Kennesaw Mountain repulse and his three thousand casualties in stride. (In comparison, Johnston had 630 casualties.) As he informed
Ellen, "I begin to regard the death and mangling of a couple of thousand
men as a small affair, a kind of morning dash, and it may be well that we
become so hardened." Cump, however, was not completely coldhearted; he
expressed profound "regret" over the death of Dan McCook. Neither Cump
nor Charley believed the outcome of the Atlanta campaign was in doubt.
Charley reported to his father that Cump continued to probe at Johnston in
an effort to turn one of his flanks and would, ultimately, be successful. Captain Emory Muenscher of the Thirtieth Ohio was not as cheery. At Kennesaw
Mountain he nearly tripped over the lifeless body of First Lieutenant Israel
White. There originally had been four members of the White family in Company F. Sergeant Thomas White, who had survived the siege of Vicksburg,
had been killed a month earlier in Dallas, Georgia. Israel White, the last of
the surviving White brothers and cousins, fell with a bullet to his head.[18]

Seeing that Cump might yet mount a successful assault, Johnston withdrew from Kennesaw Mountain without the Yankees' knowing until a day
later. Cump's victory, however, could not be savored by his men. Johnston had
constructed yet another formidable line of entrenchments. Atlanta, like Vicksburg, would have to be taken by siege. Cump's troops passed the summer of
1864 expending an enormous quantity of ammunition. Union artillery shells,
though ostensibly aimed at military targets, overshot Atlanta's rail yards and
reduced residential neighborhoods to splinters. St. Philip's Church took a number of rounds, leading Episcopal bishop Henry Lay to make a subsequent protest to the Union commander. Cump gave three responses. First, it was nearly
impossible to aim his guns accurately without having a better understanding
of Atlanta's physical layout. Second, the Confederates themselves were at fault
for placing their military operations so close to civilian structures. And third, if

God, as the rebels claimed, was really upset with Cump for his actions, then he could wait to receive divine chastisement after his death.[19]

While the besieged of Atlanta were hoping that Cump's appointment with God would come sooner than later, Union and Confederate skirmishers clashed daily. Although many Confederates proved eager to call for temporary truces so that both sides could have a respite from the heat, Texas troops seemed determined never to stop shooting. Soldiers from the Thirtieth Ohio wrote home describing the amputations they had witnessed and happily reporting that their three-year terms of enlistment were nearly completed. Captain Muenscher confided in his journal, "I find myself breaking down so rapidly that I cannot be of much service and my own interest requires that I should not expose myself any longer to so great privations."[20]

George Hildt saw a twenty-pound rebel shell blow his coffeepot into smithereens. A short while later, he and the Thirtieth Ohio discovered the freshly beheaded body of a Confederate private. The unfortunate soldier's commanding officer had hacked him apart with a saber for not advancing quickly enough against Union positions. Hildt told his parents that it was someone else's turn to fight—he had not reenlisted. Some one hundred thousand Union troops in all the theaters of operations similarly declined to reenlist. Another 136,000 Union soldiers whose three-year terms of service were nearly completed agreed to continue fighting. As an incentive, the U.S. government offered a bonus, or "bounty," to volunteers and veterans. Disturbed by the shortfall in reenlistments, Cump fretted in a letter to Ellen that "no recruits are coming, for the [next] draft is not till September, and then I suppose it will consist mostly of niggers and bought recruits that must be kept to the rear. I sometimes think our people do not deserve to succeed in war; they are so apathetic."[21]

The Union and Confederate corpses piling up outside Atlanta were nothing compared to the miseries Grant had unleashed on Virginia in the spring of 1864. Like McClellan, Burnside, and Hooker, Grant had ordered the Army of the Potomac into Virginia. In this venture, unlike previous forays, however, Grant did not have the Confederate capital of Richmond as his first objective. He anticipated that Richmond would fall to him in good time. Instead, Cump's friend had decided to destroy Lee's army. Northern newspaper readers, especially those with family members in the Army of the Potomac, would have seared in their memories several peculiarly named, and previously obscure, Virginia map points: the Wilderness, Spotsylvania, and Cold Harbor. Between May 5 and May 12, 1864, the Army of the Potomac suffered thirty-two thousand casualties. The Army of Northern Virginia claimed eighteen thousand casualties.[22]

Rather than withdrawing, which had been the past practice for the Army of the Potomac, Grant continued to maneuver and assault Lee. At Cold Harbor 7,000 Union troops were killed, wounded, or missing. Lee had 1,500 casualties. Grant made it clear to Lee that he was willing to suffer much higher losses if he could kill a few Confederates in the process. By June 18, Grant's casualties totaled 65,000 out of an army that had previously mustered 118,000 soldiers. Nearly half of Lee's original 64,000 troops were dead or wounded. The difference between the two armies, however, was that Grant had a reserve from which to draw, even if they were, from Cump's vantage, "niggers and bought recruits." Taking his final stand at the rail and road hub of Petersburg, twenty-two miles south of Richmond, Lee had no more replacements. With a greatly diminished and battered army, Lee held on for what was to become a ten-month-long siege.[23]

To many northern Democratic politicians and newspaper editors the war appeared lost. Sherman and Grant were bogged down in hopeless, bloody sieges. The Union casualties at Kennesaw Mountain were fodder for outraged editorials and congressional speeches. Antiwar Democrats fought for control of their party in 1864. They were determined to defeat Lincoln and negotiate an end to the war. More ominously, a number of Republicans faltered, staggered by Sherman and Grant's losses and seeming inability to win. Lincoln urged Grant on and told him not to worry about his reelection.

Senator John Sherman wanted Lincoln ousted from the White House. As he wrote to Cump in 1864, "The conviction is general that Lincoln has not the energy, dignity, or character to either conduct the war or to make peace." He was not alone in his low assessment of the president. Ohio general James Garfield, Kansas senator Samuel Pomeroy, Treasury secretary Salmon Chase, and Ohio senator Ben Wade were equally disenchanted. Luckily for Lincoln, his enemies within the Republican Party did not trust one another. Each also had his own share of enemies, which limited his political effectiveness. Tom Ewing and his allies in Kansas regarded Pomeroy as a brainless puppet of Senator Lane. So far as Chase was concerned, Thomas Ewing viewed him as a scheming mediocrity whose only talent was in persuading others that he was more intelligent than the facts warranted.[24]

Unionist Democrats and moderate Republicans harbored an intense dislike of Ben Wade. Ohio's senior senator was more self righteous and vindictive than was normal even for a member of Congress. Wade routinely castigated his critics as idiots and traitors. Grant himself, Wade argued, could not be trusted since the Ohio general was a Democrat and a southern sympathizer. Wade spent 1864 arrogantly drafting plans for a punitive Reconstruction of the South, even though the outcome of the war was in doubt. Lincoln, in one of his few acts that earned the Ewing family's approval, chose to "pocket veto" Wade's legislative handiwork. Since Congress had adjourned, the Constitution gave Lincoln the option of ignoring Wade's Reconstruction bill rather than vetoing it outright. Wade, and his cosponsor, Maryland Representative Henry Winter Davis, would have to try again when Congress reconvened.[25]

Lincoln saw Chase as a bigger political threat than Wade. Senators Sherman and Pomeroy made no secret of their desire to remove Lincoln and replace him with Chase. Several Ohio Republicans in the state legislature, operating with Chase's blessing, wanted to take a neutral stance toward Lincoln's renomination. The president's legislative loyalists, however, forced through a resolution within Ohio's Republican caucus endorsing Lincoln. Cousin Jimmy Blaine engineered a similar resolution in the Maine legislature.[26]

From his vantage point in Congress, Blaine tallied Chase's political strengths and weaknesses. Chase had two advantages, but these, upon reflection, proved illusory. First, Chase was not Lincoln. That gave him some support. However, once people looked at Chase more as a candidate and less as an abstraction, his support evaporated. Second, Chase "was at the head of the department which was most potential in the distribution of patronage." The problem with that proposition was that all Lincoln had to do was take away Chase's patronage purse. Cousin Jimmy had spent too much time with his Ewing kin not to see how politically weak Chase was in reality.[27]

The president understood that Chase loved titles and the public perception that he wielded great power. This meant that Chase did not have to be in the White House so long as Lincoln stroked his ego. His political solution was to promise Chase a seat on the U.S. Supreme Court. It was only a matter of time before Chief Justice Roger Taney, the frail southern partisan and author of the *Dred Scott* decision, died. Speculation as to whom Lincoln would appoint to replace Taney had been a heated topic of Washington conversation all through 1863 and into 1864. Until Taney, there had never been a Supreme Court justice whose worsening health was followed as closely and with quite so much eager anticipation. Taney's death on October 12, 1864, brought boundless joy to Senator Wade and the Radical Republican faction in Congress. Senator Charles Sumner of Massachusetts joyfully proclaimed "providence has given us a victory, in the death of Chief Justice Taney."[28]

In spite of Maria's terminal illness and his own health issues, Thomas Ewing asked Orville Browning to give him regular reports on political developments in the nation's capital. Regaining some of his strength, Ewing returned to Washington in the early spring of 1864 with his daughter Maria

Theresa and son Phil as escorts. His visits to the White House resumed as he brought the concerns of his legal clients to the attention of the president. Ewing, of course, was also in search of political intelligence. Naval Secretary Gideon Welles gripped about "old party hacks like Ewing" having ready access to Lincoln. Welles, however, was powerless to keep Thomas Ewing away. After all, an insult to Ewing was, by extension, an injury to John Sherman, Jimmy Blaine, Maryland senator Reverdy Johnson, Tennessee military governor Andrew Johnson, several members of the U.S. Supreme Court, and two attorneys with national reputations—Henry Stanbery and Orville Browning. Welles was outgunned, and he knew it.[29]

Once Ewing confirmed that Lincoln planned to make Chase the chief justice of the U.S. Supreme Court he lashed out. Writing to Lincoln, Ewing succinctly expressed his disgust: "[Chase] has no considerable reputation as a lawyer. He is a politician rather than a lawyer and unless he changes his nature always will be even if made Chief Justice. I am unwilling to see a Chief Justice of the U.S. intriguing and trading for the Presidency." Lincoln replied that he hoped Ewing would not come to the White House and "scold" him for his decision. In his heart, Lincoln knew that Ewing was right. The president of the United States had bought off a political rival with the highest judicial office in the land. To Lincoln's foes, making Chase chief justice underscored how little regard the president held for the Supreme Court. Taney had spent the past two years deprecating Lincoln for suspending the *writ of habeas corpus*. Replacing Taney with Chase could be interpreted as an expression of contempt for the judicial branch of government. Lincoln insisted that it was not out of contempt for the Supreme Court that he had elevated Chase. Rather, it was simple political expediency.[30]

Given his sinking electoral prospects, Lincoln and the moderate Republicans resorted to a few other acts of political expediency. First, Lincoln would run for reelection as the head of a "Union," rather than "Republican," ticket. Moderates wanted Unionist Democrats to think of Lincoln, rather than Ben Wade, when they voted, and deemphasizing the Republican appellation might help. Second, moderates dumped Lincoln's radical vice president, Hannibal Hamlin. (Blaine carefully avoided defending or criticizing Hamlin, who was, after all, likely to remain influential in Maine politics.) Moderate Republicans needed a Unionist Democrat, preferably one from the South who would appeal to centrists in the Old Northwest and the Border States. Admittedly, there were few who could fit that bill, and there was only one who had the support of the Ewing family and its allies.[31]

Nominating Andrew Johnson in 1864 for vice president was a sign of moderate Republicans' political cunning, as well as evidence of their desperation.

Andrew Johnson (1808–75). A protégée of Thomas Ewing, Andrew Johnson completed the ascent from poor southern boy to U.S. senator, Tennessee military governor, and, in 1864, vice presidential nominee on a Unionist ticket with Abraham Lincoln. (Courtesy of the Library of Congress.)

Johnson was an avid campaigner with the courage to defy his fellow south-erners by first remaining loyal to the Union and then embracing emancipa-tion as a necessary military measure. He had spent much time in the politi-cally vital state of Ohio and had made many friends among legislators and the throngs of small-town people who came to hear him speak. On the other hand, Johnson was confrontational and could not hold his liquor—traits the Ewing family had not seen when he stayed at the Main Hill mansion.[32]

The ascendant antiwar Democrats felt confident of victory when they convened in Chicago. Although former president Millard Fillmore had been a Whig, he endorsed the candidacy of George McClellan. William Allen, who had defeated Thomas Ewing for the Senate in 1836, stirred himself from retirement in Chillicothe to join the antiwar crusade. Lancaster's newly elected state representative, Edson Olds, still smarting from his incarcera-tion, also came to Chicago. Olds alleged that Lincoln was trying to prevent Democrats in the Old Northwest from buying guns and bullets. He did not explain why civilians needed additional arms, but it was unlikely that Olds thought they would be used against Confederate raiders.[33]

Clement Vallandigham, Ohio's exiled congressman, sneaked into Chicago to rally behind the onetime commander of the Army of the Potomac. Decry-ing Grant's unprecedented casualties, Vallandigham led the effort to con-struct a strong "Peace Platform" demanding that "immediate efforts be made for a cessation of hostilities." The Democrats charged that "the Constitution itself has been disregarded in every part, and public liberty and private right alike trodden down, and the material prosperity of the country essentially impaired." Ohio representative Samuel Cox, the leader of the congressional antiwar faction, also made a tremendous impression in Chicago. As *Harper's Weekly* later reported, Cox had thundered, "For less offenses than Mr. Lin-coln had been guilty of the English people had chopped off the head of the first [King] Charles." Whether or not Cox had intentionally called for Lin-coln's execution would be the subject of controversy in the months ahead.[34]

Given the prominence of Ohio politicians within the antiwar camp, it was not surprising that George Pendleton of Cincinnati became the Democratic vice presidential nominee. A member of the U.S. House of Representatives, Pendleton had seen his stature among Democrats rise in 1864 when he opposed congressional efforts to write a constitutional amendment abolishing slavery. Not only would such an amendment usurp private property rights, Pendleton asserted, but it would be unconstitutional to ratify it without the consent of the southern states. Tennessee, for instance, could not possibly be allowed to vote on such an amendment, since it was under the thumb of Andrew Johnson, an unelected military governor. There was little doubt that Pendleton was even more opposed to the war than McClellan. Indeed, McClellan unconvincingly disavowed the more extreme positions of his supporters.[35]

Democratic newspapers swung into action. The *New York World*, having coined the term *miscegenation* in 1863, warned throughout the 1864 election that Lincoln planned to hand white women over to sexually promiscuous black men. Samuel Medary's *Ohio Statesman* denounced Lincoln as "the tyrant, the knave, and the indecent joker." The *Cleveland Plain Dealer* was harsher, describing the president as "a third-rate lawyer from Springfield, Illinois, who once kept a whisky still up a hollow, split 3,000 rails, and now splits the American Union, and calls for Negro songs on a crimson battlefield, yet has the audacity to aspire again to the chief magistracy of the great Republic." In sum, the *Cleveland Plain Dealer* argued, Lincoln was "a miserable failure, a coarse filthy joker, a disgusting politician, a mean, cunning, and cruel tyrant and the shame and disgrace of the nation."[36]

As Lincoln had anticipated, many disenchanted Republicans felt so disgusted with McClellan and Pendleton that they temporarily set aside their opposition to the Union ticket. Senator Sumner, however, continued to grouse that Lincoln should have "patriotically withdrawn," since there were at least a hundred better alternatives. The *New York Tribune* set the rhetorical tone of the Union ticket, editorializing that "if Mr. Jeff Davis had been the platform-maker for the Chicago [Democratic] Convention, he could not have treated himself more tenderly nor his enterprise more gingerly than they have been in the actual Platform." Noah Brooks, a reporter for the *Sacramento Daily Union*, charged that the Democrats applauded the song "Dixie" when bands played it at their convention "but never cheer[ed] the patriotic airs." *Harper's Weekly* argued that a vote for McClellan and Pendleton was a vote for "shameful surrender" to the Confederacy.[37]

Ultimately it was not *Harper's Weekly*, the *Sacramento Daily Union*, or the *New York Tribune* that assured Lincoln's reelection and the continuation of the Union war effort. Rather, the Unionists won thanks to the actions of a very improbable trio: Jefferson Davis, John Bell Hood, and William T. Sherman. Neither Jefferson Davis nor his trusted military confidant Braxton Bragg appreciated Johnston's strategy of retreat and entrenchment. In the space of ten weeks Johnston had killed, wounded, or captured nearly a quarter of Cump's army. Over that same span of time, Cump had taken seventy-four days to move one hundred miles into the Confederacy. Johnston had the Yankees bogged down outside Atlanta. Moreover, the city continued to produce large quantities of ammunition and weapons for the South. Most worrisome, many of Cump's exhausted troops were counting down the days to the end of their three-year enlistments. Cump's army might just melt away under the scorching Georgia sun before Atlanta surrendered.[38]

On July 18, Davis, at Bragg's urging, replaced Johnston with General John Bell Hood. Cump could not have asked for a better enemy commander than Hood. There was no doubting that Hood had been a good division commander and that his Texas troops were among the toughest men in the war. Hood certainly did not lack grit. Despite losing a leg in combat, in addition to an arm that was rendered nearly useless, Hood kept on fighting. Hood's flaw, however, was his recklessly aggressive mind-set. Johnston's subtle defensive strategy was foreign to Hood's temperament. Davis had wanted a bold commander who would take the battle to Cump. The Confederate president got everything he wished for and more. Through the close of July and into August, Hood launched three major attacks, each one a bloody affair that progressively weakened his defense of Atlanta.[39]

Hood's intense assaults had astonished the troops on both sides and took Cump by surprise. On July 22, believing that Hood's troop movements were a prelude to retreat, Cump had sent Charley galloping through the army shouting, "The rebels have gone [!] March through Atlanta and go into camp on the other side." Cump was grossly mistaken. Hood was preparing for an assault. As the New York Times reported, despite having caught Cump ill prepared, the July 22 attack still cost the Confederates nearly three men to each Yankee put out of action. Having suffered 8,499 casualties on July 22, in addition to 4,796 on July 20, Hood increased the Confederate body count on July 28, with 4,632 killed or wounded. In his three July assaults, Hood claimed 17,927 casualties to Cump's 6,051. Hood was running out of the men whose lives and combat effectiveness Johnston had carefully preserved.[40]

Both armies were showing enormous mental and physical strains. The shocked remnants of the Thirtieth Ohio had reverted to a state of jumpiness not seen since their invasion of western Virginia in 1861. Captain Muenscher observed that after some of his men accidentally shot a hornet's nest, the angry bees had "stampeded the whole Thirtieth Ohio." A grim George Hildt wrote his parents that when he questioned a prisoner about the size of Hood's force, the soldier replied that the Confederates "had enough for one or two more killings." Another prisoner complained to Hildt that "Hood was going to fight [with his army] until the last one was killed, and [he] couldn't stand it." As Hildt concluded, "Hood's tactics suits us first rate, and if he keeps it up his army will soon be gone." Hildt was prescient. Hood abandoned Atlanta on September 2. Half of his troops were casualties. Of course, Lee's losses were little better. Then again, he still guarded Richmond.[41]

Southern newspapers were livid when they learned of Hood's abandonment of Atlanta. The *Atlanta Intelligencer*, which had earlier relocated to Macon, Georgia, charged that Cump and his depraved officers were having sexual intercourse with "nigger women." Confederate loyalists soon had even greater cause to curse Cump when he ordered 3,500 civilians to leave the city. Having learned to hate Vicksburg's hungry, demanding citizens, Cump had no intention of wasting his precious supplies feeding the desperate people of Atlanta. "War," Cump told Atlanta's mayor, "is cruelty." Few in Cump's command felt any pang of remorse. Cump's troops seized stately mansions for their lodgings, enjoying good cigars from the balconies as their military bands serenaded them in the increasingly cooler September evenings. Even Jefferson Davis became a cause for Yankee merriment, as word spread of a "sermon" to the faithful that he had delivered at a Macon church: "Our cause is not lost. Sherman cannot keep up his long line of communications, and retreat, sooner or later, he must."[42]

Although Cump had spent years denigrating politicians, he knew when he held an electoral trump card. His army had removed a major obstacle in the way of the Lincoln's reelection. That same month General Phil Sheridan gave the northern public more morale-boosting news. Sheridan had cleared Virginia's Shenandoah Valley of Confederate forces and secured Washington from future large-scale raids. He had then proceeded to destroy anything of potential military value. Although many northerners did not realize it, Thomas Ewing could claim some credit for both Cump's and Sheridan's achievements. The death of Judge Charles Sherman had given Ewing the opportunity to raise Cump and then secure his admission to West Point. Hugh's academic dismissal from West Point had opened a slot at the military academy for Sheridan. The intercession of Sheridan's parish priest with Thomas and Maria Ewing had given the son of poor Irish Catholic immigrants entry into the ranks of America's military elite. If Lincoln did not know Sheridan's story, he certainly knew Cump's.[43]

With Lee pinned at Petersburg, Atlanta eliminated as a Confederate manufacturing center, and the Shenandoah Valley in ashes, southern military prospects were grim. There was, however, one desperate gamble that might yet doom Lincoln. If a Confederate army could take a major Union city before the 1864 presidential election, then McClellan and Pendleton might yet win and negotiate recognition of the Confederacy. The weakest military link of the Union was in the West. Tom Ewing had fretted for over a year that his best troops were routinely reassigned to other theaters. Few in the East paid much heed to developments in the Kansas-Missouri theater, though the 1863 Lawrence Massacre had caught northern attention. There was, however, one militarily vital city in the West whose importance easterners recognized: St. Louis. The first major clash between rebels and Unionists had occurred in St. Louis in 1861. Perhaps the last major battle of 1864 might happen in that city as well.

Since his mother's death, Tom had returned to a region that had become somewhat calmer. Most guerrillas could now operate effectively only in conjunction with Confederate troops. Transferred to the St. Louis District, Tom had some physical distance between himself and the emotionally inflamed Kansas-Missouri border. John Schofield was not as fortunate. Because he had absorbed so much political abuse to protect Tom after the Lawrence Massacre, Schofield had to be sent away to Cump's command. It helped Tom that Hugh's friend, William Rosecrans, now led the Department of the Missouri. Rosecrans's transfer, however, had represented nothing less than a humiliating demotion for his failure to defeat Bragg in Tennessee.[44]

Although Rosecrans was generally supportive, Tom still had to contend with Senator Lane's marauding operatives. In a letter to William Dole, Lincoln's commissioner of Indian affairs, Tom observed that "locusts were never thicker in Egypt than Lane's strikers in Kansas, salaried by the Government or made rich by contracts, solely to work for Lane." Tom also continued to joust with Democratic newspaper critics of General Order Number 11. Republican newspapers, meanwhile, chastised him for permitting guerrilla families to return to western Missouri once they had sworn their allegiance to the Union. According to the Radical Republican press, any oath of allegiance sworn by a rebel had to be regarded as a lie. Like his father, Tom never hesitated to wage editorial warfare with foes that, as the saying went, "bought ink by the barrel."[45]

Cump had reached out to Tom, in spite of Ellen Sherman's demand that he disown her brother. He offered to make Tom a division commander in the Atlanta campaign. Tom declined. His aide, Major Harrison Hannahs, whom Tom informed of Cump's generosity, chided his commander. "General Ewing," Hannahs began, "you have made the mistake of your life. Sherman will not only go to Atlanta, but he will go to the sea, just as sure as there is a God in Israel." Tom's wife heartily concurred with Hannahs. She still liked Cump, in spite of the loathing she felt for Ellen Sherman. Tom would not reconsider. He then urged her to return to Lancaster with their children. As Tom told his wife and Phil Ewing, he planned to resign from the army once he knew that Missouri was sufficiently pacified. He had enough of the guerrilla war and saw little future for himself in Kansas politics so long as Lane remained entrenched. Tom, however, did not want it to appear as if he were running home in defeat.[46]

In St. Louis Tom recruited and trained troops. He had a difficult time recruiting among the white population. Some of his problems stemmed from the fact that every able-bodied *white* man willing to fight for the Union had long since enlisted. Those who remained in Missouri were not physically fit for service, did not want to wear out their privately owned horses chasing Confederate cavalry, or harbored prosouthern sympathies. As the *New York Times* reported, Tom had to be careful not to arm disloyal recruits who would then join the Confederates. Tom vowed to Missouri Unionists that he and Rosecrans would personally investigate the backgrounds of all white militia volunteers.[47]

Even though Tom was not keen to enlist blacks, they were the only physically fit recruits whose loyalties were unquestionable. The War Department, in a subsequent review of the relationships between white officers and black soldiers, found Tom to be one of the few humane commanders. He treated his black recruits with respect, even though he did not regard them as potential citizens or as social equals. Then again, unlike Cump, Tom did not casually refer to blacks as "niggers." None of the Ewings used that term of loathing.[48]

General Rosecrans had warned his superiors in Washington that so long as Confederate troops and guerrillas found sanctuary in neighboring Arkansas, Missouri would not be secure from attack. Rosecrans's grim assessment of the military and political situation was not groundless. Missouri governor Claiborne Jackson had established a pro-Confederate government in exile in Marshall, Texas, and Camden, Arkansas. After Claiborne's death in 1862 from cancer, Lieutenant Governor Thomas Reynolds exhorted General Sterling Price to liberate Missouri.[49]

The invasion that Reynolds longed for, and that Rosecrans feared, finally came on September 19, 1864. Price's band numbered twelve thousand, including a few thousand cavalry troops and eighteen cannons. Reynolds rode with Confederate forces, anticipating that he would be inaugurated governor after Price captured the state capital of Jefferson City. Price also had several hundred Missouri guerrillas with him whose mission was to sow terror among the Unionist civilian population. A few weeks earlier these same guerrillas had made an assault on a Union outpost in Oklahoma. On that raid Price's guerrillas had made a point of torturing and then executing blacks. Cries of "O! Good master, save and spare me!" only seemed to increase the pleasure with which Price's guerrillas took in their work. Reynolds had warned Price not to bring the guerrillas along, arguing that "they war not on the enemy, but on our own people." Their brutal behavior, Reynolds, insisted, would turn all of Missouri against the Confederacy.[50]

Price's men were fully primed for the Missouri campaign. They wanted to make the Yankees pay for issuing General Order Number 11. In Centralia, Missouri, the Confederates murdered two dozen white soldiers who had gone home on leave or been discharged from the service because of the severity of their wounds. "Bloody" Bill Anderson, who had served with Quantrill, had his men rape every black female they could find, including children. Pro-Confederate civilians boldly boasted to their Unionist neighbors that "their time was coming." Price's infantry and General Joe Shelby's cavalry were going to annihilate all the Yankees who stood in their way.[51]

As stories of Confederate atrocities spread through Missouri, Rosecrans ordered Tom to investigate. Having sent troops to protect Jefferson City, Rolla, and Springfield, Rosecrans could spare Tom just two hundred men from the Fourteenth Iowa. Since he did not know if the rumors of an invasion were true or, if accurate, where Price intended to go, Rosecrans would not concentrate his troops until he had better military intelligence. The possibility that Price intended to assault St. Louis before taking the state capital seemed remote, though it was worrisome. Rosecrans had barely six thousand troops to defend St. Louis. Still, if Price did advance on St. Louis, he would run into Fort Davidson's garrison of eight hundred at Pilot Knob, located eighty-six miles south of that city near the Iron Mountain Railroad. Tom would go to Fort Davidson and then report back to Rosecrans. As luck would have it, Pilot Knob proved to be on Price's invasion route. Decades earlier Thomas Ewing had given speeches in praise of freedom fighters such as King Leonidas and his three hundred Spartans holding the line against Persian "Immortals." Now his classically educated son would fight in a desperate battle that became known as "the Thermopylae of the West."[52]

As a defensive position, Fort Davidson appeared deceptively weak. It was, after all, simply an eight-sided redoubt constructed of packed dirt and sandbags. There was a ten-foot-wide, six-foot-deep dry ditch around the fort that seemed to be a parody of a medieval European castle moat. There was even a poor imitation of a retractable drawbridge across the moat that consisted of a few planks lashed together and raised and lowered with a rope. If not for the dry moat, the walls of Fort Davidson would have been only a few feet high and easily scaled. To make matters seemingly worse for the defenders, a thousand yards away Pilot Knob and Shepherd's Mountain rose six hundred feet above the fort. Price could use this high ground to rain cannon fire down on the Union troops. Once the Confederates destroyed a few sections of the Iron Mountain Railroad, Ewing would have no hope of Rosecrans coming to his assistance.[53]

Fort Davidson's garrison consisted of a few companies from the Third Missouri Cavalry and the First, Second, Forty-Seventh, and Fiftieth Missouri

Infantry. Most of the Missouri infantry had no combat experience, though the foot soldiers manning the batteries were experienced gunners. Fort Davidson's commander, Major James Wilson, was a veteran horse trooper and had been fighting Missouri guerrillas since the war began. Despite its small size, Tom's detachment greatly enhanced Pilot Knob's defenses. His troops were hardened veterans and, just as importantly, came armed with deadly accurate Springfield rifles. Experienced infantry could rapidly reload and hit their targets at distances of five hundred feet or more.[54]

A few of the Confederate officers wanted to bypass Pilot Knob and continue their advance to St. Louis. The presidential election, after all, might hang on the capture of St. Louis, but it certainly would not be decided by taking Fort Davidson. Price and his Missouri guerrillas and troopers, however, disagreed. They had learned that both Tom Ewing and Colonel Thomas Fletcher of the Forty-Seventh Missouri were at Fort Davidson. What better way to avenge General Order Number 11 than by executing Ewing as a war criminal? As for Fletcher, he was guilty of being the Republican Party's gubernatorial nominee. He had also commanded black troops, which was sufficient cause alone to merit death. There was little doubt that the rebels wanted blood. When Confederates troops captured Major Wilson during a skirmish, they made his death as painful as possible. First, the Confederates beat and shot him. Then, as Wilson bled out, the rebels left him among a herd of hungry pigs that tore him apart.[55]

In preparation for Price's attack, Tom placed a few soldiers in rifle pits outside the fort near the mountain trails. These troops would be able to impede the momentum of Price's advance and act as the eyes and ears of the troops inside Fort Davidson. Once the Confederates came too near, the soldiers in the rifle pits could retreat across the fort's "drawbridge" to relative safety. Tom also scattered logs and rocks around his redoubt with the intention of slowing down and breaking up the Confederate assault. The longer it took for Price's men to cross the open fields to the dry moat, the more likely Tom's men would be able to wound or kill them. Moreover, if the Confederates could not attack as organized regiments, concentrate their gunfire, and coordinate simultaneous assaults from all directions, they could more easily be repulsed.[56]

Tom further strengthened his hand by giving Lieutenant David Murphy complete control of the fort's four siege guns, three howitzers, three mortars, and six field guns. To counter the boredom of garrisoning an isolated post, Murphy had drilled his battery crews to the point where they did not need to fire the typical gun "bracket." Most commonly, gunnery crews fired a first shot for range to the left, a second shell for range to the right, and then the third shot scored the kill between the brackets. Murphy's crews dispensed with the brackets. They could hit any target they aimed for on Shepherd's Mountain with their first shot.[57]

Murphy's gunners quickly proved their worth. In the prelude to Price's infantry assault on September 27, the Confederates laboriously dug gun emplacements on Shepherd's Mountain. Tom, growing concerned with Murphy's nonchalant attitude, inquired as to when he might fire on the Confederates. Murphy insisted that it would be best to permit Price's men to expend time and energy emplacing their guns. "My plan," Murphy told Tom, "is to permit the enemy to fire the first shot, and after that is done there will be firing enough from our side to gratify the desires of everybody." Tom, although visibly anxious, consented: "All right, but I still think that you should open fire and prevent them from getting their guns in a good position." Seconds later, the Confederate guns opened fire on the fort. Their shots went astray. Targeting the smoke from Price's cannons, Murphy ordered his gunners to open up. Within the span of a few minutes, Murphy's crews wiped out several of Price's guns.[58]

Following the ineffective Confederate artillery bombardment, the battle of Pilot Knob commenced in deadly earnest. Twice, Price's men waved white flags of truce. Tom correctly surmised that these were ruses intended to get him to cease firing while Price infiltrated his soldiers closer to the fort. His suspicions had been initially aroused when he recognized the man who approached with the first flag of truce, Price's chief of staff, L. A. McLean. Six years earlier in "Bleeding Kansas," Tom had sworn out an arrest warrant against McLean for criminal activities relating to voting fraud, perjury, and, in general, associating with the Missouri bushwhackers. Tom curtly informed McLean that he had no intention of surrendering the fort and its ample supply of gunpowder and ammunition. When a second truce flag appeared, even while Price's men moved in closer to the fort, Tom gave Murphy permission to blast its carrier to pieces.[59]

Price attacked Fort Davidson with seven thousand men. He had deployed the balance of his forces, around five thousand soldiers, to the Missouri countryside, where they destroyed rail lines and torched farms belonging to Unionists. Even with a reduced force, however, Price outnumbered Ewing seven to one. At no other time during the war was the balance of forces so greatly in the favor of the Confederates. (The Collierville, Tennessee, skirmish in which Hugh and Charley had fought a year earlier ran a close second to Pilot Knob in terms of the relative imbalance between forces.) Price's troops rushed forward with enthusiasm, shouting out their intention to kill Tom Ewing. Enthusiasm and superior numbers, however, were not sufficient.

As Tom had planned, the logs and rocks he scattered around the fort, in addition to the rifle pits a few of his troops manned, thoroughly broke up one prong of the assault. Unable to maintain an organized line, the Confederate troops in this prong floundered in the open where Tom's best shots easily picked them off. The second prong of the attack fared worse.[60]

Having failed to make a thorough reconnaissance of the battlefield, the second assault force in Price's attack was surprised to discover Fort Davidson's dry moat. Colonel and gubernatorial candidate Thomas Fletcher recalled the ensuing carnage: "The advancing line came up to a point where the ditch encircling the fort was discovered, and then it turned in full retreat. It would have been the part of chivalry, no doubt, for the men behind the guns to have ceased firing upon the backs of their disappointed foes; but no permission was given for the indulgence of this feeling, had it existed." Hundreds of Confederates fell, covering the ground in deep piles of the dead and the dying. Others rolled into the ditch on top of each other, suffocating the wounded at the bottom. Tom ordered some of his men to crawl out among the bodies and bring back their weapons.[61]

The scene inside the fort was a mixture of chaos and order. Soldiers kept up a continuous fire thanks to a few dozen white and black civilian volunteers who reloaded extra rifles. Disregarding flying rebel bullets, Lieutenant Murphy paced the top of the fort's wall. From this dangerous vantage point, Murphy directed his gunners' canister fire, which spewed out hundreds of flesh-tearing lead balls. When a Confederate storming party crawled up the side of the ditch to the top of the redoubt, Murphy threw rocks at the rebels and screamed, "Come on! We are waiting for you!" Tom shouted at him to regain his composure and take cover.[62]

Dozens of Missouri and Iowa troops were hit. Some men grasped at their comrades with viselike death grips. Others, in the words of one soldier, took musket balls in their foreheads, "through which the brains could be seen pulsating and oozing out." In the midst of the battle, a sergeant in the Fourteenth Iowa observed with awe, "I saw the stately form of General Ewing, his arms folded, his mouth tightly closed, and his face slightly pale, but firm as a 'stone wall.' He was walking erect from side to side, looking here and there at the surging mass around us."[63]

Captain William Campbell of the Fourteenth Iowa went about the fort with Tom, redeploying squads of Hawkeyes to the growing gaps in the Missouri militia lines. Three times Price's men charged into the moat and tried to pull down the drawbridge. The grim contest was, Campbell observed, "a perfect saturnalia of the damned." At sundown, the rebels pulled back. "Everyone engaged," Campbell noted, "was tired, hot, and wet with perspiration, as if they had been fighting fire." Thanks to the immense mass of gunpowder smoke that blanketed the fort, it was nearly impossible to distinguish the white civilians from the black civilians.[64]

The cost of that moment of perfect equality, however, was steep. Tom had lost a quarter of his troops. Scores were wounded, more than a few mortally. Outside the fort, stacked in the dry moat and strewn around the field, were the remains of the rebel army. Price subsequently claimed that he had suffered a couple of hundred casualties. In truth, there were likely 1,500 Confederate soldiers dead or injured. Many of Price's wounded soldiers were left on the battlefield to die. Shocked by the intensity of their repulse, Price's men raided the liquor stocks in a nearby settlement. Many were too drunk and numb to bother rescuing their own wounded. Tom could barely help his own men, though he tried without much success to save some of the bleeding rebels.[65]

As a slight rain began to fall, Tom turned to Campbell and said, "Captain, what do you call this—a big battle or not? I have been in three or four small skirmishes and in three or four big political fights. That has been the extent of my fighting." Surprised, and impressed, by his commander's "frank acknowledgement," Campbell replied, "General, taking into account the small force on our side and the immense odds against us, this is the hottest battle I was ever in." Tom appeared satisfied with Campbell's response. He had finally joined Hugh and Charley among the ranks of the full combat veterans. Moreover, Tom had defeated enemy soldiers in open battle. He was no longer playing a frustrating game of cat and mouse with guerrillas and their families.[66]

Gesturing to his officers to join him in conversation, Tom asked them what they thought their odds of survival would be the next day. Not one expected to hold the fort. Even though Price had proven himself to be among the most incompetent generals in the Confederate Army, he would still bring up the remainder of his field guns to bear on the fort. Price would also prepare assault ladders tomorrow with which to span the dry moat. There were not sufficient able-bodied Iowa and Missouri troops left to defend the entire length of the walls. It was also obvious that Price would not take a lot of prisoners—and those who were captured could expect, like Major Wilson, to be tortured to death.[67]

Tom evacuated the fort at three o'clock in the morning, initially heading north. A squad would stay behind for an hour, blow up the fort's magazine, and then join up with Tom. Murphy spiked the heavier guns to render them useless. He then wrapped rags around the wheels of the lighter field pieces to reduce the noise made as horses quietly pulled them out of the fort.

The troops also placed canvas over the planks of the drawbridge to muffle the sounds of men and horses crossing the moat. Tom would not leave his wounded behind, so he had them loaded into wagons whose wheels were also padded. Every man drew one hundred rounds of ammunition. Campbell and the Fourteenth Iowa took the point in case they encountered Confederate patrols. Thanks to the inebriation and exhaustion of Price's troops, however, there were no patrols deployed. Even when the fort's magazine blew up, shaking the ground within a radius of twenty miles, Price's men did not arouse themselves. The rebels figured that the fort's gunpowder supplies had exploded by accident, resulting in the extermination of the Union garrison.[68]

Price did not send a scouting party over to Fort Davidson until eight o'clock in the morning. By then, Tom's diminished command had covered ten miles. Realizing that he no longer had sufficient troops to capture St. Louis, Price opted to sow even more terror in the Missouri countryside and to capture Tom. He was not, however, able to mount an immediate pursuit given the demoralized and hung-over condition of his soldiers. Once Price's men bestirred themselves, however, there remained a danger that Tom's pursuers would push his men into the waiting arms of General Shelby's marauding cavalry. Given that threat, Tom decided not to make a direct and predictable retreat to St. Louis but rather to head westward toward Rolla. He aimed for the narrowest of Ozark backroads that he could find, preferably ones with cliffs so steep that enemy horse soldiers would have no room in which to mount an ambush. Tom also roughly interrogated the occasional prisoner his men took. Placing "hanging nooses" around Confederate soldiers' necks greatly encouraged their willingness to talk.[69]

The remnant of Tom's Iowans covered the rear of his retreat, repeatedly clashing with Price's troops until the Confederate infantry collapsed in exhaustion. Then Shelby's cavalry took up the chase. Murphy rapidly unlimbered and fired his field guns over and over again. This would have seemed a peculiar moment to be transported back in time to his college days at Brown, but so it happened. As Tom observed, there was something about "the dun heather of the mountain sides" and the approach of the Confederates that "forcibly reminded" him of Sir Walter Scott's "stirring description of the chase in the 'Lady of the Lake'":

> Yelled on the view the opening pack,
> Glen, rock, and cavern paid them back.
> To many a mingled sound at once
> The wakened mountains gave response;
> The falcon, from her cairn on high,

Glanced on the rout a wondering eye,
Till, far beyond her piercing ken,
The hurricane had swept the glen.
Back limped with slow and crippled pace,
The sulky leaders of the chase;
Close to their master's side they pressed,
With drooping tail and humble crest.[70]

Dozens of Missouri refugees joined Tom's column. Many had miraculously escaped Price's guerrillas, though their farms were now charred remains. Black civilians flocked to Tom, seeing his troops as their only hope for survival. Despite being slowed down by the wounded and the increasing number of children, in the thirty-nine hours since leaving Pilot Knob Tom had marched his command sixty-six miles through driving rain and across mud-sucking streams. The longer Confederate forces pursued him, the more time Rosecrans had to find reinforcements for St. Louis and Jefferson City. Price and Shelby were also going deeper into Missouri and further away from their Arkansas base. Tom had become the bait with which to lure rebel soldiers and guerrillas to their destruction.[71]

Arriving in Leasburg, thirty-five miles from Rolla, Tom prepared for his last stand. He had found a civilian willing to take word to Rolla of his need for reinforcements. Tom could not count on their timely arrival. In the retreat so far, he had lost 150 men, in addition to the 250 killed and missing at Pilot Knob. His soldiers, their number reduced nearly in half, had just thirty rounds of ammunition apiece out of the hundred bullets they had originally taken. Although Shelby had cut the rail line, Tom's men still had access to boxcars and ties that they could use to construct a redoubt. He praised his troops and the civilian volunteers, most especially the black men, "who eagerly bore their share of labor and danger." Shelby's cavalry, outnumbering Tom five to one, went from morning to night probing Tom's defenses. The next day, the Confederates shouted to Tom that if he did not surrender then all the Union soldiers would be executed as common criminals, rather than spared as prisoners of war. Since their execution was likely to happen even if they did surrender, Tom's men defiantly burst into a chorus of "The Battle Cry of Freedom." Chastened, and learning of the approach of a Union relief column, Shelby withdrew.[72]

The military consequences of Tom's stand at Pilot Knob, and his subsequent retreat, were quick to be seen. Price's diminished force could not take St. Louis and then had to pass on attacking the reinforced capital city. As General Clinton Fisk of the District of North Missouri harshly put it, "The capital of the State had been saved from the polluting presence of her traitorous sons in arms." Union troops caught up with guerrilla leader "Bloody" Bill Anderson on October 27 and killed him. Quantrill, who had been leery of Price's invasion, abandoned Missouri, relocating his guerrilla operations to Kentucky. The remnants of Price's army disintegrated under the pressure of Union attack and desertion. Confederate military operations, whether by regular troops or guerrillas, largely ceased in the western theater.[73]

Politically, Tom's actions at Pilot Knob earned mixed reviews. Kansas gubernatorial candidate Samuel Crawford, a former colonel in the Second Kansas Cavalry and an ally of Jim Lane, minimized Tom's achievement. Price, according to Crawford, had not mounted that much of an assault, yet Tom had still abandoned Fort Davidson in defeat. Outraged correspondents wrote to Lincoln condemning Tom's orders to execute captured guerrillas in retaliation for the torture and murder of Major Wilson. An aroused Rosecrans informed Lincoln that retaliation was the best policy: "All other motive having failed to secure my soldiers who had surrendered themselves prisoners of war from cold blooded assassination or official murder by Price's Command, I felt bound to appeal to the sense of personal security by declaring to these men that I should hold them individually responsible for the treatment of my Troops while prisoners in their hands."[74]

On the positive side of the political ledger, Missouri Republicans swept Democrats at the polls, with Colonel Fletcher elected governor. For Missourians in the years to come, serving at Pilot Knob acquired the political cachet Texans reserved for those who had fought at San Jacinto in 1836. Senator Lane, learning of Tom's successful engagement with Price and Shelby, shifted mental gears midspeech to praise his greatest political enemy. Fully cognizant of the military and political stakes involved with Price's invasion, the *New York Times* and *Harper's Weekly* gave Tom full credit. The *New York Herald* even reprinted Tom's official report of the battle and retreat. St. Louis attorney and Republican politician Charles Drake wrote effusively to Lincoln that Tom deserved command of the Department of Missouri and promotion to the rank of major general: "His talents, administrative and military, eminently fit him for the position; his gallantry in the field has endeared him to Missourians; he has traversed the length and breadth of Missouri, and thoroughly knows what she is and what she needs."[75]

As Tom's aide, Major Hannahs saw a commander exhausted by, and out of patience with, the political pettiness of men like Crawford. Lincoln did arrange for Tom's promotion to major general. Tom accepted the honor but still insisted on resigning his commission. He had already decided that he would leave the military for private law practice. Tom's course of action was set in stone when he received a letter from his wife postmarked from Lancaster. She had given birth on the day of the battle for Fort Davidson. There had been complications: "Our dear little ones [were] perhaps, never, never in such danger of being left both Fatherless and Motherless in the same day."[76]

In the aftermath of Price's thwarted invasion of Missouri, Lincoln swept to victory. As he had done in the run up to his renomination, Lincoln prepared the ground for the general election. Although fourteen of the northern states permitted soldiers to vote while deployed outside their borders, others did not. Lincoln wrote to Cump after the fall of Atlanta that he had a request to make on the behalf of Indiana's Unionists: "Anything you can safely do to let her soldiers, or any part of them, go home and vote at the state election, will be greatly in point." The president also sought to enhance his Electoral College vote margin by forcing through Congress the admission of Nevada and West Virginia to the Union. Nevada did not have sufficient population to be admitted to the Union in 1864, and there was no provision in the U.S. Constitution to chop up an existing state to create a new political entity like West Virginia in 1863. Both Nevada and West Virginia, however, could be counted upon in 1864 to vote for Lincoln.[77]

The Lincoln-Johnson Union ticket rolled over the Democrats. In Ohio, despite having George Pendleton as their vice presidential candidate, the Democrats went from controlling fourteen of the state's nineteen congressional seats to holding just two. Hugh's former comrade-in-arms, Rutherford Hayes, joined the ranks of newly elected Republican members of the U.S. House of Representatives. Lincoln rejoiced when he heard that Samuel Cox would no longer be barking at his heels.[78]

There was, however, cause for concern among Republicans. Kentucky, in spite of Lincoln's best efforts to mollify the foes of emancipation, went to McClellan. The Virginia Military District in Ohio remained Democratic, and Fairfield County, despite having bred such Union heroes as Cump, Tom, Hugh, and Charley, rejected Lincoln. Electoral patterns in Pennsylvania were little different. Many of the counties bordering Maryland, as well as Philadelphia's Irish Catholic neighborhoods, voted Democratic. Adams County, for instance, which had narrowly gone to Lincoln in 1860, went Democratic in 1864. The county seat was Gettysburg. Lee's political instincts had proven correct. A few more Gettysburg bloodbaths on northern soil might have defeated Lincoln. Many northerners continued to fear that freed slaves would move into the North, where they would compete for jobs and sow social disorder. Such voters were also concerned that the federal government would continue to expand its power at the expense of states' and individuals' rights.[79]

Nationally, there was one electoral equation that Republicans could not ignore, even as they averted their eyes from the embarrassment given to them by the Democratic loyalists of Adams County, Pennsylvania, and Fairfield County, Ohio. Lincoln's 2.2 million votes and 55 percent vote share in 1864 appeared decisive. However, if the 660,000 southern white males who had cast ballots in 1860 had participated in the 1864 election, Lincoln would have lost with 47 percent of the vote. After four years of war and a monopoly of power in Washington, the Republicans had increased their actual portion of the national electorate by only seven percentage points. Once the South surrendered and received readmission to the Union, and the white Democratic males not killed in the war began voting in federal elections, the Republicans were doomed. A new Republican constituency had to be found. Enfranchising blacks—southern and northern—would have to follow the abolition of slavery if the Republicans had any hope of retaining power.

Lincoln's reelection in November 1864 removed the chief political obstacle standing in the way of Cump's desire to march across Georgia. The president had been unwilling to entertain such a bold move before the election. Grant had stressed the northern public to its breaking point, and Lincoln regarded Cump's plan as too nerve-racking. Cump reassured Grant and Lincoln that advancing through Georgia would be a lot easier than capturing Atlanta. He would not have to worry about protecting his supply line since his men could live off the land. This would have the added advantage of denying food supplies to the Confederacy. Cump also reduced the number of his troops to a hard core of sixty thousand. Those Union troops who remained in service, but did not join Cump, could be deployed to guard Tennessee.

Cump would leave the Confederates guessing as to his destination. He hoped to avoid engaging with enemy forces whenever possible. Cump wanted to wage economic and psychological war on civilians, destroying their rail lines, burning their cotton, and breaking their morale. It was not for nothing that Cump kept at his side a copy of the 1860 U.S. Census, which gave him a road map to the South's most productive lands. As a bonus, while the Yankees desecrated their homes, Lee's Georgian troops would be sitting helplessly in their Petersburg trenches contemplating desertion. This psychological factor was of some importance given that many Confederate soldiers claimed they had gone to war not to preserve slavery but to defend their homes and women from Yankee invaders. Cump's plan was made all the easier by the decision of Hood to take his remnant army away from Atlanta. Hood ultimately attempted a disastrous attack against George Thomas's troops in Tennessee. That left Georgia defended by 3,500 cavalry troops under the youthful Joe Wheeler and

3,000 militiamen who had been too old, too young, or too enfeebled to serve with Hood or Lee.[80]

He expected that slaves would abandon their work at the approach of the Union column. This was part of the economic dislocation that Cump envisioned. He would be taken aback by the joyful cries of deeply religious slaves who greeted him as Moses delivering them from Pharaoh. Cump was little moved, however, by their plight. He had loved being posted in the prewar South and had chastised Hugh years earlier for thinking that blacks were equal to whites. If there was any doubt about Cump's unwillingness to spark a social revolution, he made his views on race clear before embarking on the three-hundred-mile long March through Georgia. In September Cump posted an unequivocal letter to a Baltimore correspondent:

> Iron is iron and steel is steel; and all the popular clamor on earth will not impart to one the qualities of the other.
>
> So a nigger is not a white man, and all the Psalm-singing on earth won't make him so. It is strange to me that among a people, North and South, who have so much common sense, that you can't say "nigger" till both parties make fools of themselves, and it is hard to say which are the worst. When we settle this little fight on hand, the great "nigger" question will be settled also.[81]

In preparation for their departure from Atlanta, Cump's troops pulled down the walls of the large manufacturing buildings so that they would burn more easily. The November 15 fire illuminated the landscape for miles in every direction. To the Union troops who knew ancient history, Atlanta's blazing glow harkened back to the Roman sack of Carthage. Ohio and Indiana soldiers, however, were not likely to waste precious salt by scattering it in Atlanta's streets. Major George Nichols of Cump's staff, commenting on the "track of smoke and flame" Union forces made upon leaving Atlanta, reflected that "in the peaceful homes at the North there can be no conception how these people have suffered for their crimes."[82]

Like the enlisted men and Cump himself, Charley Ewing was in fine spirits. For the first time in his life he had been saving money and paying off debts, not that the merchants of Atlanta had presented Cump's army with bills for their cigars and bourbon. The March through Georgia, Charley subsequently enthused in a letter to his father, "has been one big picnic. No rain, or cold and plenty of good things for the mess." As for Cump, Charley observed, "During our march from Kingston to this place [Savannah] the work he had to do was only play for him. The perfect faith the army had in him, and his perfect confidence in the army left nothing to fear or to be anxious for."[83]

Charley's correspondence came up short on details. The advance from Atlanta to Savannah on the Atlantic coast had been more of a continuous festival than a staid Sunday-afternoon picnic. When Cump's infantry descended upon the state capital of Milledgeville on November 22, they had been crestfallen to see that the hamlet consisted of little more than the legislative building and a woman's penitentiary. One newspaper correspondent later described Milledgeville as "a dingy, sleepy, Rip Van Winkle sort of old town, with grass-grown streets, [that] fairly represents the spirit of southern civilization." Union soldiers were even less impressed and observed that the female prison inmates were unlikely to be sexually assaulted.[84]

Good times, however, soon rolled in the legislative chambers. Charley had helped locate the legislature's liquor and tobacco stocks. Cigars, pipe, and chewing tobacco were distributed, and the soldiers took their seats in the lavishly decorated chambers. Officers delivered speeches in the "southern political style," which, among Charley's compatriots, meant speaking loudly, slowly, and without recourse to proper grammar. Joseph Foraker, formerly of the Eighty-Ninth Ohio and now a staff officer, assisted in "drafting" a resolution to bring Georgia back into the Union. The "speaker" of the assembly, Ohio general James Robinson, took enormous gulps from a whisky flask while appointing Charley to a special committee on "Federal Relations." Charley, several officers, and a large quantity of alcohol adjourned to a caucus room. As spittoons filled and bottles emptied, several soldiers came running into the legislature. In their best imitation of hysterical southern plantation belles, they shouted in horror, "The Yankees are coming!" The "legislators" roared with delight and then adjourned.[85]

Not everyone in Cump's army was as merry as Charley Ewing and Joe Foraker. Major Henry Hitchcock, who had recently joined Cump's staff, proved to be a scold. Hitchcock's father was a friend of Hugh Ewing. It was Hugh who had made the arrangements to send Henry to Cump. While Hitchcock practiced law in St. Louis, Charley Ewing had been leading infantry assaults in Mississippi. Hitchcock had never seen combat and lacked a context for understanding what he regarded as the coarse and criminal behavior of Cump's troops. He had recoiled when Charley distributed the Georgia legislature's tobacco: "I have not taken nor received nor shall I, one cent's worth from anybody, other than my share of the subsistence gathered for the mess." Privately, Hitchcock groused, "I think Sherman is lacking in enforcing discipline. Brilliant and daring, fertile, rapid and terrible, he does not seem to me to *carry out things* in this respect."[86]

Hitchcock wasted no time getting into an argument with Charley. The latter wanted to torch a plantation house whose owner had allegedly burned a bridge over Buffalo Creek near Sandersville. Hitchcock was appalled. Overhearing the heated exchange, Cump said, "In war everything is right which prevents anything. If bridges are burned I have the right to burn all houses near it." Hitchcock, thinking more like a lawyer than a subordinate officer, retorted, "Beg pardon, General, but what I was contending for *with Colonel Ewing* was that indiscriminate punishment was not just—and that there ought to be good reason for connecting this man with the burning of the bridges before burning his house." Cump shot back, "Well, let him look to his own people, if they find that their burning bridges only destroys their own citizens' houses they'll stop it."[87]

While his relationship with Charley gradually improved, Hitchcock continued to regard him as heedless. On one occasion, for instance, Charley and the other staff officers were enjoying their cigars while Hitchcock slept in his tent. None of the officers noticed how deep and flammable the pile of pine needles was at their feet. Hitchcock groggily awoke from a nap to see Charley frantically putting out a fire that had started to burn his tent. On another occasion, Charley nearly severed his own femoral artery, which would have "bled him to death." Charley had been carrying a scalpel in his coat pocket with which to cut twine. "Mounting his horse," Hitchcock observed, Charley had his coat "doubled under [his] right thigh," and the scalpel blade was "driven into [the] inner side of this thigh to the bone." After all Charley had been through, this would have been a terribly embarrassing way to have died.[88]

Other officers and enlisted men were far more appreciative of Charley's personality and logistical skills than Hitchcock. "No one," Major Nichols insisted, "better understands the organization of this army, down to its last battalion, than he." Moreover, Nichols continued, "His position would permit an incumbent so disposed to be exacting, censorious, and hypercritical, but Colonel Ewing is of a far different character. Though firm, he is as courteous as he is efficient." Corporal Luke Clarke of the Thirteenth U.S. Infantry shared Nichols's assessment and further observed that no one in the army was a better entertainer. Charley could mimic nearly every major officer and politician in the North.[89]

Cump estimated that by the time his men assaulted Fort McAllister outside Savannah on December 13, they had confiscated ten thousand horses and mules and inflicted $100 million worth of damage to Georgia. In Savannah, the Confederates left behind twenty-five thousand bales of precious cotton. Cump's troops became adept at demolishing rail lines, taking out five-mile stretches in the span of an hour. They even devised a special tool so that after placing the iron rails over a pile of burning ties the soldiers could give them a "corkscrew" twist. The South did not have the metal fabrication facilities to straighten out the rails. His men had encountered minimal armed resistance, though General Wheeler pulled a nasty surprise by planting land mines. Cump's response was primitive but effective: he let Wheeler know that he would march Confederate prisoners ahead of the Union column. Wheeler planted no more mines.[90]

"Sherman's March" captured the imagination of the North. Correspondents sent dispatches from Savannah recounting the humbling of Georgia. *Harper's Weekly* compared Cump to Napoleon, adding that where the French had failed to conquer Russia the Union forces had subdued the South. Newspapers in the Old Northwest reported on, even as they editorialized about, what their reporters had witnessed: "The white inhabitants mostly fled precipitately before us, taking with them such of their effects as could be gotten away. Trunks and boxes containing valuable goods and wares were unearthed from gardens and confiscated by the finders. Had these people stayed at home and kept their property by them they would have fared much better. Their fleeing from us and hiding their goods was *prima facie* evidence of guilty distrust which furnished a license for our soldiers."[91]

Cump grandly offered Lincoln the city of Savannah as a "Christmas present." Lincoln admitted to Cump that he had been "*anxious, if not fearful,*" at the outset of the campaign but that "now, the undertaking being a success, the honor is all yours." The president had wasted no time, Cousin Jimmy Blaine noted, in sending an exuberant message to Congress that called Sherman's March "[the] most remarkable feature in the military operations of the year." Musicians went to work to commemorate Cump's achievement. Connecticut-born composer Henry Clay Work penned a lively tune that would subsequently follow Cump wherever he went:

> Bring the good ol' Bugle boys! We'll sing another song,
> Sing it with a spirit that will start the world along,
> Sing it like we used to sing it fifty thousand strong,
> While we were marching through Georgia!
> Hurrah! Hurrah! We bring the Jubilee!
> Hurrah! Hurrah! The flag that makes you free,
> So we sang the chorus from Atlanta to the sea,
> While we were marching through Georgia![92]

Cump and Charley settled comfortably into Savannah. Charley, joined by Hitchcock and a correspondent from *Harper's Weekly*, sailed the Ogeechee River, taking in the sights. They met up with some well-provisioned Union naval officers, who, Hitchcock noted with envy, were "luxurious rascals compared to us dwellers in tents." Thanks to the *Harper's Weekly* reporter, Charley soon had his engraved image seen by thousands of northerners. From the mansion where he was staying, a deeply satisfied Cump wrote to Ellen, "It would amuse you to see the Negroes; they flock to me, old and young, they pray and shout and mix up my name with that of Moses, and Simon, and other scriptural ones as well as "Abram Linkom," the Great Messiah of 'Dis Jubilee.'"[93]

There was, however, one sad note to Cump's pleasant sojourn. Having been cut off from communications with the North for several weeks, he did not learn until his arrival in Savannah that he had lost another child. Cump had to read in the *New York Herald* that his infant son Charles Sherman had died on December 4 while staying with relatives at Notre Dame. He had been in the field when little Charley was born and had never laid eyes on his youngest child. Ellen's cousin, Mother Angela, tried to console her, but losing two children in less than two years was a crushing blow. "Oh, blessed labor, fairest child," Ellen and Cousin Angela observed in memory of little Charley, "with spotless presence undefiled, to teach us in this desert-wild, of Heaven, that may be ours."[94]

While Ellen buried her baby, a few hundred miles away in Washington the U.S. Supreme Court was in a special session. The surviving members of the Supreme Court Club gathered to memorialize Roger Taney. Thomas Ewing, Cousin Henry Stanbery, Orville Browning, and Reverdy Johnson joined the justices. Only John Campbell, now in Richmond serving in the Confederate War Department, was absent. Ewing, who regarded the *Dred Scott* decision with loathing, nonetheless accepted the task of composing Taney's testimonial. Given the temper of the times, Ewing paid tribute to the chief justice's good character, leaving aside how disastrous his jurisprudence had been for the country: "But his was not the destiny of private life, where virtue, benevolence, and religion pursue the noiseless tenor of their way; and yet, upon the broad and lofty theatre to which he was called, and where, for more than a quarter of a century, he sat in judgment, between sovereign states as between private litigants, 'without fear and without reproach,' there was ever apparent this deep undercurrent which marked him as the model of a good man and a Christian gentleman."[95]

A week later, Ewing and his friends returned to the Supreme Court chambers to witness the debasing of their beloved club. With the ascension of

Salmon Chase to chief justice, a new era dawned. Taney, the standard-bearer of states' rights on the Court, gave way to Chase, the ambitious extender of federal power. Stanbery and Johnson would never reconcile themselves to the new order, particularly when it came to political rights for freed slaves. Ewing, having already registered his protest with Lincoln, made no public comment.[96]

It was not lost on the members of the Supreme Court Club that race had become a major issue in American politics. Northern Democrats had sought since 1861, well before Lincoln issued the Emancipation Proclamation, to depict Republicans as enemies of the white race. Once Lincoln, acting out of military exigency, made the abolition of slavery a war objective and began recruiting blacks into the Union Army, Democrats in both sections of the country often reacted angrily. Many northern Democrats, who had supported a war to preserve the Union, would not embrace Lincoln's new political agenda. Kentucky Democrats reacted harshly to Lincoln, leaving it to Hugh Ewing to deal with a hostile state government and an energized guerrilla insurgency. These were political conditions Tom Ewing knew too well in Missouri. The Ewing patriarch had predicted that there would be a backlash against emancipation that would only grow in the coming years.

Given the task of defeating a South that scorned emancipation, the war became progressively bloodier. The Lawrence Massacre in 1863, and Tom's issuance of General Order Number 11, had little precedent in American history. (Indians and slaves, however, might have found massacre and dislocation to be familiar themes.) One year later, there could be little doubt that the Union and the Confederacy had erased the line separating civilization from barbarism. No longer, thanks in good measure to Cump, Tom, Hugh, and Charley, could meaningful distinctions be made between civilians and combatants. The war for the Union was no longer just framed around soldiers on the field of battle. It had become for many a war of all against all. Very few limits remained. Execution, rape, torture, pillage, and retaliation, though not necessarily routine, were not rare occurrences either. Whether or not this trend continued depended upon the will of the South. After Pilot Knob and the March through Georgia, the North would not step back from whatever steps deemed necessary to win victory. Sterling Price, incompetent that he was, had demonstrated his commitment to fight as dirty as possible.

With the coming of the new year of 1865, few Americans could put these developments into an understandable context. Fewer still could fathom the enormous number of dead and wounded. In what proved to be the final months of the war, 1865 saw the United States lurch ever closer to a political and social abyss. The Ewing family would alternately be leading the way to, and pulling back from, that abyss.

7

"Stand on the Crater of a Living Volcano"

Processions, Trials, and Recriminations

I would as soon expect a house to stand on the crater of a living
volcano, as a State, where whites and blacks being nearly equal
in numbers, the whites are proscribed and the blacks made rulers. Such a Government cannot long have the heartfelt sympathy
of any large body of men anywhere. Blood is thicker than water,
and northern whites will sympathize with southern whites in their
struggle to shake off the incubus of Negro rule.
—Thomas Ewing Jr., 1867

Few soldiers in Cump's army could complain about the hardships they
endured while occupying Savannah. The city boasted gracious architecture
and bore no resemblance to the dismal settlements they had seen in north
Georgia. Admittedly, it took the sons of the Old Northwest some effort to
get used to eating rice. Most of Cump's troops, however, dove into the sea-
food. For the natives of Ohio and Indiana, saltwater oysters were a once-in-
a-lifetime treat. Meanwhile, Charley continued his explorations of the area,
though he failed to loosen up the censorious Major Henry Hitchcock. Charley's friend and fellow staff officer Major George Nichols was far more easy-
going. As Nichols said of Savannah: "A foreigner visiting the city would not
suppose that it was so lately a prize of battle. Ladies walk the streets with perfect confidence and security, and the public squares are filled with children at
play; the stores and theaters are open; soldiers are lounging on the doorsteps
of the houses in cheerful conversation with fair damsels; carriages whirl by,
wherein the blue coat and brass buttons are in close proximity—anything but
warlike—to jockey hats and flowering ringlets."[1]

Even Cump relaxed, socializing with Savannah's elite and sparking rumors of extramarital affairs. Irate Republican politicians, however, soon interrupted Cump's pleasant interlude. Word had reached Washington that one of Cump's generals, the unfortunately named Jeff Davis, had acted in a cruel manner toward Georgia's black populace. Davis, not wishing to remain burdened with runaway slaves who had to be fed, chose to remove a pontoon bridge that Union engineers had constructed over Ebenezer Creek. Scores of stranded slaves, mostly women, the elderly, and children who could perform no military tasks for the Union forces, either drowned or were butchered by General Joe Wheeler's cavalry. Salmon Chase, confirming Thomas Ewing's prediction that a judicial robe would never cloak his politician's skin, lashed out at Cump.[2]

Secretary of War Edwin Stanton arrived in Savannah in early January 1865 to chastise Cump. Stanton compelled him to schedule a meeting with Savannah's leading free black residents. Cump, who had little regard for minorities or clergy, had no choice but to invite several black Methodist and Baptist ministers to converse with him and the war secretary. He regarded Stanton's visit as an insult, as well as an unwarranted civilian interference with military matters. Captain Joseph Foraker, who had accidentally stumbled into one of Cump's and Stanton's interminable sessions, later observed: "Sherman was, as usual, enthusiastic, cordial, frank, and talkative. Stanton, on the contrary, was glum and had little to say. His manner was such I could not help thinking he was unfriendly to Sherman, as he afterward showed he was."[3]

Setting the stage for a later showdown with Radical Republicans, Cump dismissed Stanton's admonishments to be more solicitous of black opinion. He had no sympathy for the actual motivation behind Stanton's high-profile visit. The Thirteenth Amendment to the U.S. Constitution, which would abolish slavery, was awaiting congressional approval before being sent to the states for ratification. As events transpired, the House of Representatives approved the amendment on January 31 with the bare two-thirds majority required by the Constitution. Only one Ohio Democrat voted in its favor. In the politically critical Buckeye State the legislature subsequently ratified the Thirteenth Amendment along party lines and over the objections of Democrats who warned that Republicans intended to "Africanize" the North. Stanton and Chase needed blacks to be fully free, *Republican*-voting citizens. That would not happen if military commanders like Cump left them to the tender mercies of southern (and northern) Democrats.[4]

Five hundred miles to the north of Savannah, Assistant Secretary of War John Campbell brooded in his Richmond quarters. Since resigning from the U.S. Supreme Court in 1861, Campbell had seen his beloved South brought to ruin. With President Jefferson Davis's permission, Campbell had written to Justice Samuel Nelson. Campbell asked Nelson if Thomas Ewing could set up a meeting between Lincoln and Confederate vice president Alexander Stephens. Lincoln agreed to talk but excluded Ewing. He sent the senior Francis Blair to make arrangements for Stephens and Campbell to come to Grant's headquarters at City Point, Virginia. The February 3 meeting proved to be a futile exercise. Stephens wanted a truce, but the Confederacy was willing neither to embrace emancipation nor to surrender its self-proclaimed status as a sovereign nation. The war, Thomas Ewing fretted, would continue until Robert E. Lee met "disgraceful defeat and surrender."[5]

The last of Cump's army departed Savannah on February 1, headed relentlessly toward Columbia, the capital of South Carolina. Though the objective was 160 miles away—normally several days' march—the swampy terrain and freezing rain made the procession extremely slow. Charley wrote to his father that he was experiencing the coldest and most miserable weather since his arrival in the South two years earlier. Always thinking, Charley secured an invitation from General Frank Blair to share a spacious—and dry—house that he had commandeered in Beaufort, South Carolina. His brother Tom may have loathed Blair, but still, as Charley could attest, he possessed a keen eye for comfort. Major Hitchcock grumbled that he ended up sleeping on the plank floor of a cold shack. Most of Cump's enlisted men would have gladly traded places with Hitchcock. To speed their progress, they had left their tents behind.[6]

Charley and the troops did not have to worry much about Confederate forces. On the other hand, marching through South Carolina proved far more exhausting than the romp across Georgia. Just to get to Columbia required crossing several water-gorged rivers and at least two dozen swamps. There was also, in contrast to Georgia, not a lot of food to be foraged. In spite of these challenges, Charley had no doubt that victory was on the horizon. He wrote his father, "We all expect a hard but a successful campaign," and added that afterwards he wanted to command a combat regiment "for the final struggle of the war" outside Richmond.[7]

While Charley may have been in good spirits, Cump's chilled and muckcovered troops were in a vicious temper. Major Nichols succinctly referred to South Carolina as "this cowardly traitor state" that "with hellish haste dragged her Southern sisters into the caldron of secession." Captain Foraker was not surprised to discover that the militarily and economically insignificant towns of Robertsville and Lawtonville "were both in ashes." Having elevated eavesdropping on Cump's high-level conversations into an art form, Foraker had heard him issue a blunt directive to Major General

Henry Slocum, the commander of the Fourteenth and Twentieth Corps: "Don't forget that when you have crossed the Savannah River you will be in South Carolina. You need not be so careful there about private property as we have been. The more of it you destroy the better it will be. The people of South Carolina should be made to feel the war, for they brought it on and are responsible more than anybody else for our presence here. Now is the time to punish them."[8]

As Cump's army approached Columbia, Nichols disparaged the "population of 'poor whites' whose brain is as arid as the land they occupy." Curious white women, standing barefoot in the mud, stared wide-eyed at the Union troops. When asked what they doing, the women explained that they had never before seen so many people gathered in one place. Nichols warned them that the soldiers might think they were soliciting sex. Meanwhile, slaves laughed and shouted greetings. The gaunt and poorly dressed whites made no effort to admonish the blacks, observing that the planters had treated both races like so much trash. None of the white elite were anywhere to be seen. Major Hitchcock finally reached his moral tipping point. South Carolina's noble gentry put up no fight, whereas in Georgia at least a few privileged whites had tried to resist. He also recoiled at a system in which a wealthy few benefited from the misery of so many. "Of all mean humbugs," Hitchcock observed, "'South Carolina's chivalry' is the meanest." He would no longer be after Charley to rein in the army.[9]

Union troops pushed to the outskirts of Columbia on February 16. What happened over the course of the next day would become the subject of bitter controversy for generations. Daniel Trezevant, who had mansions in Columbia and Charleston, held Cump responsible for the destruction of the helpless capital. According to Trezevant, drunken, debased blacks began looting and burning shops and churches. Yankee soldiers, when not busy raping black women, joined the pillaging slaves. It could not be otherwise, Trezevant argued, since the soldiers were just as savage as the vicious blacks. Worsening the situation, whenever upstanding white citizens attempted to put out the fires, Cump's undisciplined soldiers shot them down. Sometime between committing wholesale rape and executing unarmed civilians, Cump's troops dug up cemeteries looking for whatever jewelry might have been left on the interred. Worse, Union soldiers beat up and robbed white women. In a matter of hours, 84 of Columbia's 124 blocks were little more than cinders.[10]

Cump and his officers conceded that the situation in Columbia was chaotic but denied there was any intent to loot and burn the city. Major Henry Clay McArthur of the Fifteenth Iowa had been among the first Union soldiers to cross the Congaree River into Columbia on the morning of February

17. His men engaged a few of General Wade Hampton's cavalry forces. The bulk of Hampton's troops, however, were not passing their time shooting at Yankees. Most were busy looting stores while others collected great piles of cotton that they set ablaze. As a member of South Carolina's planter elite, Hampton had no intention of allowing anything of value to fall into Cump's hands. Hampton, assuming the role of a Russian marshal facing Napoleon, preferred to leave scorched earth behind. He subsequently denied that this was Confederate military policy, choosing to blame Cump for the disaster that unfolded in Columbia.[11]

Ironically, the South Carolinian government had set the stage for Columbia's destruction. Convinced that *Charleston* would be the Union's key objective, South Carolina had transferred food, cotton, weapons, and military production facilities to the capital. Columbia had consequently become an enormous military target, laden with highly combustible cotton and gunpowder. Major Nichols, taking into account the importance of the Charleston and Augusta Railroad, which went through Columbia, as well as the city's manufacturing output, concluded that South Carolina's capital dwarfed Milledgeville in strategic importance.[12]

Beyond enormous food and military provisions, Columbia was blessed with massive liquor stocks, which grateful slaves handed out to Cump's troops. There was not, Major Hitchcock conceded, much of a leap from downing a fifth of whisky and lighting a bonfire to keep warm to, intentionally or not, torching the entire community. The irate Trezevant was correct in citing the drunken condition of many of the Union soldiers. On the other hand, it was unlikely that Cump's men devoted their energies to digging up graveyards; there was loot enough scattered in the streets. Moreover, Union men, surveying the large numbers of mixed-race slaves in Columbia, could point out to Trezevant that the rape of black women had been taking place long before they arrived on the scene.[13]

Union troops were not impressed with Columbia's aesthetic charms. The capitol building had not been completed, though its granite exterior was solid enough to entertain Cump's gunners as they bounced cannonballs off its walls. Major Nichols said of Columbia:

The residences of these people accorded with their personal appearance. Dirty wooden shanties, built on a river bank a few hundred feet above the factory, were the places called homes—homes where doors hung shabbily by a single hinge, or were destitute of panels; where rotten steps led to foul and close passage-ways, filled with broken crockery, dirty pots and pans, and other accumulations of rubbish; where stagnant pools of water bred disease; where half a dozen persons occupied the same bed-chamber; where old women and ragged children lolled lazily in the sunshine; where even the gaunt fowls that went desolately about the premises partook of the prevailing character of misery and dirt. These were the operatives, and these the homes produced by the boasted civilization of the South.[14]

Sister Baptista Lynch, the Mother Superior of the Ursuline Convent in Columbia, had sent a letter to Cump on the morning of February 17 pleading for his protection. It seemed that she had been one of the teachers employed by the Ewing family in Ohio to instruct Cump's daughter Minnie. Cump designated Charley as the army's ambassador to the southern Catholicism. Unfortunately for Sister Baptista, her convent ended up torched, as did the church where she and her students took refuge. She confronted Cump, accusing him of having lied to "a cloistered nun." Angry, yet wilting under her gaze, Cump ordered Charley to work out a deal with Sister Baptista. That encounter went somewhat better. Charley at first tried to maintain an unapologetic stance but quickly reverted to the poise of a chastised Catholic schoolboy. He ended up expelling Major General John Logan from a mansion that Fifteenth Corps was preparing to burn. Charley was not keen to write his father about the Ewing family reunion with Sister Baptista. Trezevant, however, would make sure that the world knew of Charley's cruel treatment of defenseless nuns.[15]

After Columbia's destruction, there was little hope that other South Carolinian towns would fare better. Winnsboro, a rail town on the line of march to North Carolina, was fortunate to have escaped with only a partial torching. Charley, along with Nichols and Foraker, urged Union troops to burn only those targets that had unquestionable military value. A house that General Charles Cornwallis had used as his headquarters while fighting Revolutionary War guerrillas survived thanks to their efforts. The Episcopal Church was not as fortunate. Still, as Charley informed his father, South Carolina was a "state of braggarts" that deserved everything it got from Cump's army. He could not understand why Confederate forces had made so little effort to defend the cradle of secession. To Charley, as well as to the other staff officers, the apparent unwillingness of South Carolina's planters to fight seemed shameful—and made the unrestrained sacking of the state even more justified.[16]

Confederate resistance finally commenced in late February. Wade Hampton's and Joe Wheeler's men executed Union troops foraging for supplies. Major Nichols was horrified to learn that eighteen Union soldiers had been found piled in a blood-drenched ravine. The Confederates had slashed their prisoners' throats. Cump ordered immediate retaliation. Confederates prisoners would be shot until the guerrilla operations ceased. Nichols cheered Cump's order and vowed that "if this murderous game is continued by these fiends, they will bitterly rue the day it was begun."[17]

By March 11, Cump's army was in Fayetteville, North Carolina, sixty-three miles south of Raleigh, the state capital. Union troops ceased the wholesale demolition of civilian dwellings once they crossed out of South Carolina. Thanks to Cump's army, South Carolina suffered the worst physical and economic despoliation of the war. South Carolina also racked up an enormous butcher's bill. By 1865, South Carolina's casualties were, proportionately, *three times* larger than those of any northern or southern state. When Charley and his fellow staff officers denigrated South Carolina's elite for failing to put up a good fight, they did not understand that there were few able-bodied men left to make a stand.[18]

Having partially recovered from his physical and mental exhaustion, Hugh wanted to get back into action. He sensed that the war was coming to a close and desired to see its end in Charley's company. Cump, however, was not supportive. At first, he refused to offer any assistance. Then, feeling pressure from Thomas Ewing, he tried to send Hugh to General George Thomas in Tennessee. If Cump did not want to be reminded of the Missionary Ridge fiasco, keeping the two best eyewitnesses far away from his theater of operations made sense. Hugh then chided Cump for writing "praise so faint and dubious, that self interest, as well as self respect, prevents the use of it." He continued, noting that the record of his troops, from South Mountain to Missionary Ridge, was faultless. Implying, as Cump did, to the contrary, was insulting. Grant ultimately gave permission for Hugh to serve under General John Schofield in the newly designated Wilmington, North Carolina, Department.[19]

Hugh's hunch that something big was going to happen in the Carolinas proved correct. Majors Nichols learned from enthusiastic civilians that Joe Johnston had returned as Confederate commander. "Our old friend," Charley respectfully noted, would attack. Nichols knew that Cump dared not regard Johnston "with the contempt" he had shown his most recent Confederate counterparts. Johnston lived up to his reputation, taking 20,000 men into combat against Cump's 60,000 at Bentonville on the road to Goldsboro. In spite of being grossly outnumbered, Johnston fought from March 19 to March 21, inflicting 2,606 casualties on Cump while sustaining losses of 1,527. The remnants of the regiments Hugh had led earlier in the war, the Thirtieth, Thirty-Seventh, and Forty-Seventh Ohio, were engaged in what turned out to be the final major battle in Cump's theater. Although Johnston claimed some success, he could not hold his position and had to retreat.[20]

Cump's army was jubilant. Against a backdrop of warmer weather and brilliantly blossoming peach and apple trees, Cump's senior officers celebrated. Blair insisted that Cump could soon make a successful run for the White House. Cump was skeptical. Ironically, if he would not contemplate a run for the White House, the White House, in the person of Lincoln, was running toward him. The president wanted Cump and Grant to meet him at City Point, Virginia, a week after the Bentonville battle. Cump stopped briefly on the way to see Hugh. As Hugh subsequently wrote his wife, "General Sherman" spared just a few minutes for conversation. Cump instead devoted his attention to the newspaper reporters, who learned from him that he was going to an important meeting with Grant. The camaraderie of past years between Cump and Hugh was gone.[21]

If abrupt with Hugh, Cump was in a fine rage with Charley. Cump's staff believed that Charley, in light of his valor at Vicksburg and many services performed on the advance through Georgia and the Carolinas, deserved promotion to the rank of brigadier general. Cump, however, insisted that in spite of Charley's record the press might believe he had been elevated in rank because of their relationship. This would have marked the first time in Cump's Civil War career that he had ever been afraid of critical newspaper coverage.[22]

Lieutenant Colonel Nicholas Owings, an Indiana lawyer and staff officer, believed Cump was behaving in a petty manner. Fortifying himself with a stiff drink, Owings slipped the order to promote Charley into a stack of papers that Cump then unknowingly signed. Senator John Sherman fully supported Charley's promotion and would smooth the way if there were any problems with the War Department. When Cump learned that Charley had been promoted, he shouted at his brother-in-law and vowed to send him to Washington with the other politicians. After calming down, he gave Charley the First Brigade, Third Division, in Blair's Seventeenth Corps.[23]

Cump came away from his meeting with Lincoln convinced that the president wanted him to make generous peace terms with Johnston when the opportunity arose. In letters to Thomas Ewing and Ellen, Cump basked in the glow of success. He assured his father-in-law that Lincoln stood behind him and that there was no need to "fear my committing a political mistake." Cump then wrote Ellen observing how delighted he was that that she and their children could enjoy his fame. Parades and speeches, of course, were not the kind of things he liked, but he knew Ellen thrived on the attention.[24]

Given that Charley and Hugh had run afoul of their ascendant brother-in-law, the purported directive Cump received from Lincoln was of no concern to either of them. The brothers met on April 3 in the coastal town of

New Bern. They pleasantly smoked cigars, drank good liquor, and shot billiards at General Schofield's headquarters. Union foragers had acquired a billiards table and all the comforts that Hugh (and Schofield) had known at Benny Haven's when they were enrolled at West Point. Charley and Hugh would soon learn that on the day of their happy reunion Lincoln had entered Richmond.[25]

Unable to hold Petersburg any longer, Lee abandoned his lines on April 2 and left the gates to Richmond open. Lincoln wasted no time visiting the prostrate Confederate capital. Jefferson Davis and nearly all the government officials had fled, leaving John Campbell as the highest-ranking Confederate representative in Richmond. Thomas Ewing's friend had now come full circle. In 1861, Campbell had sent along to Ewing the sketchy details of assassination plots against Lincoln. He then left the Supreme Court and joined the Confederate government. Campbell had renewed contact with Ewing in late 1864 to arrange for a peace conference with Lincoln. Now, on April 3, Campbell met with Lincoln. Hundreds of slaves, realizing the significance of Lincoln's appearance, had shed tears of joy. No one could have predicted that eight years after Campbell had given concurrence to the *Dred Scott* decision in 1857, he would be pledging his loyalty to the president who buried slavery.[26]

Lee surrendered to Grant at Appomattox Courthouse, Virginia, on April 9. Washington residents celebrated for days. On April 14, a jubilant crowd flocked to a production of *Our American Cousin* at Ford's Theater. City newspapers had reported that both Lincoln and Grant would be at Ford's Theater. Grant, however, begged out of the engagement, in part because his wife did not, according to observers, enjoy Mary Todd Lincoln's company. Among those who had read about Lincoln's outing was renowned actor and Confederate loyalist John Wilkes Booth. Being well familiar with Ford's Theater, Booth knew where he could position himself to kill Lincoln. After shooting Lincoln in the back of his head, Booth leapt from the presidential box and onto the stage. If Booth had intended to make a dramatic bow before striding off the stage, his hard landing gave him a limp that was anything but graceful.[27]

At first the stunned audience did not realize what had just happened. Then sorrow and anger took hold. Several individuals carried the mortally wounded Lincoln across the street to a boardinghouse owned by William Petersen. News quickly circulated that there had been an attempt on the life of Secretary of State William Seward. Stanton immediately mounted an investigation into the apparent conspiracy to decapitate the U.S. government. He summoned three well-regarded Washington trial lawyers to Petersen's house. Of the trio, Britton Hill was likely the best constitutional attorney. His political connections were equally as impressive. Hill, having worked on pre-war cases in St. Louis with Tom Ewing, had entrée to a practice that included Thomas Ewing, Orville Browning, Henry Stanbery, and Reverdy Johnson.[28]

Stanton's hastily assembled panel gathered eyewitness testimony and developed potential leads for investigators. It did not take long to identify such players as Booth, John Surratt, and David Herold. The war secretary subsequently issued a public notice that offered a large reward for the apprehension of the conspirators and threatened retribution to their sympathizers:

> All persons harboring or secreting the said persons, or either of them, or aiding or assisting their concealment or escape, will be treated as accomplices in the murder of the President and the attempted assassination of the Secretary of State, and shall be subject to trial before a military commission and the punishment of death.
>
> Let the stain of innocent blood be removed from the land by the arrest and punishment of the murderers.[29]

Even while Booth readied the final act of Lincoln's life, Joe Johnston had sent a request to Cump for a truce. While on his way to meet Johnson on April 17, Cump received a telegram from Stanton apprising him of Lincoln's murder. Johnston appeared stunned when he read the telegraph. Both agreed to negotiate an end to hostilities. By the next day, April 18, they had worked out an agreement. Convinced that he was following Lincoln's directions, Cump went beyond the demobilization of Johnston's forces to discussing recognition of southern state governments and a generous amnesty for just about every Confederate officer and government official except for Jefferson Davis and a few of his cronies. The terms made at the Bennett Place went far beyond the scope of what Grant and Lee had agreed to at Appomattox Courthouse nine days earlier.[30]

Cump sent Major Hitchcock to take the terms of Johnston's surrender to his superiors. He was shocked when an irate Stanton directed Grant to meet Cump in North Carolina and prepare for a new offensive against Johnston. Not only had Stanton sent Grant to put Cump in his place, he had launched a newspaper campaign against the conqueror of Georgia and the Carolinas. Cump's old nemesis, General Henry Halleck, joined the assault. Michigan Senator Zachariah Chandler, a vocal member of the Committee on the Conduct of the War, charged that Cump "was the coming man of the Copperheads." Given the hysterics emanating from Washington, Johnston wisely consented to less favorable terms in order to avoid more casualties.[31]

No one who had known Cump over the years had ever seen him so angry. Faced with adverse publicity in 1861 Cump had been despondent. In 1865 Cump was seething. He wrote, indiscreetly through military channels, to General Schofield. Cump charged that the Radical Republicans had become mentally unhinged by Lincoln's assassination. They had always hated him because he opposed giving former slaves the electoral power to subjugate southern whites. Cump also vented his rage with Ellen, detailing the Radical Republican plot against him: "Stanton wants to kill me because I do not favor the scheme of declaring the Negroes of the South, now free, to be loyal voters, whereby politicians may manufacture just so much more pliable electioneering material. The Negroes don't want to vote. They want to work and enjoy property, and they are no friends of the Negro who seek to complicate him with new prejudices."[32]

Cump's officers and relatives believed that Stanton, Halleck, and Chandler were acting out of petty jealousy and ideological animus. The goal of the Radical Republicans was to paint Cump as a treasonous Caesar. The Potomac, his foes insinuated, would be Cump's Rubicon across which his legions planned to overthrow the republic. Given the circumstances, it was not surprising when General Frank Blair called for President Andrew Johnson to remove Stanton from the cabinet. Charley concurred and predicted that "if Stanton should happen to fall into the hands of this army he would have a sorry time of it. He is cursed from one end of the army to the other and will feel it before his day is over." Senator John Sherman and Thomas Ewing, while more restrained in public toward Stanton, mounted a vigorous counteroffensive in the press. Both wrote stern letters defending their most famous family member.[33]

It would have been understandable if Hugh had stepped back from Cump. It was a damning indictment of Cump's character that he never brought himself to recognize Hugh in the way the New York Times did in the spring of 1865. As the Times reported, Hugh had "served honorably through most of the campaigns in the central South," fighting on even after being wounded on numerous occasions. This last bit of intelligence was something that Hugh had often omitted in his letters home, since he did not wish to worry Henrietta and the children.[34]

It was telling that when Hugh's promotion to the rank of major-general of volunteers came through in May, it was because of the support given to him by Frank Blair, not Cump. Where Cump had been tepid in his characterization of Hugh's military deeds, Blair gave effusive praise. He, at least, recognized the important role Hugh and his brigade had played at Vicksburg. Blair also observed that no possible fault could be found with Hugh and his division at Missionary Ridge. The Fourth Division had been given a thankless task that Hugh and the troops performed "with distinguished ability and merit." Even if the senior Blair and Ewing had been sniping at each other since the Jackson administration, and even if Frank and Tom had feuded over the Missouri insurgency, Hugh (and Charley) deserved recognition. Blair hoped Hugh would receive a major general's commission in the Regular Army.[35]

In spite of all that had passed between them, Hugh was not going to sit by and watch Cump destroy himself with intemperate rhetoric. Most of the family had gathered in Washington to watch Cump's army make a victory procession on May 24. When Halleck expressed concern about the prospect of Cump's troops roaming the streets freely, Cump threw a public fit. After hearing about Cump's indiscreet behavior, Hugh rushed over to Willard's hotel to find John Sherman. They then summoned Tom to round out their family meeting before involving Grant. Both Sherman and Grant visited Cump, cooling him off sufficiently so that he testified calmly on May 22 before the Committee on the Conduct of the War. Cump insisted that he had thought he was carrying out Lincoln's wishes when he agreed to generous surrender terms with Johnston. His restraint before the congressmen represented a sharp turnabout. Only three days earlier Cump had told the committee chair that Congress could wait to hear him after his troops paraded.[36]

The Army of the Potomac was all spit and polish. Cump's troops, though in freshly issued uniforms, appeared far more ruddy and wiry than their eastern counterparts. It was exactly what one would expect given that the respective armies had spent the past year quite differently: one on the march for hundreds of miles and the other in a protracted siege. Captain Foraker, who had never previously been in the nation's capital, was awestruck by the thousands of cheering civilians who lined Pennsylvania Avenue on May 24. Major Nichols wistfully recounted the scene: "With banners proudly flying, ranks in close and magnificent array, under the eye of their beloved Chief, and amid the thundering plaudits of countless thousands of enthusiastic spectators, the noble army of seventy thousand veterans paid their marching salute to the President of the Nation they had helped preserve in its integrity—and then broke ranks, and set their faces toward Home."[37]

Charley had earlier written to his father to make sure that he would attend the procession. He need not have worried. Thomas Ewing had an honored place on the reviewing stand with President Johnson. Charley mounted his horse as bystanders looked keenly at the handsome, unmarried thirty-year-old general. Suddenly, a young lady rushed up to Charley and placed a garland of flowers around the neck of his horse. All along the route of the procession

Review and victory procession of Union troops, Washington, D.C., Pennsylvania Avenue, May 1865. (Courtesy of the Library of Congress.)

women threw flowers at their conquering heroes—with the youngest and most attractive men receiving more than their fair share of bouquets. Years earlier, Thomas Ewing had read stories to his children about Roman battles and victory processions. Now his sons had lived an American *Aeneid*.[38]

Cump joined his father-in-law and President Johnson on the reviewing stand. When Stanton extended his hand in greeting, Cump coldly walked past him. For the next several hours as his troops marched by, Cump avoided conversing with his enemies. Ellen was glad Cump had exercised that much self-control. If it was of any consolation to Ellen, at least her estranged brother Tom had made himself even more despised by Radical Republicans than Cump had.[39]

Britton Hill had kept Tom apprised of the investigation into Lincoln's assassination. The fact that Hill joined the inquiry even as Lincoln was gasping for breath just a few feet away in the Petersen House had affected him deeply. Hill told his law partners that he now wanted to execute northern traitors and exile white southerners. Although not as bloody-minded, Cousin Jimmy Blaine was also moved by Lincoln's death. Addressing a crowd of mourners, Blaine said of Lincoln, "I thought his kindness of heart, his exalted patriotism, his abounding charity, his lofty magnanimity never shone more conspicuously" than when he urged charity toward the vanquished South. Tom and his father were more restrained than either Blaine or Britton. Lincoln's assassination, while regrettable, was tragic because it enabled Radical Republicans to exploit northern hysteria for political advantage. This development, rather than Lincoln's death, was what troubled the Ewings.[40]

One of the individuals caught in Stanton's dragnet was Dr. Samuel Mudd of Maryland. During his flight from Washington, Booth had stopped at Mudd's house to seek treatment for his broken leg. Mudd initially claimed that he did not know Booth and would not have recognized him in any event since he was in a disguise. He certainly had no idea that Booth had shot the president. Only after Booth had left did Mudd realize that something was amiss. He then went to the authorities. To his dismay, Mudd found himself placed under arrest. His distraught wife, Sarah Frances, pleaded with Tom to defend her husband. The Mudds and Ewings, she could point out but did not have to, had been friends for thirty years. The Ewing, Mudd, and Gillespie girls had even attended the same Catholic schools in Washington before the war.[41]

Tom, Reverdy Johnson, and five other, lesser-known attorneys agreed to serve as legal counsel for the seven men and one woman charged with being members of the conspiracy to assassinate Lincoln. Booth was spared a trial, since he had died on April 26 in a shootout with Union troops. Tom represented Mudd, Ned Spangler, and Sam Arnold. Spangler was a carpenter employed at Ford's Theater and, unfortunately for him, a friend of Booth. Arnold had known of Booth's earlier intention to kidnap Lincoln but had severed relations with him. He did not, however, apprise Union authorities of Booth's plots, which he thought were mere fantasies. Reverdy Johnson represented Mary Surratt, at whose Washington boardinghouse Booth's conspirators developed their plot.[42]

Instead of being tried in a civilian court, Stanton had the defendants placed before a military tribunal at the Washington Arsenal. Hill, having regained some of his composure by the time the military trial commenced in May, contacted President Johnson about the legality of bypassing the civilian courts. Thomas Ewing informed the president that he thought it was unconstitutional to conduct military commissions, since the civilian courts were operating and the war was over. In its outlines, Ewing's argument bore some resemblance to the points raised by Roger Taney, the late chief justice of the Supreme Court. He had often challenged Lincoln over the legality of prosecuting of civilians in military courts. Taney had failed to persuade Lincoln to change course. Ewing was no more successful with Johnson.[43]

There was no doubt that the defense attorneys were in an all-but-hopeless position. Wherever Tom went in Washington, strangers came up to him screaming and cursing. He responded with silent contempt. What transpired inside the courtroom was little better. When the tribunal convened, Brigadier General Thomas Harris questioned the patriotism of Reverdy Johnson. It seemed that Johnson had committed the sin of opposing the imposition of a loyalty oath in Maryland. The real problem with Johnson, however, was that he had criticized emancipation and been on the wrong side of the *Dred Scott* case. Those present in the courtroom reported that Johnson was "in a towering rage when replying to this imputation of disloyalty." It did not appear to matter to the tribunal that Reverdy Johnson had earlier taken the lead in urging Lincoln to abolish slavery through a constitutional amendment. A presidential proclamation, after all, could be withdrawn by a subsequent administration. He subsequently dropped out of the trial, since his presence intensified the tribunal's prejudice against Mary Surratt.[44]

Apparently, the military commissioners thought better of launching a similar attack against the man who had issued General Order Number 11. Although the officers were more civil toward Tom, it did not help Mudd. Hugh observed that the good doctor, having been slow in alerting the authorities about his most famous patient, would be lucky to escape execution.[45]

The witnesses arrayed against the defendants were a disparate lot. It was difficult to understand why Ulysses Grant was called to testify, since he had no firsthand acquaintance with either the accused or the facts of the plot. Ostensibly, Grant appeared in court so as to assert military jurisdiction over Washington at the time of the assassination. If Grant did have legal authority over Washington in April 1865, then a military, rather than civilian, trial could be imposed. There was, though, an unstated reason as to why Grant testified. Using his stature as a northern war hero was a good way for the Radical Republicans to diminish the reputations of the male defendants who had not served in the Union Army. Grant's presence also obliquely reminded the military judges that the chain of command had an interest in the outcome of the trial.[46]

Another witness, Mary Simms, had been one of Mudd's slaves. She testified that Mudd hated Lincoln, beat his slaves, and wanted to aid the Confederacy. While Simms tried to depict Mudd as a traitor, she could connect him to the conspiracy only by arguing that she had seen him meet Mary Surratt's son. Other former slaves painted a similar portrait of Mudd. If Mudd could not be convicted of being a coconspirator, then he might still hang as a cruel slave master.[47]

Tom persistently challenged the black witnesses, asking how they knew that the people who stopped by Mudd's house were Confederate agents. He also wondered whether the prospect of reward money had sharpened their memories. They tended to evade Tom's questions. The tribunal did not give Tom the leeway he would have had in a civilian court to challenge their credibility on grounds of obvious bias. No one observing the trial from afar could fail to note that black men and women had testified against a white man. Few states in the North before the Civil War encouraged—or even permitted—blacks to offer testimony against whites. It was certainly not like anything Thomas Ewing or Henry Stanbery had ever experienced in Ohio.[48]

Harper's reported that Mudd "appeared calm and attentive," while Arnold seemed "restless and nervous." Good composure notwithstanding, Mudd had a few problems. To begin with, Mudd had originally denied knowing Booth before he showed up at his house with a broken leg. Mudd subsequently recanted, admitting that he had met Booth previously but had not said anything for fear that he might look like a coconspirator. Second, Mudd, as Hugh observed, had taken far too long to go to the authorities and share his strange encounter with Booth. Mudd claimed he had not immediately stepped forward because he might appear complicit in Lincoln's death. Tom insisted that Mudd's behavior during and after he treated Booth was hardly sinister. He also contended that the prosecution sought to transform innocent coincidences—like Mudd knowing Booth—into a criminal conspiracy.[49]

After a seven-week trial, four of the defendants were sentenced to hang and the other four given prison terms. Under the circumstances it was a major victory for Tom that his clients avoided execution. Tom, however, was not satisfied with the outcome, informing the tribunal: "Congress has not 'ordained and established' you as a court, or authorized you to call these parties before you and sit upon their trial, and you are not 'judges' who hold offices during good behavior. You are, therefore, no court under the Constitution, and have no jurisdiction in these cases, unless you obtain it from some other source, which overrules this constitutional provision."[50]

Tom continued his indictment of the tribunal. He insisted that the president had no constitutional right to create military courts with jurisdiction over civilians who were citizens of the United States. Not surprisingly, his arguments went nowhere. U.S. Attorney General James Speed, an ally of Stanton's, replied, first, that Congress had been remiss in providing for the adequate protection of the country, and second, that civilians engaged in disloyal activities, even if they were citizens, had to be regarded as enemy combatants. Given the circumstances as Speed described them, the military had no choice but to assert its authority by creating tribunals and prosecuting traitors. Paradoxically, Thomas Ewing had advanced a similar argument a few years earlier when advocating the military trial and execution of Missouri guerrillas. With any prospect of appeal summarily closed off, Surratt and her compatriots mounted the gallows and were hanged on July 7, 1865. Tom's clients headed to jail.[51]

Calling upon Hugh's in-laws, Tom arranged for Father Nicholas Young to write General Phil Sheridan. Since the two men were fellow members of the Catholic communion, Father Young asked Sheridan to look after Mudd during his imprisonment at Fort Jefferson in the isolated Florida Keys outpost of Dry Tortugas. Sheridan gladly accepted the task.[52]

The Lincoln conspiracy trial greatly added to Tom's fame—and infamy. It also set him, his father, Hugh, and the partners in the Washington firm on a collision course with the Republican radicals. The Ewings and their allies viewed the trial as a ploy by Stanton to become the de facto head of the U.S. government. By circulating unsubstantiated charges that Jefferson Davis was implicated in Lincoln's assassination, Stanton allegedly sought to fuel hysteria and thereby impose the power of the War Department over American politics. Many of the Ewings' friends were also convinced that Stanton would accuse Andrew Johnson of being a Confederate agent if he thought it would weaken the White House.[53]

Having failed to prevent the War Department from orchestrating the military trial of Mudd, the Ewings moved quickly to isolate Stanton. Their strategy was to swarm the White House. Cousin Hamp Denman became an Interior Department superintendent for Indian relations. Denman's frequent western trips afforded him the opportunity to send political intelligence to his cousins. Reverdy Johnson became minister to Great Britain. Hugh joined the administration as minister to The Hague. Tom went to work for the president as a speechwriter and policy advisor. His wartime Kansas buddy Edmund Ross ascended to the U.S. Senate after Jim Lane committed suicide. The senior Ewing served as presidential adviser. Orville Browning joined the cabinet as secretary of the Interior. Most importantly, Henry Stanbery replaced Joshua Speed as U.S. attorney general. Only Stanton remained, kept in place by congressional radicals.[54]

Thomas Ewing urged the president to distinguish between Confederate leaders and the mass of ordinary white southerners when deciding which individuals to deprive of their voting rights. At least fifty thousand whites in Maryland, Kentucky, and Missouri who had fought for the Confederacy "were mere material of war," not the instigators of the rebellion. Ewing also made another claim relative to southern white voting rights. According to the Patriarch, since the rebellion was not legal, the authority of the Constitution had remained in effect during the war. Consequently, white southerners had never relinquished their citizenship and right to representation in Congress. Republican radicals, therefore, had no legal authority to revoke the voting rights of more than a handful of treasonous leaders. Even then, those few individuals had to be charged with treason, tried in a *civilian* court, and convicted before their voting rights could be curtailed.[55]

The senior Ewing also advised Johnson to temper the radicals' push for black voting rights. As Ewing subsequently wrote to Hugh, many moderate Republicans and Unionist Democrats in the North were not prepared to endorse an enlargement of the franchise. He had a point. By a comfortable margin of fifty thousand votes in 1867, Ohio rejected amending the state constitution to permit black suffrage. Ohio Democrats mobilized their political base with appeals against "niggerism." Hugh's comrade-in-arms Rutherford Hayes had barely won the governorship by three thousand votes. ("Landslide" Hayes carried Ohio in the 1876 presidential election by just seven thousand votes.) Even Jacob Cox, Hayes's Republican gubernatorial predecessor and former commander in the Kanawha Division, had advocated shipping Ohio's blacks to the Deep South. Such sentiments were no different in Kansas, Missouri, and New York, which also rejected black suffrage.[56]

In 1866, Radical Republicans authorized the creation of the Freedmen's Bureau and passed a civil rights act. The intention of the Freedman's Bureau was to provide education and job training to the former slaves. As for the

1866 Civil Rights Act, this legislation was in response to those southern states that had passed laws prohibiting blacks from moving and changing jobs. Republicans regarded such southern ordinances as thinly veiled efforts to reestablish slavery. Tom and Henry Stanbery drafted President Johnson's vetoes of both measures. Their objections, which Congress brushed aside when overriding Johnson's veto, were, first, that the former Confederate states had not been given the opportunity to approve or disapprove the legislation; second, the Constitution did not grant Congress the authority to make particular groups of people wards of the state; and third, that the Constitution did not empower Congress to compel members of one race to underwrite the educational expenses of another race.[57]

Congressional radicals, in spite of a presidential veto threat, also enacted a Military Reconstruction bill. This legislation placed the former Confederate states in five military districts for a period of what turned out to be ten years. Both Cousin Jimmy Blaine and John Sherman tried to soften the psychological impact of federal occupation by holding out the prospect of a speedy path of readmission to the Union. Tom, in a letter subsequently published in the *New York Times*, decried the imposition of military rule and promotion of black enfranchisement: "The North already groans under the punishment now being inflicted on the South, and must, besides, pay for the whip. The Negro governments, when formed, must be propped up with Northern bayonets; and, however costly, they can never be safely withdrawn. When reconstructed, each one of those States will be like a magazine—all secure while carefully guarded outside, but, when left, unguarded, a chance spark will blow it, and all about it, to the devil."[58]

Several months after Johnson's unsuccessful veto of the Freedman's Bureau and the 1866 Civil Rights Act, Tom took part in a Cleveland convention of Union military veterans. The delegates, who included several Union generals, issued a call for President Johnson to fire Stanton. Both Tom and his father publicly, as well as Cump privately, wanted Jacob Cox to become war secretary. Radical Republicans responded by hosting a Pittsburgh convention of pro-Stanton Union veterans. Escalating the rhetorical civil war between the two factions of Union veterans, Tom's allies subsequently resolved that "Stanton has disgraced and dishonored [the War Department] ever since his appointment to that office, by his many acts of cruelty—both to the Union and Confederate soldiers—and by his official acts of tyranny; and . . . the soldiers and sailors should, on all occasions, meet him with the same feelings of outraged dignity and patriotism that he was received with, on an ever-memorable occasion, in the city of Washington, from that great and glorious soldier—General William Tecumseh Sherman."[59]

Although Tom and the family circle were disgusted with Stanton and his congressional backers, they also felt considerable scorn for the Democrats. The Ewings wanted northern Democrats to renounce their Copperhead past and recognize that the South had lost the war. If the Democrats wanted to become a viable national party again, then they needed to emphasize economic issues and acknowledge that the states were not independent of the federal government. Democrats also had to figure out how to oppose civil rights while accepting that slavery was abolished. Longtime Ewing foe and former Democratic senator William Allen, however, would not let go of his anger. He viewed Salmon Chase as a "disappointed Negro worshipper" who had plunged America into an unnecessary war. Allen won the 1874 Ohio gubernatorial election with a pledge to oppose Reconstruction. For the sons of Ohio's Virginia Military District, Robert E. Lee would always be one battle away from complete victory. Their war never ended.[60]

Former Ohio congressman Samuel Cox, whose 1864 electoral defeat had made Lincoln rejoice, managed to obtain a new U.S. House seat—this time representing New York City's Tammany Hall political machine. Samuel Cox simply picked up where he had left off in his fight against federal authority and the Thirteenth Amendment. He was not alone. Thomas Ewing wrote to Hugh that congressional Democrats were not willing to ally with moderate Republicans against the radicals. "The Democracy," Ewing lamented, "are irredeemable and unmitigated fools."[61]

More than two years into Reconstruction, President Johnson finally moved against Stanton, knowing full well that Radical Republicans would react angrily. Indeed, Senator Ben Wade had earlier pushed through legislation to bar President Johnson from removing cabinet members who had been appointed by Lincoln. Thomas Ewing had warned Johnson that he had waited too long. Further, "It will not do to adopt rash measures," he informed the president. "It is better to let Stanton alone. Public opinion is against him and his backers, and by an imprudent act you may turn it in his favor." Among his family and friends, Ewing observed that Johnson "has a strong sense of right, and a stubborn determination to do it, but his action, when he acts, is never in the right time. It is spasmodic. For example, he knew for more than a year that Stanton was false to him and in daily conference with those who sought to destroy him but he kept his position against the earnest advice of all his friends."[62]

By the end of 1867, the struggle between Andrew Johnson and the Republican Congress over Reconstruction policy entered its final act. The president approached both Ewing and Cump to join his cabinet as the new war secretary—the Congress be damned. Tom and his father, as well as Henry

Stanbery, recommended that Cump decline the offer and keep a low profile as he moved about Washington. It was good advice. The House Judiciary
Committee decided to launch impeachment proceedings against Johnson for
violating the 1867 Tenure of Office Act. As Ewing pithily commented, the
Constitution permitted Johnson to fire Stanton just as it allowed him "to
face a herd of wild bulls and shake a scarlet cloak at them, and just the same
amount of presidential wisdom were exhibited in one case as in the other."[63]

Henry Stanbery resigned as attorney general in order to defend Johnson at his Senate impeachment trial. Having had his nomination to the U.S.
Supreme Court blocked by the Radical Republicans, Stanbery was in a fighting mood. The trial itself emitted a bad odor for any number of reasons, not
least of which was the congressional assertion that the president could not
select his own cabinet. There was also a major congressional conflict of interest attached to the impeachment proceedings. Senator Ben Wade of Ohio
had taken the lead in demanding Andrew Johnson's ouster. The problem was
that since Johnson did not have a vice president, Ben Wade, as president *pro
tem* of the Senate, was next in the line of presidential succession. Samuel Cox
expressed the opinion that Wade was playing Oliver Cromwell to Johnson's
Charles I. If anyone could save Johnson, Cox believed, it was Stanbery. Next
to Thomas Ewing, Cox noted admiringly, "A more magnificent presence
never graced a court nor adorned a public rostrum."[64]

In the Senate, Stanbery pushed back against the radicals, continuously citing constitutional precedent in his typically calm and conversational manner. This only appeared to enrage Wade. The senator seemingly did not know
the difference between cajoling influential politicians to his side and making
implicit threats. Although distrustful of Wade, John Sherman was sufficiently
frustrated with Johnson's gracelessness to consider his impeachment. Cump,
who joined Thomas Ewing in the Senate gallery, warned John that the Radical Republicans looked like "a prejudiced jury." Senator Sherman assured his
family that he would be fair. He ultimately voted for impeachment.[65]

Most of the Ewings' family and friends stood by Johnson. Thomas Ewing
accurately predicted that a sufficient number of senators would "hold their
judicial oaths paramount to party obligations and by their votes save what
is left of the Constitution." Tom Ewing played his own important part in the
impeachment trial, encouraging Senator Ross to save the president. Drawing upon their shared experience in the Eleventh Kansas, Tom reforged
their wartime bond. To the immense ire of Radical Republicans, Ross cast
the deciding vote against impeachment. Former Leavenworth mayor Daniel Anthony lashed out at Ross. "Your vote is dictated by Tom Ewing, not
your oath," Anthony cried, "Kansas repudiates you as she does all perjurers

and skunks." Admitting defeat, Stanton ceased his war against Johnson. Tom and Hugh's friend and ally, John Schofield, subsequently became secretary of war.[66]

After 1868 the struggle to shape the contours of postwar American politics continued, though without the drama Johnson's impeachment trial had offered. Stanbery and Reverdy Johnson teamed up to thwart radical Republican Reconstruction. Even before the impeachment trial, Johnson had opposed legislative efforts to permit blacks to serve on juries. He had asked the U.S. Senate "whether we are willing to have ourselves tried by a jury of black men for the most part just emerged from slavery, without the capacity absolutely necessary to a faithful and intelligent discharge of that duty." While sympathetic to Johnson's stance, John Sherman had expressed his dismay that all-white juries in the postwar South appeared unwilling to convict white defendants of crimes against blacks.[67]

In 1866, the advent of the Ku Klux Klan, a southern-based, clandestine group devoted to the intimidation of black and white Republicans, brought the issue of civil rights to the forefront. It also gave Johnson and Stanbery a large number of clients to defend. Former Confederate general Wade Hampton, who had been Cump's personal demon in South Carolina, opened up his wallet to Johnson and Stanbery in the defense of Klansmen. Facing off against newly elected President Ulysses Grant, who advocated the prosecution of Klansmen in the South, Stanbery and Johnson went to trial. Their performance was masterful. They calmly questioned the veracity of prosecution witnesses and sowed suspicions that blacks were exaggerating (if not inventing) their accounts of persecution. There was also the problem that authorities were seeking to prosecute 169 Klansmen in York County, South Carolina, alone. Stanbery and Johnson were accomplished in the art of dragging out proceedings and wearing down their rivals. The prospect of repeating the same proceedings several hundred times over demoralized judges and prosecutors, making subsequent trials less likely to happen.[68]

Stanbery and Johnson's prewar legal and political careers became all but forgotten in the aftermath of the 1871 Klan trials. Few commentators in the 1870s knew that Stanbery and Johnson had been longtime law partners with Thomas Ewing. Even fewer realized that Stanbery was related to Thomas Ewing and, by extension, to General Sherman. Phil Stanbery, who had served under Cump at Vicksburg, retreated from view, opting not to share the stage with his controversial father, who died in 1881, or with Johnson, who passed away in 1876. The younger Stanbery, chastened by his war wounds, settled into a quiet existence as a southern Ohio attorney. His thirst for adventure

Virginia Miller Ewing (1845–1937). The daughter of an Ohio Democratic politician, Virginia Miller Ewing married Washington, D.C.'s, most eligible bachelor, Charles Ewing, in 1870. As if Charley were making up for lost time, he and Virginia had eight children in a span of a dozen years. Prematurely widowed, Virginia Ewing ultimately came to rest with her husband at Arlington National Cemetery. (Courtesy of the University of Notre Dame Archives.)

had been quenched, and he had chosen not live among the Washington political set—which included his Ewing, Gillespie, and Blaine cousins.

Thomas Ewing managed to outlive nearly all his enemies and friends. Other than providing unheeded advice to Andrew Johnson, Ewing did not take a visible political role after the Civil War. He let Stanbery and Johnson wreak havoc on Radical Republican Reconstruction. Only once did he openly enter the national political area. In 1867, following newspaper stories that Hugh had looted Jefferson Davis's Mississippi plantation, Ewing composed a scathing letter published in the *Cincinnati Commercial* and the *New York Times*. He insisted that his son had committed no larceny, conveniently forgetting that Hugh had sent Davis's checkers set to Lancaster. Ewing also did not count Davis's personal correspondence and letter of appointment to West Point, all of which Hugh had collected, as stolen property. It was a strange oversight for one of America's most prominent attorneys to make, but when it came to his children Ewing had never allowed logic to trump sentiment.[69]

Reporters from the *Boston Daily Advertiser* and the *New York Times* wrote fondly of seeing "good old Tom Ewing with his bald head and jovial double chin" at the U.S. Supreme Court. The *New York Times* reprinted an interview with the Patriarch as he told stories about President Zachary Taylor, Daniel Webster, and Henry Clay. There was not likely any other American still alive who had been friends with all three national political figures. Ewing fondly recalled how he and Webster would challenge each other's knowledge of Latin classics, rummaging through every bookstore and private library in Boston, Baltimore, and Washington looking for obscure quotations. As for Henry Clay, Ewing slyly revealed that the Kentuckian's rhetorical flourishes sometimes got the best of him to the point where he invented words. Ewing recounted that he had learned to position himself at Clay's elbow and whisper the correct words for which he was searching.[70]

Ewing did not live long enough to see Charley fully blossom into a devoted family man, a successful Washington attorney, and one of America's most prominent Catholic laymen. In 1870 Charley married Virginia Miller of Mount Vernon, Ohio, who was eleven years his junior. Her father had been a prewar Democratic member of the U.S. House of Representatives, as well as a descendant of the Brownsville, Pennsylvania, Gillespies. Although Cincinnati archbishop John Purcell performed the wedding ceremony, Virginia did not convert to Catholicism until a few years later. As Virginia confided to her Blaine cousins, she had become enchanted with elaborate Catholic rituals, especially communion, which stood in stark contrast to the austere Presbyterianism of her childhood. Of course, there was also a history of the Ewings, Blaines, and Gillespies moving back and forth between the Catholic and Presbyterian churches, so Virginia's conversion had precedent. She certainly embraced the Catholic exhortation to go forth and multiply, bearing eight children within a span of a dozen years.[71]

At the end of the war Charley had launched a Washington legal career. Unlike his father, brothers, and cousins, however, Charley avoided the paths of the trial lawyer and politician. Instead, he became a patent attorney. It was one of the least glamorous legal pursuits he could have chosen, as well as the most detailed oriented. In addition to a keen focus, patent attorneys had to have minds nimble enough to understand the science behind new inventions. They also had to follow the intricacies of corporate law. At first brush, it would have seemed an unlikely, and dull, career choice for a man who had charged headlong into the thrill and terror of combat. As Cump's staff officer, logistical troubleshooter, and military law expert, however, Charley had exhibited the same mental qualities that quickly made him one of the top patent attorneys in the United States.[72]

President Grant, in an effort to improve relations with the western Indian tribes, had launched a program to expand the role of Christian mission work. Even though the American Catholic Church had spent years laboring nearly alone in the field of Indian missions, Grant favored, with funds and political access, Protestant organizations. This was a rude slap in the face of the Catholic Church, given that there were one hundred thousand Indian converts to Catholicism, compared to fifteen thousand Protestant Indians. Ellen Sherman, who objected with equal vigor to the Grant administration's religious bias and to her own husband's hatred of Indians, recruited Charley to place the Catholic missions on an equal political footing with the Protestants. Baltimore archbishop James Bayley gave Charley the authority to represent the Catholic Church and protect its Indian schools from Protestant interference.[73]

As was the Ewing family custom when tasked with an assignment, Charley went to work with vigor. Irate Protestant organizations, fearing the loss of their federal funds, leveled baseless charges of corruption against Charley. Not only did Charley not receive any financial advantage from his jousting with Grant's Interior Department, he actually gave money out of his own pocket to help fund the Catholic missions. He took the insults in stride but did, on one occasion, announce that he would not associate with those in the Washington political elite who made abusive statements about the Vatican.[74]

Recognizing what a valuable advocate the church had found in Charley Ewing, Pope Pius IX in 1877 made him a Knight of the Order of Saint Gregory the Great. It was the highest honor that the Vatican could bestow upon a member of the laity. "Good-Time" Charley, the man who had once liberated the tobacco and liquor stocks of the Georgia legislature, became the moral exemplar of American Catholicism.

Charley, Virginia, and their brood settled comfortably into Washington, often dining with Cousin Jimmy Blaine, who had been elected Speaker of the House in 1869. They even named one of their sons James Gillespie Blaine Ewing. While Charley's family and professional lives thrived, Washington's humid summers and soggy winters exacted a toll on his health. During the Vicksburg, Georgia, and Carolinas campaigns, soldiers and staff had frequently seen Charley cough so hard that he would spit up blood. His already compromised lungs were in no condition to fight off pneumonia when it struck in June 1883. After twelve days of labored breathing, Charley died.[75]

His funeral Mass and burial in Washington's Mt. Olivet Cemetery received nearly as much political and media attention as his father's. The *New York Times* reported that Charley's casket stood under the Seventeenth Corps' headquarters flag while generals and senators lined up as pallbearers. Cousin

Jimmy Blaine and all but one member of the Ewing family attended the funeral. Citing pressing military business in Buffalo, New York, Cump had departed Washington. He did, however, issue a brief letter to the press attesting to Charley's good character. At the gravesite, as the *Philadelphia Press* subsequently reported, a painful drama unfolded: "The four eldest [children] stood about his grave yesterday. His beautiful widow, broken-hearted, was on the arm of General Tom Ewing. The children were in the charge of Eliza, a faithful servant. When the priest took the shovel and threw dirt upon the coffin, after it had been lowered in the grave, the poor widow fainted away and was laid on the grass, and the four little ones gathered about Eliza and sobbed as though their hearts were breaking."[76]

Her little brother's death was a severe blow to Ellen Sherman. She had largely withdrawn from public view after her father's death in 1871. Charley's passing, however, saw her recede almost completely into the background. Cump, on the other hand, thrived as the center of national attention. Although his behavior during the illnesses and deaths of Thomas and Charley Ewing stirred some hushed commentary, Cump made no apologies for finally escaping from the shadow of his in-laws. He attended theatrical performances and dances, made dinner speeches, and allegedly had several affairs, while a reclusive Ellen stayed home. His brother John, rising in prominence as a Republican Party leader, maintained the Sherman family's ties to the Ewings.[77]

In spite of becoming one of America's most famous generals, Cump had his share of disappointments. He held the Ewings responsible for ruining his son Tom. Since Willie's death, Cump had wanted Tom Sherman to go to West Point with Grant's son. Tom Sherman, however, followed the Ewing path—first to law school and then, to Cump's enormous distress, to seminary. His son, instead of becoming an American soldier, joined the "Pope's Marines" as a Jesuit priest. Cump refused to witness Tom Sherman's ordination. Some commentators speculated that Tom Sherman had taken to the cloth as penance for his father's sins on the March through Georgia and the Carolinas. Given his mother's anti-Confederate militancy, though, that scenario seemed unlikely. Moreover, the Catholic Church had a well-articulated conception of "just war" that recognized that destruction of property was morally better than the destruction of life.[78]

Three years after Ellen's death in 1888, Cump succumbed to pneumonia. Tom Ewing and John Sherman were with Cump when he passed away in New York City. Tens of thousands of spectators turned out for his funeral procession before his body went to St. Louis. Cump had been adamant about not being buried in Lancaster. In death Cump was finally free of his in-laws.[79]

Although Tom had been with Cump on his deathbed, his postwar relationships with John Sherman and Cousin Jimmy had been much warmer. Tom and his wife often dined with the Blaines in Washington. He also enlisted his cousin in a major business venture—the $25 million development of rail lines and coal fields in southern Ohio. Blaine enjoyed the lifestyle that his Ohio profits afforded but did not care for the negative publicity generated when miners complained of low wages and hazardous working conditions. As someone with presidential aspirations, the last thing Cousin Jimmy needed was the *New York Times* making visits to hardscrabble mining towns like Nelsonville, Ohio.[80]

Cousin Jimmy had set his eyes on the White House. To secure the Republican Party nomination, however, he had to pass ideological muster. Having been lukewarm toward radical Republican Reconstruction in the South, Blaine had to demonstrate his political fitness on the cultural-religious front. Demonstrating his anti-Catholic *bona fides*, however, was difficult. His cousins, after all, were Mother Angela Gillespie, who had established Catholic-sponsored military hospitals during the war, and Charley Ewing, one of America's most distinguished members of the laity. To shore up his political prospects, in 1875 Cousin Jimmy introduced a constitutional amendment to Congress that would prohibit federal and state governments from subsidizing religious education. The "Blaine Amendment" was transparently directed against the Catholic Church. Though it did not pass through Congress, in spite of President Grant's endorsement, dozens of states subsequently enacted their own version of Cousin Jimmy's legislation.[81]

His Catholic cousins did not turn on him, understanding that Blaine was still more sympathetic to Catholicism than most Republican politicians. Even Rutherford Hayes, in spite of his long association with Thomas and Hugh Ewing, warned during his quest for the presidency in 1876 that Catholic immigrants were invading Ohio and displacing real Americans. Sadly for Cousin Jimmy, when his turn finally came in 1884 and he received the Republican presidential nomination, a Protestant clergyman brought him down. At a campaign event in New York that Blaine attended, Rev. Samuel Burchard denounced "Rum, Romanism, and Rebellion." Burchard had smeared American Catholics as drunkards and traitors. For the thousands of northern Catholics who had served in the Union Army, and whose ranks included Charley and Hugh Ewing, this Republican attack was too much. Blaine, having chosen to ignore Burchard's gaffe, lost sufficient Catholic votes to throw an extremely close presidential election to the Democrats.[82]

As was true with Cousin Jimmy, Tom Ewing had presidential ambitions. By leaving Kansas and eventually resettling in Lancaster, Tom created a potentially strong political base. For a distinguished Union war veteran with political aspirations, Ohio perfectly suited Tom's purposes. Over three hundred thousand Ohio men, the third largest number in the North, had fought for the Union. Moreover, four Civil War veterans from Ohio ascended to the White House between 1869 and 1897: Ulysses Grant, Rutherford Hayes, James Garfield, and William McKinley. Although their margins of victory were often narrow, a win was still a win. Two of the four used the governorship of Ohio as a stepping-stone to the White House. The one sticking point for Tom was that each one of these successful politicians was Republican. Tom's years in Kansas, on top of his Washington service to President Johnson, had given him an extreme distaste for the "Party of Lincoln."[83]

Initially, being an Ohio Democrat worked for Tom. He denounced Radical Reconstruction and black voting rights, while exhorting Democrats to move past the war and focus on economic issues. If northern and southern Democrats were to reunite successfully, then it was time for the party to accept the end of slavery and look toward federal and state policies to promote investment and job growth. Tom believed that one of the keys to economic development was to increase the supply of paper currency in order to make more credit available to the people in America's Heartland. He took his economic agenda with him to Congress, representing Lancaster in the U.S. House of Representatives from 1877 to 1880. His widely circulated criticism of the Republican policy of restricting the money supply and keeping credit tight enraged former President Grant. Like his father before him, Tom knew how to get under the skin of a rival politician.[84]

In 1879 Tom made a strategic political move by running for Ohio governor. The next step, if he was successful in obtaining the governorship, would be a run for the presidency. Unfortunately for Tom, his war record proved to be both an asset and a liability. As early as 1871, when he left Washington for Ohio, Tom had heard rumblings from some Democrats regarding General Order Number 11. He had sent out letters to former military subordinates in Kansas seeking their help. Wyllis Ransom, a former major in the Sixth Kansas Cavalry, wrote back, insisting that "this order was executed in no cruel or vindictive spirit." Given the viciousness of the guerrillas, and the food, shelter, military intelligence, and weapons they received from their relatives, Tom had acted properly in removing thousands of Missouri civilians from the Kansas border. General Order Number 11, Ransom, insisted, had crushed the guerrilla insurgency and saved the lives of countless innocents.[85]

Tom's tactics in the struggle against Missouri guerrillas came up again during his first campaign for Congress. General Schofield gave Tom a rousing defense. As the *New York Times* paraphrased Schofield:

Presidential portrait artist George Caleb Bingham of Missouri (1811–79) got his political revenge against Tom Ewing with *Order No. 11* (1865–70, oil on canvas). (Courtesy Cincinnati Art Museum, Ohio, USA, The Edwin and Virginia Irwin Memorial. The Bridgeman Art Library.)

Civilization and humanity alike demanded a prompt suppression of this border war. There were only two methods of stopping it. One was to largely increase the military force in the district, which was found impracticable because of the necessity of sending reinforcements to Grant's army at Vicksburg. The other was to remove from the Missouri border the few remaining farmers whose crops and stores furnished the guerrillas their subsistence. . . . [General Order Number 11] was an act of wisdom, courage, and humanity by which hundreds of innocent lives were saved and a barbarous and disgraceful warfare brought to a summary close. Not a life was sacrificed nor any great discomfort inflicted in executing it. The necessities of all the poor people were provided for, and none were permitted to suffer.[86]

Once Tom declared his gubernatorial candidacy, an old enemy, Missouri portrait painter George Bingham, finally had the opportunity to exact his revenge. Bingham exclaimed that the "day of retribution for General Tom Ewing has arrived." Just after the war Bingham had painted a special picture that he entitled *Order No. 11*. In his compelling portrait, Union troops burned the homes of innocent Missourians and committed acts of murder and torture. Seated on horseback approvingly watching the horrible scene unfold was none other than Tom Ewing. Bingham engraved his painting so that it could be mass produced. From his deathbed, Bingham made sure that copies of *Order No. 11* circulated throughout Ohio. Tom's political career was finished.[87]

Tom's misfortune, however, could not solely be blamed on Bingham's propaganda. Given the partisan divisions of the Civil War, which continued into the postwar years, it was easier for a Republican in the North to boast of his military record. Conversely, northern Democrats who fought for the Union had to be very careful how they played their service records. Their party, after all, had been bitterly divided on the merits of fighting, and the antiwar wing had taken control in 1864.

In Tom's case, paradoxically, he would have been better off as a Democrat to have had a lackluster service record. Instead, Tom had distinguished himself. Worse, he had distinguished himself fighting a dirty guerrilla war. This war had been far from the honorable field of battle fought between noble warriors. Compounding his troubles, from the point of view of many northern Democrats, Tom had followed up General Order Number 11 by humiliating a Confederate force several times larger than his own. Although Democrats should have regarded Pilot Knob as a "legitimate" battlefield like Gettysburg, its lopsided outcome made it look like a slaughter pen. To put Tom's dilemma somewhat differently, he had exiled ten thousand likely Democrats in 1863 and then killed two thousand likely Democrats in 1864. No matter how much he opposed Republican Reconstruction and civil rights, Tom could never be a Democrat in good standing—especially in a state like Ohio with its southern culture and sympathies.

After his disheartening gubernatorial bid, Tom and his family left Ohio. He settled in New York City, where he built a successful corporate law practice and, like his father, made numerous appearances before the U.S. Supreme Court. Tom never got past the sting of political defeat, spending the remainder of his life soliciting letters from former commanders and subordinates defending his conduct in Missouri. In 1896, while he was crossing a street, a streetcar struck him down. He died a few days from internal bleeding. Where Sterling Price had failed to kill him, New York transportation had succeeded.[88]

Hugh Ewing had no ambition to hold political office. He was, however, more than happy to serve his country, whether as a soldier or as a diplomat. When Hugh arrived as the U.S. ambassador to The Hague in 1866, he learned that the European monarchies expected diplomats to wear courtly uniforms with gold piping. He complied, going about in a colorful ensemble that put his tailored general's uniform to shame. Hugh also discovered, courtesy of his predecessor, that the only good thing about the Netherlands was its proximity to London and Paris. If one wanted good food, spirits, and music, the Dutch were not going to provide it—and Hugh, judging from his expanding waistline, was fond of fine dining. In contrast to some of the other American diplomats, Hugh took his duties seriously. He saw himself as more than a mere political appointee. Hugh conscientiously observed the increasingly aggressive Kingdom of Prussia and filed reports with Washington regarding its military capabilities.[89]

After Hugh and his family left the Netherlands in 1870 they spent the next four years in Washington. Where Tom and Charley enjoyed practicing law in the nation's capital, however, Hugh did not. He decided to settle permanently in Lancaster, where his brother Phil and sister Maria Theresa still lived. Hugh and Henrietta quickly became pillars of Ohio's Catholic community. Indeed, two of their seven children, a son and a daughter, took religious vows in the church.

Tom occasionally enticed Hugh away from his "gentleman's farm" to hit the campaign trail. Both traveled with Democratic presidential nominee Winfield Hancock in 1880. Hancock, a native of Pennsylvania, had been a competent Union general. His stand at Gettysburg had greatly enhanced his national profile. Hancock's subsequent military record, however, had not been as outstanding—thereby making him marginally palatable to southerners. Like the Ewings, Hancock ran afoul of Radical Republicans because he was not sufficiently supportive of civil rights. Hancock's loss to Ohio's James Garfield was all the confirmation Tom needed to follow Hugh's example and disengage from politics.[90]

Hugh had long aspired to become a writer, an avocation that his inheritance permitted him to pursue. He published fictional essays and novels, some with Catholic publishers and others with major New York houses, including Henry Holt and Peter Collier. The action in his 1888 novel *A Castle in the Air* was set in what southern Ohioans would have recognized as a thinly disguised bar and brothel called the Red Lion. Luckily for Hugh, by this point anyone who had traveled to Chillicothe for whiskey and sex was long since dead.

A Castle in the Air received good reviews, since Hugh knew how to depict disreputable taverns and lawyers very well. His father, mother, and Ellen Sherman had always recognized his talent for close observation—and penchant for engaging in "primary research." While the Red Lion had been Hugh's obvious literary inspiration, it was difficult to ascertain which

dishonest Appalachian attorney Hugh had used as the model for his vil-
lain. There were many conniving attorneys to choose from among Thomas
Ewing's rivals, though William Allen would have been a good candidate.[91]

His 1893 novel *The Black List: A Tale of Early California*, received equally
good publication notices. Its scenes of prewar California and Mexico were
vivid and far more appealing than anything Chillicothe could offer. This
novel also had an action hero, a decent man fleeing from a Mormon assassination squad. Hugh obviously loved Mexican culture, Catholicism, and food.
Given the racial and religious politics of the 1890s, *The Black List* stood out
for its positive depiction of Mexicans and equal loathing for Mormons. His
own adventures in crossing Mexico, prospecting the California goldfields,
and surviving a military rescue mission shaped the contours of this novel
and made it a more engaging read than *A Castle in the Air*.[92]

Though Hugh waxed eloquent on vicious Appalachian lawyers and Mormon death squads, he had more difficulty writing about his military experiences. One attempt at an autobiography went well from childhood to West
Point, the California Gold Rush, Bleeding Kansas, and the 1861 western Virginian campaign. His expansive narrative began to falter when he arrived at
South Mountain and grew terser at Vicksburg. Hugh's wartime correspondence with Henrietta had followed a similar trajectory. A contemporaneous campaign diary revealed the same pattern. He seemed unable to find
the words to describe in detail what he and his "Forlorn Hope" had gone
through in Mississippi. Missionary Ridge apparently shut him down nearly
completely. His brother Tom had mostly been able to rein in his emotions.
Though the Lawrence Massacre had thrown Tom off his stride, he had recovered. Hugh, in contrast, had always been the most romantic, and emotional,
of the boys. His pain showed through clearly.

If Hugh's combat history caused him mental anguish, the physical ail-
ments connected with his military service were at least as severe. He had
always lived hard, actively seeking adventure—fighting, and dining, with
gusto. A few leg and back injuries that he had sustained in the California
goldfields were made worse by the hardships of campaigning in Virginia,
Maryland, Mississippi, and Tennessee. Over the years his rheumatism worsened to the point where he would be confined to his bed for weeks at a time.
During the war he had worked through his pain with alcohol. This therapy
continued afterwards. Of the three Ewing brothers who went off to war,
Hugh had come back in the worst physical, and mental, condition. Given
these circumstances, it was remarkable that Hugh outlived most of family,
dying in 1905.[93]

Hugh's children ensured that he would rest beside Henrietta and his parents in Lancaster's St. Mary's Cemetery. They erected a large monument that loomed above Thomas and Maria Ewing, almost as if they did not want Hugh spending eternity in his father's shadow. Six years later, the federal government, in setting aside the Vicksburg battlefield as a national park, honored Hugh Ewing with a bronze-cast portrait marker. If, by the time he died, many youths in southern Ohio did not know of Hugh's military exploits, at least the U.S. government had remembered. He was the last of the dynasty to have made such a mark on American history. The third generation, having watched their parents burned in the postwar order, kept a lower profile and largely stayed away from electoral politics. In time, even the exploits of Thomas Ewing faded away. Only William T. Sherman lived on in the public memory.

Postscript

In the years following Hugh Ewing's death, Ohio, the Old Northwest, and the nation underwent a dramatic economic transformation. Railroads replaced the canals Thomas Ewing had helped to build. Each new mode of transportation, from wagon to canal boat and locomotive to automobile, was simply layered over the same narrow route through the Hocking Valley. Just a few remnants of the past poked through the brush; a crumbling canal lock here, a deeply wagon-rutted stretch of Zane's Trace there. Otherwise the infrastructure of the pre-Civil War era was all but gone.

Oak forests gave way to coal mines. Eventually, even the coalfields that Thomas Ewing, Tom, and Cousin Jimmy Blaine had brought into existence immediately before and after the Civil War fell victim to an economy that had moved on to alternative fuels. By the beginning of the twentieth century the economic action in the Old Northwest clustered in the cities that refined oil and manufactured steel, tires, and automobiles. Cleveland, Youngstown, Toledo, Detroit, and Chicago boomed, while pre-Civil War settlements in what is now known as the Lower Midwest became backwaters.

Today, semi trucks speed through Lancaster's two-hundred-year-old downtown on their way to the sprawling strip malls at the periphery of Columbus. As busy commuters and truckers blow down Main Hill with little regard for their forward momentum and the traffic lights below, they pass by the stately mansions of Thomas Ewing and Henry Stanbery. Commuters might give a quick double-take when driving by the Sherman House Museum, if only because of the Civil War-era cannon pointed toward them. Out of their immediate sight line are the squares filled with homes and churches built by Pennsylvania and Virginian settlers in the 1820s and 1830s. Out of sight, such structures, along with their cobblestone and brick-paved alleys, remain mostly out of mind.

While it is a sad commentary on the state of historical knowledge that not many Americans would recognize the names Ewing and Stanbery, even many residents in southern Ohio would be flummoxed. At best, they might recognize Ewing and Stanbery as the names of a Lancaster school or street. William T. Sherman would more likely evoke national and local recognition than Ewing or Stanbery. However, even that acknowledgment would come with a major caveat. It took 135 years after the conclusion of the Civil War before Lancaster erected a statue honoring General Sherman. In contrast, Somerset's statue of General Philip Sheridan was dedicated forty years after the war.

Lancaster may have cradled dozens of accomplished Union Army officers and nationally prominent Unionist politicians, but that did not mean that the Shermans, Ewings, Stanberys, Gillespies, and Blaines were locally popular even in their own time. Thanks to early nineteenth-century settlement patterns, the lower reaches of the Old Northwest Territory had a deeply engrained southern culture. Ohio, Indiana, and Illinois remained a part of the Union only by virtue of an enormous Pennsylvania, New Jersey, and New England settlement in the central and northern reaches of those states. Most of that migration came after the opening of the Erie Canal in 1825, a generation after Virginians had stamped the West with their cultural, political, and racial values. For the majority of people living in southern Ohio, the Civil War was an illegitimate Republican war. Ohio provided the North with the largest number of nationally prominent antiwar politicians. Far from being heroes, William Sherman, Hugh Ewing, Tom Ewing, and Charley Ewing were, to antiwar Democrats, the armed agents of a despotic Abraham Lincoln.

If Cump, Tom, and Charley had merely been good soldiers on the glorious battlefields of Fredericksburg or Gettysburg, they might have had some begrudging respect from southern Ohio Democrats. Their problem, however, was twofold. First, each proved to be an exceptional warrior. Second, fighting guerrillas in Missouri and pillaging Georgia and the Carolinas was not the good, clean war. It mattered little to the antiwar citizens of the Old Northwest, any more than it did to southerners, that George Meade at Gettysburg and Ulysses Grant on the Overland Campaign inflicted far greater casualties than Cump and the two Ewing brothers had racked up in their theaters. Even Hugh could not escape the odium of the dirty war given his record in fighting Confederate insurgents in western Virginia and Kentucky.

Of course, Hugh's military career went far beyond fighting guerrillas. Given his record of standing shoulder to shoulder with his men at South Mountain, Antietam, Vicksburg, and Missionary Ridge, Hugh had clearly fought in the good war. That fact, however, mattered less and less for the public memory as the years passed. The shock of losing over six hundred thousand Americans in the Civil War, followed by the social and political disruption caused by the end of slavery, was difficult for many northerners to absorb. In the nexus between grief and racism came a growing desire for national reconciliation in the North. Southerners, having seen their own land fertilized with the blood of their sons, seemed intent upon winning a victory that eluded them on the battlefield. This desire defined the Lost Cause in historical memory.

Viewed through the quasi-religious lens of the Lost Cause, all Confederates were noble warriors. To advance that narrative, however, a great deal of historical distortion would be required. Lee would be remembered for fighting against great odds at Gettysburg, not kidnapping Pennsylvania blacks and taking them south into slavery. The desperate fighting at South Mountain became a minor prelude to Antietam and Lee's outmaneuvering of McClellan. All but forgotten would be the Confederate troops at South Mountain who pretended to surrender and then fired on Union troops. Wounded Confederate troops even shot at Yankees who tried to offer them medical assistance. Subsequently, many Union soldiers shot every Confederate soldier who came across their path. South Mountain in 1862, and to an extent Vicksburg in 1863, did not look like battles between gentlemen knights. As Hugh bore witness, noble Confederate knights would not have murdered his orderly for the crime of joining a black regiment. If anything, Hugh Ewing's war had more than a few characteristics that would have been familiar to the American soldiers and Marines who fought Japan in World War II.

The Lost Cause, as mythical and as inaccurate as it was, at least imparted a deep reverence for the Confederate fallen that has persisted to this very day. In 1861, the men who founded a Texas frontier settlement that became known as Granbury went to war. If it was true anywhere in the South that the fear of an expansionist federal government, rather than slavery and racism, drove Confederate enlistment, it would be in the Fort Worth region. This section of Texas had no plantations and few if any slaves. In the Granbury cemetery the Confederate dead, from a general down to a private, have their graves lovingly maintained.

In contrast, overgrown and nearly forgotten cemeteries dot Lancaster. There the graves of the Union troops sit in neglect, tombstones often knocked down. Even if it took 135 years for southern Ohio to honor General Sherman, at least he has a statue. Other Union soldiers have not fared so well. They were the veterans of an unpopular war. Black freedom, followed by a Radical Reconstruction policy that championed citizenship and voting rights for the former slaves, made Union veterans even less popular. In Boston, Union veterans might still be honored, but not in the southern reaches of the Old Northwest.

As veterans of a war that most of their neighbors opposed, the Ewings were not destined to be popular. But then, the family had not been popular before the war. The Patriarch had held true to his Whig Party embrace of a strong federal government. Thomas Ewing believed that federal, state, and local government should partner with private business interests to improve transportation, industrial, and educational infrastructure. His own life, after all, embodied the Whig belief in the striving individual of the frontier who, by dint of hard work and intellectual self-improvement, became a successful businessman and politician. Ewing and Lincoln shared at least that much in common, even if they disliked each other personally. To Democrats, however, Ewing was the partisan of an over-reaching, coercive government that he used to enrich himself. They saw Lincoln in the same light. Never mind that Andrew Jackson Democrats pioneered patronage politics, or that if there was Whig graft, at least canals, roads, and schools were a visible by-product of its governance.

In such a political environment Thomas Ewing could not prevail in the electoral arena. His political mark would be made in appointed national office and as a ranking member of the Supreme Court Club. As a moderate who sought to split the difference between Radical Republicans and secessionist Democrats over the issue of the expansion of slavery and emancipation, Thomas Ewing was destined for failure. The Patriarch had no use for Republican radicals or for civil rights. Thomas Ewing opposed the expansion of slavery, not the institution itself so long as it remained contained in what was to him an economically and socially regressive South. All his politically connected friends, relatives, and law partners, notably Orville Browning, Reverdy Johnson, and Henry Stanbery, concurred. None of the so-called "fossil Whigs" welcomed a war to abolish slavery, and none were keen to give blacks the right to sit on juries and vote.

Tom largely shared his father's view, though by virtue of serving in a combat command he recognized emancipation as a useful military tool. He also had no problem recruiting and leading black troops. Even Edwin Stanton's War Department, which was no friend of the Ewings, acknowledged that Tom was more humane in his treatment of black volunteers than most Union officers. Still, while Tom may have respected individual blacks and praised their service to the Union, he did not want them voting. He most certainly did not want blacks voting for Republican radicals like Ben Wade, Jim Lane, or Zachariah Chandler. Cump agreed with Tom on this score, while Hugh, who had always taken the side of underdogs, whether they were Catholic West Point cadets, Mexican ranchers, or fugitive southern slaves, did not. His mother's Catholic injunction "to do unto me as you would do unto the least of my people" set Hugh apart from his Protestant brother and brother-in-law.

Ultimately, Tom shared his father's political fate. He could not reorient a Democratic Party that remained divided between its Unionist and antiwar factions for decades. Sectional divisions only worsened the Democrats' problems. Tom offered a way out for the Democratic Party: put the Civil War behind it, admit slavery was over, become more Whig-like in its economic philosophy, and oppose civil rights, but not to the extent that racism became the only thing that glued the northern and southern wings together. Democrats would have none of it, least of all coming from the man who had executed General Order Number 11.

From the vantage point of modern times Andrew Johnson and his Ewing allies appear to be racial and political reactionaries. It is important to recall, however, that they occupied the center between Republican radicals and die-hard Confederate Democrats. Most Americans from Tennessee and the lower portions of the Old Northwest held views similar to those put forward by Johnson, Stanbery, and the Ewing family. They had fought a war to preserve the Union, not to abolish slavery. If forced to accept the end of slavery, the prowar Democrats and "fossil Whigs" of America's Heartland rejected nearly every facet of Republican Reconstruction. Their disdain for Confederates, antiwar Democrats, and blacks could not find political expression in either major political party. Like the Ewings, such voters were without a home, their allegiance available to whichever candidate could best represent their views. These disaffected, independent voters had the power to swing state and national elections but not enough strength to control the agendas of either the Democrats or the Republicans. As the Ewings went, so did independent voters—influential but not in control of the agenda.

Religion played an important role in the Ewing's political and military experiences. The Ewings were one of the rare religiously blended families in nineteenth-century America. This was especially noteworthy given that their ancestors had fought against each other in Ireland's sectarian wars. Indeed, Irish Catholics and Scots-Irish Presbyterians often continued their warfare against each other on America's shores. Remarkably, in an era when Catholics faced discrimination and much rhetorical abuse, the Ewings rose to near the top of America's economic and political summit. They achieved this stature in spite of nativist opposition. It was nativists, after all, who denied Thomas Ewing the Whig Party's vice presidential nomination in 1848 because he was married to a Catholic.

Lancaster's attitude toward Catholics, like that of America at large, was mixed. Mother Angela Gillespie, the woman who helped found the American Catholic nursing tradition, became largely forgotten in her hometown. Her only memorial, if it may be called that, is the Mount Carmel Hospital system in Columbus, which is a direct legacy of her Civil War nursing work. The fact that Charley Ewing received the highest honor the Vatican could award to a member of the laity does not register at all in the community's history. What did become recorded in southern Ohio's history was a Civil War-era Republican Party and press that denigrated Catholics, most especially the Ewings, as servants of a dangerous foreign power. For their part, envious Catholic Democrats in southern Ohio resented the Ewings' material and political success. Such Catholics often did not regard the Ewings as fellow members of the communion.

Catholic religious association not only created a political roadblock for Thomas Ewing but also halted Cousin Jimmy Blaine's progress toward the White House. Blaine had difficulty asserting his Protestant *bona fides* with Republicans. When he finally had appeared to mollify Protestant Republicans, he inadvertently alienated Catholics outside his family in 1884 and lost the presidential election. Tom Ewing faced a problem similar to that of Cousin Jimmy. Catholic Democrats in Kansas expressed open hatred of Tom for having gone over to the Presbyterian Church—which was actually not that much of a journey given the family's religious and ethnic history. These same people also despised Tom for, paradoxically, being problack, by which they meant opposed to the expansion of slavery to the West.

The Ewing family tried to find the middle ground between Catholics and Protestants, just as they had sought the moderate path in politics. Neither effort proved successful. In a postwar America where anti-Catholicism was growing in strength and intensity, there was little prospect for a family that bridged the religious divide. This was as true nationally as it was locally. By the 1920s, a second, explicitly anti-Catholic Ku Klux Klan had come into existence. This second Klan took control of Lancaster and Fairfield County's public schools, political offices, and law enforcement agencies. Ironically, from the steps of St. Mary's Church that the Ewing family helped build, one could see the nighttime glow of the Klan crosses being burned on Lancaster's Standing Stone Mountain. It would be decades before Catholics, whether in southern Ohio or nationally, would be able to scale the political and economic heights reached in the Civil War era by the Ewings. By then, the Ewing name would largely be forgotten.

NOTES

ABBREVIATIONS

KSHS   Kansas State Historical Society
LOC   Library of Congress
NYT   *New York Times*
OR   *Official Records of the War of the Rebellion*
OHS   Ohio Historical Society (OHS)
UNDA   University of Notre Dame Archives (UNDA)

NOTES TO THE INTRODUCTION

1. Lee Kennett, *Sherman: A Soldier's Life* (New York: HarperCollins, 2001), 207–9; Silvia Tammisto Zsoldos, "The Political Career of Thomas Ewing, Sr." (PhD diss., University of Delaware, 1977), 270; John F. Marszalek, *Sherman: A Soldier's Passion for Order* (New York: Free Press, 1993), 234.

2. Marszalek, *Sherman*, 15–16; *Memorial of Thomas Ewing of Ohio* (New York: Catholic Publication Society, 1873), 33.

3. Theodore Calvin Pease, ed., *The Diary of Orville Hickman Browning*, vol. 1, *1850–1864* (Springfield: Illinois State Historical Library, 1925), 615–16; Roy Nichols, "William Tecumseh Sherman in 1850," *Pennsylvania Magazine of History and Biography* 75 (1951): 424–35.

4. Zsoldos, "Political Career," 20, 22–23; Michael F. Holt, *The Rise and Fall of the American Whig Party: Jacksonian Politics and the Onset of the Civil War* (New York: Oxford University Press, 1999), 22–23, 137–38; "The Story of a Noble Life," in *The Catholic Record: A Miscellany of Catholic Knowledge and General Literature, Volume 8* (Philadelphia: Hardy and Mahony, 1874), 1–12; "Hon. Mr. Ewing," *Liberator*, March 1, 1834.

5. Hervey Scott, *A Complete History of Fairfield County, Ohio, 1795–1876* (1877; repr., Marceline, MO: Walsworth, 1983), 148–49.

6. State of Ohio, Fairfield County, Court of Common Pleas, March Term, 1828, Thomas Ewing, Attorney for Plaintiff (copy in author's possession); M. Whitcomb Hess, "Portrait of an Early American Jurist: Thomas Ewing," *Contemporary Review* 215 (1969): 264–67.

7. Pease, *Diary of Orville Hickman Browning*, 1:527; Thomas Ewing to Abraham Lincoln, November 18, 1861 (Abraham Lincoln Papers, LOC, transcribed

and annotated by the Lincoln Studies Center, Knox College, Galesburg, IL); Thomas Ewing to Abraham Lincoln, November 28, 1861, *OR*, 2:1103–4; "Story of a Noble Life"; Hess, "Portrait."

8. Thomas Ewing obituary, *Harper's Weekly* 15 (1871): 1171; Zsoldos, "Political Career," 190; Hess, "Portrait"; "Story of a Noble Life."

9. Zsoldos, "Political Career," 85–86, 181–82, 189; David R. Contosta, *Lancaster, Ohio: Frontier Town to Edge City* (Columbus: Ohio State University Press, 1999), 38, 70–71.

10. Zsoldos, "Political Career," 85–86, 181; "Labyrinth of Falsehood," *NYT*, October 13, 1884; David G. Taylor, "Hocking Valley Railroad Promotion in the 1870's: The Atlantic and Lake Erie Railway," *Ohio History* 81 (1972): 263–78.

11. Contosta, *Lancaster, Ohio*, 42; Zsoldos, "Political Career," 226, 253; Ellen Ewing Sherman to William T. Sherman, October 10, 1862 (William T. Sherman Family Papers, UNDA, Box 38); Nichols, "William Tecumseh Sherman"; Katherine Burton, *Three Generations: Maria Boyle Ewing, Ellen Ewing Sherman, and Minnie Sherman Fitch* (New York: Longmans, Green, 1947), 73.

12. Marszalek, *Sherman*, 8, 10; Anne C. Rose, *Beloved Strangers: Interfaith Families in Nineteenth-Century America* (Cambridge, MA: Harvard University Press, 2001), 30–32.

13. Zsoldos, "Political Career," 103–4; Marszalek, *Sherman*, 9, 41, 98.

14. Rose, *Beloved Strangers*, 32–33; Lorie Ann Porter, "Not So Strange Bedfellows: Thomas Ewing II and the Defense of Samuel Mudd," *Lincoln Herald* 90 (1988): 91–101; Burton, *Three Generations*, 73; "Our Founders: Catherine Mudd, O.P.," Dominican Sisters St. Mary of the Springs, Columbus, OH, www.columbusdominicans.org/ourhistory/founders.htm.

15. Burton, *Three Generations*, 74. For a representative example of Ellen Ewing's observational skills, see Ellen Ewing to Hugh Boyle Ewing, June 30, 1847 (Hugh Ewing Papers, OHS, Box 1).

16. Contosta, *Lancaster, Ohio*, 57, 60–61; Scott, *Complete History*, 113–14.

17. Ulysses S. Grant, *Personal Memoirs* (New York: Modern Library, 1999), 14.

18. Nicole Etcheson, "The Southern Influence on Midwestern Political Culture: Ohio, Indiana, and Illinois from Frontier to Disunion" (PhD diss., Indiana University, 1991), 11, 24–25, 28.

19. David A. Gerber, *Black Ohio and the Color Line, 1860–1915* (Urbana: University of Illinois Press, 1976), 9, 27–28; Mary Alice Mairose, "Thomas Worthington and the Quest for Statehood and Gentility," in *Builders of Ohio: A Biographical History*, ed. Warren Van Tine and Michael Pierce (Columbus: Ohio State University Press, 2003), 65; Stephen E. Maizlish, *The Triumph of Sectionalism: The Transformation of Ohio Politics, 1844–1856* (Kent: Kent State University Press, 1983), 7; John D. Barnhart, "Sources of Southern Migration into the Old Northwest," *Mississippi Valley Historical Review* 22 (June 1935): 49–62.

20. Maizlish, *Triumph of Sectionalism*, 3, 8; Eugene H. Roseboom, *The Civil War Era, 1850–1973*, History of the State of Ohio 4 (Columbus: Ohio Historical Society, 1968), 408; Eugene H. Roseboom, "Southern Ohio and the Union in 1863," *Mississippi Valley Historical Review* 39 (June 1952): 29–44; Jennifer L. Weber, *Copperheads: The Rise and Fall of Lincoln's Opponents in the North* (New York: Oxford University Press, 2006), 2–3.

21. V. Jacque Voegeli, *Free but Not Equal: The Midwest and the Negro during the Civil War* (Chicago: University of Chicago Press, 1967), 55, 68, 77–79.

22. Ibid., 11, 14–15, 76; Remarks of Hon. George Pendleton, *Congressional Globe*, 37th Cong., 3rd sess., January 31, 1864, 654; Speech of Hon. Samuel S. Cox, *Congressional Globe*, 37th Cong., 2nd sess., June 3, 1862, 242–49; Remarks of Samuel S. Cox, *Congressional Globe*, 37th Cong., 3rd sess., December 15, 1862, 94–100.

23. Arnold M. Shankman, "Candidate in Exile: Clement Vallandigham and the 1863 Ohio Gubernatorial Election" (MA thesis, Emory University, 1969), 256–58; Webber, *Copperheads*, 193, 119–21.

24. Roseboom, *Civil War Era*, 401, 404, 408, 411; Eric J. Cardinal, "The Democratic Party of Ohio and the Civil War: An Analysis of a Wartime Political Minority" (PhD diss., Kent State University, 1981), 122, 159.

25. Williston H. Lofton, "Northern Labor and the Negro during the Civil War," *Journal of Negro History* 34 (July 1949): 251–73; Contosta, *Lancaster, Ohio*, 65–66.

26. Nina Silber, *Daughters of the Union: Northern Women Fight the Civil War* (Cambridge, MA: Harvard University Press, 2005), 16–17, 20, 35; Drew Gilpin Faust, *This Republic of Suffering: Death and the American Civil War* (New York: Alfred A. Knopf, 2008), 3.

27. David Herbert Donald, *Lincoln* (New York: Simon and Schuster, 1995), 571.

28. John Jose Patrick, "John Sherman: The Early Years, 1823–1865," (PhD diss., Kent State University, 1982), 39–40, 146–47; Roseboom, *Civil War Era*, 430; Pease, *Diary of Orville Hickman Browning*, 1:605, 613; Zsoldos, "Political Career," 255–56, 264–65, 271–72; Bruce Tap, *Over Lincoln's Shoulder: The Committee on the Conduct of the War* (Lawrence: University of Kansas Press, 1998), 24, 30, 190, 234; Donald, *Lincoln*, 481.

29. Cardinal, "Democratic Party of Ohio," 235; "Obituary: Hon. Thomas Ewing, Sr.," *NYT*, October 28, 1871; John H. Cox and LaWanda Cox, "Andrew Johnson and His Ghost Writers: An Analysis of the Freedmen's Bureau and Civil Rights Veto Messages," *Mississippi Valley Historical Review* 48 (December 1961): 460–79.

30. "Story of a Noble Life"; Holt, *Rise and Fall*, 328, 340; William E. Van Horne, "Lewis D. Campbell and the Know Nothing Party in Ohio," *Ohio History* 76 (1967): 202–21.

31. Hans L. Trefousse, *Rutherford B. Hayes* (New York: Times Books, 2002), 23–29, 56; "Obituary: Hon. Thomas Ewing, Sr.," *NYT*, October 28, 1871; *Memorial of Thomas Ewing*, 36.

32. *Memorial of Thomas Ewing*, 39.
33. There is a vast literature on historical memory and the Civil War. An edited collection by Gabor Borritt, *The Lincoln Enigma: The Changing Faces of an American Icon* (New York: Oxford University Press, 2001), does a fine job of discussing the evolving scholarly and popular culture interpretations of Abraham Lincoln. On the impact of death on the American psyche during and after the Civil War, the most recent, and profound, scholarly contribution has been Faust, *This Republic of Suffering*. Nina Silber, *The Romance of Reunion: Northerners and the South, 1865–1900* (Chapel Hill: University of North Carolina Press, 1997), makes a strong case for the roles gender and race played in shaping the postwar reconciliation of the two sections.
34. Faust, *This Republic of Suffering*, xii.

NOTES TO CHAPTER ONE

The chapter epigraph is from Thomas Ewing Sr., "Commencement on the Ohio Canal at the Licking Summit, July 4, 1825," *Ohio History* 34 (1925): 66–99.

1. Clement L. Martzolff, ed., "The Autobiography of Thomas Ewing," *Ohio History* 22 (1913): 126–204.
2. James G. Leyburn, *The Scotch-Irish: A Social History* (Chapel Hill: University of North Carolina Press, 1962), 124–25.
3. Ibid., 197, 207, 301.
4. Ibid., 199, 201, 205–206; James T. Lemon, *The Best Poor Man's Country: Early Southeastern Pennsylvania* (Baltimore: Johns Hopkins University Press, 2002).
5. George Ewing, *The Military Journal of George Ewing (1754–1824), a Soldier of Valley Forge* (Yonkers, NY: Thomas Ewing Family, Privately Printed, 1928).
6. Martzolff, "Autobiography of Thomas Ewing."
7. G. Ewing, *Military Journal*; Martzolff, "Autobiography of Thomas Ewing"; George F. Scheer and Hugh Rankin, *Rebels and Redcoats: The American Revolution through the Eyes of Those That Fought and Lived It* (New York: Da Capo, 1987), 308; Hugh F. Rankin, *The North Carolina Continentals* (Chapel Hill: University of North Carolina Press, 2006).
8. Martzolff, "Autobiography of Thomas Ewing"; James Ewing, Affidavit of James Ewing, State of New Jersey, Cumberland County, October 16, 1819, Pertaining to the Military Service of "George Ewing" (Thomas Ewing Family Papers, Box 262, LOC); Statement and Account of Military Service of "George Ewing," ca. 1820 (Thomas Ewing Family Papers, Box 262, LOC).
9. Martzolff, "Autobiography of Thomas Ewing."
10. Ibid.
11. Ibid.; Samuel Prescott Hildreth, *Pioneer History: Being an Account of the First Examinations of the Ohio Valley and the Early Settlement of the North West*

Territory (Cincinnati: H. W. Derby [and the Cincinnati Historical Society], 1848), 470–73.

12. Martzolff, "Autobiography of Thomas Ewing."

13. Ibid., 139; "The Story of a Noble Life," in *The Catholic Record: A Miscellany of Catholic Knowledge and General Literature,* vol. 8 (Philadelphia: Hardy and Mahony, 1874), 1–12.

14. Martzolff, "Autobiography of Thomas Ewing"; Ohio Historical Society, "Coonskin Library," in *Ohio History Central: An Online Encyclopedia of Ohio History,* http://ohiohistorycentral.org.

15. Martzolff, "Autobiography of Thomas Ewing."

16. Ibid.

17. Ibid.; John Edmund Stealey III, *The Antebellum Kanawha Salt Business and Western Markets* (Lexington: University of Kentucky Press, 1993), 8, 10, 13–14, 15–17; Lloyd Lewis, *Sherman, Fighting Prophet* (New York: Harcourt, Brace, 1932), 14–15.

18. Stealey, *Antebellum Kanawha Salt Business,* 19, 133–35, 137, 140–43; John Edmund Stealey III, ed., *Kanawhan Prelude to Nineteenth-Century Monopoly in the United States: The Virginian Salt Combination* (Richmond: Virginia Historical Society, 2000); Martzolff, "Autobiography of Thomas Ewing"; John Edmund Stealey III, "Slavery in the Kanawha Salt Industry," in *Appalachians and Race: The Mountain South from Slavery to Segregation,* ed. John C. Inscoe (Lexington: University of Kentucky Press, 2001), 50–73.

19. Martzolff, "Autobiography of Thomas Ewing"; Lewis, *Sherman, Fighting Prophet,* 15–17; Emanuel Spencer, "Glimpses of Log-Cabin Life in Early Ohio," in *Magazine of American History with Notes and Queries, Volume 24,* ed. Martha J. Lamb (New York: J. J. Little, 1890), 101–11.

20. R. Douglas Hurt, *The Ohio Frontier: Crucible of the Old Northwest, 1720–1830* (Bloomington: Indiana University Press, 1996).

21. Hurt, *Ohio Frontier,* 4–5; David R. Contosta, *Lancaster, Ohio, 1800–2000: Frontier Town to Edge City* (Columbus: Ohio State University Press, 1999), 10.

22. Contosta, *Lancaster, Ohio,* 13.

23. Hurt, *Ohio Frontier,* 257–58; Contosta, *Lancaster, Ohio,* 15, 20–22.

24. Contosta, *Lancaster, Ohio,* 14, 24, 25, 27.

25. Hurt, *Ohio Frontier,* 223–24, 257–58, 260–61; Contosta, *Lancaster, Ohio,* 29; Lewis, *Sherman, Fighting Prophet,* 18; Richard Lingeman, *Small Town America: A Narrative History, 1620–Present* (New York: G. P. Putnam's Sons, 1980), 106.

26. Martzolff, "Autobiography of Thomas Ewing"; Katherine Burton, *Three Generations: Maria Boyle Ewing, Ellen Ewing Sherman, Minnie Sherman Fitch* (New York: Longmans, Green, 1947), 18; "Philemon Beecher," in *Biographical Directory of the United States Congress, 1774–Present,* Bioguide.congress.gov.

27. Burton, *Three Generations,* 3–4.

28. Anne C. Rose, *Beloved Strangers: Interfaith Families in Nineteenth-Century America* (Cambridge, MA: Harvard University Press, 2001), 30–31; Gail Hamilton, *Biography of James G. Blaine* (Norwich, CT: Henry Brill, 1895), 78.

29. Burton, *Three Generations*, 4–8.

30. Ibid., 10–14.

31. Martzolff, "Autobiography of Thomas Ewing"; Burton, *Three Generations*, 18–23; Silvia Tammisto Zsoldos, "The Political Career of Thomas Ewing, Sr." (PhD diss., University of Delaware, 1977), 8.

32. Martzolff, "Autobiography of Thomas Ewing"; Burton, *Three Generations*, 22–26.

33. Martzolff, "Autobiography of Thomas Ewing"; Burton, *Three Generations*, 26–27; Rose, *Beloved Strangers*, 32.

34. Martzolff, "Autobiography of Thomas Ewing"; Lewis, *Sherman, Fighting Prophet*, 23–27.

35. Henry Howe, ed., *Historical Collections of Ohio in Two Volumes: An Encyclopedia of the State* (State of Ohio: Laning, 1898), 652–53; Bruce Tap, "Henry Stanbery," in *American National Biography On-Line*, February 2000, American Council of Learned Societies, www.anb.org.

36. George Irving Reed, ed., *Bench and Bar of Ohio: A Compendium of History and Biography* (Chicago: Century Publishing and Engraving, 1897), 1:84; State of Ohio, Fairfield County, Court of Common Pleas, March Term, 1828, Thomas Ewing, Attorney for Plaintiff (copy in author's possession); Howe, *Historical Collections of Ohio*, 652–53; Tap, "Henry Stanbery."

37. Reed, *Bench and Bar*, 1:66–67.

38. Zsoldos, "Political Career," 18; Reed, *Bench and Bar*, 1:62–68, 75–83.

39. Martzolff, "Autobiography of Thomas Ewing."

40. Ibid.; Michael F. Holt, *The Rise and Fall of the American Whig Party: Jacksonian Politics and the Onset of the Civil War* (New York: Oxford University Press, 1999), 2–5; Ronald P. Formisano, "State Development in the Early Republic: Substance and Structure, 1780–1840," in *Contesting Democracy: Substance and Structure in American Political History*, ed. Byron E. Shafer and Anthony J. Badger (Lawrence: University of Kansas Press, 2001), 7–35.

41. Martzolff, "Autobiography of Thomas Ewing"; Holt, *Rise and Fall*, 2–5; Formisano, "State Development," 7–35; Melvyn Dubofsky, "Daniel Webster and the Whig Theory of Economic Growth: 1828–1848," *New England Quarterly* 42 (December 1969): 551–72.

42. Larry L. Miller, *Ohio Place Names* (Bloomington: Indiana University Press, 1996), 7–13, 169–77, 194; Jeffrey P. Brown, "The Ohio Federalists, 1803–1815," *Journal of the Early Republic* 2 (Autumn 1982): 261–82; Nicole Etcheson, "The Southern Influence on Midwestern Political Culture: Ohio, Indiana, and Illinois from Frontier to Disunion" (PhD diss., Indiana University, 1991), 2.

43. John D. Barnhart, "The Southern Influence in the Formation of Ohio," *Journal of Southern History* 3 (February 1937): 28–42; John D. Barnhart, "The Southern Element in the Leadership of the Old Northwest," *Journal of Southern History* 1 (May 1935): 186–92; Mary Alice Mairose, "Thomas Worthington and the Quest for Statehood and Gentility," in *Builders of Ohio: A Biographical History*, ed. Warren Van Tine and Michael Pierce (Columbus: Ohio State University Press, 2003), 63–68.

44. Etcheson, "Southern Influence," 60–61; Formisano, "State Development," 7–35; H. Roger Grant, *Ohio on the Move: Transportation in the Buckeye State* (Athens: Ohio University Press, 2000), 3.

45. Donald J. Ratcliffe, "The Market Revolution and Party Alignments in Ohio, 1828–1840," in *The Pursuit of Public Power: Political Culture in Ohio, 1787–1861*, ed. Jeffrey P. Brown and Andrew R. L. Cayton (Kent: Kent State University Press, 1994), 100; Harold E. Davis, "Economic Basis of Ohio Politics, 1820–1840," *Ohio History* 47 (1938): 288–318.

46. Grant, *Ohio on the Move*, 5–6; George W. Knepper, *Ohio and Its People* (Kent: Kent State University Press, 2003), 144.

47. Grant, *Ohio on the Move*, 55–56; Davis, "Economic Basis," 288–318; T. Ewing, "Commencement"; Knepper, *Ohio and Its People*, 147.

48. Grant, *Ohio on the Move*, 52–53; T. Ewing, "Commencement."

49. Grant, *Ohio on the Move*, 72; Lingeman, *Small Town America*, 138–40.

50. Ratcliffe, "Market Revolution," 106, 112; Reed, *Bench and Bar*, 1:75–83; Contosta, *Lancaster, Ohio*, 25.

51. Burton, *Three Generations*, 36–37; Zsoldos, "Political Career," 137.

52. Henry G. Connor, *John Archibald Campbell, Associate Justice of the United States Supreme Court, 1853–1861* (New York: Da Capo, 1971), 83. For a good discussion of the culture of the U.S. Supreme Court in the first half of the nineteenth century, see Brian McGinty, *Lincoln and the Court* (Cambridge, MA: Harvard University Press, 2008). The correspondence between Reverdy Johnson and Thomas Ewing attests to their friendship and alliance, which extended to Tom Ewing Jr. when Johnson and the younger Ewing defended the Lincoln assassination conspirators (Thomas Ewing Family Papers, LOC, Box 159).

53. Everett P. Wheeler, "Constitutional Law of the United States as Molded by Daniel Webster," *Yale Law Journal* 13 (May 1904): 366–90; Maurice G. Baxter, "Daniel Webster," in *American National Biography On-Line*, February 2000, American Council of Learned Societies, www.anb.org.

54. Baxter, "Daniel Webster"; Harlow W. Sheidley, "The Webster-Hayne Debate: Recasting New England's Sectionalism," *New England Quarterly* 67 (March 1994): 5–29; Wayne Fields, "The Reply to Hayne: Daniel Webster and the Rhetoric of Stewardship," *Political Theory* 11 (February 1983): 5–28.

55. Zsoldos, "Political Career," 22–23; Burton, *Three Generations*, 35; "Anecdote," *Liberator*, August 31, 1833.

56. Zsoldos, "Political Career," 22–23, 137; Robert V. Remini, "Henry Clay," in *American National Biography On-Line*, February 2000, American Council of Learned Societies, www.anb.org; Burton, *Three Generations*, 35.

57. Hamilton Andrews Hill, *Memoir of Abbott Lawrence* (Boston: Little, Brown, 1884), 29–30; Carl E. Prince and Seth Taylor, "Daniel Webster, the Boston Associates, and the U.S. Government's Role in the Industrializing Process, 1815–1830," *Journal of the Early Republic* 2 (Autumn 1982): 283–99; Abby L. Gilbert, "Thomas Ewing, Sr.: Ohio's Advocate for a National Bank," *Ohio History* 82 (1973): 4–24.

58. Prince and Taylor, "Daniel Webster."

59. Contosta, *Lancaster, Ohio*, 38; Grant, *Ohio on the Move*, 61; Hervey Scott, *A Complete History of Fairfield County, Ohio, 1795–1876* (1877; repr., Marceline, MO: Walsworth, 1983), 150–51.

60. Francis P. Weisenburger, "Charles Hammond: The First Great Journalist of the Old Northwest," *Ohio History* 43 (October 1934): 337–427.

61. David F. Ericson, "The Nullification Crisis, American Republicanism, and the Force Bill Debate," *Journal of Southern History* 61 (May 1995): 249–70.

62. Thomas Ewing Speech on the Tariff, *Register of Debates, U.S. Senate, 22nd Congress, 1st Session, February 17, 1832* (Washington, DC: Gales and Seaton's Register, 1832), 416–38.

63. Ibid.

64. Ibid.

65. Ibid.

66. Perry M. Goldman, "Political Virtue in the Age of Jackson," *Political Science Quarterly* 87 (March 1972): 46–62; Burton, *Three Generations*, 43; Robert V. Remini, *Andrew Jackson: The Course of American Democracy, 1833–1845*, 3 vols. (New York: History Book Club, 1984), 3:175, 240.

67. Remini, *Andrew Jackson*, 3:240; Zsoldos, "Political Career," 38–47.

68. David P. Currie, "The Constitution in Congress: The Public Lands, 1829–1861," *University of Chicago Law Review* 70 (Summer 2003): 783–820; David J. Russo, "The Major Political Issues of the Jacksonian Period and the Development of Party Loyalty in Congress, 1830–1840," *Transactions of the American Philosophical Society* 62 (1972): 3–51.

69. Richard H. Timberlake Jr., "The Specie Standard and Central Banking in the United States before 1860," *Journal of Economic History* 21 (September 1961): 318–41; Russo, "Major Political Issues."

70. Gilbert, "Thomas Ewing, Sr."

71. Zsoldos, "Political Career," 49, 85–86.

72. Russo, "Major Political Issues."

73. Zsoldos, "Political Career," 53–66; Russo, "Major Political Issues"; Gilbert, "Thomas Ewing, Sr."

74. Gilbert, "Thomas Ewing, Sr."; Zsoldos, "Political Career," 69–71.

75. Zsoldos, "Political Career," 131–33.

76. Ibid., 131–32.

77. William H. Riker, "The Senate and American Federalism," *American Political Science Review* 49 (June 1955): 452–69.

78. Weisenburger, "Charles Hammond"; Richard C. Rohrs, "Partisan Politics and the Attempted Assassination of Andrew Jackson," *Journal of the Early Republic* 1 (Summer 1981): 149–63.

79. Henry Clay Hubbart, "'Pro-Southern' Influences in the Free West, 1840–1865," *Mississippi Valley Historical Review* 20 (June 1933): 45–62; Gilbert, "Thomas Ewing, Sr."; Barnhart, "Southern Element"; Timberlake, "Specie Standard."

80. Zsoldos, "Political Career," 132–33.

81. Reginald Charles McGrane, *William Allen: A Study in Western Democracy* (Columbus: Ohio State Archeological and Historical Society, 1925), 47–52; Hubbart, "'Pro-Southern' Influences"; Thomas E. Powell, *The Democratic Party of the State of Ohio* (Columbus: Ohio Publishing, 1913), 216.

82. McGrane, *William Allen*, 47–52; Miller, *Ohio Place Names*, 14, 39; Hubbart, "'Pro-Southern' Influences."

83. Henry Clay to Francis Brooke, February 10, 1837, in *The Private Correspondence of Henry Clay*, ed. Calvin Colton (New York: A. S. Barnes, 1855), 410–11.

84. Hill, *Memoir of Abbott Lawrence*, 60; Sydney Nathans, "Daniel Webster, Massachusetts Man," *New England Quarterly* 39 (June 1966): 161–81.

85. Zsoldos, "Political Career," 137–43; Gilbert, "Thomas Ewing, Sr."

86. Zsoldos, "Political Career," 137–43; Gilbert, "Thomas Ewing, Sr."

87. Zsoldos, "Political Career," 146–49; Holt, *Rise and Fall*, 127.

88. William Greene to Thomas Corwin, May 12, 1841, in *Quarterly Publication of the Historical and Philosophical Society of Ohio, 1918–1920, Volumes XIII–XV* (Cincinnati: Historical and Philosophical Society of Ohio, 1920), 4; Gilbert, "Thomas Ewing, Sr."; Zsoldos, "Political Career," 146–49; Lewis, *Sherman, Fighting Prophet*, 29.

89. Everett S. Brown and Ruth C. Silva, "Presidential Succession and Inability," *Journal of Politics* 11 (February 1949): 236–56; "Diary of Thomas Ewing, August and September 1841," *American Historical Review* 18 (October 1912): 97–112.

90. Holt, *Rise and Fall*, 127–33; Nathans, "Daniel Webster"; Gilbert, "Thomas Ewing, Sr."

91. "Diary of Thomas Ewing"; Holt, *Rise and Fall*, 132–35.

92. George E. Badger to J. J. Crittenden, February 4, 1842, in *The Life of John J. Crittenden: With Selections from His Correspondence and Speeches*, ed. Chapman Coleman and Ann Mary Butler Coleman, 2 vols. (Philadelphia: J. B. Lippincott, 1871), 2:167–68; Holt, *Rise and Fall*, 133–38; Zsoldos, "Political Career," 172–79.

93. Holt, *Rise and Fall,* 133–38; Zsoldos, "Political Career," 172–79; Nathans, "Daniel Webster"; Gilbert, "Thomas Ewing, Sr."; "Diary of Thomas Ewing."
94. Zsoldos, "Political Career," 181–82.
95. Zsoldos, "Political Career," 189–90; Philemon Beecher Ewing to Thomas Ewing, July 25, 1849 (Thomas Ewing Family Papers, LOC, Box 159).
96. Mary Land, "Ben Wade," in *For the Union: Ohio Leaders in the Civil War,* ed. Kenneth W. Wheeler (Columbus: Ohio State University Press, 1968), 159.
97. Stephen E. Maizlish, *The Triumph of Sectionalism: The Transformation of Ohio Politics, 1844–1856* (Kent: Kent State University Press, 1983), 6, 8.
98. Norman A. Graebner, "Thomas Corwin and the Election of 1848: A Study in Conservative Politics," *Journal of Southern History* 17 (May 1951): 162–79; Maizlish, *Triumph of Sectionalism,* 58–60; Hubbart, "'Pro-Southern' Influences"; Barnhart, "Southern Element"; Thomas E. Jeffrey, "George Edmund Badger," in *American National Biography On-Line,* February 2000, American Council of Learned Societies, www.anb.org.
99. Thomas Ewing to Oran Follett, April 28, 1854, in *Quarterly Publication of the Historical and Philosophical Society of Ohio, 1918–1920, Volumes XIII–XV* (Cincinnati: Historical and Philosophical Society of Ohio, 1920), 50–51.
100. Ewing to Oran Follett, April 28, 1854, 50–51.
101. Report of R. S. Finley, November 12, 1830, in *The African Repository and Colonial Journal,* vol. 6 (Washington, DC: American Colonization Society, 1831), 312; Maizlish, *Triumph of Sectionalism,* 17; Graebner, "Thomas Corwin."
102. Holt, *Rise and Fall,* 294–97, 307; Maizlish, *Triumph of Sectionalism,* 96; Zsoldos, "Political Career," 192; Stephen E. Maizlish, "Ohio and the Rise of Sectional Politics," in Brown and Cayton, *Pursuit of Public Power,* 127; Graebner, "Thomas Corwin."
103. Robert P. Ludlum, "Joshua R. Giddings, Radical," *Mississippi Valley Historical Review* 23 (June 1936): 49–60.
104. Maizlish, *Triumph of Sectionalism,* 96; Holt, *Rise and Fall,* 328; William E. Van Horne, "Lewis D. Campbell and the Know-Nothing Party in Ohio," *Ohio History* 76 (1968): 202–21; Charles R. Morris, *American Catholic: The Saints and Sinners Who built America's Most Powerful Church* (New York: Times Books, 1997), 54–80; Jay P. Dolan, *The American Catholic Experience: A History from Colonial Times to the Present* (Notre Dame: University of Notre Dame Press, 1992), 201–2.
105. Contosta, *Lancaster, Ohio,* 55–57.
106. Eugene H. Roseboom, "Salmon P. Chase and the Know Nothings," *Mississippi Valley Historical Review* 25 (December 1938): 335–50; Eugene H. Roseboom, *The Civil War Era, 1850–1873,* History of the State of Ohio 4 (Columbus: Ohio Historical Society, 1968), 323; David Donald, "Abolitionist Leadership: A Displaced Social Elite," in *The Abolitionists: Reformers or Fanatics?* ed. Richard O. Curry (New York: Holt, Rinehart, and Winston, 1965), 42–48.

107. Maizlish, *Triumph of Sectionalism*, 139–141; Holt, *Rise and Fall,* 400–401; Thomas Cecil Mulligan, "Lest the Rebels Come to Power: The Life of William Dennison, 1815–1882, Early Ohio Republican" (PhD diss., Ohio State University, 1994), 87.

108. William D. Hoyt Jr., "Zachary Taylor and the Military Establishment, 1835," *American Historical Review* 51 (April 1946): 480–84.

109. Holt, *Rise and Fall,* 344–45, 443–44; "The New Cabinet," *Liberator*, March 16, 1849.

110. Zsoldos, "Political Career," 196; Theodore Calvin Pease, ed., *The Diary of Orville Hickman Browning*, vol. 1, *1850–1864* (Springfield: Illinois State Historical Library, 1925), 615–16.

111. Zsoldos, "Political Career," 199–200; Holt, *Rise and Fall,* 421.

112. Pease, *Diary of Orville Hickman Browning*, 1:592–93, 617; Nathans, "Daniel Webster"; Holt, *Rise and Fall,* 425–26.

113. Paul M. Angle and Earl Schenck Miers, eds., *The Living Lincoln: The Man, His Mind, His Times, and the War He Fought, Reconstructed from His Own Writings* (New York: Barnes and Noble Books, 1992), 137; Benjamin P. Thomas, *Abraham Lincoln: A Biography* (New York: Barnes and Noble Books, 1994), 129; Zsoldos, "Political Career," 203–9; Josiah M. Lucas to Abraham Lincoln, May 9, 1849 (Abraham Lincoln Papers, LOC, transcribed and annotated by the Lincoln Studies Center, Knox College, Galesburg, IL); Abraham Lincoln to Thomas Ewing, April 7, 1849 (Abraham Lincoln Papers, LOC, transcribed and annotated by the Lincoln Studies Center, Knox College, Galesburg, IL). There are many more letters in the LOC pertaining to the Ewing-Lincoln encounter of 1849.

114. Dale L. Morgan, "The Administration of Indian Affairs in Utah, 1851–1858," *Pacific Historical Review* 17 (November 1948): 383–409; Henry Barrett Learned, "The Establishment of the Secretaryship of the Interior," *American Historical Review* 16 (July 1911): 751–73.

115. Morgan, "Administration of Indian Affairs"; Learned, "Establishment of the Secretaryship"; William H. Seward and George E. Baker, eds., *The Works of William H. Seward*, vol. 3 (New York: Redfield, 1853), 443–44.

116. Joseph Richard Werne, "Partisan Politics and the Mexican Boundary Survey, 1848–1853," *Southwestern Historical Quarterly* 90 (1987): 329–46; Janet R. Fireman, ed., "R. P. Effinger's Excellent Adventure: The Unknown Letters of a Young Ohio Lawyer, 1849–1850," *California History* 82 (January 2004): 2–75. Effinger's father was born in Virginia, and the younger Effinger was a Democratic Party activist.

117. Zsoldos, "Political Career," 216, 348.

118. Ibid., 220–23, 233–38; James M. Landis, "Constitutional Limitations on the Congressional Power of Investigation," *Harvard Law Review* 40 (December 1926): 153–221.

119. Thomas Maitland Marshall, "Diary and Memoranda of William L. Marcy, 1849–1851," *American Historical Review* 24 (April 1919): 444–62.

120. Zsoldos, "Political Career," 225–27.

121. Ibid., 237; *"Speech of Mr. Ewing of Ohio, on Mr. Bradbury's Resolutions," Delivered in the Senate of the United States, January 7, 1851* (Washington, DC: Gideon, 1851).

122. Mulligan, "Lest the Rebels Come," 42, 56–57; Williston H. Lofton, "Abolition and Labor: Appeal of the Abolitionists to the Northern Working Classes: Part I," *Journal of Negro History* 33 (July 1949): 249–61; Williston H. Lofton, "Abolition and Labor: Reaction of Northern Labor to the Anti-Slavery Appeal, Part II," *Journal of Negro History* 33 (July 1948): 261–83; John F. Hume, *The Abolitionists, Together with Personal Memories of the Struggle for Human Rights, 1830–1864* (New York: G. P. Putnam's Sons, 1905), 21–25. Hume was a native of southern Ohio and an abolitionist.

123. Miller, *Ohio Place Names*, 4; Mulligan, "Lest the Rebels Come," 56–57; Phyllis F. Field, "William Dennison," in *American National Biography On-Line*, February 2000, American Council of Learned Societies, www.anb.org.

124. William Dennison to Thomas Ewing, November 12, 1850 (Thomas Ewing Family Papers, Box 159, LOC); Thomas Ewing to William Dennison, November 13, 1850 (Thomas Ewing Family Papers, Box 159, LOC).

125. Tremaine McDowell, "Memoranda and Documents: Webster's Words on Abolitionists," *New England Quarterly* 7 (June 1934): 315.

126. Thomas Ewing, Remarks, "Slave Trade in the District of Columbia," Appendix to the *Congressional Globe*, U.S. Senate, 31st Cong., 1st sess., September 12, 1850, 1639.

127. Ibid., 1667; Holt, *Rise and Fall,* 570.

128. Henry Clay to James Harlan, March 16, 1850, in, Colton, *Private Correspondence of Henry Clay,* 603–4.

129. Holman Hamilton, "Texas Bonds and Northern Profits: A Study in Compromise, Investment, and Lobby Influence," *Mississippi Valley Historical Review* 43 (March 1957): 579–94.

130. Ibid.

131. Charles Warren, *The Supreme Court in United States History,* vol. 2, *1836–1918* (Boston: Little, Brown, 1926), 221; Holt, *Rise and Fall,* 536; Zsoldos, "Political Career," 230–31.

132. Thomas Ewing, Remarks, "The Compromise Bill," Appendix to the *Congressional Globe*, U.S. Senate, 31st Cong., 1st sess., July 29, 1850, 1453–55, 1460; Zsoldos, "Political Career," 229–30.

133. Holt, *Rise and Fall,* 569, 657–59, 770; Zsoldos, "Political Career," 232–32; Land, "Ben Wade."

NOTES TO CHAPTER TWO

The chapter epigraph is from Hugh Ewing, *The Black List: A Tale of Early California* (New York: Peter Fenelon Collier, 1893), 3.

1. Charles Bracelen Flood, *Grant and Sherman: The Friendship that Won the Civil War* (New York: Harper Perennial, 2005), 21.
2. John F. Marszalek, *Sherman: A Soldier's Passion for Order* (New York: Free Press, 1993), 9.
3. "Philemon B. Stanbery," *A Biographical Record of Fairfield County, Ohio* (New York: S. J. Clarke, 1902), 153–55.
4. William T. Sherman to Ellen Ewing, December 10, 1838 (William T. Sherman Family Papers, Box 20, UNDA).
5. Sherman to Ellen Ewing, December 10, 1838; William T. Sherman to Ellen Ewing, November 24, 1838 (William T. Sherman Family Papers, Box 20, UNDA); Hugh Boyle Ewing, "The Autobiography of a Tramp" (Hugh Boyle Ewing Papers, Box 9, OHS), 20.
6. Marszalek, *Sherman*, 13; Lloyd Lewis, *Sherman, Fighting Prophet* (New York: Harcourt, Brace, 1932), 45; H. Ewing, "Autobiography of a Tramp," 12.
7. William T. Sherman to Ellen Ewing, May 10, 1839 (William T. Sherman Family Papers, Box 21, UNDA); H. Ewing, "Autobiography of a Tramp," 9, 21.
8. Lewis, *Sherman, Fighting Prophet*, 65; Sister Mary Rita, *A Story of Fifty Years: From the Annals of the Congregation of the Sisters of the Holy Cross* (Notre Dame, IN: Ave Maria, 1905), 137.
9. C. M. Wiseman, *Pioneer Period and Pioneer Period of Fairfield County, Ohio* (Columbus: P. J. Heer, 1901), 75–76; Gail Hamilton, *Biography of James G. Blaine* (Norwich, CT: Henry Brill, 1895), 66–70, 581–82.
10. Gail Hamilton, *Biography of James G. Blaine*, 66–70.
11. William T. Sherman to Ellen Ewing, January 22, 1839 (William T. Sherman Family Papers, Box 21, UNDA); Katherine Burton, *Three Generations: Maria Boyle Ewing, Ellen Ewing Sherman, Minnie Sherman Fitch* (New York: Longmans, Green, 1947), 51, 53–54; Luke Clarke, *In Memoriam: Charles Ewing* (Philadelphia: J. B. Lippincott, 1888), 9–10.
12. William T. Sherman to Ellen Ewing, May 4, 1839 (William T. Sherman Family Papers, Box 21, UNDA); Clarke, *In Memoriam*, 10–11.
13. Marszalek, *Sherman*, 13.
14. H. Ewing, "Autobiography of a Tramp," 37.
15. Thomas Ewing to A. T. Goodman, May 1870, in *The Historical Magazine and Notes and Queries, Concerning Antiquities, History, and Biography of America, Volume 21*, ed. H. B. Dawson (Morrisania, NY: Henry B. Dawson, Library of Congress, 1872–73), 71–73; Marszalek, *Sherman*, 10–11; Burton, *Three Generations*, 54–55.
16. Wiseman, *Pioneer Period*, 156; Marszalek, *Sherman*, 12.
17. Wiseman, *Pioneer Period*, 65; Phil Ewing to Thomas Ewing, December 31, 1849 (Thomas Ewing Family Papers, Box 159, LOC); John Jose Patrick, "John Sherman: The Early Years, 1823–1865 (PhD diss., Kent State University, 1982),

13–15; Lewis, *Sherman, Fighting Prophet*, 46; H. Ewing, "Autobiography of a Tramp," 36.

18. Patrick, "John Sherman," 19, 22, 26; Lewis, *Sherman, Fighting Prophet*, 31; John Sherman, *Recollections of Forty Years in the House, Senate, and Cabinet* (Chicago: Werner, 1895), 1:44–46.

19. Thomas Ewing Sr., "Commencement on the Ohio Canal at the Licking Summit, July 4, 1825," *Ohio History* 34 (1925): 66–99.

20. Silvia Tammisto Zsoldos, "The Political Career of Thomas Ewing, Sr." (PhD diss., University of Delaware, 1977), 104; H. Ewing, "Autobiography of a Tramp," 13–14.

21. Zsoldos, "Political Career," 137–38; Nicole Etcheson, "The Southern Influence on Midwestern Political Culture: Ohio, Indiana, and Illinois from Frontier to Disunion" (PhD diss., Indiana University, 1991), 56, 417; Nicole Etcheson, "Manliness and the Political Culture of the Old Northwest, 1790–1860," *Journal of the Early Republic* 15 (Spring 1995): 59–77.

22. Zsoldos, "Political Career," 230–31; Flood, *Grant and Sherman*, 22.

23. Burton, *Three Generations*, 31–35, 48–49.

24. Ibid., 30–31.

25. Ibid., 39; William T. Sherman to Ellen Ewing, August 21, 1839 (William T. Sherman Family Papers, Box 21, UNDA).

26. H. Ewing, "Autobiography of a Tramp," 11, 16–17.

27. Marszalek, *Sherman*, 11; H. Ewing, "Autobiography of a Tramp," 10–11, 27–31.

28. Wiseman, *Pioneer Period and Pioneer Period,* 64; Hervey Scott, *A Complete History of Fairfield County, Ohio, 1795–1876* (1877; repr., Marceline, MO: Walsworth, 1983), 138.

29. Marszalek, *Sherman*, 9–10, 14; Burton, *Three Generations*, 39–40.

30. Anne C. Rose, *Beloved Strangers: Interfaith Families in Nineteenth-Century America* (Cambridge, MA: Harvard University Press, 2001), 30–33; Sister Mary Rita, *Story of Fifty Years*, 135–36.

31. Rose, *Beloved Strangers*, 30–33; Stephen E. Boyer, "The Theology of the Battlefield: William Tecumseh Sherman and the U.S. Civil War," *Journal of Military History* 64 (October 2000): 1005–34.

32. Burton, *Three Generations*, 44–45; Roy Morris Jr., *Sheridan: The Life and Wars of General Phil Sheridan* (New York: Crown, 1992), 13; Rose, *Beloved Strangers*, 32–33; Lorie Ann Porter, "Not So Strange Bedfellows: Thomas Ewing II and the Defense of Samuel Mudd," *Lincoln Herald* 90 (1988): 91–101.

33. Morris, *Sheridan*, 13; Porter, "Not So Strange Bedfellows"; William T. Sherman to Ellen Ewing, December 8, 1839 (William T. Sherman Family Papers, Box 21, UNDA).

34. Porter, "Not So Strange Bedfellows"; Rose, *Beloved Strangers*, 32; Burton, *Three Generations*, 58–59, 73.

35. Porter, "Not So Strange Bedfellows"; J. H. Clay Mudd to Thomas Ewing, May 10, 1849 (Thomas Ewing Family Papers, Box 159, LOC); Rose, *Beloved Strangers*, 32; Burton, *Three Generations*, 58–59, 73.

36. William T. Sherman to Ellen Ewing, December 8, 1839; William T. Sherman to Ellen Ewing, February 8, 1844 (William T. Sherman Family Papers, Box 23, UNDA).

37. H. Ewing, "Autobiography of a Tramp," 38.

38. Ibid., 39–40.

39. Ibid.

40. Ibid., 45.

41. Ibid., 40.

42. Ibid., 41; Ellen Ewing to Hugh Ewing, January 8, 1847 (Hugh Ewing Papers, Box 1, OHS).

43. H. Ewing, "Autobiography of a Tramp," 42; Ellen Ewing to Hugh Ewing, January 8, 1847; Eugene C. Tidball, *"No Disgrace to My Country": The Life of John C. Tidball* (Kent: Kent State University Press, 2002), 49.

44. H. Ewing, "Autobiography of a Tramp," 42; John C. Waugh, *The Class of 1846 from West Point to Appomattox: Stonewall Jackson, George McClellan, and their Brothers* (New York: Ballantine Books, 1994), 56–58. Waugh, Ewing, and Tidball mistakenly confused George for William Crittenden—an understandable error given that they were cousins, the passage of time, and George Crittenden's prominence as a Confederate general.

45. H. Ewing, "Autobiography of a Tramp," 42–43; Waugh, *Class of 1846,* 57.

46. H. Ewing, "Autobiography of a Tramp," 44; Emory M. Thomas, *Robert E. Lee: A Biography* (New York: W. W. Norton, 1995), 152.

47. Marszalek, *Sherman*, 26–27; Ellen Ewing to Hugh Ewing, January 8, 1847; Ellen Ewing to Hugh Ewing, June 30, 1847 (Hugh Ewing Papers, Box 1, OHS).

48. H. Ewing, "Autobiography of a Tramp," 26–27, 48; Tidball, *"No Disgrace to My Country,"* 49.

49. H. Ewing, "Autobiography of a Tramp," 26–27; Tidball, *"No Disgrace to My Country,"* 49; Porter, "Not So Strange Bedfellows"; Morris, *Sheridan*, 15; Philip H. Sheridan, *Personal Memoirs of P. H. Sheridan* (New York: Charles Webster, 1888), 1:7, 9.

50. H. Ewing, "Autobiography of a Tramp," 26–27; Sheridan, *Personal Memoirs,* 1:7, 9; Paul Andrew Hutton, *Phil Sheridan and His Army* (Norman: University of Oklahoma Press, 1999), 274.

51. H. Ewing, "Autobiography of a Tramp," 48–49; Hugh Ewing, "The Gold Plague," *Rosary: A Monthly Magazine* 3 (May 1893–April 1894): 828–32.

52. Gary G. Hamilton, "The Structural Sources of Adventurism: The Case of the California Gold Rush," *American Journal of Sociology* 83 (May 1978): 1466–90; Janet R. Fireman, ed., "R. P. Effinger's Excellent Adventure: The Unknown Letters of a Young Ohio Lawyer, 1849–1850," *California History* 82 (January

2004): 2–75; H. Ewing, "Autobiography of a Tramp," 50–51; Wiseman, *Pioneer Period*, 82–83.

53. Gary Hamilton, "Structural Sources of Adventurism," 1466–90; H. Ewing, "Autobiography of a Tramp," 51; Maria Ewing to Thomas Ewing, February 15, 1849 (Thomas Ewing Family Papers, Box 159, LOC); Tom Ewing to Hugh Ewing, January 3, 1849 (Hugh Ewing Papers, Box 1, OHS); Tom Ewing to Hugh Ewing, January 19, 1849 (Hugh Ewing Papers, Box 1, OHS); Ellen Ewing to Thomas Ewing, February 15, 1849 (Thomas Ewing Family Papers, Box 159, LOC).

54. H. Ewing, "Gold Plague"; Ellen Ewing to Hugh Ewing, March 3, 1849 (Hugh Ewing Papers, Box 1, OHS); H. Ewing, "Autobiography of a Tramp," 51.

55. "R. P. Effinger's Excellent Adventure," 2–75; Dale L. Morgan and James R. Scobie, eds., *Three Years in California: William Perkins' Journal of Life at Sonora, 1849–1852* (Berkeley: University of California Press, 1964), 73–74; H. Ewing, "Autobiography of a Tramp," 52.

56. H. Ewing, "Autobiography of a Tramp," 54–89.

57. Ibid., 54–56.

58. Ibid., 57–66; Morgan and Scobie, *Three Years in California*, 77–80.

59. H. Ewing, "Autobiography of a Tramp," 57–66; Morgan and Scobie, *Three Years in California*, 77–80.

60. Paul W. Gates, "Adjudication of Spanish-Mexican Land Claims in California," *Huntington Library Quarterly* 21 (May 1958): 213–36; Ulysses S. Grant, *Personal Memoirs* (New York: Modern Library, 1999), 101–2.

61. H. Ewing, "Autobiography of a Tramp," 103–18; Ellen Ewing to Hugh Ewing, August 10, 1849 (Hugh Ewing Papers, Box 1, OHS); Ellen Ewing to Hugh Ewing, September 12, 1849 (Hugh Ewing Papers, Box 1, OHS); Ellen Ewing to Hugh Ewing, May 18, 1849 (Hugh Ewing Papers, Box 1, OHS); Marszalek, *Sherman*, 75; William T. Sherman, *Memoirs of General William T. Sherman*, vol. 1 (New York: D. Appleton, 1891), 81.

62. H. Ewing, "Autobiography of a Tramp," 103–18; Journal of Brevet Major D. H. Rucker, U.S. Army, "Operations for the Relief of the Overland Emigrants to California, 1849" (Hugh Ewing Papers, Box 1, OHS).

63. Ellen Ewing to Hugh Ewing, May 18, 1849; Ellen Ewing to Hugh Ewing, July 8, 1849 (Hugh Ewing Papers, Box 1, OHS).

64. Burton, *Three Generations*, 76–77; W. Sherman, *Memoirs*, 1:82–83; Roy Nichols, "William Tecumseh Sherman in 1850," *Pennsylvania Magazine of History and Biography* 75 (1951): 424–35.

65. William T. Sherman to Ellen Ewing, August 21, 1839; Boyer, "Theology of the Battlefield," 1005–34; Burton, *Three Generations*, 76.

66. Marszalek, *Sherman*, 114–15; Lee Kennett, *Sherman: A Soldier's Life* (New York: HarperCollins, 2001), 98–99.

67. William T. Sherman to John Sherman, January 14, 1851, in *The Sherman Letters: Correspondence between General and Senator Sherman from 1837 to 1891,*

ed. Rachel Sherman Thorndike (New York: Charles Scribner's Sons, 1894), 48–49; W. Sherman, *Memoirs*, 85–87; Zsoldos, "Political Career," 230–31; Marszalek, *Sherman*, 82–83.

68. Zsoldos, "Political Career," 243–44.

69. H. Roger Grant, *Ohio on the Move: Transportation in the Buckeye State* (Athens: Ohio University Press, 2000), 66; Charles Richard Williams, *The Life of Rutherford Birchard Hayes* (Boston: Houghton Mifflin, 1914), 1:91–93; Rutherford B. Hayes to Thomas Ewing, February 11, 1853 (Thomas Ewing Family Papers, Box 159, LOC).

70. Lida Rose McCabe, "The 'Martha Washington' Case," *English Illustrated Magazine* 16 (October 1896–March 1897): 695–703; George Irving Reed, ed., *Bench and Bar of Ohio: A Compendium of History and Biography* (Chicago: Century Publishing and Engraving, 1897), 1:75–83; *The Methodist Church Property Case* (Cincinnati: Swormstedt and Poe, 1852).

71. *Methodist Church Property Case*; Henry G. O'Connor, *John Archibald Campbell: Associate Justice of the United States Supreme Court, 1853–1861* (Boston: Houghton Mifflin, 1920), 24; John S. Goff, "The Rejection of United States Supreme Court Appointments," *American Journal of Legal History* 5 (October 1961): 357–68.

72. Stephen E. Maizlish, *The Triumph of Sectionalism: The Transformation of Ohio Politics, 1844–1856* (Kent: Kent State University Press, 1983), 192; Stephen E. Maizlish, "Ohio and the Rise of Sectional Politics," in *The Pursuit of Public Power: Political Culture in Ohio, 1787–1861*, ed. Jeffrey P. Brown and Andrew R. L. Cayton (Kent: Kent State University Press, 1994), 134; Zsoldos, "Political Career," 249.

73. Etcheson, "Southern Influence," 56, 417; Zsoldos, "Political Career," 247; Michael F. Holt, *The Rise and Fall of the American Whig Party: Jacksonian Politics and the Onset of the Civil War* (New York: Oxford University Press, 1999), 660, 752.

74. Eugene H. Roseboom, *The Civil War Era, 1850–1973*, History of the State of Ohio 4 (Columbus: Ohio Historical Society, 1968), 293.

75. Ibid., 282, 295; J. Sherman, *Recollections*, 1:102–3; Joseph P. Smith, *History of the Republican Party in Ohio* (Chicago: Lewis, 1898), 1:17.

76. Jed Dannenbaum, *Drink and Disorder: Temperance Reform in Cincinnati from the Washington Revival to the WCTU* (Urbana: University of Illinois Press, 158–60; Eugene H. Roseboom, "Salmon P. Chase and the Know Nothings," *Mississippi Valley Historical Review* 25 (December 1938): 335–50; Eric J. Cardinal, "The Democratic Party of Ohio and the Civil War: An Analysis of a Wartime Political Minority" (PhD diss., Kent State University, 1981), 14; Roseboom, *Civil War Era*, 282, 303.

77. Roseboom, "Salmon P. Chase," 335–50; Daryl Pendergraft, "Thomas Corwin and the Conservative Republican Reaction, 1858–1861," *Ohio History*

57 (1948): 1–23; Cardinal, "Democratic Party of Ohio," 14; Maizlish, "Ohio," 139–40.

78. Dannenbaum, *Drink and Disorder*, 161, 163, 16; Roseboom, "Salmon P. Chase," 335–50; Cardinal, "Democratic Party of Ohio," 14–18; Roseboom, *Civil War Era*, 322.

79. *Memorial of Thomas Ewing of Ohio* (New York: Catholic Publication Society, 1873), 49.

80. Fireman, "R. P. Effinger's Excellent Adventure," 27; "The Story of a Noble Life," in *The Catholic Record: A Miscellany of Catholic Knowledge and General Literature, Volume 8* (Philadelphia: Hardy and Mahony, 1874), 1–12.

81. Tom Ewing to Thomas Ewing, May 1, 1853 (Thomas Ewing Family Papers, Box 159, LOC); Tom Ewing to Thomas Ewing, May 17, 1853 (Thomas Ewing Family Papers, Box 159, LOC); Obituary, "General Thomas Ewing," *NYT*, January 22, 1896; "General Thomas Ewing," in *A Biographical Record of Fairfield County, Ohio* (New York: S. J. Clarke, 1902), 476–77.

82. Zsoldos, "Political Career," 246, 251; Rose, *Beloved Strangers*, 32–33.

83. Morris, *Sheridan*, 13; Hugh Ewing to Thomas Ewing, February 8, 1853 (Thomas Ewing Family Papers, Box 159, LOC).

84. Tony R. Mullis, *Peacekeeping on the Plains: Army Operations in Bleeding Kansas* (Columbia: University of Missouri Press, 2004), 26, 38; Floyd Shoemaker, "Missouri's Pro-Slavery Fight for Kansas, Part I," *Missouri Historical Review* 48 (1954): 221–36.

85. Shoemaker, "Missouri's Pro-Slavery Fight [Part I]"; Thomas Goodrich, *War to the Knife: Bleeding Kansas, 1854–1861* (Mechanicsburg, PA: Stackpole Books, 1998), 15; Albert Castel, *A Frontier State at War: Kansas, 1861–1865* (Ithaca: Cornell University Press, 1958), 7.

86. Mullis, *Peacekeeping on the Plains*, 49–50, 56; Goodrich, *War to the Knife*, 27–28, 32.

87. Goodrich, *War to the Knife*, 23–24, 27; Robert A. Carter, *Buffalo Bill Cody: The Man behind the Legend* (Edison, NJ: Castel Books, 2000), 18–21.

88. Christopher Phillips, "'The Crime against Missouri': Slavery, Kansas, and the Cant of Southernness in the Border West," *Civil War History* 48 (2002): 60–81; Samuel A. Johnson, "The Emigrant Aid Company in Kansas," *Kansas Historical Quarterly* 1 (1932): 429–41; Shoemaker, "Missouri's Pro-Slavery Fight [Part I]"; Louise Barry, "The Emigrant Aid Company Parties of 1854," *Kansas Historical Quarterly* 12 (1943): 115–55; Goodrich, *War to the Knife*, 70–72.

89. Mullis, *Peacekeeping on the Plains*, 23–24; Goodrich, *War to the Knife*, 34, 38.

90. Goodrich, *War to the Knife*, 47, 56; Salmon P. Chase, reference letter for John Brown, December 20, 1856 (John Brown Collection, Box 1, KSHS).

91. Patrick, "John Sherman," 58–63; J. Sherman, *Recollections*, 1:129.

92. Goodrich, *War to the Knife*, 110, 114–17; Edgar Langsdorf, "S. C. Pomeroy and the New England Emigrant Aid Company, 1854–1858," *Kansas Historical Quarterly* 7 (1938): 379–98; Shoemaker, "Missouri's Pro-Slavery Fight for Kansas, Part III," *Missouri Historical Review* 49 (1954): 41–54.

93. J. Sherman, *Recollections*, 1:131; Patrick, "John Sherman," 63–66.

94. Goodrich, *War to the Knife*, 119, 123, 143; Castel, *Frontier State at War*, 19–20.

95. Thomas Goodrich, *Black Flag: Guerrilla Warfare on the Western Border, 1861–1865* (Bloomington: Indiana University Press, 1995), 16; William Stanley Hoole, ed., "A Southerner's Viewpoint of the Kansas Situation, 1856–1857: The Letters of Lieut. Col. A. J. Hoole, CSA," *Kansas Historical Quarterly* 3 (1934): 43–56; V. E. Gibbens, ed., "Letters on the War in Kansas in 1856," *Kansas Historical Quarterly* 10 (1941): 369–79.

96. Thomas Ewing, *The Struggle for Freedom in Kansas* (New York: Cosmopolitan Magazine Press, 1894).

97. Castel, *Frontier State at War*, 4, 13; Floyd Shoemaker, "Missouri's Pro-Slavery Fight for Kansas, Part II," *Missouri Historical Review* 48 (1954): 325–40.

98. Castel, *Frontier State at War*, 7–8, 10–11; James R. Shortridge, *Cities on the Plains: The Evolution of Urban Kansas* (Lawrence: University of Kansas Press, 2004), 58.

99. Paul Wallace Gates, *Fifty Million Acres: Conflicts over Kansas Land Policy, 1854–1890* (Ithaca: Cornell University Press, 1954), 50–51; Thomas Ewing Jr. to Thomas Ewing, July 25, 1857 (Thomas Ewing Letter Press Book 1, KSHS); Shortridge, *Cities on the Plains*, 60.

100. Gates, *Fifty Million Acres*, 128–30, 157–58.

101. David G. Taylor, "Thomas Ewing, Jr., and the Origins of the Kansas Pacific Railway Company," *Kansas Historical Quarterly* 42 (1976): 155–79; Thomas Ewing Jr. to Thomas Ewing, July 14, 1857 (Thomas Ewing Letter Press Book 1, KSHS); Thomas Ewing Jr. to William F. Roelofson, March 26, 1859 (Thomas Ewing Letter Press Book 2, KSHS); Shortridge, *Cities on the Plains*, 99–100.

102. Thomas Ewing Jr. to John Sherman, December 16, 1859 (Thomas Ewing Letter Press Book 3, KSHS); Marion Mills Miller, ed., *Great Debates in American History* (New York: Current Literature Publishing, 1913), 5:107.

103. Thomas Ewing Jr. to Thomas Ewing, October 26, 1859 (Thomas Ewing Family Papers, Box 161, LOC); Thomas Ewing Jr. to Thomas Ewing, July 14, 1857 (Thomas Ewing Letter Press Book 1, KSHS); Thomas Ewing Jr. to Thomas Ewing, May 11, 1859 (Thomas Ewing Letter Press Book 3, KSHS); Marszalek, *Sherman*, 116.

104. Thomas Ewing Jr. to Thomas Ewing, October 20, 1859 (Thomas Ewing Family Papers, Box 161, LOC); Goodrich, *Black Flag*, 7; Castel, *Frontier State at War*, 14.

105. Thomas Ewing Jr. to Thomas Ewing, September 5, 1859 (Thomas Ewing Family Papers, Box 161, LOC); Sherman, Ewing & McCook to George B. Parker, April 4, 1859 (Thomas Ewing Letter Press Book 2, KSHS).

106. Thomas Ewing Jr. to Thomas Ewing, May 11, 1859; Thomas Ewing Jr. to Thomas Ewing, January 6, 1859 (Thomas Ewing Family Papers, Box 161, LOC).

107. George W. Brown, *Reminiscences of Gov. R. J. Walker: With the True Story of the Rescue of Kansas from Slavery* (1902; repr., Westport, CT: Negro Universities Press, 1970), 164–65; Castel, *Frontier State at War*, 5, 25; T. Ewing, *Struggle for Freedom.*

108. Brown, *Reminiscences,* 164–65; T. Ewing, *Struggle for Freedom;* Reed, *Bench and Bar,* 1:116.

109. William Elsey Connelley, *The Life of Preston B. Plumb, 1837–1891: United States Senator for Kansas for the Fourteen Years from 1877 to 1891* (Chicago: Brown and Howell, 1913), 80–82, 84, 90; Brown, *Reminiscences,* 136–49.

110. Castel, *Frontier State at War*, 25–26; Thomas Ewing Jr. to the Seward Club of Lawrence, Kansas, October 24, 1859 (Thomas Ewing Correspondence, Box 3, KSHS).

111. Thomas Ewing Jr. to R. B. Mitchell, December 15, 1858 (Thomas Ewing Letter Press Book 2, KSHS); Thomas Ewing Jr. to Thomas Ewing, August 5, 1857 (Thomas Ewing Letter Press Book 1, KSHS); Brown, *Reminiscences,* 140–41.

112. Thomas Ewing Jr. to James G. Blaine, *NYT,* May 28, 1858.

113. Thomas Ewing Jr. to Thomas Ewing, July 14, 1857 (Thomas Ewing Letter Press Book 1, KSHS); Thomas Ewing Jr. to Thomas Ewing, November 17, 1858 (Thomas Ewing Family Papers, Box 161, LOC); Deshler Welch, "The City of Columbus," *Harper's Weekly* 76 (December 1887–May 1888): 715–26; Ronald D. Smith, *Thomas Ewing, Jr.: Frontier Lawyer and Civil War General* (Columbia: University of Missouri Press, 2008), 48.

114. Burton, *Three Generations,* 94; Marszalek, *Sherman,* 114–15.

115. Burton, *Three Generations,* 119–20; Marszalek, *Sherman,* 114–16.

116. Ellen Sherman to Hugh Ewing, January 15, 1859 (Thomas Ewing Family Papers, Box 161, LOC); Thomas Ewing Jr. to Thomas Ewing, November 9, 1859 (Thomas Ewing Family Papers, Box 161, LOC); Thomas Ewing Jr. to Maria Maher, September 14, 1859 (Thomas Ewing Letter Press Book 3, KSHS); Lewis, *Sherman, Fighting Prophet,* 110.

117. Marszalek, *Sherman,* 117; Lewis, *Sherman, Fighting Prophet,* 105–6; Shortridge, *Cities on the Plains,* 60–61.

118. Burton, *Three Generations,* 117–18; R. Smith, *Thomas Ewing, Jr.,* 72–73.

119. "General Hugh Ewing" (Thomas Ewing Family Papers, Box 262, LOC); Ellen Ewing Sherman to Hugh Ewing, May 18, 1858 (Thomas Ewing Family Papers, Box 161, LOC); Maria Ewing to Hugh Ewing, May 4, 1858 (Hugh Ewing Papers, Box 1, OHS).

120. Burton, *Three Generations,* 117–18; R. Smith, *Thomas Ewing, Jr.,* 80–81.

121. Shortridge, *Cities on the Plains,* 58; Sister Julia Gilmore, *Come North! The Life Story of Mother Xavier Ross, Valiant Pioneer and Foundress of the Sisters of*

Charity of Leavenworth (New York: McMullen Books, 1951), 81, 113, 116, 119, 122; Thomas Ewing Jr. to Hugh Ewing, July 27, 1859 (Thomas Ewing Letter Press Book 3, KSHS); R. Smith, *Thomas Ewing, Jr.*, 41–42.

122. Clarke, *In Memoriam*, 18–19.

123. Charles Ewing to Thomas Ewing, February 3, 1859 (Thomas Ewing Family Papers, Box 161, LOC); Clarke, *In Memoriam*, 20–21; Burton, *Three Generations*, 123–14.

124. S. A. Bronson, *John Sherman: What He Said and Done, Being a History of the Life and Public Services of the Hon. John Sherman* (Columbus: H. W. Derby, 1880), 59–61; Patrick, "John Sherman," 1–2.

125. Brian McGinty, *Lincoln and the Court* (Cambridge, MA: Harvard University Press, 2008), 20–21, 44, 47.

126. Roseboom, *Civil War Era*, 326–27, 341–42; Frank L. Klement, *The Limits of Dissent: Clement L. Vallandigham and the Civil War* (Lexington: University Press of Kentucky, 1970), 15.

127. Roseboom, *Civil War Era*, 344–46; C. L. Martzolff, ed., "Thomas Ewing: Address at Marietta, Ohio, 1858," *Ohio History* 28 (1919): 186–207; Patrick, "John Sherman," 68–69.

128. McGinty, *Lincoln and the Court*, 33–34; Thomas Cecil Mulligan, "Lest the Rebels Come to Power: The Life of William Dennison, 1815–1882, Early Ohio Republican" (PhD diss., Ohio State University, 1994), 101, 122.

129. Mary Land, "Ben Wade," in *For the Union: Ohio Leaders in the Civil War*, ed. Kenneth W. Wheeler (Columbus: Ohio State University Press, 1968), 161; Frank L. Klement, "Clement L. Vallandigham," in Wheeler, *For the Union*, 5.

130. Mulligan, "Lest the Rebels Come," 123; Roseboom, *Civil War Era*, 359; David R. Contosta, *Lancaster, Ohio, 1800–2000: Frontier Town to Edge City* (Columbus: Ohio State University Press, 1999), 59–60.

NOTES TO CHAPTER THREE

The chapter epigraph is from a letter from Thomas Ewing Jr. to Hugh Ewing, April 15, 1861 (Hugh Ewing Papers, Box 2, OHS).

1. David G. Taylor, "Boom Town Leavenworth: The Failure of the Dream," *Kansas Historical Quarterly* 38 (1972): 389–415; Thomas Ewing Jr. to A. J. Isacks, May 20, 1860 (Thomas Ewing Letter Press Book 4, KSHS); Thomas Ewing Jr. to Thomas Ewing, April 21, 1860 (Thomas Ewing Family Papers, Box 161, LOC); Thomas Ewing Jr. to Thomas Ewing, April 7, 1860 (Thomas Ewing Family Papers, Box 161, LOC).

2. Taylor, "Boom Town Leavenworth"; Thomas Ewing Jr. to Thomas Ewing, March 2, 1860 (Thomas Ewing Family Papers, Box 161, LOC).

3. Thomas Ewing Jr. to Hamp Denman, February 23, 1860 (Thomas Ewing Letter Press Book 3, KSHS); Thomas Ewing Jr. to Thomas Ewing, February 2, 1860 (Thomas Ewing Family Papers, Box 161, LOC).

4. Joseph G. Gambone, "Samuel C. Pomeroy and the Senatorial Election of 1861, Reconsidered," *Kansas Historical Quarterly* 37 (1971): 15–32; Thomas Ewing Jr. to Thomas Ewing, February 2, 1860; Thomas Ewing Jr. to John Hanna, January 26, 1860 (Thomas Ewing Letter Press Book 3, KSHS); Thomas Ewing Jr. to J. J. Combs, January 22, 1861 (Thomas Ewing Letter Press Book 4, KSHS).

5. Gambone, "Samuel C. Pomeroy"; Albert Castel, *A Frontier State at War: Kansas, 1861–1865* (Ithaca: Cornell University Press, 1958), 24.

6. Thomas Ewing Jr. to Abraham Lincoln, May 6, 1860 (Abraham Lincoln Papers, LOC, transcribed and annotated by the Lincoln Studies Center, Knox College, Galesburg, IL); Thomas Ewing Jr. to Thomas Vernon, February 23, 1860 (Thomas Ewing Letter Press Book 3, KSHS); Allan Nevins, *The War for the Union: The Improvised War, 1861–1862* (New York: Charles Scribner's Sons, 1959), 51.

7. Thomas Ewing Jr. to Charley Ewing, May 1, 1860 (Thomas Ewing Letter Press Book 3, KSHS); Hugh Ewing to Thomas Ewing, April 23, 1860 (Thomas Ewing Family Papers, Box 161, LOC); Ronald D. Smith, *Thomas Ewing, Jr.: Frontier Lawyer and Civil War General* (Lawrence: University of Kansas Press, 2008), 112–113.

8. Thomas Ewing, *Speech of the Hon. Thomas Ewing at Chillicothe, Ohio, before a Republican Mass Meeting, September 29th, 1860* (Cincinnati: Rickey, Mallory, 1860).

9. Allen C. Guelzo, *The Crisis of the American Republic: A History of the Civil War and Reconstruction Era* (New York: St. Martin's Press, 1995), 73.

10. Harold Holzer, *Lincoln President-Elect: Abraham Lincoln and the Great Secession Winter, 1860–1861* (New York: Simon and Schuster, 2008), 20.

11. Ewing, *Speech of the Hon. Thomas Ewing*; Silvia Tammisto Zsoldos, "The Political Career of Thomas Ewing, Sr." (PhD diss., University of Delaware, 1977), 255.

12. Ewing, *Speech of the Hon. Thomas Ewing*; Zsoldos, "Political Career," 256.

13. George W. Julian, *The Life of Joshua R. Giddings* (Chicago: A. C. McClurg, 1892), 377–83; Zsoldos, "Political Career," 255–56.

14. Ellen Ewing Sherman to Hugh Ewing, September 7, 1860 (Thomas Ewing Family Papers, Box 161, LOC).

15. Eugene H. Roseboom, *The Civil War Era, 1850–1973*, History of the State of Ohio 4 (Columbus: Ohio Historical Society, 1968), 365–66, 371.

16. John Jose Patrick, "John Sherman: The Early Years, 1823–1865" (PhD diss., Kent State University, 1982), 112; Ollinger Crenshaw, "The Speakership Contest of 1859–1860: John Sherman's Election a Cause of Disruption?" *Mississippi Valley Historical Review* 29 (December 1942): 323–38.

17. Joseph Medill to Abraham Lincoln, December 18, 1860 (Abraham Lincoln Papers, LOC, transcribed and annotated by the Lincoln Studies Center, Knox

College, Galesburg, IL); John Sherman, *Recollections of Forty Years in the House, Senate, and Cabinet* (Chicago: Werner, 1895), 1:226.

18. Charles R. Wilson, "Cincinnati, a Southern Outpost in 1860–1861?" *Mississippi Valley Historical Review* 24 (March 1938): 473–82; Thomas Cecil Mulligan, "Lest the Rebels Come to Power: The Life of William Dennison, 1815–1882, Early Ohio Republican" (PhD diss., Ohio State University, 1994), 131–32.

19. Jerry R. Desmond, "Maine and the Elections of 1860," *New England Quarterly* 67 (September 1994): 455–75; Holzer, *Lincoln President-Elect*, 42.

20. Michael Fellman, *Inside War: The Guerrilla Conflict in Missouri During the American Civil War* (New York: Oxford University Press, 1989), 8.

21. William E. Parrish, *Turbulent Partnership: Missouri and the Union, 1861–1865* (Columbia: University of Missouri Press, 1963), 5–7.

22. Worthington G. Snethen to Abraham Lincoln, December 8, 1860 (Abraham Lincoln Papers, LOC, transcribed and annotated by the Lincoln Studies Center, Knox College, Galesburg, IL); Thomas Ewing Jr. to W. R. Griffith, December 18, 1860 (Thomas Ewing Letter Press Book 4, KSHS).

23. Zsoldos, "Political Career," 258–59.

24. Richard H. Abbott, "Henry Wilson," in *American National Biography On-Line*, February 2000, American Council of Learned Societies, www.anb.org; Henry Wilson, *History of the Rise and Fall of the Slave Power in America*, vol. 3 (Boston: James R. Osgood, 1877), 92–93; Robert G. Gunderson, "The Washington Peace Conference of 1861: Selection of Delegates," *Journal of Southern History* 24 (August 1958): 347–59; Robert Gray Gunderson, "Letters from the Washington Peace Conference of 1861," *Journal of Southern History* 17 (August 1951): 382–92.

25. Gunderson, "Washington Peace Conference"; Gunderson, "Letters"; Nevins, *War for the Union*, 121.

26. Gunderson, "Washington Peace Conference"; David M. Potter, *Lincoln and His Party in the Secession Crisis* (Baton Rouge: Louisiana University Press, 1995), 36–37; Samuel S. Cox, *Three Decades of Federal Legislation, 1855 to 1885* (Providence, RI: J. A. and R. A. Reid, 1885), 88.

27. Gunderson, "Washington Peace Conference"; Potter, *Lincoln and His Party*, 353; "Domestic Intelligence," *Harper's Weekly* 5 (February 16, 1861): 102–3; Kenneth M. Stampp, "Letters from the Washington Peace Conference of 1861," *Journal of Southern History* 9 (August 1943): 394–403; Eric J. Cardinal, "The Democratic Party of Ohio and the Civil War: An Analysis of a Wartime Political Minority" (PhD diss., Kent State University, 1981), 56.

28. "Incendiary Publications," *Liberator*, June 25, 1836; "Rare Impudence," *Liberator*, September 13, 1850; "Our Washington Correspondence," *Charleston Mercury*, February 15, 1861.

29. Gunderson, "Letters"; George S. Boutwell, *Reminiscences of Sixty Years in Public Affairs* (New York: McClure, Phillips, 1902), 1:268–69.

30. Zsoldos, "Political Career," 259–62; L. E. Chittenden, *A Report of the Debates and Proceedings in the Secret Sessions of the Conference Convention for Proposing Amendments to the Constitution of the United States Held at Washington, DC, in February 1861* (New York: D. Appleton, 1864), 141–44.

31. Chittenden, *Report of the Debates*, 141–44; Howard C. Westwood, "The Real Lost Cause: The Peace Convention of 1861," *Military Affairs* 27 (Autumn 1963): 119–30.

32. Chittenden, *Report of the Debates*.

33. David Herbert Donald, *Lincoln* (New York: Simon and Schuster, 1995), 268, 280; Westwood, "Real Lost Cause."

34. Thomas Ewing Jr. to Hugh Ewing, January 17, 1861 (Thomas Ewing Letter Press Book 4, KSHS); Thomas Ewing Jr. to Thomas Ewing, January 20, 1861 (Thomas Ewing Letter Press Book 4, KSHS); Thomas Ewing Jr. to James Lane, January 25, 1861 (Thomas Ewing Letter Press Book 4, KSHS).

35. Maria Theresa Ewing to Thomas Ewing, January 26, 1860 (Thomas Ewing Family Papers, Box 161, LOC).

36. Nathan Sargent to Abraham Lincoln, November 12, 1860 (Abraham Lincoln Papers, LOC, transcribed and annotated by the Lincoln Studies Center, Knox College, Galesburg, IL); Brian McGinty, *Lincoln and the Court* (Cambridge, MA: Harvard University Press, 2008), 27, 93; Nevins, *War for the Union*, 22. Nathan Sargent was quoting Campbell's opinion of Thomas Ewing.

37. Thomas Ewing to Andrew Johnson, June 29, 1865, in *The Papers of Andrew Johnson*, vol. 7, *1864–1865*, ed. Leroy P. Graf, Patricia P. Clark, and Marion O. Smith (Knoxville: University of Tennessee Press, 1986), 311–12; Nevins, *War for the Union*, 72.

38. McGinty, *Lincoln and the Court*, 76–78, 93–94, 205–6; Thomas E. Jeffrey, "George Edmund Badger," in *American National Biography On-Line*, February 2000, American Council of Learned Societies, www.anb.org.

39. Westwood, "Real Lost Cause"; Benjamin Tuska, "Know-Nothingism in Baltimore, 1854–1860," *Catholic Historical Review* 11 (July 1925): 217–51; William L. Barney, "Reverdy Johnson," in *American National Biography On-Line*, February 2000, American Council of Learned Societies, www.anb.org.

40. Thomas E. Stephens, "John Jordan Crittenden," in *American National Biography On-Line*, February 2000, American Council of Learned Societies, www.anb.org; Thomas Ewing to John J. Crittenden, June 25, 1861, in , *The Life of John J. Crittenden: With Selections from His Correspondence and Speeches*, ed. Chapman Coleman and Ann Mary Butler Coleman, 2 vols. (Philadelphia: J. P. Lippincott, 1970), 2:322–33.

41. Thomas Ewing Jr. to Hugh Ewing, April 15, 1861; Jay Monaghan, *Civil War on the Western Border, 1854–1865* (Boston: Little, Brown, 1955), 128; "General

Lane and His Army," *Harper's Weekly* 5 (November 23, 1861): 738; Castel, *Frontier State at War*, 34–35.

42. Katherine Burton, *Three Generations: Maria Boyle Ewing, Ellen Ewing Sherman, Minnie Sherman Fitch* (New York: Longmans, Green, 1947), 129.

43. Lloyd Lewis, *Sherman, Fighting Prophet* (New York: Harcourt, Brace, 1932), 157–58; Edward O. C. Ord to Abraham Lincoln, December 28, 1860 (Abraham Lincoln Papers, LOC, transcribed and annotated by the Lincoln Studies Center, Knox College, Galesburg, IL).

44. Burton, *Three Generations*, 131; William T. Sherman, *Memoirs of General William T. Sherman*, vol. 1 (New York: D. Appleton 1891), 167–68.

45. Richard S. Brownlee, *Gray Ghosts of the Confederacy: Guerrilla Warfare in the West, 1861–1865* (Baton Rouge: Louisiana State University Press, 1958), 12; Donald B. Connelly, *John M. Schofield and the Politics of Generalship* (Chapel Hill: University of North Carolina Press, 2006), 25–27; Albert Castel, *General Sterling Price and the Civil War in the West* (Baton Rouge: Louisiana State University Press, 1968), 12; Charles Ewing to Hugh Ewing, December 19, 1860, in *In Memoriam: Charles Ewing*, by Luke Clarke (Philadelphia: J. B. Lippincott, 1888), 29.

46. William Ernest Smith, *The Francis Preston Blair Family in Politics* (New York: Da Capo, 1969), 2:26; Brownlee, *Gray Ghosts*, 14; Connelly, *John M. Schofield*, 23–24; Castel, *General Sterling Price*, 11.

47. Parrish, *Turbulent Partnership*, 7; Snethen to Lincoln, December 8, 1860.

48. William T. Sherman to Thomas Ewing Jr., May 23, 1861, in *Home Letters of General Sherman*, ed. M. A. DeWolfe Howe (New York: Charles Scribner's Sons, 1909), 197–98; W. Smith, *Francis Preston Blair Family*, 32, 45, 114.

59. Christopher Phillips, *Damned Yankee: The Life of General Nathaniel Lyon* (Baton Rouge: Louisiana State University Press, 1996); Connelly, *John M. Schofield*, 24.

50. Parrish, *Turbulent Partnership*, 20; W. Smith, *Francis Preston Blair Family*, 32.

51. Connelly, *John M. Schofield*, 27; Brownlee, *Gray Ghosts*, 13; Fellman, *Inside War*, 9.

52. W. Sherman, *Memoirs*, 1:173–74; Connelly, *John M. Schofield*, 27; Brownlee, *Gray Ghosts of the Confederacy*, 13–14; Ellen Ewing Sherman to Hugh Ewing, September 19, 1860 (Thomas Ewing Family Papers, Box 161, LOC). The Union generals were Frank Blair, Charley Ewing, Hugh Ewing, Ulysses Grant, Nathaniel Lyon, John Schofield, and William Sherman. The Confederate generals were Sterling Price and Joe Shelby.

53. Ellen Ewing Sherman to Thomas Ewing, May 11, 1861 (William T. Sherman Family Papers, UNDA, Box 15); W. Sherman, *Memoirs*, 1:173–74; Castel, *General Sterling Price*, 13–14; Brownlee, *Gray Ghosts*, 13–14.

54. Castel, *General Sterling Price*, 14. Four Union soldiers and twelve Baltimore civilians had died as a result of the April 19, 1861 riot.

55. Mulligan, "Lest the Rebels Come," 146, 148, 169; Roseboom, *Civil War Era*, 385; Whitelaw Reid, *Ohio in the War: Her Statesmen, Her Generals, and Soldiers* (Cincinnati: Moore, Wilstach, and Baldwin, 1868), 1:770–71.

56. Mulligan, "Lest the Rebels Come," 122, 133, 198; Roseboom, *Civil War Era*, 385–86; Brian D. McKnight, *Contested Borderland: The Civil War in Appalachian Kentucky and Virginia* (Lexington: University Press of Kentucky, 2006), 25.

57. Mulligan, "Lest the Rebels Come," 152, 207; Richard Nelson Current, *Lincoln's Loyalists: Union Soldiers from the Confederacy* (Boston: Northeastern University Press, 1992), 6–7; Guelzo, *Crisis of the American Republic*, 143.

58. Gerald J. Prokopowicz, *All for the Regiment: The Army of the Ohio, 1861–1862* (Chapel Hill: University of North Carolina Press, 2001), 31, 39; Noel Fisher, "Groping toward Victory: Ohio's Administration of the Civil War," *Ohio History* 105 (1996): 25–45.

59. Mulligan, "Lest the Rebels Come," 150, 161, 164.

60. Ibid., 164, 178–79; Joseph P. Smith, *History of the Republican Party in Ohio, 2 Volumes* (Chicago: Lewis, 1898), 211[au: which volume is it in?]; Reid, *Ohio in the War*, 1:771.

61. David R. Contosta, *Lancaster, Ohio, 1800–2000: Frontier Town to Edge City* (Columbus: Ohio State University Press, 1999), 60–61; Burton, *Three Generations*, 134–35; Hervey Scott, *A Complete History of Fairfield County, Ohio, 1795–1876* (1877; repr., Marceline, MO: Walsworth, 1983), 114; Maria Ewing to Charles Ewing, April 18, 1861, in Clarke, *In Memoriam*, 33.

62. Contosta, *Lancaster, Ohio*, 59, 64; Jacque Voegeli, *Free but Not Equal: The Midwest and the Negro during the Civil War* (Chicago: University of Chicago Press, 1967), 9.

63. Taylor, "Boom Town Leavenworth"; David G. Taylor, "Thomas Ewing, Jr., and the Origins of the Kansas Pacific Railway Company," *Kansas Historical Quarterly* 42 (1976): 155–79; Lewis, *Sherman, Fighting Prophet*, 251.

64. Richard Orr Curry, *A House Divided: A Study of Statehood Politics and the Copperhead Movement in West Virginia* (Pittsburgh: University of Pittsburgh Press, 1964), 9, 35–36; Virgil Carrington Jones, *Gray Ghosts and Rebel Raiders* (New York: Galahad Books, 1995), 14–19, 26.

65. T. H. Barton, *Autobiography of Thomas H. Barton, the Self-Made Physician of Syracuse, Ohio, including a History of the Fourth Regiment, West Virginia Volunteer Infantry* (Charleston: West Virginia Printing, 1890), 74–75; Curry, *House Divided*, 2, 38; Current, *Lincoln's Loyalists*, 9; "The First West Virginia Infantry," *West Virginia History* 55 (1996): 41–96, repr. of *Annual Report of the Adjutant General of the State of West Virginia for the Year Ending December 31, 1864*.

66. Mulligan, "Lest the Rebels Come," 153; Roseboom, *Civil War Era*, 384; George McClellan to William Dennison, May 13, 1861, in *The Civil War Papers of George B. McClellan*, ed. Stephen W. Sears (New York: Da Capo, 1992), 18–19.

67. Curry, *House Divided*, 55; Harvey S. Ford, ed., *John Beatty, Memoirs of a Volunteer, 1861–1863* (New York: W. W. Norton, 1946), 17.

68. John Alexander Williams, *West Virginia: A History* (New York: W. W. Norton, 1984), 59; Ruth Woods Dayton, "The Beginning—Philippi 1861," *West Virginia History* 13 (1952): 254–66.

69. Michael J. Snaufer, "The Thirteenth Ohio Volunteer Infantry" (MA thesis, Baylor University, 2005), 1–4, 23, 26, 35.

70. Ibid., 20, 26; Otis K. Rice, "Coal Mining in the Kanawha Valley to 1861: A View of Industrialization in the Old South," *Journal of Southern History* 31 (November 1965): 393–416; John E. Stealey III, "Slavery in the Kanawha Salt Industry," in *Appalachians and Race: The Mountain South from Slavery to Segregation,* ed. John C. Inscoe (Lexington: University Press of Kentucky, 2001), 50–73.

71. Val Husley, "'Men of Virginia—Men of Kanawha—to Arms!': A History of the Twenty-Second Virginia Volunteer Infantry Regiment, C.S.A.," *West Virginia History* 35 (1973–74): 220–36; Richard O. Curry, "Crisis Politics in West Virginia, 1861–1870," in *Radicalism, Racism, and Party Realignment: The Border States during Reconstruction,* ed. Richard O. Curry (Baltimore: Johns Hopkins University Press, 1969), 82–84. Captain George S. Patton of the Kanawha Rifles was the grandfather of World War II general George S. Patton.

72. Husley, "Men of Virginia"; Roy Bird Cook, "The Civil War Comes to Charleston," *West Virginia History* 23 (1962): 153–67; William T. Price, *Historical Sketches of Pocahontas County, West Virginia* (Marlinton, WV: Price Brothers, 1901), 176–77; Emory M. Thomas, *Robert E. Lee: A Biography* (New York: W. W. Norton, 1995), 194–95.

73. Rutherford Hayes to Lucy Hayes, July 27, 1861, in *Diary and Letters of Rutherford Birchard Hayes,* vol. 2, *1861–1865,* ed. Charles Richard Williams (Columbus: Ohio State Historical Society, 1922), 45–46; Hans L. Trefousse, *Rutherford B. Hayes* (New York: Times Books, 2002), 22.

74. Robert B. Boehm, "The Battle of Rich Mountain, July 11, 1861," *West Virginia History* 20 (1959): 5–15; Dallas B. Shaffer, "Rich Mountain Revisited," *West Virginia History* 28 (1966): 16–34; General Hugh Ewing [Personal Military History], Report, to the Adjutant General of the Army, Washington, DC, 1864 (Hugh Ewing Papers, Box 4, OHS), 3.

75. Thomas, *Robert E. Lee,* 199; Hugh Ewing to Henrietta Ewing, July 1, 1861 (Hugh Ewing Papers, Box 2, OHS); Hugh Ewing to Henrietta Ewing, July 12, 1861 (Hugh Ewing Papers, Box 2, OHS); Jacob Dolson Cox, *Military Reminiscences of the Civil War,* vol. 1, *April 1861–November 1863* (New York: Charles Scribner's Sons, 1900), 47.

76. H. Ewing, [Personal Military History], Report, 4; Price, *Historical Sketches,* 133, 151, 176–77; Hugh Ewing to Henrietta Ewing, July 20, 1861 (Hugh Ewing Papers, Box 2, OHS); Curry, "Crisis Politics," 84–85.

77. H. Ewing, [Personal Military History], Report, 4; Hugh Ewing to Henrietta Ewing, July 20, 1861.

78. Ford, *John Beatty,* 36.

79. Boehm, "Battle of Rich Mountain"; Ford, *John Beatty,* 24, 36; "General Rosecrans' Division," *NYT,* July 31, 1861.

80. Clarice Lorene Bailes, "Jacob Dolson Cox in West Virginia," *West Virginia History* 6 (1944): 5–58; Frank Klement, "General John B. Floyd and the West Virginia Campaigns of 1861," *West Virginia History* 8 (1946): 319–33; Cook, "Civil War Comes to Charleston."

81. Husley, "Men of Virginia"; Bailes, "Jacob Dolson Cox"; Klement, "General John B. Floyd," 319–33; Cook, "Civil War Comes to Charleston"; J. Cox, *Military Reminiscences,* 1:69.

82. Current, *Lincoln's Loyalists,* 8; Bailes, "Jacob Dolson Cox"; Klement, "General John B. Floyd"; J. Williams, *West Virginia,* 62.

83. Bailes, "Jacob Dolson Cox"; Klement, "General John B. Floyd"; J. Cox, *Military Reminiscences,* 1:70, 78–79; John M. Belohlavek, "John B. Floyd and the West Virginia Campaign of 1861," *West Virginia History* 29 (1967): 283–91.

84. Hugh Ewing to Henrietta Ewing, 26 August 1861 (Hugh Ewing Papers, Box 2, OHS); Martha B. Caldwell, ed., "The Diary of George H. Hildt, June to December 1857," *Kansas Historical Quarterly* 10 (1941): 260–98.

85. H. Ewing, [Personal Military History], Report, 5; Hugh Boyle Ewing, "The Autobiography of a Tramp" (Hugh Boyle Ewing Papers, Box 9, OHS), 4–5 (or 205–6). Hugh Ewing's unpublished autobiography has eccentric numbering, so that after the initial couple of hundred pages the numbers revert to lower ones and then go back up to the 200s.

86. C. Williams, *Diary and Letters,* 2:63–65, 68–70.

87. Ibid., 60; Charles Richard Williams, *The Life of Rutherford Birchard Hayes, Nineteenth President of the United States* (Boston: Houghton Mifflin, 1914), 1:146.

88. Thomas, *Robert E. Lee,* 209; A. L. Long, ed., *Memoirs of Robert E. Lee: His Military and Personal History* (Secaucus, NJ: Blue and the Grey Press, 1983), 124–27. A. L. Long was military secretary to Lee and published the original version of his superior's memoirs in 1886.

89. David L. Phillips and Rebecca L. Hill, *War Diaries: The 1861 Kanawha Valley Campaigns* (Leesburg, VA: Gauley Mount Press, 1990), 113–14, 137–39.

90. C. Williams, *Diary and Letters,* 2:90; H. Wayne Morgan, ed., "A Civil War Diary of William McKinley," *Ohio History* 69 (1960): 272–90.

91. Husley, "Men of Virginia"; Belohlavek, "John B. Floyd"; E. Kidd Lockard, "The Unfortunate Military Career of Henry A. Wise in West Virginia," *West Virginia History* 31 (1969): 40–54; Klement, "General John B. Floyd"; Assistant Surgeon Horace Wirtz, USA, Statement of the Killed and Wounded at the Battle of Carnifex Ferry, September 10, 1861, *OR,* 5:146.

92. Colonel Hugh Ewing, Thirtieth Ohio Infantry, Report, September 1861, *OR*, 5:145–46; H. Ewing, [Personal Military History], Report, 5–6.

93. Thomas, *Robert E. Lee*, 200; Belohlavek, "John B. Floyd."

94. Thomas, *Robert E. Lee*, 202–10; Klement, "General John B. Floyd"; John B. Floyd, "General Floyd," *NYT*, January 10, 1862.

95. J. Cox, *Military Reminiscences*, 1:127–28; C. Williams, *Diary and Letters*, 2:103.

96. H. Ewing, "Autobiography of a Tramp," 251–52; Robert Schenk to Abraham Lincoln, December 23, 1861 (Hugh Ewing Papers, Box 2, OHS); J. Williams, *West Virginia*, 66.

97. C. Williams, *Diary and Letters*, 2:76–77, 97–101.

98. James G. Blaine, *Twenty Years of Congress: From Lincoln to Garfield, with a Review of the Events Which Led to the Political Revolution of 1860, Volume I* (Norwich, CT: Henry Brill, 1884), 459–60; Hugh Ewing to Henrietta Ewing, October 22, 1861 (Hugh Ewing Papers, Box 2, OHS).

99. Hugh Ewing to Henrietta Ewing, October 31, 1861 (Hugh Ewing Papers, Box 2, OHS); Hugh Ewing to Henrietta Ewing, November 28, 1861 (Hugh Ewing Papers, Box 2, OHS).

100. Sister Mary Rita, *A Story of Fifty Years: From the Annals of the Congregation of the Sisters of the Holy Cross* (Notre Dame, IN: Ave Maria, 1905), 90–92, 94.

101. Ibid., 90–92, 94; Nina Silber, *Daughters of the Union: Northern Women Fight the Civil War* (Cambridge, MA: Harvard University Press, 2005), 113–14, 197–98.

102. Ellen Ewing Sherman to Hugh Ewing, October 8, 1861 (Thomas Ewing Family Papers, Box 161, LOC); Ellen Ewing Sherman to Hugh Ewing, November 20, 1861 (Thomas Ewing Family Papers, Box 161, LOC).

103. Ford, *John Beatty*, 35–36; Ellen Ewing Sherman to Hugh Ewing, November 3, 1861 (Thomas Ewing Family Papers, Box 161, LOC); Ellen Ewing Sherman to Hugh Ewing, October 8, 1861.

104. David A. Gerber, *Black Ohio and the Color Line, 1860–1915* (Urbana: University of Illinois Press, 1976), 27–28.

105. S. Cox, *Three Decades*, 314–15; Voegeli, *Free but Not Equal*, 4, 6; Frank L. Klement, "Clement L. Vallandigham," in *For the Union: Ohio Leaders in the Civil War*, ed. Kenneth W. Wheeler (Columbus: Ohio State University Press, 1968), 11.

106. J. Smith, *History of the Republican Party*, 1:186–88; Cardinal, "Democratic Party of Ohio," 194.

107. Mulligan, "Lest the Rebels Come," 157–58, 210; Cardinal, "Democratic Party of Ohio," 88, 100; Smith, *History of the Republican Party*, 1:188.

108. Mary Land, "Ben Wade," in Wheeler, *For the Union*, 169, 172; Cardinal, "Democratic Party of Ohio," 102–3.

109. Ellen Ewing Sherman to Hugh Ewing, October 8, 1861, in *The Papers of Andrew Johnson,* vol. 5, *1861–1862,* ed. Leroy P. Graf and Ralph W. Haskins (Knoxville: University of Tennessee Press, 1979), xiii–xxiv.
110. Ellen Ewing Sherman to Hugh Ewing, October 8, 1861.
111. Lee Kennett, *Sherman: A Soldier's Life* (New York: HarperCollins, 2001), 118–26.
112. James Lee McDonough, *War in Kentucky: From Shiloh to Perryville* (Knoxville: University of Tennessee Press, 1994), 63; Lowell H. Harrison, "The Civil War in Kentucky: Some Persistent Questions," *Register of the Kentucky Historical Society* 76 (1978): 1–21; McKnight, *Contested Borderland*, 32.
113. Ellen Ewing Sherman to Hugh Ewing, October 8, 1861; Ellen Ewing Sherman to Hugh Ewing, November 3, 1861; Oliver P. Morton to Abraham Lincoln, September 20, 1861 (Abraham Lincoln Papers, LOC, transcribed and annotated by the Lincoln Studies Center, Knox College, Galesburg, IL); Andrew Johnson to William T. Sherman, October 30, 1861, in Graf and Haskins, *Papers of Andrew Johnson,* 5:29–30.
114. Prokopowicz, *All for the Regiment,* 14–16; E. Merton Coulter, *The Civil War and Readjustment in Kentucky* (Gloucester, MA: Peter Smith, 1966), 128–30; McKnight, *Contested Borderland,* 36–37; Kennett, *Sherman,* 137.
115. John F. Marszalek, *Sherman: A Soldier's Passion for Order* (New York: Free Press, 1993), 164.
116. Kennett, *Sherman,* 139–41; James M. Perry, *A Bohemian Brigade: The Civil War Correspondents—Mostly Rough, Sometimes Ready* (New York: John Wiley and Sons, 2000), 111–18, 125.
117. Ellen Ewing Sherman to Hugh Ewing, December 30, 1861 (Thomas Ewing Family Papers, Box 161, LOC).
118. Marszalek, *Sherman,* 165–67; Charles Bracelen Flood, *Grant and Sherman: The Friendship That Won the Civil War* (New York: Harper Perennial, 2005), 74–76; P. B. Ewing to Henry Halleck, with enclosure to the *Cincinnati Commercial,* December 13, 1861, *OR,* 52:200–201.
119. Jeannette P. Nichols, "John Sherman," in Wheeler, *For the Union,* 413–14; Patrick, "John Sherman," 146–47; Marszalek, *Sherman,* 166.
120. Nevins, *War for the Union,* 307, 331–39.
121. Thomas Ewing to Abraham Lincoln, September 17, 1861 (Abraham Lincoln Papers, LOC, transcribed and annotated by the Lincoln Studies Center, Knox College, Galesburg, IL); Thomas Ewing to Hugh Ewing, November 2, 1861 (Hugh Boyle Ewing Papers, Box 2, OHS).
122. Glyndon G. Van Deusen, *William Henry Seward* (New York: Oxford University Press, 1967), 341; Nevins, *War for the Union,* 61–62, 384, 387–90.
123. John Hay to William H. Seward, December 3, 1861, *OR,* 2:1103–4; Thomas Ewing to Abraham Lincoln, November 18, 1861 (Abraham Lincoln Papers, LOC, transcribed and annotated by the Lincoln Studies Center, Knox College, Galesburg, IL).

124. Marszalek, *Sherman*, 166–67; W. Sherman, *Memoirs*, 1:216–17; Flood, *Grant and Sherman*, 76–77; Zsoldos, "Political Career," 264–65; Perry, *Bohemian Brigade*, 119; Burton, *Three Generations*, 138–39; Kennett, *Sherman*, 143–44.

125. Theodore Calvin Pease, ed., *The Diary of Orville Hickman Browning*, vol. 1, *1850–1864* (Springfield: Illinois State Historical Library, 1925), 527.

126. Back east, Union soldiers spoke of "seeing the elephant," meaning they had been in combat. In the Ohio River Valley, pirates had lured curious travelers to their dens (and often to their deaths) by charging them to see a "cave-dwelling varmint." For a Hollywood treatment of this aspect of Ohio history see the 1962 film *How the West Was Won.*

NOTES TO CHAPTER FOUR

The chapter epigraph is from a letter from Hugh Ewing to Henrietta Ewing, July 17, 1862 (Hugh Ewing Papers, Box 2, OHS).

1. Ellen Ewing Sherman to William T. Sherman, January 29, 1862 (William T. Sherman Family Papers, Box 38, UNDA).

2. Ellen Ewing Sherman to Abraham Lincoln, January 9, 1862 (Abraham Lincoln Papers, LOC, transcribed and annotated by the Lincoln Studies Center, Knox College, Galesburg, IL); Ellen Ewing Sherman to William T. Sherman, January 8, 1862 (William T. Sherman Family Papers, Box 38, UNDA); Ellen Ewing Sherman to William T. Sherman, January 29, 1862.

3. William T. Sherman to Thomas Ewing, April 27, 1862, in *Home Letters of General Sherman,* ed. M. A. DeWolfe Howe (New York: Charles Scribner's Sons, 1909), 225–26; Ellen Ewing Sherman to William T. Sherman, March 12, 1862 (William T. Sherman Family Papers, Box 38, UNDA).

4. John F. Marszalek, *Sherman: A Soldier's Passion for Order* (New York: The Free Press, 1993), 184–85.

5. Charles and Barbara Whalen, *The Fighting McCooks: America's Famous Fighting Family* (Bethesda, MD: Westmoreland Press, 2006), 129–30; Sister Mary Rita, *A Story of Fifty Years: From the Annals of the Congregation of the Sisters of the Holy Cross* (Notre Dame, IN: Ave Maria, 1905), 93–111; Anna Shannon McAllister, *Flame in the Wilderness: Life and Letters of Mother Angela Gillespie, 1824–1887, American Foundress of the Sisters of the Holy Cross* (Paterson, NJ: St. Anthony Guild Press, 1944), 167–92.

6. *Letter of the Hon. Thomas Ewing to His Excellency Ben J. Stanton, Lieutenant Governor of Ohio,* Columbus: B. Nevins Printer, 1862 (OHS Collections); Ellen Ewing Sherman to William T. Sherman, June 1, 1862 (William T. Sherman Family Papers, Box 38, UNDA).

7. *"Battle of Pittsburg Landing—Volunteers of Ohio,"* Remarks of Hon. John Sherman of Ohio, in Senate of the United States, May 9, 1862 (Washington, DC: Scammell, 1862) (OHS Collections).

8. Ellen Ewing Sherman to Hugh Ewing, April 21, 1862 (Thomas Ewing Family Papers, Box 161, LOC); Ellen Ewing Sherman to Hugh Ewing, May 23, 1862 (Thomas Ewing Family Papers, Box 161, LOC).

9. William L. Burton, *Melting Pot Soldiers: The Union's Ethnic Regiments* (New York: Fordham University Press, 1998), 203–4.

10. Thomas P. Lowry, *Tarnished Eagles: The Courts-Martial of Fifty Union Colonels and Lieutenant Colonels* (Mechanicsburg, PA: Stackpole Books, 1997), 136–40.

11. Francis H. Peirpont to Abraham Lincoln, September 12, 1861 (Abraham Lincoln Papers, LOC, transcribed and annotated by the Lincoln Studies Center, Knox College, Galesburg, IL); F. H. Peirpoint to General William Rosecrans, October 8, 1861, *OR*, 5:615; Richard Lowe, "Francis Harrison Pierpoint," in *American National Biography On-Line*, February 2000, American Council of Learned Societies, www.anb.org. Pierpont spelled his name in various ways: Peirpont, Pierpont, and Peirpoint.

12. Richard Orr Curry, *A House Divided: A Study of Statehood Politics and the Copperhead Movement in West Virginia* (Pittsburgh: University of Pittsburgh Press, 1964), 75; Rutherford Hayes to S. Birchard, September 14, 1861, in *Diary and Letters of Rutherford Birchard Hayes,* vol. 2, *1861–1865,* ed. Charles Richard Williams (Columbus: Ohio State Historical Society, 1922), 92–93.

13. John Alexander Williams, *West Virginia: A History* (New York: W. W. Norton, 1984), 65; Virgil Carrington Jones, *Gray Ghosts and Rebel Raiders* (New York: Galahad Books, 1995), 66–71; Private William Murphey, Thirtieth Ohio, to his brother, January 10, 1862 (William Murphey, Thirtieth Ohio, Correspondence, OHS).

14. J. Williams, *West Virginia*, 66; Ellen Ewing Sherman to Hugh Ewing, March 29, 1862 (Thomas Ewing Family Papers, Box 161, LOC).

15. Clarice Lorene Bailes, "Jacob Dolson Cox in West Virginia," *West Virginia History* 6 (1944): 5–58.

16. Captain Elijah Warner, Company E, Thirtieth Ohio, report to Colonel Hugh Ewing, May 1, 1862 (Hugh Ewing Papers, Box 2, OHS).

17. Second Lieutenant Ezra McConnell, Company B, Thirtieth Ohio, report to Colonel Hugh Ewing, May 13, 1862 (Hugh Ewing Papers, Box 2, OHS).

18. Ibid.

19. Major George Hildt, Thirtieth Ohio, letters to his parents, April 19, 1862, April 30, 1862, May 12, 1862 (George Hildt, Thirtieth Ohio, Correspondence, OHS).

20. Hugh Ewing to Henrietta Ewing, March 6, 1862 and May 25, 1862 (Hugh Ewing Papers, Box 2, OHS).

21. Silvia Tammisto Zsoldos, "The Political Career of Thomas Ewing, Sr." (PhD diss., University of Delaware, 1977), 264.

22. Benjamin J. Blied, *Catholics and the Civil War* (Milwaukee, WI: Bruce, 1945), 20–51, 70–82.

23. Hugh Ewing to Henrietta Ewing, June 25, 1862, and August 10, 1862 (Hugh Ewing Papers, Box 2, OHS). In his correspondence during this time frame, Hugh reacted firmly, and sometimes apologetically, to Henrietta's distress. But her letters, responding to Hugh on this topic were not deposited with this collection.

24. Hugh Ewing to Henrietta Ewing, June 2, 1862, June 25, 1862, and August 10, 1862; Nina Silber, *Daughters of the Union: Northern Women Fight the Civil War* (Cambridge, MA: Harvard University Press, 2005, 23–24.

25. Ellen Ewing Sherman to William T. Sherman, April 23, 1862 (William T. Sherman Family Papers, Box 38, UNDA).

26. Thomas Ewing to Abraham Lincoln, April 9, 1862 (Abraham Lincoln Papers, LOC, transcribed and annotated by the Lincoln Studies Center, Knox College, Galesburg, IL); Ellen Ewing Sherman to William T. Sherman, March 26, 1862, and April 13, 1862 (William T. Sherman Family Papers, Box 38, UNDA).

27. Hugh Ewing to Henrietta Ewing, June 2, 1862; Hugh Ewing to Gilbert (?), June 21, 1862 (Hugh Ewing Papers, Box 2, OHS).

28. Hugh Ewing to Henrietta Ewing, July 17, 1862; Ellen Ewing Sherman to Hugh Ewing, June 17, 1862 (Thomas Ewing Family Papers, Box 161, LOC).

29. Ellen Ewing Sherman to Hugh Ewing, June 7, 1862, July 3, 1862, and July 9, 1862 (Thomas Ewing Family Papers, Box 161, LOC).

30. Maria Ewing to Hugh Ewing, April 11, 1862, and June 25, 1862 (Hugh Ewing Papers, Box 2, OHS); Ellen Ewing Sherman to Hugh Ewing, July 11, 1862 (Thomas Ewing Family Papers, Box 161, LOC).

31. Charles Ewing to William T. Sherman, February 11, 1862 (Thomas Ewing Family Papers, Box 161, LOC); Charles Ewing to Thomas Ewing, April 24, 1862 (Thomas Ewing Family Papers, Box 161, LOC); Ellen Ewing Sherman to Charles Ewing, March 22, 1862 (Thomas Ewing Family Papers, Box 161, LOC).

32. Ellen Ewing Sherman to Charles Ewing, April 10, 1862 and April 18, 1862 (Thomas Ewing Family Papers, Box 161, LOC); Ellen Ewing Sherman to William T. Sherman, July 12, 1862 (William T. Sherman Family Papers, Box 38, UNDA).

33. Ellen Ewing Sherman to Charles Ewing, April 13, 1862 (Thomas Ewing Family Papers, Box 161, LOC); Ellen Ewing Sherman to William T. Sherman, February 22, 1862, February 24, 1862, April 13, 1862, April 19, 1862, April 26, 1862, May 2, 1862, June 9, 1862, and July 17, 1862 (William T. Sherman Family Papers, Box 38, UNDA).

34. Michael S. Green, *Freedom, Union, and Power: Lincoln and his Party during the Civil War* (New York: Fordham University Press, 2004), 302.

35. Donald B. Connelly, *John M. Schofield and the Politics of Generalship* (Chapel Hill: University of North Carolina Press, 2006), 29.

36. Ibid., 29; Arthur Roy Kirkpatrick, "Missouri's Secessionist Government, 1861–1865," *Missouri Historical Review* 45 (1951): 124–37.

37. Connelly, *John M. Schofield,* 16.
38. Richard S. Brownlee, *Gray Ghosts of the Confederacy: Guerrilla Warfare in the West, 1861–1865* (Baton Rouge: Louisiana State University Press, 1958), 18, 26; Connelly, *John M. Schofield,* 36; Sceva Bright Laughlin, "Missouri Politics during the Civil War: The Struggle for Emancipation," *Missouri Historical Review* (1929): 87–113.
39. Brownlee, *Gray Ghosts,* 15, 22–23.
40. Ibid., 21.
41. Thomas Ewing to Henry Halleck, December 30, 1861, *OR,* 1:242; Thomas Ewing to Henry Halleck, January 5, 1862, *OR,* 1:251; Henry Halleck to Thomas Ewing, January 1, 1862, *OR,* 1:247.
42. Henry Halleck to General John Pope, December 31, 1861, *OR,* 1:242–43.
43. Albert Castel, *A Frontier State at War: Kansas, 1861–1865* (Ithaca: Cornell University Press, 1958), 50–54; Brownlee, *Gray Ghosts,* 38–39; Dudley Taylor Cornish, "Kansas Negro Regiments in the Civil War," *Kansas Historical Quarterly* 20 (1953): 417–29; Hildegarde Rose Herklotz, "Jayhawkers in Missouri, 1858–1863," *Missouri Historical Review* 18 (1923): 64–101.
44. Castel, *Frontier State at War;* Brownlee, *Gray Ghosts,* 46; Mark Grimsley, *The Hard Hand of War: Union Military Policy toward Southern Civilians, 1861–1865* (Cambridge: Cambridge University Press, 1995), 124.
45. Thomas Goodrich, *Black Flag: Guerrilla Warfare on the Western Border, 1861–1865* (Bloomington: Indiana University Press, 1995), 13, 52; Robert A. Carter, *Bill Cody: The Man behind the Legend* (Edison, NJ: Castle Books, 2000), 65–68.
46. Brownlee, *Gray Ghosts,* 30; Homer Croy, *Cole Younger: Last of the Great Outlaws* (Lincoln: University of Nebraska Press, 1999), 3–7, 11, 16.
47. Tom Ewing to Philemon Ewing, February 16, 1862 (Philemon Ewing Papers, Box 6, OHS).
48. William Elsey Connelley, *The Life of Preston B. Plumb, 1837–1891: United States Senator for Kansas for the Fourteen Years from 1877 to 1891* (Chicago: Brown and Howell, 1913), 103–7.
49. James McPherson, *Crossroads of Freedom: Antietam* (New York: Oxford University Press, 2002), 88–89, 91.
50. Ibid., 88–89; Walter Geer, *Campaigns of the Civil War* (1926; repr., Old Saybrook, CT: Konecky and Konecky, 2001), 150.
51. General Hugh Ewing, [Personal Military History], Report to the Adjutant General of the Army, Washington, DC, 1864 (Hugh Ewing Papers, Box 4, OHS), 9; Hugh Ewing to Henrietta Ewing, August 10, 1862; Jack D. Welsh, *Medical Histories of Union Generals* (Kent: Kent State University Press, 1996), 111; Jacob Dolson Cox, *Military Reminiscences of the Civil War,* vol. 1 (New York: Charles Scribner's Sons, 1900), 228.
52. Ellen Ewing Sherman to William T. Sherman, August 24, 1862, and August 30, 1862 (William T. Sherman Family Papers, Box 38, UNDA).

53. Geer, *Campaigns of the Civil War*, 152; Gideon Welles, *Diary of Gideon Welles: Secretary of the Navy under Lincoln and Johnson*, vol. 1, *1861–March 30, 1864* (Boston: Houghton Mifflin, 1911), 115.

54. H. Ewing, [Personal Military History], Report, 9; Cox, *Military Reminiscences*, 1:226–29.

55. Hugh Ewing, "The Autobiography of a Tramp" (Hugh Ewing Papers, Box 9, OHS), 274.

56. Ibid., 274.

57. McPherson, *Crossroads of Freedom*, 98; "The Invasion of Maryland," *Harper's Weekly* 6 (September 27, 1862): 618.

58. Cox, *Military Reminiscences*, 1:264–67.

59. Charles Richard Williams, *The Life of Rutherford Birchard Hayes, Nineteenth President of the United States* (Boston: Houghton Mifflin, 1914), 1:193–94.

60. Ibid., 1:194; C. Williams, *Diary and Letters*, 2:347.

61. Cox, *Military Reminiscences*, 1:269–70; C. Williams, *Diary and Letters*, 2:348–49.

62. Cox, *Military Reminiscences*, 1:271–73.

63. Geer, *Campaigns of the Civil War*, 153.

64. Ibid., 156; H. Ewing, [Personal Military History], Report, 10–11; Cox, *Military Reminiscences*, 1:286.

65. H. Ewing, [Personal Military History], Report, 11–12; John Michael Priest, *Before Antietam: The Battle for South Mountain* (Shippensburg, PA: White Mane, 1992), 155–51; Cox, *Military Reminiscences*, 1:282–83.

66. Hans L. Trefousse, *Rutherford B. Hayes* (New York: Times Books, 2002), 29; C. Williams, *Life of Rutherford Birchard Hayes*, 197–99; Priest, *Before Antietam*, 141–45, 150–51; C. Williams, *Diary and Letters*, 2:355–57.

67. H. Ewing, [Personal Military History], Report, 11.

68. Colonel Hugh Ewing, Thirtieth Ohio Infantry, Report of the Battle of South Mountain, September 14, 1862, *OR*, 19:469; George Hildt to his parents, September 22, 1862 (George Hildt Letters, Thirtieth Ohio, OHS).

69. Priest, *Before Antietam*, 170; Francis Winthrop Palfrey, *Campaigns of the Civil War*, vol. 5, *Antietam and Fredericksburg* (Edison, NJ: Castle Books, 2002), 35–38.

70. James V. Murfin, *The Gleam of Bayonets: The Battle of Antietam and the Maryland Campaign of 1862* (New York: Thomas Yoseloff, 1965), 175; Cox, *Military Reminiscences*, 1:292–93; Brigadier General Jacob D. Cox, Kanawha Division, Report of the Battle of South Mountain, September 20, 1862, *OR*, 19:458–61; "The Victory of Sunday," *NYT*, September 17, 1862; James Longstreet, *From Manassas to Appomattox: Memoirs of the Civil War in America* (New York: Barnes and Noble, 2004), 169–70.

71. H. Ewing, [Personal Military History], Report, 11; Palfrey, *Campaigns of the Civil War*, 5:39; Cox, Report of the Battle of South Mountain, September 20, 1862, 458–61.

72. "The Late General Reno," *Harper's Weekly* 6 (October 4, 1862): 634; "General Reno's Death," *NYT*, March 30, 1879; Priest, *Before Antietam*, 215–16; H. Ewing, "Autobiography of a Tramp," 275.

73. McPherson, *Crossroads of Freedom*, 111.

74. Geer, *Campaigns of the Civil War*, 159; McPherson, *Crossroads of Freedom*, 115.

75. Jeffrey D. Wert, *General James Longstreet: The Confederacy's Most Controversial Soldier* (New York: Simon and Schuster, 1993), 191.

76. Palfrey, *Campaigns of the Civil War*, 5:58–59, 118.

77. Stephen W. Sears, *Landscape Turned Red: The Battle of Antietam* (New Haven, CT: Ticknor and Fields, 1983), 296; McPherson, *Crossroads of Freedom*, 116–119, 124; Jeffrey D. Wert, *The Sword of Lincoln: The Army of the Potomac* (New York: Simon and Schuster, 2005), 159–60; Geer, *Campaigns of the Civil War*, 163, 171.

78. Robert R. Krick, "It Appeared as Though Mutual Extermination Would Put a Stop to the Awful Carnage: Confederates in Sharpsburg's Bloody Lane," in *The Antietam Campaign,* ed. Gary W. Gallagher (Chapel Hill: University of North Carolina Press, 1999), 223–58.

79. McPherson, *Crossroads of Freedom*, 125–27; Palfrey, *Campaigns of the Civil War*, 5:111; Geer, *Campaigns of the Civil War*, 168; Cox, *Military Reminiscences*, 1:301.

80. H. Ewing, [Personal Military History], Report, 12; Brigadier General Jacob D. Cox, Kanawha Division, Special Orders No. 8, September 28, 1862, *OR*, 51:870–71; Colonel Hugh Ewing, Report of Col. Hugh Ewing, Thirtieth Ohio Infantry, Commanding First Brigade, of the Battle of Antietam, September 22, 1862, *OR*, 19:463; John Michael Priest, *Antietam: The Soldiers' Battle* (New York: Oxford University Press, 1989), 257.

81. Palfrey, *Campaigns of the Civil War*, 5:112; Sears, *Landscape Turned Red*, 277; J. H. Horton and Solomon Teverbaugh, *A History of the Eleventh Regiment, Ohio Volunteer Infantry* (Dayton, OH: W. J. Shuey, 1866), 75–76; Priest, *Antietam,* 268; Wert, *General James Longstreet,* 194.

82. Richard Wheeler, *Voices of the Civil War* (New York: Meridian, 1990), 194; McPherson, *Crossroads of Freedom*, 126–27.

83. McPherson, *Crossroads of Freedom*, 126–27; Priest, *Antietam,* 280; Sears, *Landscape Turned Red*, 289–90.

84. Major George H. Hildt, Report of Major George H. Hildt, Thirtieth Ohio Infantry, of the Battle of Antietam, September 20, 1862, *OR*, 19:469–71; Colonel Eliakim Scammon, Headquarters Kanawha Division, Report, September 22, 1862, *OR*, 19:462–63; Cox, Special Orders No. 8, 870–71; Cox, *Military Reminiscences,* 1:350–51; Sears, *Landscape Turned Red*, 290.

85. Longstreet, *From Manassas to Appomattox*, 195–96, 213–14; Sears, *Landscape Turned Red*, 295–96; Wert, *Sword of Lincoln*, 169.

86. Hugh Ewing to Henrietta Ewing, September 20, 1862 (Hugh Ewing Papers, OHS, Box 2); Hildt to his parents, September 22, 1862; Sears, *Landscape Turned Red*, 292, 296; Palfrey, *Campaigns of the Civil War*, 5:71.

87. Ellen Ewing Sherman to William T. Sherman, October 1, 1862 (William T. Sherman Family Papers, Box 38, UNDA); Hugh Ewing to Philemon Ewing, October 18, 1862 (Philemon Ewing Papers, Box 6, OHS).

88. Reverdy Johnson to George McClellan, March 9, 1864, in *The Civil War Papers of George B. McClellan*, ed. Stephen W. Sears (New York: Da Capo, 1992), 568–69; Bruce Tap, *Over Lincoln's Shoulder: The Committee on the Conduct of the War* (Lawrence: University of Kansas Press, 1998), 30; H. L. Trefousse, *Benjamin Franklin Wade: Radical Republican from Ohio* (New York: Twayne, 1963), 252; "The Conduct of the War: Report of the Congressional Committee," *NYT*, April 6, 1863.

89. "The New War Program–A New Cabinet Demanded," *New York Herald*, September 25, 1862.

90. Thomas Calvin Pease, ed., *The Diary of Orville Hickman Browning*, vol. 1, *1850–1864* (Springfield: Illinois State Historical Library, 1925), 605–6; Glyndon G. Van Deusen, *William Henry Seward* (New York: Oxford University Press, 1967), 333; David Donald, ed., *Inside Lincoln's Cabinet: The Civil War Diaries of Salmon P. Chase* (New York: Longmans, Green, 1954), 152; "Conservative Meeting in New York," *Weekly Vincennes (Indiana) Western Sun*, July 12, 1862.

91. Thomas Ewing to Abraham Lincoln, June 2, 1862 (Abraham Lincoln Papers, LOC, transcribed and annotated by the Lincoln Studies Center, Knox College, Galesburg, IL); Border State congressmen to Abraham Lincoln, July 14, 1862 (Abraham Lincoln Papers, LOC, transcribed and annotated by the Lincoln Studies Center, Knox College, Galesburg, IL).

92. William D. Mallam, "Lincoln and the Conservatives," *Journal of Southern History* 28 (February 1962): 31–45; Zsoldos, "Political Career," 271.

93. Pease, *Diary of Orville Hickman Browning*, 1:608–9; Brian McGinty, *Lincoln and the Court* (Cambridge, MA: Harvard University Press, 2008), 115.

94. Williston H. Lofton, "Northern Labor and the Negro during the Civil War," *Journal of Negro History* 34 (July 1949): 251–73.

95. V. Jacque Voegeli, *Free but Not Equal: The Midwest and the Negro during the Civil War* (Chicago: University of Chicago Press, 1967), 14–15, 36, 88; V. Jacque Voegeli, "The Northwest and the Race Issue, 1861–1862," *Mississippi Valley Historical Review* 50 (September 1863): 235–51; Lofton, "Northern Labor."

96. Eugene H. Roseboom, "Southern Ohio and the Union in 1863," *Mississippi Valley Historical Review* 39 (June 1952): 29–44; Eric J. Cardinal, "The Democratic Party of Ohio and the Civil War: An Analysis of a Wartime Political Minority," (PhD diss., Kent State University, 1981), 110, 124; Voegeli, *Free but Not Equal*, 76.

97. Roseboom, "Southern Ohio"; Cardinal, "Democratic Party," 115–18.
98. Voegeli, "Northwest and the Race Issue"; John C. Waugh, *Reelecting Lincoln: The Battle for the 1864 Presidency* (New York: Crown, 1997), 334–35; Speech of Hon. S.S. Cox of Ohio, *Congressional Globe*, 37th Cong., 2nd sess., Appendix, June 3, 1862, 242–49; Jeanette P. Nichols, "John Sherman," in *For the Union: Ohio Leaders in the Civil War,* ed. Kenneth W. Wheeler (Columbus: Ohio State University Press, 1968), 384.
99. George H. Porter, *Ohio Politics during the Civil War Period* (New York: AMS Press, 1968), 151–52.
100. Ibid.; *Letter of Lieutenant Governor Stanton in Reply to Hon. Thomas Ewing* (Columbus: Ohio State Journal, 1862) (OHS Collections).
101. Mark E. Neeley Jr., *The Fate of Liberty: Abraham Lincoln and Civil Liberties* (New York: Oxford University Press, 1992), 192, 234; John Sherman, Remarks on Edson Olds and Civil Liberties, *Congressional Globe*, U.S. Senate, 37th Cong., 3rd sess., December 9, 1862, 30–31.
102. John Sherman to Andrew Johnson, April 27, 1862 (Abraham Lincoln Papers, LOC, transcribed and annotated by the Lincoln Studies Center, Knox College, Galesburg, IL).
103. Roseboom, "Southern Ohio"; Voegeli, "Northwest and the Race Issue"; Albert Castel, *Decision in the West: The Atlanta Campaign of 1864* (Lawrence: University of Kansas Press, 1992), 5–6; Jennifer L. Weber, *Copperheads: The Rise and Fall of Lincoln's Opponents in the North* (New York: Oxford University Press, 2006), 68–69; Voegeli, *Free but Not Equal,* 62; Charles R. Wilson, "Cincinnati's Reputation during the Civil War," *Journal of Southern History* 2 (November 1936): 468–79.
104. Porter, *Ohio Politics,* 157–58; Ellen Ewing Sherman to William T. Sherman, September 3, 1862, and October 10, 1862 (William T. Sherman Family Papers, Box 38, UNDA).
105. Maria Ewing to Hugh Ewing, December 7, 1862 (Hugh Ewing Papers, Box 2, OHS); Maria Ewing to Henrietta Ewing, October 3, 1862 (Hugh Ewing Papers, Box 2, OHS).
106. Homer L. Kerr, "Battle of Elkhorn: The Gettysburg of the Trans-Mississippi West," in *Essays on the American Civil War: The Walter Prescott Webb Memorial Lectures,* ed. William F. Holmes and Harold M. Hollingsworth (Austin: University of Texas Press, 1968), 31–44; Castel, *Frontier State at War,* 82.
107. Connelley, *Life of Preston B. Plumb,* 107–8.
108. Ibid., 108; Jay Monaghan, *Civil War on the Western Border, 1854–1865* (Boston: Little, Brown, 1955), 258.
109. Connelley, *Life of Preston B. Plumb,* 104–5; Kim Allen Scott, "The Preacher, the Lawyer, and the Spoils of War," *Kansas History* 13 (1991): 206–17.
110. Scott, "Preacher, the Lawyer."

111. Brigadier General James G. Blunt, Commanding First Division, Army of the Frontier, Report, Cane Hill, Arkansas, December 3, 1862, *OR*, 22:43–46.

112. Colonel Thomas Ewing Jr., Eleventh Regiment Kansas Volunteers, Report, Benton County, Arkansas, December 1, 1862, *OR*, 22:52; Scott, "Preacher, the Lawyer." The letter from Tom Ewing to Ellen Cox Ewing, December 2, 1862, is cited in Scott, "Preacher, the Lawyer."

113. Brigadier General James G. Blunt, Commanding First Division, Army of the Frontier, Report, Rhea's Mills, Arkansas, December 20, 1862, *OR*, 22:71–77; Colonel Thomas Ewing Jr., Eleventh Regiment Kansas Volunteers, Report, Camp at Cane Hill, Arkansas, December 12, 1862, *OR*, 22:97–98; Tom Ewing to Phil Ewing, December 19, 1862 (Philemon Ewing Papers, Box 6, OHS).

114. Monaghan, *Civil War*, 277–78.

115. George Hildt to his parents, November 22, 1862 (George Hildt Letters, Thirtieth Ohio, OHS).

NOTES TO CHAPTER FIVE

The chapter epigraph is from Henry Champion Deming, *The Life of Ulysses S. Grant, General of the United States Army* (Hartford, CT: S. S. Scranton, 1868), 268.

1. Walter Geer, *Campaigns of the Civil War* (1926; repr., Old Saybrook, CT: Konecky and Konecky, 2001), 266–69; Charles Bracelen Flood, *Grant and Sherman: The Friendship That Won the Civil War* (New York: Harper Perennial, 2005), 152; Lee Kennett, *Sherman: A Soldier's Life* (New York: HarperCollins, 2001), 188.

2. Thomas Ewing to Hugh Ewing, February 8, 1863 (Hugh Ewing Papers, Box 3, OHS); Hugh Ewing to Henrietta Ewing, November 10, 1862 (Hugh Ewing Papers, Box 2, OHS); Hugh Ewing to Philemon Ewing, November 7, 1862 (Philemon Ewing Papers, Box 6, OHS); Nina Silber, *Daughters of the Union: Northern Women Fight the Civil War* (Cambridge, MA: Harvard University Press, 2005), 20.

3. Ellen Ewing Sherman to William T. Sherman, January 19, 1863, and January 29, 1863 (William T. Sherman Family Papers, Box 39, UNDA).

4. Charles Ewing to Philemon Ewing, December 25, 1862 (Philemon Ewing Papers, Box 6, OHS); William T. Sherman to John Sherman, January 6, 1863, in *The Sherman Letters: Correspondence between General and Senator Sherman from 1837 to 1891*, ed. Rachel Sherman Thorndike (New York: Scribner's Sons, 1894), 179–80; Flood, *Grant and Sherman*, 148–52.

5. Ellen Ewing Sherman to William T. Sherman, January 14, 1863 (William T. Sherman Family Papers, Box 39, UNDA).

6. William T. Sherman to John Sherman, January 6, 1863; Geer, *Campaigns of the Civil War*, 268–69; Flood, *Grant and Sherman*, 148–52.

7. Flood, *Grant and Sherman*, 149–50.
8. Hugh Boyle Ewing, "The Autobiography of a Tramp" (Hugh Boyle Ewing Papers, Box 9, OHS), 292; Joseph T. Glatthaar, *Partners in Command: The Relationship between Leaders in the Civil War* (New York: Free Press, 1994), 153; Flood, *Grant and Sherman*, 149–50; Kennett, *Sherman,* 200–201; Ellen Ewing Sherman to William T. Sherman, January 28, 1863 (William T. Sherman Family Papers, Box 39, UNDA).
9. George Hildt to his parents, January 31, 1863 (George Hildt Letters, Thirtieth Ohio, OHS); Thomas White to his sister, January 21, 1863 (Thomas K. White Letters, Thirtieth Ohio, OHS).
10. Ellen Ewing Sherman to William T. Sherman, February 4, 1863 (William T. Sherman Family Papers, Box 39, UNDA); Charles Ewing to Maria Ewing, January 14, 1863 (Charles Ewing Family Papers, Box 6, LOC); Kennett, *Sherman,* 196–97, 245.
11. Luke Clarke, *In Memoriam: Charles Ewing* (Philadelphia: J. B. Lippincott, 1888), 42–43; Charles Ewing to Maria Ewing, January 14, 1863; Ellen Ewing Sherman to William T. Sherman, March 7, 1863 (William T. Sherman Family Papers, Box 39, UNDA).
12. General Hugh Ewing, [Personal Military History], Report to the Adjutant General of the Army, Washington, DC, 1864 (Hugh Ewing Papers, Box 4, OHS), 15; Geer, *Campaigns of the Civil War*, 270.
13. H. Ewing, [Personal Military History], Report, 15–16.
14. Ibid.; Thomas White to his mother, April 10, 1863 (Thomas K. White Letters, 30th Ohio, OHS) .
15. H. Ewing, [Personal Military History], Report, 16–17; Flood, *Grant and Sherman*, 153–54.
16. H. Ewing, [Personal Military History], Report, 16–17; Flood, *Grant and Sherman*, 153–58; George Hildt to his parents, April 28, 1863 (George Hildt Letters, Thirtieth Ohio, OHS).
17. H. Ewing, [Personal Military History], Report, 19; Hildt to his parents, April 28, 1863.
18. H. Ewing, [Personal Military History], Report, 18–20; Flood, *Grant and Sherman*, 160–162.
19. Thomas White to his mother, June 8, 1863 (Thomas K. White Letters, Thirtieth Ohio, OHS); Geer, *Campaigns of the Civil War*, 279–82; Phillip M. Thienel, *Seven Story Mountain: The Union Campaign at Vicksburg* (Jefferson, NC: McFarland, 1995), 214; Richard Wheeler, *Voices of the Civil War* (New York: Meridian, 1990), 340.
20. Clarke, *In Memoriam*, 48–49; Flood, *Grant and Sherman*, 167-68; Theodore R. Davis, "The Siege of Vicksburg," *Harper's Weekly* 7 (July 4, 1863): 427; Colonel Giles A. Smith, Eighth Missouri Infantry, commanding First Brigade, Report, Including Operations since May 16, May 26, 1863, *OR,* 24:262–65; Lloyd

Lewis, *Sherman, Fighting Prophet* (New York: Harcourt, Brace, 1932), 278-79; William T. Sherman to Ellen Ewing Sherman, May 25, 1863, in *Home Letters of General Sherman,* ed. M. A. DeWolfe Howe (New York: Charles Scribner's Sons, 1909), 262-63.

21. Clarke, *In Memoriam,* 48–49; Charles Ewing to Thomas Ewing, May 22, 1863 (Charles Ewing Family Papers, Box 6, LOC); Flood, *Grant and Sherman,* 167–68; William T. Sherman to Ellen Ewing Sherman, May 25, 1863, in *Home Letters,* 262–63; Ellen Ewing Sherman to William T. Sherman, June 5, 1863 (William T. Sherman Family Papers, Box 39, UNDA); Ellen Ewing Sherman to William T. Sherman, July 26, 1863 (William T. Sherman Family Papers, Box 39, UNDA).

22. Clarke, *In Memoriam,* 46–47.

23. Major General Frank P. Blair Jr., U.S. Army, Commanding Second Division, Report, Including Operations since May 7, before Vicksburg, Mississippi, May 24, 1863, *OR,* 24:254–60.

24. Lewis, *Sherman, Fighting Prophet,* 279; H. Ewing, [Personal Military History], Report, 21; Brigadier General Hugh Ewing, U.S. Army, Commanding Third Brigade, Report, Battlefield near Vicksburg, May 27, 1863, *OR,* 24:281–83.

25. Flood, *Grant and Sherman,* 168; Clarke, *In Memoriam,* 51–52; H. Ewing, [Personal Military History], Report, 21; Thienel, *Seven Story Mountain,* 214–15; Lewis, *Sherman, Fighting Prophet,* 280; Michael B. Ballard, *Vicksburg: The Campaign That Opened the Mississippi* (Chapel Hill: University of North Carolina Press, 2004), 338; Private John S. Kountz, Thirty-Seventh Ohio, in *Ninth Reunion of the 37th Regiment, OVI, St. Mary's, Ohio, September 10 and 11, 1889* (Toledo, OH: Montgomery and Vrooman, 1890), 21–22.

26. Flood, *Grant and Sherman,* 168; Ballard, *Vicksburg,* 338–39; H. Ewing, [Personal Military History], Report, 21–22.

27. Flood, *Grant and Sherman,* 168; Clarke, *In Memoriam,* 52–53; H. Ewing, [Personal Military History], Report, 21; Lewis, *Sherman, Fighting Prophet,* 280; Ballard, *Vicksburg,* 338; Thienel, *Seven Story Mountain,* 214–15.

28. H. Ewing, [Personal Military History], Report, 22; Flood, *Grant and Sherman,* 168.

29. T. H. Barton, *Autobiography of Thomas H. Barton, the Self-Made Physician of Syracuse, Ohio, Including a History of the Fourth Regiment, West Virginia Volunteer Infantry* (Charleston: West Virginia Printing, 1890), 153; George Irving Reed, ed., *Bench and Bar of Ohio: A Compendium of History and Biography* (Chicago: Century Publishing and Engraving, 1897), 1:302–4; James Marshall-Cornwall, *Grant as Military Commander* (New York: Barnes and Noble Books, 1970), 114; H. Ewing, Commanding Third Brigade, Report, Battlefield near Vicksburg, May 27, 1863.

30. George Hildt to his parents, June 19, 1863 (George Hildt Letters, Thirtieth Ohio, OHS); Ellen Ewing Sherman to William T. Sherman, May 25, 1863 (William T. Sherman Family Papers, Box 39, UNDA).

31. Robert Norris to his wife, June 25, 1863 (Robert Norris Letters, Thirtieth Ohio, OHS).

32. Osborn H. Oldroyd, *A Soldier's Story of the Siege of Vicksburg from the Diary of Osborn H. Oldroyd* (Springfield, IL: H. W. Rokker, 1885), 39–40; Flood, *Grant and Sherman*, 171.

33. Oldroyd, *Soldier's Story*, 43; Kennett, *Sherman*, 199–201; Whitelaw Reid, *Ohio in the War: Her Statesmen, Generals and Soldiers* (New York: Moore, Wilstach, and Baldwin, 1868), 1:854; David Herbert Donald, *Lincoln* (New York: Simon and Schuster, 1995), 409.

34. Ballard, *Vicksburg*, 363; Robert Norris to his wife, June 25, 1863; Thienel, *Seven Story Mountain*, 216.

35. H. Ewing, [Personal Military History], Report, 22–23.

36. Marshall-Cornwall, *Grant as Military Commander*, 117; John F. Marszalek, *Sherman: A Soldier's Passion for Order* (New York: Free Press, 1993), 234–35.

37. H. Ewing, [Personal Military History], Report, 24–25; Marshall-Cornwall, *Grant as Military Commander*, 117; H. Ewing, "Autobiography of a Tramp," 299; Hugh Ewing to Henrietta Ewing, July 14, 1863 (Ewing letter, M105, Manuscript Collection, McCain Library and Archives, University of Southern Mississippi).

38. H. Ewing, [Personal Military History], Report, 25–26; William T. Sherman to John Sherman, July 19, 1863, in Thorndike, *Sherman Letters*, 208–9; John Bennett Walters, "General William T. Sherman and Total War," *Journal of Southern History* 14 (November 1948): 447–80.

39. Flood, *Grant and Sherman*, 162–63; Hugh Ewing to Henrietta Ewing, July 13, 1863, August 2, 3, and 8, 1863 (Hugh Ewing Papers, Box 3, OHS); H. Ewing, [Personal Military History], Report, 25–26; Walters, "General William T. Sherman," 447–80.

40. H. Ewing, [Personal Military History], Report, 26; Felicity Allen, *Jefferson Davis: Unconquerable Heart* (Columbia: University of Missouri Press, 1999), 359–60.

41. Lewis, *Sherman, Fighting Prophet*, 299.

42. National Park Service, "Vicksburg Medal of Honor Recipients," nps.gov/vick/index.htm.

43. Thomas Ewing to Abraham Lincoln, June 6, 1863, and August 12, 1863 (Abraham Lincoln Papers, LOC, transcribed and annotated by the Lincoln Studies Center, Knox College, Galesburg, IL); George Hildt to Harriett Baer, September 3, 1863 (George Hildt Letters, Thirtieth Ohio, OHS).

44. Michael E. Banasik, *Cavaliers of the Brush: Quantrill and His Men*, Unwritten Chapters of the Civil War West of the River 5 (Iowa City: Press of the Camp Polk Bookshop, 2003), 175.

45. Thomas Ewing to Abraham Lincoln, June 27, 1863 (Abraham Lincoln Papers, LOC, transcribed and annotated by the Lincoln Studies Center, Knox College, Galesburg, IL).

46. Samuel J. Crawford, *Kansas in the Sixties* (Chicago: A. C. McClurg, 1911), 69.

47. "General Blunt's Account of His Civil War Experiences," *Kansas Historical Quarterly* 1 (1932): 211–65; Sceva Bright Laughlin, "Missouri Politics during the Civil War: Chapter IV, The Struggle for Emancipation," *Missouri Historical Review* 24 (1929): 87–113; Edward Bates to Abraham Lincoln, June 5, 1863 (Abraham Lincoln Papers, LOC, transcribed and annotated by the Lincoln Studies Center, Knox College, Galesburg, IL); Abraham Lincoln to James H. Lane, July 17, 1863 (Abraham Lincoln Papers, LOC, transcribed and annotated by the Lincoln Studies Center, Knox College, Galesburg, IL).

48. James C. Malin, "Theatre in Kansas, 1858–1869: Background for the Coming of the Lord Dramatic Company to Kansas, 1869," *Kansas Historical Quarterly* 23 (1957): 10–53; W. B. Hesseltine, "Military Prisons of St. Louis, 1861–1865," *Missouri Historical Review* 23 (1929): 380–99; Raymond L. Welty, "Supplying the Frontier Military Posts," *Kansas Historical Quarterly* 7 (1938): 154–69; Thomas Goodrich, *Black Flag: Guerrilla Warfare on the Western Border, 1861–1865* (Bloomington: Indiana University Press, 1995), 113.

49. Jay Monaghan, *Civil War on the Western Border, 1854–1865* (Boston: Little, Brown, 1955), 277–78; W. Wayne Smith, "An Experiment in Counterinsurgency: The Assessment of Confederate Sympathizers in Missouri," *Journal of Southern History* 35 (1969): 361–80; Goodrich, *Black Flag*, 15, 52, 56, 59, 61, 147; Homer Croy, *Cole Younger: Last of the Great Outlaws* (Lincoln: University of Nebraska Press, 1999), 31; Dudley Taylor Cornish, "Kansas Negro Regiments in the Civil War," *Kansas Historical Quarterly* 20 (1953): 417–29.

50. Croy, *Cole Younger*, 29; W. Smith, "Experiment in Counterinsurgency," 361–80; Goodrich, *Black Flag*, 36, 58.

51. Goodrich, *Black Flag*, 36–37; Albert Castel, *A Frontier State at War: Kansas, 1861–1865* (Ithaca: Cornell University Press, 1958), 96, 139; Thomas Ewing Jr., Brigadier-General, to Colonel C. W. Marsh, Headquarters District of the Border, Kansas City, Missouri, June 19, 1863, *OR*, 22:327–28.

52. Castel, *Frontier State at War*, 111–13; William Elsey Connelley, *The Life of Preston B. Plumb, 1837–1891: United States Senator for Kansas for the Fourteen Years from 1877 to 1891* (Chicago: Brown and Howell, 1913), 138–39.

53. Castel, *Frontier State at War*, 113; Thomas Ewing Jr., Brigadier-General, Headquarters District of the Border, Report to Lieutenant Colonel C. W. Marsh, Assistant Adjunct General, Department of Missouri, St. Louis, July 22, 1863, *OR*, 22:388; Mayor Daniel R. Anthony to Brigadier-General Thomas Ewing Jr., July 22, 1863, *OR*, 22:390–92.

54. Castel, *Frontier State at War*, 122–23; Brigadier-General Thomas Ewing Jr., Commanding District of the Border, Report to Lieutenant Colonel C. W. Marsh, Assistant Adjunct-General, Department of the Missouri, Louis, Missouri, June 20, 1863, *OR*, 22:375–76; "Speech of General Ewing at Olathe,

Johnson County," *Leavenworth Times*, June 1863 (Thomas Ewing Family Papers, Box 212, LOC).

55. Castel, *Frontier State at War*, 121; Goodrich, *Black Flag*, 43; Reed, *Bench and Bar*, 1:117; Brigadier-General Thomas Ewing Jr., Report to Lieutenant Colonel C. W. Marsh, Assistant Adjunct-General, Department of the Missouri, Louis, Missouri, August 3, 1863, *OR*, 22:428–29.

56. Monaghan, *Civil War*, 280; Croy, *Cole Younger*, 3–4.

57. Monaghan, *Civil War*, 280; Croy, *Cole Younger*, 31; Barbara S. Groseclose, "Painting, Politics, and George Caleb Bingham," *American Art Journal* 10 (1978): 5–19; Richard S. Brownlee, *Gray Ghosts of the Confederacy: Guerrilla Warfare in the West, 1861–1865* (Baton Rouge: Louisiana University Press, 1958), 118–19; Connelley, *Life of Preston B. Plumb*, 147–49; Nancy Rash, *The Painting and Politics of George Caleb Bingham* (New Haven: Yale University Press, 1991), 189, 211–13; George Caleb Bingham to John M. Schofield, June 4, 1863 (John McAllister Schofield Papers, Box 2, LOC).

58. Goodrich, *Black Flag*, 76; Castel, *Frontier State at War*, 125–27; Brownlee, *Gray Ghosts*, 122–24; Monaghan, *Civil War*, 279; Edward E. Leslie, *The Devil Knows How to Ride: The True Story of William Clarke Quantrill and His Confederate Raiders* (New York: Da Capo, 1998), 193; Brigadier-General Thomas Ewing Jr., Headquarters District of the Border, Report of Brigadier-General Thomas Ewing Jr., Commanding District of the Border, to Colonel C. W. Marsh, Assistant Adjunct-General, Department of the Missouri, Saint Louis, August 31, 1863, *OR*, 22:579–85.

59. Burton J. Williams, "Erastus D. Ladd's Description of the Lawrence Massacre," *Kansas Historical Quarterly* 29 (1963): 113–21; Castel, *Frontier State at War*, 125–32; Brownlee, *Gray Ghosts*, 122–24; Croy, *Cole Younger*, 35–36; Leslie, *Devil Knows How to Ride*, 193–244.

60. "A Story of Lawrence," *Harper's Weekly* 8 (May 14, 1864): 310–11; Castel, *Frontier State at War*, 125–32; Brownlee, *Gray Ghosts*, 122–24; Leslie, *Devil Knows How to Ride*, 193–244.

61. William E. Unrau, ed., "In Pursuit of Quantrill: An Enlisted Man's Response," *Kansas Historical Quarterly* 39 (1973): 379–91; Connelley, *Life of Preston B. Plumb*, 158–67; Castel, *Frontier State at War*, 133–35.

62. Goodrich, *Black Flag*, 96; Noel C. Fisher, "'Prepare Them for My Coming': General William T. Sherman, Total War, and Pacification in West Tennessee," *Tennessee Historical Quarterly* 51 (1992): 74–86.

63. Thomas Ewing Jr., U.S. Army, Commanding District of the Border, Report to Colonel C. W. Marsh, Adjunct General, Department of the Missouri, Saint Louis, August 31, 1863, *OR*, 22:579–85.

64. Major General John M. Schofield, U.S. Army, Commanding Department of the Missouri, Report to E. D. Townsend, Assistant Adjunct-General, Washington, DC, September 14, 1863, *OR*, 22:572–75; J. M. Schofield,

Major-General, Report of Major General John M. Schofield, U.S. Army, Commanding Department of the Missouri, of Operations May 24–December 10, 1863, to Colonel E. D. Townsend, Assistant Adjunct-General, Washington, DC, December 10, 1863, *OR*, 22:12–17.

65. Charles R. Mink, "General Orders No. 11: The Forced Evacuation of Civilians during the Civil War," *Military Affairs* 34 (1970): 132–37; "The War in Kansas," *NYT*, September 6, 1863; "Consternation among the Border Ruffians," *Harper's Weekly* 7 (September 19, 1863): 595.

66. Castel, *Frontier State at War*, 144–49; John M. Schofield, *Forty-Six Years in the Army* (Norman: University of Oklahoma Press, 1998), 79; Brigadier-General Thomas Ewing Jr., Report to Major General John M. Schofield, Department of the Missouri, August 26, 1863, *OR*, 22:477; Abraham Lincoln, Note to Honorable A.C. Wilder, Honorable J. H. Lane, Washington, DC, August 27, 1863, *OR*, 22:479; John McAllister Schofield, "Diary of Events in the Department of Missouri," August 31, 1863, September 8, 1863 (John McAllister Schofield Papers, Box 1, LOC).

67. Lincoln, "Note to Honorable A. C. Wilder."

68. H. Hannahs, Acting Assistant Adjunct-General, by the Order of Brigadier-General Ewing, General Orders No. 11, District of the Border, August 25, 1863, *OR*, 22:473.

69. Schofield, *Forty-Six Years*, 83; S. A. Thatcher to Thomas Ewing Jr., September 1, 1863 (Thomas Ewing Family Papers, Box 212, LOC); H. B. Denman to Thomas Ewing Jr., September 3, 1863 (Thomas Ewing Family Papers, Box 212, LOC); John McAllister Schofield, "Diary of Events in the Department of Missouri," September 6, 1863 (John McAllister Schofield Papers, Box 1, LOC).

70. Charles W. Blair to Thomas Ewing Jr., November 19, 1863, November 22, 1863, May 23, 1871 (Thomas Ewing Family Papers, Box 212, LOC).

71. Sarah Bohl, "A War on Civilians: Order Number 11 and the Evacuation of Western Missouri," *Prologue: The Journal of the National Archives* 36 (2004): 44–51; Groseclose, "Painting, Politics," 5–19; Jeremy Neely, *The Border between Them: Violence and Reconciliation on the Kansas-Missouri Line* (Columbia: University of Missouri Press, 2007), 123–24; Brownlee, *Gray Ghosts*, 126; Castel, *Frontier State at War*, 142–43, 152–53; Ann Davis Niepman, "General Orders Number 11 and Border Warfare during the Civil War," *Missouri Historical Review* 66 (1972): 185–210.

72. Abraham Lincoln to John M. Schofield, October 1, 1863 (Abraham Lincoln Papers, LOC, transcribed and annotated by the Lincoln Studies Center, Knox College, Galesburg, IL); Bill R. Lee, "Missouri's Fight over Emancipation in 1863," *Missouri Historical Review* 45 (1951): 256–74; Mink, "General Orders No. 11"; John McAllister Schofield, "Diary of Events in the Department of Missouri," October 2, 1863, October 4, 1863" (John McAllister Schofield Papers, Box 1, LOC).

73. Paul B. Hatley and Noor Ampssler, "Army General Orders Number 11: Final Valid Option or Wanton Act of Brutality?" *Journal of the West* 33 (1994): 77–87; W. C. Ransom to Thomas Ewing Jr., May 30, 1871 (Thomas Ewing Family Papers, Box 212, LOC); Donald B. Connelly, *John M. Schofield and the Politics of Generalship* (Chapel Hill: University of North Carolina Press, 2006), 77; Mink, "General Orders No. 11," 132–37; Castel, *Frontier State at War*, 153.

74. Leslie, *Devil Knows How to Ride*, 268.

75. Connelly, *John M. Schofield*, 76; Monaghan, *Civil War*, 298; Jack D. Welsh, *Medical Histories of Union Generals* (Kent: Kent State University Press, 1996), 111–12.

76. Katherine Burton, *Three Generations: Maria Boyle Ewing, Ellen Ewing Sherman, and Minnie Sherman Fitch* (New York: Longman's, Green, 1947), 147–53; Flood, *Grant and Sherman*, 192; Lewis, *Sherman, Fighting Prophet*, 299.

77. Burton, *Three Generations*, 147–53; H. Ewing, "Autobiography of a Tramp," 305; Ellen Ewing Sherman, *The Soldier's Casket* (Philadelphia: C. W. Alexander, 1865), 1:515–22.

78. Burton, *Three Generations*, 147–53.

79. Jeffrey D. Wert, *General James Longstreet: The Confederacy's Most Controversial Soldier* (New York: Simon and Schuster, 1993), 328–31.

80. Ibid., 328–31; Theodore Calvin Pease, ed., *The Diary of Orville Hickman Browning*, vol. 1, *1850–1864* (Springfield: Illinois State Historical Library, 1925), 615–16.

81. Flood, *Grant and Sherman*, 205; Patrick J. Carmody, *The Battle of Collierville: A Reminiscence* (Baton Rouge: Ortlibb's Printing House, 1910); D. C. Anthony, Colonel, Sixty-Sixth Indiana, Report, Collierville, Tennessee, October 21, 1863, *OR*, 30:752–54.

82. Carmody, *Battle of Collierville*.

83. Ibid.; H. Ewing, "Autobiography of a Tramp," 306; Flood, *Grant and Sherman*, 205; E. O. Hurd, "The Battle of Collierville," in *Sketches of War History, 1861–1865: Papers Prepared for the Commandery of the State of Ohio, Military Order of the Loyal Legion of the United States,* ed. W. H. Chamberlin, A. M. Van Dyke, and George A. Thayer (Cincinnati: Robert Clarke, 1903), 243–54.

84. Michael Fellman, *Citizen Sherman: A Life of William Tecumseh Sherman* (New York: Random House, 1995), 197–205; Ellen Ewing Sherman to William T. Sherman, October 16 and 19, 1863 (William T. Sherman Family Papers, Box 39, UNDA.)

85. Greer, *Campaigns of the Civil War*, 311; Wiley Sword, *Mountains Touched with Fire: Chattanooga Besieged, 1863* (New York: St. Martin's Press, 1995), 157–59; Wheeler, *Voices of the Civil War*, 364–65; George Hildt to his parents, January 2, 1864 (George Hildt Letters, Thirtieth Ohio, OHS).

86. Sword, *Mountains Touched with Fire*, 58, 160–61, 243; Marszalek, *Sherman*, 244–45.

87. William F. G. Shanks, *Personal Recollections of Distinguished Generals* (New York: Harper and Brothers, 1866), 27, 38; Hugh Ewing to Henrietta Ewing, October 22, 1863 (Hugh Ewing Papers, Box 3, OHS); "Grant's Victories," *New York Herald*, November 26, 1863.

88. Kountz, in *Ninth Reunion of the 37th Regiment*, 27–28.

89. H. Ewing, [Personal Military History], Report, 31–32; Sword, *Mountains Touched with Fire*, 257–58; Brigadier Hugh Ewing, Report of Brigadier General Hugh Ewing, U.S. Army, Commanding Fourth Division, Including Operations since September 28, November 28, 1863, *OR*, 31:630–32; Colonel John M. Loomis, Reports of Colonel John M. Loomis, Twenty-Sixth Illinois Infantry, Commanding First Brigade, Fourth Division, Eleventh Army Corps, December 6, 1863, *OR*, 1:633–35.

90. Greer, *Campaigns of the Civil War*, 311–26; Sword, *Mountains Touched with Fire*, 280–81, 302–5, 322, 347; Kennett, *Sherman*, 214–16; Major General William T. Sherman, Report of Major General William T. Sherman, U.S. Army, Commanding Army of the Tennessee, Including Operations since September 23, and March to the Relief of Knoxville, with Field Dispatches, November 18–29, and Thanks of Congress, December 19, 1863, *OR*, 31:568–82; William T. Sherman, *Memoirs of General William T. Sherman,* vol. 1 (New York: D. Appleton, 1891), 375–79; Ulysses S. Grant, *Personal Memoirs* (New York: Modern Library, 1999), 347–52; Benson Bobrick, *Master of War: The Life of General George H. Thomas* (New York: Simon and Schuster, 2009), 228.

91. Greer, *Campaigns of the Civil War*, 311–26; Sword, *Mountains Touched with Fire*, 280–81, 302–5, 322, 347; Kennett, *Sherman*, 214–16, 218; Sherman, Report of Major General William T. Sherman, December 19, 1863, 568–82; Sherman, *Memoirs*, 1:375–79; Grant, *Personal Memoirs*, 347–52; M. D. Gage, *From Vicksburg to Raleigh: Or, A Complete History of the Twelfth Regiment Indiana Volunteer Infantry and the Campaigns of Grant and Sherman* (Chicago: Clarke, 1865), 137–46.

92. Kennett, *Sherman*, 238; Major General William T. Sherman to Major General S. A. Hurlbut, Headquarters Department of the Tennessee, December 21, 1863, *OR*, 31:459; William T. Sherman to Major General H. W. Halleck, December 26, 1863, *OR*, 31:497; Ellen Ewing Sherman to William T. Sherman, October n.d., 1863, December 2, 1863 (William T. Sherman Family Papers, Box 39, UNDA); Welsh, *Medical Histories*, 111.

93. Thomas Ewing to Abraham Lincoln, August 6, 1863 (Abraham Lincoln Papers, LOC, transcribed and annotated by the Lincoln Studies Center, Knox College, Galesburg, IL).

94. John Sherman to William T. Sherman, July 18, 1863, in Thorndike, *Sherman Letters*, 207–8; Silvia Tammisto Zsoldos, "The Political Career of Thomas Ewing, Sr." (PhD diss., University of Delaware, 1977), 270; Leroy P. Graf and Ralph W. Haskins, eds., *The Papers of Andrew Johnson*, vol. 5, *1861–1862*

(Knoxville: University of Tennessee Press, 1979), 159–62; William D. Mallam, "Lincoln and the Conservatives," *Journal of Southern History* 28 (1962):
31–45.

95. Neil Rolde, *Continental Liar from the State of Maine: James G. Blaine* (Gardiner, ME: Tilbury House, 2006), 97–99; Samuel S. Cox, Remarks, "Meaning
of the Late Elections," *Congressional Globe*, U.S. House of Representatives,
37th Cong., 3rd sess., December 15, 1862, 94–100.

96. William H. Lofton, "Northern Labor and the Negro during the Civil War,"
Journal of Negro History 34 (1949): 251–73; Kenneth H. Wheeler, "Local
Autonomy and Civil War Draft Resistance: Holmes County, Ohio," *Civil War
History* 45 (1999): 147–59; Jennifer L. Weber, *Copperheads: The Rise and Fall of
Lincoln's Opponents in the North* (New York: Oxford University Press, 2006),
80, 104, 112, 178–79; Eric J. Cardinal, "The Democratic Party of Ohio and the
Civil War: An Analysis of a Wartime Political Minority" (PhD diss., Kent
State University, 1981), 134; Edgar Cowan to Abraham Lincoln, June 17, 1863
(Abraham Lincoln Papers, LOC, transcribed and annotated by the Lincoln
Studies Center, Knox College, Galesburg, IL); Albert Castel, *Decision in the
West: The Atlanta Campaign of 1864* (Lawrence: University of Kansas Press,
1992), 8; Silber, *Daughters of the Union*, 138, 158–59.

97. Henry Clyde Hubbart, "'Pro-Southern' Influences in the Free West, 1840–
1865," *Mississippi Valley Historical Review* 20 (1933): 45–62; Weber, *Copper-
heads*, 113; Thomas Ewing to Hugh Ewing, July 26, 1863 (Hugh Ewing Papers,
Box 3, OHS); Cardinal, "Democratic Party of Ohio," 141; David R. Contosta,
Lancaster, Ohio, 1800–2000: Frontier Town to Edge City (Columbus: Ohio
State University Press, 1999), 65.

98. Weber, *Copperheads*, 120–21; Cardinal, "Democratic Party of Ohio," 161–65.

99. Gideon Welles, *Diary of Gideon Welles,* vol. 1, *1861–March 30, 1864* (Boston:
Houghton Mifflin, 1911), 321; James G. Blaine, *Twenty Years of Congress: From
Lincoln to Garfield, with a Review of the Events Which Led to the Political
Revolution of 1860* (Norwich, CT: Henry Bill, 1884), 1:489.

100. Mark E. Neeley Jr., *The Fate of Liberty: Abraham Lincoln and Civil Liberties*
(New York: Oxford University Press, 1992), 199; John Sherman, Remarks,
Congressional Globe, U.S. Senate, 37th Cong., 2nd sess., July 9, 1862, 3198–
3200; V. Jacque Voegeli, *Free but Not Equal: The Midwest and the Negro during
the Civil War* (Chicago: University of Chicago Press, 1967), 81–82; G. T. Beauregard to Hon. Charles J. Villere, Mobile, Alabama, May 26, 1863, *OR*, 14:955;
Joseph Benson Foraker, *Notes of a Busy Life* (Cincinnati: Stewart and Kidd,
1916), 1:37.

101. Cardinal, "Democratic Party of Ohio," 222; H. Ewing, "Autobiography of a
Tramp," 22.

102. Joseph P. Smith, *History of the Republican Party in Ohio,* 2 vols. (Chicago:
Lewis, 1898), 1:153–66; Arnold Shankman, "Soldier Voters and Clement L.

Vallandigham in the 1863 Ohio Gubernatorial Election," *Ohio History* 82 (1979): 88–104; Weber, *Copperheads*, 121, 191; George H. Porter, *Ohio Politics during the Civil War Period* (New York: AMS Press, 1968), 183; Arnold M. Shankman, "Candidate in Exile: Clement Vallandigham and the 1863 Ohio Gubernatorial Election" (M.A. thesis, Emory University, 1969), 218–20; Eugene H. Roseboom, "Southern Ohio and the Union in 1863," *Mississippi Valley Historical Review* 39 (1952): 29–44.

103. Shankman, "Candidate in Exile," 225; Welles, *Diary of Gideon Welles*, 1:470.

NOTES TO CHAPTER SIX

The chapter epigraph is from a letter from William T. Sherman to James M. Calhoun, Mayor, and E. E. Pawson and S. C. Wells, representing the City Council of Atlanta, September 12, 1864, *OR*, 39:418–19.

1. William T. Sherman to General U.S. Grant, December 29, 1863, *OR*, 31:527–28; Stephen E. Bower, "The Theology of the Battlefield: William Tecumseh Sherman and the U.S. Civil War," *Journal of Military History* 64 (October 2000): 1005–34.

2. "A Speech by Gen. W.T. Sherman," *NYT*, January 10, 1864.

3. Hugh Boyle Ewing, "The Autobiography of a Tramp" (Hugh Boyle Ewing Papers, Box 9, OHS), 322; Thomas Ewing to Hugh Ewing, January 31, 1864 (Hugh Ewing Papers, Box 3, OHS); Katherine Burton, *Three Generations: Maria Boyle Ewing, Ellen Ewing Sherman, Minnie Sherman Fitch* (New York: Longmans, Green, 1947), 154–55.

4. Ellen Ewing Sherman to William T. Sherman, April 15, 1864 (William T. Sherman Family Papers, Box 40, UNDA); Thomas Ewing to U.S. Grant, March 30, 1864, in John Y. Simon, ed., *The Papers of Ulysses S. Grant*, vol. 16, *1866* (Carbondale,: Southern Illinois University Press, 1988), 483–84.

5. Ellen Ewing Sherman to William T. Sherman, February 16, 1864, April n.d., 1864, and April 9, 1864 (William T. Sherman Family Papers, Box 61, UNDA); Jack D. Welsh, *Medical Histories of Union Generals* (Kent: Kent State University Press, 1996), 111; Drew Gilpin Faust, *This Republic of Suffering: Death and the American Civil War* (New York: Alfred A. Knopf, 2008), 32–33.

6. Lloyd Lewis, *Sherman, Fighting Prophet* (New York: Harcourt, Brace, 1932), 346–47; General Hugh Ewing, [Personal Military History], Report to the Adjutant General of the Army, Washington, DC, 1864 (Hugh Ewing Papers, Box 4, OHS), 33; H. Ewing, "Autobiography of a Tramp," 324.

7. Elizabeth R. Bullitt and Joshua Speed to Abraham Lincoln, August 26, 1864 (Abraham Lincoln Papers, LOC, transcribed and annotated by the Lincoln Studies Center, Knox College, Galesburg, IL); E. Polk Johnson, *A History of Kentucky and Kentuckians: The Leaders and Representative Men in Commerce, Industry, and Modern Activities* (Chicago: Lewis, 1912), 1:121; "From Kentucky," *NYT*, March 30, 1864.

8. H. Ewing, [Personal Military History], Report, 34; "Trouble in Kentucky," *NYT*, September 11, 1864; Thomas Dionysius Clark and Margaret A. Lane, *The People's House: Governors' Mansions of Kentucky* (Lexington: University Press of Kentucky, 2002), 48–50; E. Merton Coulter, *The Civil War and Readjustment in Kentucky* (Gloucester, MA: Peter Smith, 1966), 196–99; Captain and Acting Assistant Adjutant-General J. S. Grier, Order to Lieutenant Colonel Fairleigh to Execute Prisoners by Command of Brigadier General Hugh Ewing, September 2, 1864, *OR*, 39:339.

9. Russell S. Bonds, *Stealing the General: The Great Locomotive Chase and the First Medal of Honor* (Yardley, PA: Westholme, 2007).

10. Jacob Dolson Cox, *Military Reminiscences of the Civil War,* vol. 2, *November 1863–June 1865* (New York: Charles Scribner's Sons, 1900), 278–79; Errol MacGregor Clauss, "Sherman's Rail Support in the Atlanta Campaign," *Georgia Historical Quarterly* 50 (1966): 413–20; Armin E. Mruck, "The Role of Railroads in the Atlanta Campaign," *Civil War History* 7 (1961): 264–71.

11. Noel C. Fisher, "'Prepare Them for My Coming': General William T. Sherman, Total War, and Pacification in West Tennessee," *Tennessee Historical Quarterly* 51 (1992): 74–86; Major General William T. Sherman to General Leslie Coombs, Frankfort, Kentucky, August 11, 1864, *OR*, 39:240–41; Luke Clarke, *In Memoriam, Charles Ewing* (Philadelphia: J. B. Lippincott, 1888), 58, 60.

12. "From Marietta," *Harper's Weekly* 8 (July 23, 1864): 467; Lee Kennett, *Marching through Georgia: The Story of Soldiers and Civilians during Sherman's Campaign* (New York: HarperCollins, 1995), 42–43.

13. Charley Ewing to Thomas Ewing, May 20, 1864 (Charles Ewing Family Papers, Box 6, LOC); Lee Kennett, *Sherman: A Soldier's Life* (New York: HarperCollins, 2001), 241–42.

14. Charley Ewing to Thomas Ewing, May 20, 1864; Joseph T. Glatthaar, *Partners in Command: The Relationship between Leaders in the Civil War* (New York: Free Press, 1994), 156; Clauss, "Sherman's Rail Support"; Mruck, "Role of Railroads."

15. George Hildt to his parents, February 26, 1864 (George Hildt Letters, Thirtieth Ohio, OHS); Emory W. Muenscher, Private Journal, March 1, 1864, and March 22, 1864 (Emory W. Muenscher Papers, Clark Historical Research Library, Central Michigan University).

16. Lieutenant George H. Hildt, Thirtieth Ohio, Report of Operations of the Thirtieth OVI, in Campaign from May 21st up to and Including the Occupation of Atlanta, September 9, 1864 (George Hildt Letters, Thirtieth Ohio, OHS); George H. Hildt, Diary of the Siege of Atlanta, May 28–October 7, 1864, June 5, 1864, entry (George Hildt Letters, Thirtieth Ohio, OHS).

17. Hildt, Diary of the Siege of Atlanta, June 27, 1864, entry; George H. Hildt to his parents, June 28, 1864 (George Hildt Letters, Thirtieth Ohio, OHS);

Charley Ewing to Thomas Ewing, July 9, 1864 (Charles Ewing Family Papers, Box 6, LOC); Kennett, *Sherman,* 246–48.

18. Kennett, *Sherman,* 248; Charley Ewing to Thomas Ewing, June 30, 1864 (Charles Ewing Family Papers, Box 6, LOC); Muenscher, Private Journal, June 27, 1864; Charles Whalen and Barbara Whalen, *The Fighting McCooks: America's Famous Fighting Family* (Bethesda, MD: Westmoreland Press, 2006), 276–78; John Keegan, *The American Civil War: A Military History* (New York: Alfred A. Knopf, 2009), 262.

19. Bower, "Theology of the Battlefield"; Kennett, *Marching through Georgia,* 151; Kennett, *Sherman,* 248–49.

20. Muenscher, Private Journal, July 6, 1864; Kennett, *Marching through Georgia,* 166–67; Robert Norris to Susan Norris, July 26, 1864 (Robert Norris Letters, Thirtieth Ohio, OHS).

21. George H. Hildt to his parents, July 31, 1864, and September 22, 1864 (George Hildt Letters, Thirtieth Ohio, OHS); Hildt, Diary of the Siege of Atlanta, August 6, 1864, entry; James M. McPherson, *Battle Cry of Freedom: The Civil War Era* (New York: Ballantine Books, 1988), 720; William T. Sherman to Ellen Ewing Sherman, August 2, 1864, in *Home Letters of General Sherman,* ed. M. A. DeWolfe Howe (New York: Charles Scribner's Sons, 1909), 305–6.

22. McPherson, *Battle Cry of Freedom,* 724–742; James Marshall-Cornwall, *Grant as Military Commander* (New York: Barnes and Noble Books, 1970), 145–82.

23. McPherson, *Battle Cry of Freedom,* 724–42; Marshall-Cornwall, *Grant as Military Commander,* 145–82.

24. V. Jacque Voegeli, *Free but Not Equal: The Midwest and the Negro during the Civil War* (Chicago: University of Chicago Press, 1967), 147; David Herbert Donald, *Lincoln* (New York: Simon and Schuster, 1995), 481; Jeannette P. Nichols, "John Sherman," in *For the Union: Ohio Leaders in the Civil War,* ed. Kenneth W. Wheeler (Columbus: Ohio State University Press, 1968), 414–15.

25. Mary Land, "Ben Wade," in Wheeler, *For the Union,* 203; Eugene H. Roseboom, *The Civil War Era, 1850–1873,* History of the State of Ohio 4 (Columbus: Ohio Historical Society, 1968), 430–34.

26. Elizabeth F. Yager, "The Presidential Campaign of 1864 in Ohio," *Ohio History* 34 (1925): 548–89; Joseph P. Smith, *History of the Republican Party in Ohio* (Chicago: Lewis, 1898), 172.

27. Yager, "Presidential Campaign of 1864"; James G. Blaine, *Twenty Years of Congress: From Lincoln to Garfield,* vol. 1 (Norwich, CT: Henry Bill, 1884), 514–15.

28. Brian McGinty, *Lincoln and the Court* (Cambridge, MA: Harvard University Press, 2008); Charles Fairman, *Reconstruction and Reunion,* vol. 6, *1864–1888* (New York: Macmillan, 1971), 6.

29. Gideon Welles, *Diary of Gideon Welles,* vol. 2, *April 1, 1864–December 31, 1866* (New York: Houghton Mifflin, 1911), 203; Theodore Calvin Pease, ed., *The Diary of Orville Hickman Browning,* vol. 1, *1850–1864* (Springfield: Illinois

State Historical Library, 1925), 661, 668; Silvia Tammisto Zsoldos, "The Political Career of Thomas Ewing, Sr." (PhD diss., University of Delaware, 1977), 271.

30. Zsoldos, "Political Career," 271–72; Thomas Ewing to Abraham Lincoln, December 3, 1864 (Abraham Lincoln Papers, LOC, transcribed and annotated by the Lincoln Studies Center, Knox College, Galesburg, IL); McGinty, *Lincoln and the Court*, 212–35.

31. Blaine, *Twenty Years of Congress*, 1:520–23; Harold M. Dudley, "The Election of 1864," *Mississippi Valley Historical Review* 18 (March 1932): 500–518; Lewis L. Gould, *Grand Old Party: A History of the Republicans* (New York: Random House, 2003), 39; John C. Waugh, *Reelecting Lincoln: The Battle for the 1864 Presidency* (New York: Crown, 1997), 196–97.

32. Leroy P. Graf and Ralph W. Haskins, eds., *The Papers of Andrew Johnson*, vol. 6, *1862–1864* (Knoxville: University of Tennessee Press, 1983), 159–61, 81.

33. J. Smith, *History of the Republican Party*, 180; Blaine, *Twenty Years of Congress*, 1:524–25; Dudley, "Election of 1864."

34. J. Smith, *History of the Republican Party*, 182; "Pleasing Political Reminiscences," *Harper's Weekly* 9 (September 2, 1865): 547.

35. J. Smith, *History of the Republican Party*, 182; Voegeli, *Free but Not Equal*, 142; Hon. George H. Pendleton, Remarks, *Congressional Globe*, U.S. House of Representatives, 38th Cong., 1st sess., June 15, 1864, 2992; Eric J. Cardinal, "The Democratic Party of Ohio and the Civil War: An Analysis of a Wartime Political Minority" (PhD diss., Kent State University, 1981), 205; Thomas Stuart Mach, "'Gentleman George' Hunt Pendleton: A Study in Political Continuity" (PhD diss., University of Akron, 1996).

36. Yager, "Presidential Campaign of 1864"; Roseboom, *Civil War Era*, 434–35; Waugh, *Reelecting Lincoln*, 318–20.

37. Noah Brooks to Abraham Lincoln, August 29, 1864 (Abraham Lincoln Papers, LOC, transcribed and annotated by the Lincoln Studies Center, Knox College, Galesburg, IL); "The Chicago Convention," *Harper's Weekly* 8 (September 3, 1864): 573; Yager, "Presidential Campaign of 1864."

38. Dudley, "Election of 1864"; Kennett, *Marching through Georgia*, 113–14; Keegan, *American Civil War*, 265.

39. Kennett, *Sherman*, 248–51.

40. "General Sherman's Army," *NYT*, August 11, 1864; Keegan, *American Civil War*, 265–67; Benson Bobrick, *Master of War: The Life of General George H. Thomas* (New York: Simon and Schuster, 2009), 254.

41. George H. Hildt to his parents, July 31, 1864, and August 15, 1864 (George Hildt Letters, Thirtieth Ohio, OHS); Muenscher, Private Journal, July 28, 1864.

42. Marc Wortman, *The Bonfire: The Siege and Burning of Atlanta* (New York: Public Affairs, 2009), 323–24, 326, 332–34; William T. Sherman to James M.

Calhoun, Mayor, E. E. Pawson and S. C. Wells, Representing City Council of Atlanta, September 12, 1864.

43. Waugh, *Reelecting Lincoln*, 297–98.

44. Daniel E. Sutherland, *A Savage Conflict: The Decisive Role of Guerrillas in the American Civil War* (Chapel Hill: University of North Carolina Press, 2009), 197; William Frank Zornow, "The Missouri Radicals and the Election of 1864," *Missouri Historical Review* 45 (1951): 354–70.

45. Thomas Ewing Jr. to William P. Dole, August 26, 1864 (Abraham Lincoln Papers, LOC, transcribed and annotated by the Lincoln Studies Center, Knox College, Galesburg, IL); Tom Ewing to J. G. Vaughan, July 1, 1864 (Thomas Ewing Family Papers, Box 212, LOC); "Colonel Ford's Opinion," *Daily Journal*, June 28, 1864 (Thomas Ewing Family Papers, Box 212, LOC).

46. Harrison Hannahs, "General Thomas Ewing, Jr.," *Kansas State Historical Society* 12 (1912): 276–82; Tom Ewing to Phil Ewing, March 8, 1864, and July 16, 1864 (Philemon Beecher Ewing Papers, Box 6, OHS).

47. "Speech of General Ewing," *NYT*, August 4, 1864; Brigadier-General Thomas Ewing Jr., Order to Lieutenant-Colonel Burris, July 19, 1864, *OR*, 41:266.

48. L. Thomas, Adjutant-General, Report to Edwin M. Stanton, Secretary of War, October 5, 1865, *OR*, 5:118–24.

49. William S. Rosecrans, Major-General, to Major-General Henry Halleck, March 16, 1864, *OR*, 34:632; Arthur Roy Kirkpatrick, "Missouri's Secessionist Government, 1861–1865," *Missouri Historical Review* 45 (1951): 124–37; Sutherland, *Savage Conflict*, 199–200.

50. Kirkpatrick, "Missouri's Secessionist Government"; Jay Monaghan, *Civil War on the Western Border, 1854–1865* (Boston: Little Brown, 1955), 307–8.

51. Thomas Goodrich, *Black Flag: Guerilla Warfare on the Western Border, 1861–1865* (Bloomington: Indiana University Press, 1995), 139–40, 147; W. Wayne Smith, "An Experiment in Counterinsurgency: The Assessment of Confederate Sympathizers in Missouri," *Journal of Southern History* 35 (August 1969): 361–80; Albert Castel, *General Sterling Price and the Civil War in the West* (Baton Rouge: Louisiana State University Press, 1968), 208.

52. Richard S. Brownlee, "The Battle of Pilot Knob, Iron County, Missouri, September 27, 1864," *Missouri Historical Review* 92 (1998): 271–96; Castel, *General Sterling Price*, 209.

53. Brownlee, "Battle of Pilot Knob"; Joseph Thompson, "The Great Little Battle of Pilot Knob, Part II," *Missouri Historical Review* 83 (1989): 271–94; Castel, *General Sterling Price*, 211.

54. Thompson, "Great Little Battle"; Brownlee, "Battle of Pilot Knob."

55. Thompson, "Great Little Battle"; Brownlee, "Battle of Pilot Knob"; Castel, *General Sterling Price*, 210, 214.

56. Thompson, "Great Little Battle"; Brownlee, "Battle of Pilot Knob"; Castel, *General Sterling Price*, 212–13.

57. Thompson, "Great Little Battle"; Brownlee, "Battle of Pilot Knob."

58. Cyrus A. Peterson and Joseph Mills Hanson, *Pilot Knob: The Thermopylae of the West* (New York: Neale, 1914), 149–50. Peterson and Hanson's book drew extensively upon interviews with the survivors of the battle of Pilot Knob.

59. Thomas Ewing, *The Struggle for Freedom in Kansas* (New York: Cosmopolitan Magazine Press, 1894); Monaghan, *Civil War,* 312; Peterson and Hanson, *Pilot Knob,* 156.

60. Thompson, "Great Little Battle"; Brownlee, "Battle of Pilot Knob"; Castel, *General Sterling Price,* 216; Sarah Bohl, "A War on Civilians: Order Number 11 and the Evacuation of Western Missouri," *Prologue: The Journal of the National Archives* 36 (2004): 44–51.

61. Castel, *General Sterling Price,* 216; Peterson and Hanson, *Pilot Knob,* 169–70.

62. Peterson and Hanson, *Pilot Knob,* 174; Brownlee, "Battle of Pilot Knob."

63. Peterson and Hanson, *Pilot Knob,* 165–67.

64. Ibid., 177–78.

65. Castel, *General Sterling Price,* 216; Brownlee, "Battle of Pilot Knob"; Peterson and Hanson, *Pilot Knob,* 214–15.

66. Peterson and Hanson, *Pilot Knob,* 211.

67. Ibid., 217; Thompson, "Great Little Battle."

68. Thompson, "Great Little Battle"; Brownlee, "Battle of Pilot Knob"; Castel, *General Sterling Price,* 216–17; Peterson and Hanson, *Pilot Knob,* 217–20; Report of Brigadier General Thomas Ewing Jr., U.S. Army, commanding District of Saint Louis, to Colonel J. V. Du Bois, Chief of Staff, Headquarters Department of the Missouri, October 20, 1864, *OR,* 41:445–52.

69. Castel, *General Sterling Price,* 217–18; Peterson and Hanson, *Pilot Knob,* 252–53; Thompson, "Great Little Battle"; Tom Ewing, "Speech of General Ewing at St. Louis, October 1864" (Thomas Ewing Family Papers, Box 212, LOC).

70. Castel, *General Sterling Price,* 217–18; Brownlee, "Battle of Pilot Knob"; Ewing, "Speech of General Ewing at St. Louis."

71. Castel, *General Sterling Price,* 217–18; Monaghan, *Civil War,* 314; Report of Brigadier General Thomas Ewing Jr., U.S. Army, commanding District of Saint Louis, to Colonel J. V. Du Bois, Chief of Staff, Headquarters Department of the Missouri, October 20, 1864.

72. Report of Brigadier General Thomas Ewing Jr., U.S. Army, commanding District of Saint Louis, to Colonel J. V. Du Bois, Chief of Staff, Headquarters Department of the Missouri, October 20, 1864; Peterson and Hanson, *Pilot Knob,* 280–94; Castel, *General Sterling Price,* 218.

73. Peterson and Hanson, *Pilot Knob,* 52; Albert Castel, *A Frontier State at War: Kansas, 1861–1865* (Ithaca: Cornell University Press, 1958), 186–92; Brownlee, "Battle of Pilot Knob."

74. Samuel J. Crawford, *Kansas in the Sixties* (Chicago: A. C. McClurg, 1911), 139, 165, 180; John F. Frazer to Abraham Lincoln, November 3, 1864 (Abraham

Lincoln Papers, LOC, transcribed and annotated by the Lincoln Studies Center, Knox College, Galesburg, IL); Zadok Street to Abraham Lincoln, November 9, 1864 (Abraham Lincoln Papers, LOC, transcribed and annotated by the Lincoln Studies Center, Knox College, Galesburg, IL); Williams S. Rosecrans to Abraham Lincoln, November 11, 1864 (Abraham Lincoln Papers, LOC, transcribed and annotated by the Lincoln Studies Center, Knox College, Galesburg, Illinois).

75. Charles D. Drake to Abraham Lincoln, November 2, 1864 (Abraham Lincoln Papers, LOC, transcribed and annotated by the Lincoln Studies Center, Knox College, Galesburg, IL); John F. Humes, *The Abolitionists: Together with Personal Memories of the Struggle for Human Rights, 1830–1864* (New York: G. P. Putnam's Sons, 1905), 194–97; "The Invasion of Missouri," *Harper's Weekly* 8 (October 22, 1864): 875; "The War in Missouri," *NYT,* October 7, 1864; "From Missouri," *NYT,* October 16, 1864; William E. Parrish, "Reconstruction Politics in Missouri, 1865–1870," in , *Radicalism, Racism, and Party Realignment: The Border States during Reconstruction,* ed. Richard O. Curry (Baltimore: Johns Hopkins University Press, 1969), 5–6; "The Missouri Campaign, General Ewing's Official Report," *New York Herald,* November 13, 1864.

76. Monaghan, *Civil War,* 314–15; Hannahs, "General Thomas Ewing, Jr.," 276–82.

77. Abraham Lincoln to William T. Sherman, September 19, 1864, in *The Living Lincoln: The Man and His Times in His Own Words,* ed. Paul M. Angle and Earl Schenck Miers (New York: Barnes and Noble Books, 1992), 620–21; J. Smith, *History of the Republican Party,* 186.

78. Yager, "Presidential Campaign of 1864"; Waugh, *Reelecting Lincoln,* 334–35.

79. Waugh, *Reelecting Lincoln,* 334–35; Dudley, "Election of 1864."

80. Keegan, *American Civil War,* 272–76; John Bennett Walters, "General William T. Sherman and Total War," *Journal of Southern History* 14 (November 1948): 447–80; Nina Silber, *Daughters of the Union: Northern Women Fight the Civil War* (Cambridge, MA: Harvard University Press, 2005), 23–24.

81. W. T. Sherman to J. A. R., September 12, 1864, in *The Historical Magazine, and Notes and Queries, Concerning Antiquities, History, and Biography of America, Volume 21,* ed. H. B. Dawson (Morrisania, NY: Henry B. Dawson, Office of the Librarian of Congress, 1872–73), 113.

82. Wortman, *Bonfire,* 335; George Ward Nichols, *The Story of the Great March from the Diary of a Staff Officer* (New York: Harper and Brothers, 1865), 37–38.

83. Charles Ewing to Thomas Ewing, August 24, 1864, December 15, 1864, December 31, 1864 (Charles Ewing Family Papers, Box 6, LOC).

84. Kennett, *Marching through Georgia,* 259–61; A. T. Sechand, "Notes in Dixie," *Delaware (Ohio) Gazette,* January 13, 1865.

85. Kennett, *Marching through Georgia,* 259–61; Joseph Benson Foraker, *Notes of a Busy Life* (Cincinnati: Stewart and Kidd, 1916), 1:44–45; M. A. DeWolfe

Howe, ed., *Marching with Sherman: Passages from the Letters and Campaign Diaries of Henry Hitchcock, Major and Assistant Adjunct General of Volunteers, November 1864–May 1865* (New Haven: Yale University Press, 1927), 87. Foraker subsequently served as Ohio's governor and U.S. senator. Robinson became Ohio's secretary of state and member of Congress. Both were Republicans.

86. Howe, *Marching with Sherman*, 86–87.

87. Ibid., 92–93.

88. Ibid., 110–11, 137–38.

89. Nichols, *Story of the Great March*, 44; Clarke, *In Memoriam*, 102–3.

90. Walters, "General William T. Sherman," 447–80; Keegan, *American Civil War*, 274; Kennett, *Marching through Georgia*, 136–37; Mark Grimsley, *The Hard Hand of War: Union Military Policy toward Southern Civilians, 1861–1865* (Cambridge: Cambridge University Press, 1995), 199–200.

91. Sechand, "Notes in Dixie;" "Sherman's March through Georgia," *Harper's Weekly* 9 (January 7, 1865): 5–6.

92. Blaine, *Twenty Years of Congress*, 1:533; Abraham Lincoln to William T. Sherman, December 26, 1864 (Abraham Lincoln Papers, LOC, transcribed and annotated by the Lincoln Studies Center, Knox College, Galesburg, IL).

93. "The Capture of Savannah," *Harper's Weekly* 9 (January 7, 1865): 12; William T. Sherman to Ellen Ewing Sherman, December 25, 1864, in Howe, *Home Letters*, 319–20; Howe, *Marching with Sherman*, 188.

94. Ellen Ewing Sherman, *The Soldier's Casket* (Philadelphia: C. W. Alexander, 1865), 1:515–22; Burton, *Three Generations*, 158–60.

95. "Roger B. Taney," *American Law Register* (1865–91) 13 (January 1865): 179–82; McGinty, *Lincoln and the Court*, 235.

96. McGinty, *Lincoln and the Court*, 235.

NOTES TO CHAPTER SEVEN

The chapter epigraph is from "General Ewing on General Grant," *NYT,* December 2, 1867.

1. Anne J. Bailey, *War and Ruin: William T. Sherman and the Savannah Campaign* (Wilmington, DE: SR Books, 2003), 117–27; Joseph T. Glatthaar, *The March to the Sea and Beyond: Sherman's Troops in the Savannah and Carolinas Campaigns* (New York: New York University Press, 1986), 92, 96–97; George Ward Nichols, *The Story of the Great March from the Diary of a Staff Officer* (New York: Harper and Brothers, 1865), 108.

2. Michael Fellman, *Citizen Sherman: A Life of William Tecumseh Sherman* (New York: Random House, 1995), 162–63; Charles Bracelen Flood, *Grant and Sherman: The Friendship That Won the Civil War* (New York: Harper Perennial, 2005), 278–79.

3. John G. Barrett, *Sherman's March through the Carolinas* (Chapel Hill: University of North Carolina Press, 1956), 30–31; Fellman, *Citizen Sherman*, 164; Flood, *Grant and Sherman*, 279; Joseph Benson Foraker, *Notes of a Busy Life* (Cincinnati: Stewart and Kidd, 1916), 1:50.

4. Fellman, *Citizen Sherman*, 165; Flood, *Grant and Sherman*, 279–80; Eric J. Cardinal, "The Democratic Party of Ohio and the Civil War: An Analysis of a Wartime Political Minority," (PhD diss., Kent State University, 1981), 224, 228–29; Eugene H. Roseboom, *The Civil War Era, 1850–1873*, History of the State of Ohio 4 (Columbus: Ohio Historical Society, 1968), 435; James G. Blaine, *Twenty Years of Congress*, vol. 1, *From Lincoln to Garfield* (Norwich, CT: Henry Bill, 1884), 538.

5. Geoffrey Perret, *Lincoln's War: The Untold Story of America's Greatest President as Commander in Chief* (New York: Random House, 2004), 395–97; William Henry Smith, *A Political History of Slavery: Being an Account of the Slavery Controversy from the Earliest Agitations in the Eighteenth Century to the Close of the Reconstruction Period in America* (New York: G. P. Putnam's Sons, 1903), 2:207; Glyndon G. Van Deusen, *William Henry Seward* (New York: Oxford University Press, 1967), 382–83; Thomas Ewing to Edwin Stanton, February 22, 1865, *OR*, 46:669.

6. Charles Ewing to Thomas Ewing, January 27, 1865 (Charles Ewing Family Papers, Box 6, LOC); M. A. DeWolfe Howe, ed., *Marching with Sherman: Passages from the Letters and Campaign Diaries of Henry Hitchcock, Major and Assistant Adjunct General of Volunteers, November 1864–May 1865* (New Haven: Yale University Press, 1927), 225–26; Luke Clarke, *In Memoriam, Charles Ewing* (Philadelphia: J. B. Lippincott, 1888), 61–62; Manning F. Force, *General Sherman* (New York: D. Appleton and Co., 1899), 265–66. General Manning Force, the former colonel of the Twentieth Ohio, commanded the First Division, Seventeenth Corps, during Sherman's March and received the Medal of Honor.

7. John Keegan, *The American Civil War: A Military History* (New York: Alfred A. Knopf, 2009), 278; Charles Ewing to Thomas Ewing, January 29, 1865, and January 31, 1865 (Charles Ewing Family Papers, Box 6, LOC); Foraker, *Notes of a Busy Life*, 1:54.

8. Foraker, *Notes of a Busy Life*, 1:53; Nichols, *Story of the Great March*, 131.

9. Howe, *Marching with Sherman*, 266; Nichols, *Story of the Great March*, 132–36.

10. D. H. Trezevant, *The Burning of Columbia, S.C.: A Review of Northern Assertions and Southern Facts* (Columbia: South Carolinian Power Press, 1866); Barrett, *Sherman's March*, 89.

11. Trezevant, *Burning of Columbia*; H. C. McArthur, *The Capture and Destruction of Columbia, South Carolina, February 17, 1865: Personal Experiences and*

Recollections of Major H. C. McArthur (Washington, DC: 15th Iowa Regimental Association, 1911. Available from the OHS).

12. Barrett, *Sherman's March*, 63; Nichols, *Story of the Great March*, 152–53.

13. Barrett, *Sherman's March*, 73; Howe, *Marching with Sherman*, 268–69.

14. Nichols, *Story of the Great March*, 158–59; John G. Barrett, *Sherman's March through the Carolinas* (Chapel Hill: University of North Carolina Press, 1956), 61.

15. Burke Davis, *Sherman's March* (New York: Vintage Books, 1980), 160, 176–77; William T. Sherman, *Memoirs of General William T. Sherman*, vol. 2 (New York: D. Appleton, 1891), 1093–95; Trezevant, *Burning of Columbia*.

16. Charles Ewing to Thomas Ewing, March 12, 1865 (Charles Ewing Family Papers, Box 6, LOC); Nichols, *Story of the Great March*, 173–74; Davis, *Sherman's March*, 188–89.

17. Nichols, *Story of the Great March*, 181–82; B. Davis, *Sherman's March*, 187–89; Barrett, *Sherman's March*, 95–98.

18. Foraker, *Notes of a Busy Life*, 1:53.

19. Lieutenant-General U.S. Grant to Major-General [Henry] Halleck, February 20, 1865, *OR*, 47:501; E. D. Townsend, Assistant Adjutant-General, Special Orders No. 93, February 25, 1865, *OR*, 7:564; William T. Sherman to George Thomas, January 20, 1865 (Hugh Ewing Papers, Box 4, OHS); Hugh Ewing to William T. Sherman, February 7, 1865 (Hugh Ewing Papers, Box 4, OHS).

20. Nichols, *Story of the Great March*, 197; Charles Ewing to Thomas Ewing, March 21, 1865 (Charles Ewing Family Papers, Box 6, LOC).

21. Foraker, *Notes of a Busy Life*, 1:66–67; Nichols, *Story of the Great March*, 260; Hugh Ewing to Henrietta Ewing, March 27, 1865 (Hugh Ewing Papers, Box 4, OHS); "Sherman, His Personal Movements," *New York Herald*, March 31, 1865.

22. Matilda Gresham, *Life of Walter Quintin Gresham, 1832–1895*, 2 vols. (Chicago: Rand McNally, 1919), 1:314–16.

23. Ibid.

24. B. Davis, *Sherman's March*, 242–45; William T. Sherman to Thomas Ewing, March 31, 1865, in M. A. DeWolfe Howe, ed., *Home Letters of General Sherman* (New York: Charles Scribner's Sons, 1909), 337–38; William T. Sherman to Ellen Ewing Sherman, April 5, 1865, in Howe, *Home Letters*, 338–40.

25. Hugh Ewing to Henrietta Ewing, April 5, 1865 (Hugh Ewing Papers, Box 5, OHS); Hugh Ewing to Henrietta Ewing, March 27, 1865 (Hugh Ewing Papers, Box 4, OHS); Hugh Boyle Ewing, "The Autobiography of a Tramp" (Hugh Boyle Ewing Papers, Box 9, OHS), 342.

26. James M. McPherson, *Battle Cry of Freedom: The Civil War Era* (New York: Ballantine Books, 1988), 846–47, 851.

27. Michael W. Kaufmann, *American Brutus: John Wilkes Booth and the Lincoln Conspiracies* (New York: Random House, 2004), 3–8; Edward Steers Jr., *Blood*

on the Moon: The Assassination of Abraham Lincoln (Lexington: University of Kentucky Press, 2005), 96–98.

28. Britton A. Hill to Thomas L. Ewing Jr., March 5, 1860 (Thomas Ewing Family Papers, Box 161, LOC); Britton A. Hill, *Liberty and Law under Federative Government* (Philadelphia: J. B. Lippincott, 1874); Britton A. Hill to Abraham Lincoln, October 3, 1864 (Abraham Lincoln Papers, LOC, transcribed and annotated by the Lincoln Studies Center, Knox College, Galesburg, IL); Kaufmann, *American Brutus*, 41–42, 64–65, 247, 258. Britton Hill's first name is commonly misspelled as "Britten."

29. Edwin M. Stanton, Secretary of War, $100,000 Reward, Washington, April 20, 1865, *OR*, 46:847–48.

30. Mark L. Bradley, *This Astounding Close: The Road to Bennett Place* (Chapel Hill: University of North Carolina Press, 2000), 170–75; B. Davis, *Sherman's March*, 258–260.

31. B. Davis, *Sherman's March*, 269–272; Bradley, *This Astounding Close*, 227–29; Foraker, *Notes of a Busy Life,* 1:67–68; Force, *General Sherman*, 299–306; Nichols, *Story of the Great March,* 317–19; Michael S. Green, *Freedom, Union, and Power: Lincoln and His Party during the Civil War* (New York: Fordham University Press, 2004), 241.

32. William T. Sherman to Ellen Ewing Sherman, May 10, 1865, in Howe, *Home Letters,* 352–54; Major General William T. Sherman to Major General John Schofield, May 28, 1865, *OR*, 47:585–86; Green, *Freedom, Union, and Power,* 238.

33. Bradley, *This Astounding Close*, 230–32; Foraker, *Notes of a Busy Life,* 1:67–68; Force, *General Sherman*, 299–306; Nichols, *Story of the Great March,* 317–19; B. Davis, *Sherman's March*, 272; Charles Ewing to Thomas Ewing, April 24, 1865 (Charles Ewing Family Papers, Box 6, LOC). The date on Charley Ewing's letter at the LOC is incorrectly given as April 4, 1865; he meant to write April 24, 1865. The date becomes clear in the context of the letter and reference to the end of the war.

34. "A Quartette of Generals," *NYT*, March 12, 1865.

35. General Frank Blair to President Andrew Johnson, June 1, 1865 (Hugh Ewing Papers, Box 4, OHS).

36. Lee Kennett, *Sherman: A Soldier's Life* (New York: HarperCollins, 2001), 286–87; Flood, *Grant and Sherman*, 364–65; Major General William T. Sherman to the Chairman of the Committee on the Conduct of the War, May 19, 1865, *OR*, 47, 532; John F. Marszalek, *Sherman: A Soldier's Passion for Order* (New York: Free Press, 1993), 353; Lloyd Lewis, *Sherman, Fighting Prophet* (New York: Harcourt, Brace, 1932), 567. Hugh Ewing kept a small datebook/diary that recorded this incident. It may be found with his papers at the OHS.

37. Nichols, *Story of the Great March,* 322; Foraker, *Notes of a Busy Life,* 1:73; B. Davis, *Sherman's March*, 288–92.

38. Charles Ewing to Thomas Ewing, April 28, 1865 (Charles Ewing Family Papers, Box 6, LOC); Clarke, *In Memoriam,* 62–63.
39. Katherine Burton, *Three Generations: Maria Boyle Ewing, Ellen Ewing Sherman, Minnie Sherman Fitch* (New York: Longmans, Green, 1947), 164–66; Marszalek, *Sherman,* 356–57.
40. Thomas Reed Turner, *Beware the People Weeping: Public Opinion and the Assassination of Abraham Lincoln* (Baton Rouge: Louisiana State University Press, 1982), 47; Neil Rolde, *Continental Liar from the State of Maine: James G. Blaine* (Gardiner, ME: Tilbury House, 2006), 108.
41. James L. Swanson, *Manhunt: The 12-Day Chase for Lincoln's Killer* (New York: William Morrow, 2006), 129–31, 152–58; Lorie Ann Porter, "Not So Strange Bedfellows: Thomas Ewing II and the Defense of Samuel Mudd," *Lincoln Herald* 90 (1988): 91–101.
42. Steers, *Blood on the Moon,* 170, 178.
43. Britton Hill to Andrew Johnson, June 19, 1865, in Turner, *Beware the People Weeping,* 141; Thomas Ewing to Andrew Johnson, July 4, 1865, in *The Papers of Andrew Johnson,* vol. 7, *1864–1865,* ed. Leroy P. Graf, Patricia P. Clark, and Marion O. Smith (Knoxville: University of Tennessee Press, 1986), 350.
44. Elizabeth D. Leonard, *Lincoln's Avengers: Justice, Revenge, and Reunion after the Civil War* (New York: W. W. Norton, 2004), 77–79; George Fort Milton, *The Age of Hate: Andrew Johnson and the Radicals* (New York: Coward and McCann, 1930), 200–201; Lewis, *Sherman, Fighting Prophet,* 571; "The Constitutional Abolition of Slavery," *New York Herald,* April 8, 1864; "The Right Way to Abolish African Slavery," *New York Herald,* February 13, 1864; R. A. Watts, "The Trial and Execution of the Lincoln Conspirators," *Michigan History Magazine* 6 (1922): 81–110. Watts was a Union soldier assigned to carry messages among the military commissioners and government authorities.
45. Leonard, *Lincoln's Avengers,* 77–79; Milton, *Age of Hate,* 200–201; Lewis, *Sherman, Fighting Prophet,* 571; H. Ewing, "Autobiography of a Tramp," 344–45; Watts, "Trial and Execution."
46. Ibid.
47. Ibid.; U.S. War Department, Transcript, "Testimony of Samuel A. Mudd," Surratt House Museum, www.surratt.org.
48. "Testimony of Samuel A. Mudd"; Watts, "Trial and Execution."
49. Leonard, *Lincoln's Avengers,* 125–27; "Trial of the Conspirators," *Harper's Weekly* 9 (June 3, 1865): 340–43.
50. "Argument on the Plea to the Jurisdiction of the Military Commission by Thomas Ewing, Jr., June 23, 1865," Surratt House Museum, www.surratt.org.
51. Ibid.; "Opinion on the Constitutional Power of the Military to Try and Execute the Assassins of the President, by Attorney General James Speed, July 1865," Surratt House Museum, www.surratt.org.
52. Porter, "Not so Strange Bedfellows."

53. Milton, *Age of Hate*, 356–57; Seymour J. Frank, "The Conspiracy to Implicate the Confederate Leaders in Lincoln's Assassination," *Mississippi Valley Historical Review* 40 (March 1954): 629–56.

54. Eugene H. Berwanger, *The West and Reconstruction* (Urbana: University of Illinois Press, 1981), 87–88, 93.

55. Thomas Ewing to Andrew Johnson, June 1865, in Graf, Clark, and Smith, *Papers of Andrew Johnson* (Knoxville: University of Tennessee Press, 1986), 7:196–97; W. Smith, *Political History of Slavery*, 289–90.

56. Thomas Ewing to Andrew Johnson, June 1865; Milton, *Age of Hate*, 468–69; Cardinal, "Democratic Party of Ohio," 228–29, 241–42; Robert Selph Henry, *The Story of Reconstruction* (New York: Konecky and Konecky, 1999), 210–11.

57. John H. Cox and LaWanda Cox, "Andrew Johnson and His Ghost Writers: An Analysis of the Freedmen's Bureau and Civil Rights Veto Messages," *Mississippi Valley Historical Review* 48 (December 1961): 460–79.

58. Robert D. Sawrey, *Dubious Victory: The Reconstruction Debate in Ohio* (Lexington: University of Kentucky Press, 1992), 97; "General Ewing on General Grant," *NYT*.

59. Henry, *Story of Reconstruction*, 196; Milton, *Age of Hate*, 356; "Soldiers and Sailors, at New York City, July [1868], Resolution, in Edward McPherson, ed., *The Political History of the Untied States of America during the Period of Reconstruction, from April 15, 1865, to July 15, 1870* (1875; repr., New York: Negro Universities Press, 1969), 368–69; "The Cleveland Convention," *NYT*, September 18, 1866.

60. Felice A. Bonadio, *North of Reconstruction: Ohio Politics, 1865–1870* (New York: New York University Press, 1970), 161, 163.

61. Milton, *Age of Hate*, 371; Albert V. House Jr., "Northern Congressional Democrats as Defenders of the South during Reconstruction," *Journal of Southern History* 6 (February 1940): 46–71.

62. Sawrey, *Dubious Victory*, 123; Milton, *Age of Hate*, 491.

63. Sawrey, *Dubious Victory*, 129; William T. Sherman to Ellen Ewing Sherman, October 7, 1867, in Howe, *Home Letters*, 360–61; Milton, *Age of Hate*, 490.

64. Samuel S. Cox, *Three Decades of Federal Legislation, 1855 to 1885* (Providence, RI: J. A. & R. A. Reid, 1885), 88, 588; P. S. Ruckman Jr., "The Supreme Court, Critical Nominations, and the Senate Confirmation Process," *Journal of Politics* 55 (August 1993): 793–805; Lewis L. Gould, *Grand Old Party: A History of the Republicans* (New York: Random House, 2003), 53; Michael Les Benedict, "A New Look at the Impeachment of Andrew Johnson," *Political Science Quarterly* 88 (September 1973): 349–67.

65. David Miller Dewitt, *The Impeachment and Trial of Andrew Johnson, Seventeenth President of the United States* (1903; repr., Whitefish, MT: Kessinger., 2006), 422; William T. Sherman to John Sherman, February 25, 1868, in *The Sherman Letters: Correspondence between General and Senator Sherman*

from 1837 to 1891, ed. Rachel Sherman Thorndike (New York: Scribner's Sons, 1894), 312–13; Roger D. Bridges, "John Sherman and the Impeachment of Andrew Johnson," *Ohio History* 82 (1973): 176–91; H. L. Trefousse, *Benjamin Franklin Wade: Radical Republican from Ohio* (New York: Twayne, 1963), 300–301.

66. "Impeachment," *NYT*, May 3, 1868; Dewitt, *Impeachment and Trial,* 539–45; Sawrey, *Dubious Victory,* 174.

67. James Forman Jr., "Juries and Race in the Nineteenth Century," *Yale Law Journal* 113 (January 2004): 895–938.

68. Mark S. Weiner, *Black Trials: Citizenship from the Beginnings of Slavery to the End of Caste* (New York: Alfred A. Knopf, 2004), 198–201, 204–13; Francis B. Simkins, "The Ku Klux Klan in South Carolina, 1868–1871," *Journal of Negro History* 12 (October 1927): 606–47; Charles Lane, *The Day Freedom Died: The Colfax Massacre, the Supreme Court, and the Betrayal of Reconstruction* (New York: Henry Holt, 2008), 116–17, 196–97, 236–41; "The Ku Klux Klan Trials," *NYT*, December 25, 1871.

69. "Hon. Thomas Ewing and His Family," *NYT*, July 16, 1867.

70. "America's Statesmen," *NYT*, August 1, 1869; Charles Warren, *The Supreme Court in United States History,* vol. 2, *1836–1918* (Boston: Little, Brown, , 1926), 461–62.

71. "Brigadier-General Charles Ewing, USV," Obituary (Thomas Ewing Family Papers, Box 262, LOC); Clarke, *In Memoriam,* 111–12; H. Augusta Dodge, ed., *Gail Hamilton's Life in Letters* (Boston: Lee and Shepard, 1901), 2:752.

72. "Brigadier-General Charles Ewing, USV"; Clarke, *In Memoriam,* 105–6.

73. "Catholics among the Indians," *NYT*, June 6, 1880; Patrick W. Carey, *Catholics in America: A History* (Westport, CT: Praeger, 2004), 51, 74; J. C. Imoda and Francis J. Weber, "Grant's Peace Policy: A Catholic Dissenter," *Montana: The Magazine of Western History* 19 (Winter 1969): 56–63.

74. Imoda and Weber, "Grant's Peace Policy"; "Brigadier-General Charles Ewing, USV"; Clarke, *In Memoriam,* 108–9.

75. Jack D. Welsh, *Medical Histories of Union Generals* (Kent: Kent State University Press, 1996), 110–11; John H. Eicher and David J. Eicher, *Civil War High Commands* (Stanford: Stanford University Press, 2001), 229.

76. H. J. R., "The Late General Ewing," *Philadelphia Press*, June 24, 1883 (Thomas Ewing Family Papers, Box 262, LOC); "The Late General Ewing," *NYT*, June 22, 1883; "General Ewing's Funeral," *NYT*, June 23, 1883. Charley Ewing was later reinterred in Arlington National Cemetery.

77. Kennett, *Sherman,* 330–31; Fellman, *Citizen Sherman,* 352–89; "Senator Sherman," *NYT*, October 4, 1871.

78. Edmund Wilson, *Patriotic Gore: Studies in the Literature of the American Civil War* (New York: W. W. Norton, 1994), 208–13; Kennett, *Sherman,* 326–27; Fellman, *Citizen Sherman,* 381–82, 397.

79. Lewis, *Sherman, Fighting Prophet*, 650; Fellman, *Citizen Sherman*, 413–15; "Along the Line of March," *NYT*, February 20, 1891; "On the Way to His Rest," *NYT*, February 20, 1891.

80. "A Labyrinth of Falsehood," *NYT*, October 13, 1884; Harriet Blaine to Walker Blaine, February 18, 1872, in *Letters of Mrs. James G. Blaine*, ed. Harriet S. Blaine Beale (New York: Duffield, 1908), 1:89–93. Mrs. Blaine's large correspondence helps document the close relationship among the Blaine and Ewing cousins in postwar Washington.

81. Marie Carolyn Klinkhamer, "The Blaine Amendment of 1875: Private Motives for Political Action," *Catholic Historical Review* 42 (April 1956): 15–49.

82. Ibid.

83. Roseboom, *Civil War Era*, 440–41.

84. "Union Soldiers and the Democratic Party," *NYT*, July 12, 1868; "The Governorship of Ohio—General Ewing and the Democratic Party," *NYT*, June 27, 1869; "Democratic Hatred of the East," *NYT*, January 25, 1878; "Grant's Opinion of Ewing," *NYT*, October 16, 1879; "Waggery in Politics," *Harper's Weekly* 15 (October 14, 1871): 954; "Speech of General Thomas Ewing, Delivered at Ironton, Ohio, June 24, 1875," (Columbus, OH: Democratic State Executive Committee, 1875, OHS Archives); Thomas E. Powell, *The Democratic Party of the State of Ohio* (Columbus: Ohio Pub., 1913), 218.

85. Wyllis C. Ransom to General Thomas Ewing Jr., May 30, 1871 (Thomas Ewing Family Papers, Box 212, LOC).

86. "A Scrap of War History," *NYT*, February 17, 1877.

87. Barbara S. Groseclose, "Painting, Politics, and George Caleb Bingham," *American Art Journal* 10 (November 1978): 5–19; Nancy Rash, *The Painting and Politics of George Caleb Bingham* (New Haven: Yale University Press, 1991), 211–13; Robert L. Gale, "George Caleb Bingham," in *American National Biography On-Line*, February 2000, American Council of Learned Societies, www.anb.org.

88. "General Thomas Ewing," *NYT*, January 22, 1896. Box 212, Thomas Ewing Family Papers, LOC, overflows with Tom Ewing's correspondence and press clippings related to General Order Number 11, the Missouri guerrilla insurgency, and the battle of Pilot Knob.

89. Robert F. Durden, "James S. Pike: President Lincoln's Minister to the Netherlands," *New England Quarterly* 29 (September 1956): 341–64; Harold A. Davis, "From the Diaries of a Diplomat, James S. Pike," *New England Quarterly* 14 (March 1941): 83–112. See *Papers Relating to the Foreign Relations of the United States, 1867* (Washington, DC: Government Printing Office, 1868) for examples of Hugh Ewing's reports to the U.S. Secretary of State.

90. *Historical Papers and Addresses of the Lancaster County Historical Society, Volume 19* (Lancaster, PA: Lancaster County Historical Society, 1915), 110–13.

91. Hugh Ewing, *A Castle in the Air* (New York: Henry Holt, 1888).

92. Hugh Ewing, *The Black List: A Tale of Early California* (New York: Peter Fenelon Collier, 1893).

93. Ronald D. Smith, *Thomas Ewing, Jr.: Frontier Lawyer and Civil War General* (Columbia: University of Missouri Press, 2008), 252–53; Welsh, *Medical Histories,* 111.

INDEX

Page numbers in *italics* refer to illustrations.

Kenneth J. Heineman, Professor of History and Department Chair at Angelo State University, is a student of American political and social history. He received the Philip S. Klein Book Prize from the Pennsylvania Historical Association for *A Catholic New Deal: Religion and Reform in Depression Pittsburgh.*